SECOND EDITION

The Elementary Principal's Handbook

A Guide to Effective Action

Larry W. Hughes
University of Houston

Gerald C. Ubben
University of Tennessee

ALLYN AND BACON, INC.
Boston   London   Sydney   Toronto

To Our Wives

Copyright © 1984, 1978 by Allyn and Bacon, Inc.
7 Wells Avenue, Newton, Massachusetts 02159

Library of Congress Cataloging in Publication Data

Hughes, Larry W., 1931–
    The elementary principal's handbook.

    Includes bibliographies and index.
    1. Elementary school administration—United States—
Handbooks, manuals, etc.   2. Elementary school principals
—United States—Handbooks, manuals, etc.   I. Ubben,
Gerald C.   II. Title.
LB2822.5.H83   1984   372.12   83–15732
ISBN 0–205–08107–X

Printed in the United States of America

10 9 8 7 6 5 4 3   87 86 85

Contents

Preface to the Second Edition   xiii

**PART ONE   ORGANIZATIONAL AND SOCIETAL
IMPINGEMENTS   1**

**1 The Elementary School Principal: A Complex Role in a
Dynamic Society   3**

INTRODUCTION   3
Five Functions of the Principalship   4
SPECIAL DEMANDS ON ELEMENTARY PRINCIPALS   4
Educational Engineer   5
The Motivating Work Environment   7
School-Community Relations Specialist   10
SUMMARY   13
BIBLIOGRAPHY   13

**2 The School Organization and Good Internal
Communication   15**

INTRODUCTION   15
Conditions Affecting Individual Behavior in Organizations   15
Bulletins, Briefings, and Benevolent and Brainy Benedictions   16
THE MULTIDIMENSIONAL ORGANIZATION   17
Personal Dimension of the School Organization   18
Informal Groups   19
LEVELS OF COMMUNICATION   21
Feedback   22
SUMMARY   22
BIBLIOGRAPHY   24

3 Students, Staff, and Administrator Rights and Responsibilities: A Legal Focus 25

INTRODUCTION 25
    Legal Structure of the Schools in the United States 26
STUDENT AND STAFF RIGHTS: ESTABLISHING A
FRAMEWORK 27
ISSUES OF EDUCATIONAL EQUITY 31
    Sex Discrimination 31
    Mainstreaming 32
    The Individualized Education Program 34
    The Desegregated School Environment 35
    Integration/Desegregation: A Distinction 35
    Grouping Children 36
    Maintaining the Equitable Environment 37
RULES AND REGULATIONS 39
    The Out-of-Date Rule 40
    Establishing Good Rules and Regulations 41
DUE PROCESS 42
    Substantive Due Process 42
    Guidelines to Insure Adherance to Substantive Due Process 43
    Procedural Due Process 44
COMMON TORT LIABILITY SETTINGS 45
    Pupil Injuries 46
    Regulating Student Conduct 50
    Privacy and the Confidentiality of Student Records 55
SUMMARY 57
BIBLIOGRAPHY 57

4 Understanding the Community 61

INTRODUCTION 61
SOCIETY IN PERSPECTIVE 62
    A Slowly Dying Myth 62
    Ideological Disunity 63
    Role of the School 64
COMMUNITY INFLUENCE SYSTEMS 65
    Community Power Structures 66
    Two Views of Community Influence Systems 67
    The Pluralistic School Community 70
    Neighborhood Influence Systems 70
    Negotiating with Pressure Groups 74
NEED FOR WELL-DEVELOPED POLICIES 76
SUMMARY 78
BIBLIOGRAPHY 78

PART TWO   ADMINISTRATIVE TASKS AND
FUNCTIONS   81

5 Guidelines and Goals for Planning School Programs   83

INTRODUCTION   83
  Interdependence of the School's Organizational Components   84
PROGRAM COMPATIBILITY   84
ORGANIZATIONAL BALANCE   85
ORGANIZATIONAL FLEXIBILITY   85
SETTING PROGRAM GOALS   86
  Goal Determination   87
DEVELOPING APPROPRIATE OBJECTIVES   88
ELEMENTARY SCHOOL GOALS AND OBJECTIVES   88
SUMMARY   90
BIBLIOGRAPHY   90

6 Individual Differences and Student Grouping   91

INTRODUCTION   91
  Achievement *vs.* Ability Differences   91
DIFFERENCES IN LEARNING STYLES   92
LEARNING INTERESTS   95
STUDENT GROWTH AND MATURITY   95
GROUPING STUDENTS   98
  Group Size   98
  Administrative Decision Making about Group Size   100
  Group Composition   100
  Retention   103
  Appropriate Bases for Grouping   103
  Group Flexibility   106
  Grouping Guidelines   108
BIBLIOGRAPHY   108

7 Organizing the Elementary School Curriculum   111

INTRODUCTION   111
CURRICULAR FLEXIBILITY   112
  Varying Curricular Emphasis   113
CURRICULAR CONTINUITY   113
  A Curricular Model   114
INDIVIDUAL VERTICAL CURRICULAR SELECTION   117
SPECIAL PROGRAMS FOR SPECIAL STUDENTS   118
  Gifted Students   118
  Handicapped Students   118
SUMMARY   119
BIBLIOGRAPHY   121

8 Organizing Elementary School Instruction   123

INTRODUCTION   123
  Instructional Processes   124
ALLOWANCE FOR INDIVIDUAL DIFFERENCES   125
OVERTONES OF INSTRUCTION   126
INSTRUCTIONAL IMPLICATIONS FOR PROGRAM
ORGANIZATION   126
INDIVIDUALIZED SYSTEMS OF INSTRUCTION   126
INSTRUCTIONAL TOOLS FOR INDIVIDUALIZATION   128
  Learning Packages   129
  Learning Centers   129
  Independent-Study Contracts   130
  External School Independent Study   131
SUMMARY   131
BIBLIOGRAPHY   132

9 Using Student Records and Reporting to Parents   135

INTRODUCTION   135
GUIDELINES FOR STUDENT RECORDS   135
  Procedures for Developing New Record Forms   136
  Record Maintenance   136
  Sample Records   137
REPORTING TO PARENTS   151
  Report Cards   151
  Parent-Teacher Conferences   155
SUMMARY   159
BIBLIOGRAPHY   159

10 Creating a Positive Learning Climate:
Student Services and Student Control   161

INTRODUCTION   161
MAINTAINING POSITIVE STUDENT CONTROL   162
  Development of a Preventive Program   163
  "Time Out" Areas and In-School Suspensions   164
  Ten Steps to Help Students Achieve Good Behavior   164
THE COUNSELING PROGRAM   166
  Advisor-Advisee Systems   167
  Developmental Guidance and Counseling   169
  Selection of an Advisor   170
  Tips for Establishing a Good Advisement Program   171
  The Role of the Guidance Counselor   173
  Pupil-Personnel Referral Services   175
SUMMARY   176
BIBLIOGRAPHY   177

11 Effective Staff Organization   179

INTRODUCTION   179
  Staffing Analysis   179
  Considerations for Selecting Particular Staffing Models   183
DISCIPLINARY VERSUS INTERDISCIPLINARY TEAM
DESIGN   184
TEAM PLANNING   186
DIFFERENT STAFFING PATTERNS   189
  Traditional Self-Contained Classrooms   190
  Teachers Plus Specialists   190
  Team Teaching   190
  Team Teaching with Aides   191
  Teams, Aides, and Multi-Age Grouping   191
  Utilization of Staff Specialists   193
  Team Integration   195
  Schoolwide Staffing   196
PARAPROFESSIONALS   197
  Types of Aides   198
  Recruitment and Selection of Aides   198
  Creating a Supportive Atmosphere for the Aides   200
  Administration of the Aide Program   200
  Liability Implications for Aides   200
SUMMARY   200
BIBLIOGRAPHY   201

12 Scheduling Staff and Students   203

INTRODUCTION   203
  Schedule Flexibility   203
  Simplicity and Complexity   204
  Timeliness of Scheduling Decisions   204
  Decision Level   204
SCHEDULING TECHNIQUES   204
SAMPLE SCHEDULE   207
TEAM PLANNING TIME   209
MIDDLE-SCHOOL SCHEDULES   210
SUMMARY   214
BIBLIOGRAPHY   215

13 Staffing the School: Recruitment, Selection, and Termination   215

INTRODUCTION   215
RECRUITMENT   215
FEDERAL REGULATIONS TO PREVENT DISCRIMINATION
OF EMPLOYMENT   219

EEOC Regulations 219
THE SELECTION PROCESS 220
    The Job Interview 220
EMPLOYEE PROBATIONARY STATUS 221
TEACHER TENURE 222
INVOLUNTARY TERMINATION 222
    Preparation for Dismissal 223
    Due Process 223
    Appropriatness of Evidence 224
    Equal Rights 225
    Reduction in Force 225
VOLUNTARY TERMINATIONS 227
SUMMARY 227
BIBLIOGRAPHY 228

14 **The Principal as Supervisor and Evaluator** 229

INTRODUCTION 229
    Characteristics of a Good Evaluation Plan 229
ATTRIBUTES OF AN EVALUATION MODEL 230
THE STAFF EVALUATION CYCLE 231
    The Identification and Integration of Individual and Institutional
    Goals 231
    Preobservation Conference 236
ANNUAL EVALUATION CONFERENCE AND
RECOMMENDATIONS 244
SUMMARY 245
BIBLIOGRAPHY 246

15 **Staff Development** 249

INTRODUCTION 249
    Purposes of Staff Development 250
    Characteristics of a Good Staff Development Plan 251
PLANNING FOR STAFF DEVELOPMENT 251
    Sources for Staff Development Ideas 251
PLANNING MODEL 252
    Planning Steps 252
    Implementation 255
    Evaluation 255
ORIENTATION OF NEW STAFF 256
SUMMARY 258
BIBLIOGRAPHY 258

16 **The Principal's Role in Contract Administration** 261

INTRODUCTION 261
    How to Handle Grievances 262
    Appealed Grievances 265

THE PRINCIPAL'S ROLE IN NEGOTIATION   265
PRINCIPAL INVOLVEMENT IN TEACHER ORGANIZATIONS   268
SUMMARY   268
BIBLIOGRAPHY   268

17 **Building Management and Facility Utilization**   269

INTRODUCTION   269
  New Buildings   269
  Open Space   270
  The Use of Traditional Buildings for Flexible Programs   273
  Renovating Existing Facilities   274
EFFECTIVE CARE OF THE SCHOOL PLANT   274
SITE UTILIZATION   277
DESIRABLE SITE DEVELOPMENT   278
MAINTENANCE OF THE BUILDING   278
  Routinizing Custodial Functions   279
  Scheduling the Work   279
SUPPLIES AND EQUIPMENT MANAGEMENT   281
  Storage and Inventory Control   281
  Staff Work Areas   284
  Using Equipment   284
  Central Warehousing   285
NONACADEMIC SUPPORT PERSONNEL   285
SUMMARY   286
BIBLIOGRAPHY   286

18 **Fiscal Planning and Record Keeping**   289

INTRODUCTION   289
  The Budgeting Process   290
  Setting Priorities—Where the Dollars Should Go   292
IMPLEMENTING A SYSTEMATIC BUDGET BUILDING
PROCESS   293
FINANCIAL RECORDKEEPING   300
  The Transgressing Staff Member   302
  Regular Review   304
  Activity and Other Funds   304
  The Audit   308
SUMMARY   309
BIBLIOGRAPHY   309

19 **Pupil Transportation and Auxiliary Services and
     Activities**   311

INTRODUCTION   311
STUDENT CONTROL ON BUSES   312
FIELD TRIPS   314
INSTRUCTIONAL MATERIALS CENTER   315

FOOD SERVICES   317
   Satellite Food Services   317
   Nutrition and Learning   317
HEALTH SERVICES   318
   School Nurses   318
   The Clinic   319
SUMMARY   321
BIBLIOGRAPHY   322

20 Public Relations Processes and Techniques   323

INTRODUCTION   323
   The Folks Raise a Question   324
ONE-WAY PUBLIC RELATIONS EFFORTS   325
   Newspapers and Other Mass Media   325
   The Public Information Officer   326
   Techniques for Dealing with the Mass Media   326
   Newsletters, Bulletins, and Report Cards   329
   The Message Was Sent—What Happened?   330
TWO-WAY COMMUNICATION EFFORTS   330
   Parent-Teacher Organizations   331
   Principal-Organized "Gripe" Sessions   332
   Key Communicators   333
   Neighborhood Seminars   333
   Program Analysis by Special Groups   334
   Citizen Committees   334
   Parent-Teacher Conferences   335
   Miniboards and Advisory Councils   335
   Questionnaires and Opinionaires   336
SUMMARY   336
BIBLIOGRAPHY   337

PART THREE   MANAGEMENT PROCESSES   339

21 Initiating Executive Action and Decision Processing   341

INTRODUCTION   341
THREE DECISION PROCESSES   341
   Unilateral Decision Making   342
   Majority Opinion   342
   Consensus Decision Making   343
   A Case in Point   345
PARTICIPATORY DECISION MAKING   348
   Assumptions about the Staff   348
   Cooperative Goal Setting Facilitates Decision Making   350
   Defining the Tasks   351
   Job Target Setting   353
   Job Thickening   354
   Why Participatory Decision Making   355

When to Involve Others in Decision Making   356
ROUTINE AND NON ROUTINE DECISION-MAKING   358
   Routine Decision Making   358
   Nonroutine Decision Making   360
   Brainstorming   360
GUIDELINES FOR EXECUTIVE DECISION MAKING   362
   What Is the Problem?   362
   Alternative Actions   362
   Organizational and Personal Barriers   363
   Good Communication Is Essential   364
SUMMARY   364
BIBLIOGRAPHY   364

22 Systematic Planning and Project Management   367

INTRODUCTION   367
PROBLEM IDENTIFICATION OR GOAL STATEMENT   369
PURPOSE OF THE PROJECT   369
FORCE FIELDING THE PROBLEM   372
THE PROJECT PLAN   371
   Component Coordinators and Other Key Personnel   372
   Putting the Specific Components into Operation   372
   Establishing Realistic Completion Dates   374
   The Project Calendar: Gantt Charting   374
   The Master Project Document   377
EVALUATION   377
SUMMARY   380
BIBLIOGRAPHY   380

23 Managing Executive Time   381

INTRODUCTION   381
   Distinguishing Between the Principal and the Principalship   381
   How to Get It Done: Time Management   382
THE ACTIVITY TRAP   382
IDEAL/PERCEIVED/REAL USE OF TIME   384
   Job Analysis   384
   Reducing the Discrepancies   388
   The Administrative Log   388
   Task Analysis   389
PRIORITY SETTING   391
WHAT GETS IN THE WAY   395
   Delegation   396
   The Myth of the Open Door   398
SUMMARY   399
BIBLIOGRAPHY   399

Index   401

Preface

to the Second Edition

In the years that have elapsed between the first and second editions of this book many things have happened, but none has reduced the need for good leadership in the elementary schools. The elementary school principal remains in a critical role on the education management team. Politicians come and go, national administrations change, new cabinet offices are created, others are closed down or diminished, and new state and national priorities emerge; but the fundamental work of the educator and the educational institution and the primary mission of the school in a free society continue. Certainly, new demands are made, and just as certainly school people must respond to these new demands with creative approaches and better-designed curricula. The mission remains the same however: to provide for an enlightened citizenry and to provide the basis for "everyperson's" child to achieve his or her potential, unfettered by station at birth.

Providing the leadership so that such a mission can be carried out has never been easy. In these later years, good leadership at the elementary school level has become even more crucial. Study after study, ranging from the banner work, *Elementary Principals and Their Schools: Beacons of Brilliance and Potholes of Pestilence*[1] to the more recent Phi Delta Kappa inquiry about elementary schools, *Why Do Some Urban Schools Succeed?*[2] reveal that the greatest single contributing factor to excellence of individual schools is the existence of good leadership.

Basic to good leadership is a repertoire of managerial skills that provide a productive climate in which teaching and learning are facilitated. Thus, when the job of the principal is done well, great things can happen; when the school is inadequately managed, young people are materially hindered in achieving their potential. It is not a job in which one can hide. Yet, persons of

---

[1]Keith Goldhammer et al., *Elementary School Principals and Their Schools: Beacons of Brilliance and Potholes of Pestilence* (Eugene, Oregon: Center for the Advanced Study of Educational Administration, 1971).

[2]*Why Do Some Urban Schools Succeed?*, Phi Delta Kappa Study of Exceptional Urban Elementary Schools (Bloomington, Ind.: Phi Delta Kappa, 1980).

Homeric proportions are not required; indeed, few such persons exist. What is required are well-trained, intelligent, and humane individuals who have the necessary human, conceptual, and technical skills to lead groups of professionals and clients into rich educational adventures.

This book attempts to focus on those necessary dimensions of good school management. There are three parts to the book. The focus of the first part is on organizational and societal impingements. Described in the four chapters that comprise Part One is the role of the elementary principal, aspects about the school organization, the community it serves, and the legal framework within which the schools operate. Part Two contains chapters describing the various functional aspects of the principalship. Guidelines for action are suggested in each chapter. Part Three is composed of three chapters that focus on important management processes. Decision making, project management, and the management of executive time are the topics in this section.

It is hoped that readers will find the book to be a practical guide and useful reference. The effort has been to provide a comprehensive and straightforward treatment of the roles and functions of the principalship. We have attempted to provide help to practitioners and those preparing to be practitioners in the development and refinement of necessary skills and techniques. The book relies heavily on exemplary practice now occurring in the field.

It is our hope that those who study the material in this book find it to be immediately useful and sufficient to the task. Best wishes.

LWH
GCU

PART ONE

Organizational and Societal Impingements

What does it take to be a successful elementary school principal? Knowledge, skill, and humaneness would seem to be basic. (In addition, a finely honed sense of one's own dispensability also provides a needed perspective and frees one to act in a rational manner.) The four chapters that comprise Part One of this book focus on intra- and extraorganizational demands made on the principal.

Chapter One describes the complexities and the multifaceted responsibilities of the elementary school principal. An important distinction is made between the *principal* and the *principalship*. Chapter Two examines organizational realities and the impact these have on the internal communications process. Chapter Three contains an extensive review of the legal principles and practices that undergird the well-operated, humane school. Part One concludes with a discussion of the effect of changing community dynamics on the elementary school.

1

The Elementary School Principal—
A Complex Role in
a Dynamic Society

INTRODUCTION

The role of the elementary school principal has never been simple. From the start, when all it meant was extra duties for the "head teacher," the expectations of boards of education, superintendents, and parents have been demanding. Parents viewed the principal as a being imbued with great authority and endowed with omniscience. This mantle has always been nervously worn. Superintendents and boards on the other hand more frequently viewed the person as some kind of glorified clerk. This didn't do much for the self-concept of principals, either. The position has developed to the point where it is now one of the most important in the school system, occupied by neither paragons of leadership nor Uriah Heeps. The former are hard to find; the latter are no longer desired by most superintendents.

Elementary schools vary in size and complexity, of course. Similarly, the role of the principal and organizational and community expectations may vary from place to place, but the functions performed by the elementary principal are quite similar irrespective of where that principalship is located or how large the school is. And this job, which is crucial to the success of the school system, can be performed successfully by mortals. The necessary human, conceptual, and technical skills can be learned.[1]

---

[1]Regarding this point Drucker wrote: Service institutions can, no more than businesses, depend on supermen or lion tamers to staff their managerial and executive positions. There are far too many institutions to be staffed. It is absurd to expect that the administrator . . . would be a genius or even a great man. If service institutions cannot be run and managed by men of normal . . . [ability]; if, in other words, we cannot organize the task so that it will be done adequately by men who only try hard, it cannot be done at all." Peter F. Drucker, *Management* (New York: Harper and Row Publishers, 1974), p. 139.

Five Functions of the Principalship

No enterprise will function well for long without a competent chief executive with well-defined tasks and responsibilities to be accomplished. Effectively executing the responsibilities of the elementary principal will require better deployment of staff, participatory decision making, better utilization of time, and a better understanding of the forces on and in the school. These define the role of the principal.

Five functions comprise the principalship: school-community relations; staff personnel development; pupil personnel development; educational program development; and business and building management. These rubrics categorize the array of tasks and responsibilities that accrue to the principalship.

Moreover, the principalship has two dimensions. One of these dimensions has to do with effectively managing the enterprise. It is composed of those activities concerned with procuring, coordinating, and deploying the matériél and personnel needed to accomplish the goals of the school.

The other dimension is somewhat more difficult to define but can be summed up in one word: leadership. This is a dimension of quality. It is distinguished by the ways a principal uses himself/herself to create a school climate characterized by staff productivity, creative thought, and efficient and effective movement toward the goals of the school organization.

The good principal must be a good manager of the enterprise, but this does not mean that the principal must personally perform each specific management task. The principal who does not have time for teachers or children or for community relations activities because the ledgers need balancing is either defining the job too narrowly or is mismanaging time. Boards of education or superintendents of schools who evaluate principals primarily on the basis of balanced ledgers and quiet classrooms would achieve greater economies if they would simply employ husky bookkeepers rather than pay the price for well-trained, lettered school executives.

This handbook focuses on the five functions and two dimensions of the modern principalship. Guidelines for action are contained in all chapters.

SPECIAL DEMANDS ON ELEMENTARY PRINCIPALS

The nature and location of the educational enterprise places special demands on the designated leader. Inside the organization the principal is expected to stimulate and nurture a positive and productive climate. The demand here is for an "educational engineer."

Yet, the school—building or district—does not exist as a closed system; rather, it is a part of an open system and is in constant interaction with the larger community. Thus, a second demand is that the principal be able to develop positive relationships with the community to be served.

Educational Engineer

Some elementary schools are uptight places, fraught with frustration for children and teachers alike. The principal sets the tone and standard for the elementary school, and there is much good research from which to conclude this. Goldhammer and Becker, for example, reporting a study of more than 300 elementary principals representing every state in the United States, concluded:

> In schools that were extremely good we inevitably found an aggressive, professionally alert, dynamic principal determined to provide the kind of educational program he deemed necessary, *no matter what.*[2]

Goldhammer and his associates examined the status of the elementary principalship early in the 1970s, conducting wide-ranging interviews with principals throught the nation and reviewing the spectrum of conditions existent in elementary schools. Elementary schools that were outstandingly good were labeled "beacons of brilliance"; those that were extremely poor were called "potholes of pestilence." They found both kinds of schools throughout the nation in all types of settings but, in their judgment, not a sufficient number of "beacons."

The potholes of pestilence invariably suffered from weak leadership. The buildings were dirty and in disrepair, teacher and student morale were low, and fear was the basic control strategy. "The schools were characterized by unenthusiasm, squalor, and ineffectiveness. The principals are just serving out their time."

More recently Lipham[3] and Hughes[4] conducted separate, although related, reviews of research in an effort to discover what direct links, if any, there were between principal behavior and student learning. While no specific direct relationship could be found, there was no little evidence to show that the way in which the school was administered and the manner in which teachers were treated did seem to affect learner outcomes. Citing an array of recent research, Lipham concluded that

> The nature and quality of leadership provided by administrators is directly and positively related to the following outcomes of the schools: perceived effectiveness of the decisionmaking process . . .; perceived effectiveness of instruction . . . ; and staff satisfaction and morale.[5]

[2]Keith Goldhammer and Gerald L. Becker, "What Makes a Good Elementary Principal," *American Education* VI, 3 (April 1970): 11.

[3]James Lipham, *Review and Discussion of the Research of Educational Practices, Administrative and Supervisory Personnel* (Atlanta: Georgia Department of Education, 1979).

[4]Larry W. Hughes, *Critique of Lipham's Review of the Research, Administrative and Supervisory Personnel* (Atlanta: Georgia Department of Education, 1979).

[5]Lipham, op. cit., p. 15.

Hughes concluded his inquiry by reporting on the Rutter study, *Fifteen Thousand Hours*.[6] Stating that the Rutter study showed that, irrespective of the degree of social disadvantage experienced by pupils, schools can indeed make a difference. Hughes went on to point out that Rutter and his associates seem to indicate that "what really matters . . . is the 'ethos' of the school—'the general tone of the place." In the twelve London schools in "poor neighborhoods" that were studied, the tone of the school seemed to have more effect on pupil performance than such factors as the age of the school plant or the strictness of the discipline. Among other things that were discovered was that when a school was good in one aspect (student achievement, fewer behavior problems, or less vandalism, for example) it tended to be good in other aspects. The researchers concluded that it really is "how a school is run that makes the difference." Importantly, while the Rutter study found that good teaching was a strong factor in the good schools in comparison to the bad, it was also found that "it was very much easier to be a good teacher in some schools than others."

The study of the relationship of principal behavior and administrative style to a productive school climate is not a recent phenomenon. Probably the best-known studies are the highly respected inquiries conducted by Halpin and Croft in the late 1950s and early 1960s.[7] Halpin and Croft developed an instrument to portray the organizational climate of an elementary school. "Climates," identified by their Organizational Climate Descriptive Questionnaire (OCDQ), range from "Open" on the positive or productive end of the scale to "Closed" on the negative or nonproductive end.[8] The instrument examines the nature of the interaction between principals and teachers.

Halpin and Croft posit two dimensions to organizational climate: work group characteristics and leader behavior. Developing out of much previous research depicting the successful administrator as one concerned about both organizational task and goal achievement and the personal needs satisfaction of workers, the OCDQ taps both of these dimensions. In schools where both task and personal needs are addressed positively the organizational climate is "open," change acceptant, productive, and adaptive. Discussing this concept, Hughes states:

> The operational definition given to open climate emphasizes that this is a situation in which organizational members derive high levels of satisfac-

---

[6]Michael Rutter *et al.*, *Fifteen Thousand Hours* (Cambridge, Mass.: Harvard University Press, 1979).

[7]Andrew W. Halpin and Don B. Croft, *The Organizational Climate of Schools* (Chicago: Midwest Administration Center, University of Chicago, 1963). The original studies focused on the elementary principalship only; later inquiries examined administrative behavior in other positions.

[8]Halpin and Croft indicate that their use of these labels was influenced by the work of Rokeach in *The Open and Closed Mind* (New York: Basic Books, 1961). They liken climate in organizations to personality in individuals. Thus, an open climate is one that is receptive to new ideas.

tion both from interpersonal relations with fellow workers and from accomplishing tasks assigned to them within the organization.[9]

Further, he points out that

> One of the guiding assumptions of the work of Halpin and Croft is that the most effective organizational climate will be one in which it is possible for acts of leadership to emerge easily from whatever source. An essential determinant of a school's effectiveness noted by Halpin and Croft was the ascribed leader's ability, or his lack of ability, to create a climate in which he and other group members could initiate and consummate acts of leadership.[10]

The role of educational engineer requires a principal who is able to deal effectively with the human side of the educational enterprise while at the same time facilitating maximum organizational goal attainment. "Production orientation" is crucial to effective building leadership, but a high-quality product will not be obtained over the long haul unless great attention is given to the needs and aspirations of the people—pupils and staff—who make up the organization.

The Motivating Work Environment

Apropos to the previous discussion is the work of Rensis Likert. Likert, a pioneer in the field of modern supervision and administration, for years headed the Institute for Social Research at the University of Michigan. While at the Institute, Likert and his associates conducted a plethora of studies of management in government, industry, and schools. The major findings of these research endeavors included:

1. Employee-centered supervisors tend to be higher producers than production-centered supervisors.
2. Close supervision tends to be associated with lower productivity and more general supervision with higher productivity.
3. Within a particular organization, there is little relationship between employees' overall attitudes toward the organization and their productivity. (There is, however, a relationship between the overall attitude toward the organization and the absentee rate; those with a favorable attitude are absent less often.)
4. High morale (defined as the total satisfaction a worker gets from the work situation) does *not* necessarily mean high productivity. However,

---

[9]From *Performance Objectives for School Principals: Concepts and Instruments* by Jack A. Culbertson, Curtis Henson and Ruel Morrison, materials from Chapter 5, "Achieving Effective Human Relations and Morale" by Larry W. Hughes, © 1974 permission by McCutchan Publishing Corporation.
[10]Ibid.

the kind of supervision which results in high productivity also tends to result in high morale.[11]

One must note the last point in the Likert summary presented above. High morale does not necessarily mean high productivity; it may describe only what Blake and Mouton call a "9-1" management style; that is, one where there is great consideration for workers but little attention to organizational goal accomplishment.[12] Characteristic of a good working environment is notable progress toward goals. High morale is thus an outcome of an already productive environment rather than the cause of a productive environment.

The question then becomes, how should an administrator behave in order to assure a productive teaching-learning environment? In an effort to provide some insight as well as some evaluative indicators of effective behavior in the human dimensions of school enterprise, Hughes[13] developed a list of performance criteria which spoke to various elements of organizational life. Ten performance statements were developed, based on four organizational concepts that seemed to relate to productive work relationships. Each performance statement was explicated by one or more observable indicators of its accomplishment. For example:

Concept 1: The school organization is multi-functional and some of the functions are a product of the personal needs and wants of individual organizational members.

Performance statement: The principal recognizes that the private goals of organizational members affect the achievement of the public goals of the school.

Indicators: The principal—

1. Recognizes and supports differing teaching styles.
2. Flexibly schedules institutional demands on employee time.
3. Is able to identify personal needs of individual colleagues and provides intra-organizational ways in which these needs may be satisfied, consistent with organizational goals.
4. Matches teaching skills with teaching arrangements.[14]

---

[11]Rensis Likert, *Motivation: The Core of Management* (New York: American Management Association, Personnel Series #155, 1953). Such findings are consistent with Blake and Mouton (1964), McGregor (1960), Herzberg (1966) and Peters and Waterman (1982), among others, moreover, for a specific application of Likert to school administration, the reader is directed also to Sergiovanni and Starratt (1971), p. 15–24, and Sergiovanni and Carver (1973), p. 55–118.

[12]This is a management style that Blake and Mouton label the "country club." In the country club, people probably go home at night very tired from all the good morale but with no discernible product or with no discernible progress made toward organizational goals. These same people will not manifest high job satisfaction or high motivation. Robert Blake and Jane S. Mouton, *The Managerial Grid* (Houston: Gulf Publishing Co., 1964).

[13]From *Performance Objectives for School Principals: Concepts and Instruments* by Jack A. Culbertson, Curtis Henson and Ruel Morrison, materials from Chapter 5, "Achieving Effective Human Relations and Morale" by Larry Hughes, © 1974 permission by McCutchan Publishing Corporation.

[14]Hughes, *op. cit.*, p. 141–42.

This particular performance statement simply recognizes the uniqueness of individual teachers and suggests that in order to get the best out of teachers, administrators should arrange the teaching environment in a manner consistent with the style, attitude, and orientation of the teacher. This does not mean team teaching for all, or open spaces for all, or committees for all. If anything, research about human beings tells us that there is no one consistently productive pattern, and this knowledge may be the key to the way administrative behavior can positively affect teacher and learner behavior. It is to this point that Fiedler's leadership research and contingency theory speak most directly.[15]

The reason that the issue is a difficult one can be clarified best of all by Fiedler's research. His model clearly reveals the situational nature of effective leadership and helps explain why some studies have shown that a directive, task-oriented leadership style may promote effective group performance, while other studies have revealed that a nondirective human-relations-oriented style is desirable for effective group performance.[16] From a large number of studies, Fiedler has concluded that three leadership dimensions are crucial factors in leader effectiveness:

1. *Leader-member Relations.* This refers to the *leader's* feeling of being accepted by his or her subordinates.
2. *Task Structure.* This is to the degree to which the subordinates' jobs are routine and precisely defined as opposed to being relatively unstructured and loosely defined.
3. *Power Position.* This refers to the power inherent in the leadership position and includes the means available to the leader to grant or withhold rewards, support of the leader by those in upper management and official authority, and a number of other similar characteristics.

Fiedler's research indicates that effective leadership (i.e., leadership that relates to high productivity) varies according to the nature of these factors in a given work environment. How might this relate to leader-member activities in the school situation? Generally speaking, one can assume the teacher's job to be relatively "unstructured," as defined by Fiedler. Job descriptions are not highly prescriptive, and there is wide latitude permitted individual teacher decisions affecting classroom activities. Figure 1-1 depicts a summary of Fiedler's research as it relates to productive leadership styles in work situations that could be labeled "unstructured."

---

[15]Fred E. Fiedler, *A Theory of Leadership Effectiveness* (New York: McGraw-Hill, 1967).

[16]Fred E. Fiedler, *Leadership* (New York: General Learning Press, University Program Module Series, 1971). Others interested in pursuing this may find the work of Hersey and Blanchard to be helpful.

Paul Hersey and Kenneth H. Blanchard, *Management of Organizational Behavior: Utilizing Human Resources*, 2nd ed. (New York: Prentice-Hall, 1972).

Group Work Environment

Leader-member relations	Task structure*	Power position	Leadership style correlating with productivity
Good	Unstructured	Strong	Directive
Good	Unstructured	Weak	Permissive
Moderately poor	Unstructured	Strong	Permissive
Moderately poor	Unstructured	Weak	Directive

*Situations which can be depicted as a "structured" task result in a different array of productive leadership styles (Fiedler, 1971).

FIGURE 1-1. Group Work Environment.

An examination of Figure 1-1 shows that, given a particular "power position" and degree of "leader-member relations," the productive leadership style might vary.

Much research continues to focus on the situational aspects of leadership and on Fiedler's contingency theory. Our point here is not to explicate this research but rather to suggest that effective leadership requires a continual focus on the goals of the enterprise as well as on the maintenance of the work group. The way in which one goes about doing this is in large part stylistic and the result of what one perceives the group's needs to be.

School-Community Relations Specialist

Schools seem to be increasingly under attack and criticism. Why? And what does it mean? How is it possible that groups or individuals can attack such a sanctified institution as education and such a saintly collection of individuals as administrators and teachers? What do people mean when they say that "schools should be *accountable*"? Why does there seem to be an "educational credibility gap"? What is this uncertainty? What has happened to education? The answers to these questions lie in an understanding of the growth of and changes in society, which require a new sort of administrator.

The increasing complexity of society, coupled with the increasing esotericism of the science and art of education, has had a great effect on the relations of the school with its community. A major role that the elementary principal must perform, and is uniquely located to perform, is political and occurs outside, in the communities served by the school. This is the role of school-community relations specialist. This implies more than an occasional talk at Kiwanis, more than a monthly PTA meeting. It means the development of mechanisms to engage in information exchanges with the many sectors of the typical school attendance area. Neighborhood leaders need to be identified and heard. Neighborhood seminars, parent-teacher conferences, special advisory groups to focus on single problems are all devices that the principal can employ in addition to the usual bulletins and newsletters that alone are insufficient communication devices.

Four factors contribute to an educational credibility gap: the high cost of public education and other necessary public services; changing values; asser-public education and other necessary public services; assertive teacher organizations; social discontent; and population mobility.

agency is visible, it is scrutinized. School administrators have not been very successful at showing how extra dollars have resulted in a better product. This is what "accountability" is all about.

In an economy of scarce resources, citizens are often forced to make painful choices—a new car or higher pay for teachers; a new school or more highly trained and paid police and fire personnel. This dilemma is a reality with obvious implications for school practices in school-community relations programs. Implicitly, it means administrators and teachers ought to be able to point out some results, now. It can't be done with a bulletin sent home, and it can't be done without specific facts. Blind-faith goodwill is not characteristic of society today.

Secondly, professional educators, as a group, are losing the affectionate regard of the public. This has occurred primarily because educators have thrown off a "cloak of sanctity" and a "vow of poverty" in an attempt to gain economic advantages. Many of society's members are shocked and resentful at the assertive attitude teachers' groups are adopting.[17] Educators ought to recognize that society at large will not accord them the advantages of both sainthood and personal economic advances. Goodwill toward teachers, administrators, and schools will have to be actively sought and based on something more substantial than the sanctity of the educational enterprise.

Third, social discontent continues. This factor focuses on the motivation of the poor and culturally different elements of our society. The polyglot nature of our society only recently has been viewed as a positive feature and the melting pot theory put to rest. The implications to the school of a multiethnic, culturally diverse population are many indeed.[18]

Two purposes of American mass public education are generally accepted as guideposts. First, public schools are to pass on the accumulated wisdom of the world and teach those skills necessary for continued personal growth. Second, public schools have been viewed as the vehicle whereby social mobility could be achieved so that no one's child need be victimized by the state of his or her birth. In this regard the implications of a culturally diverse multiethnic

---

[17]"Assertiveness" on the part of teacher groups (associations or unions) has other implications for the elementary school principal as well. The principal plays a crucial role in the implementation of master contracts and is the "front line" in grievance proceedings. See Chapter 16, "The Principal's Role in Contract Administration."

[18]Insight about the various ways the school principal can capitalize on the richness of cultural diversity and multiethnicity in our society and the implications such diversity has for school programming and inservice training can be gained from a two-part cassette-tape series published by Cassette Services, Inc., St. Paul, Virginia 24283. Request "The Multi-Ethnic Curriculum," *Principals' Audio Journal* (November 1974 and December 1974), Side B.

society are manifest. In the eyes of some, the public school system has often operated to discourage participation in or achievement of the "good life" by many in society's understructure. Members of these groups have argued so persuasively for changed practices in the schools that the courts, legislatures, and educators have been dealing with the issue for the past two decades. The result has been desegregated schools, bilingual programs, breakfast at public expense, Headstart, Upward Bound, alternative education, magnet schools, mainstreaming, and neighborhood miniboards, among a host of other programs and procedures designed to reduce blatant inequities and require, as well, closer school-community relationships.

The fourth condition that impels the elementary principal into an outside role is population mobility. If any one factor characterizes most of American society today, it is mobility. America continues on the move, and highly stable school populations are difficult to find. Two kinds of population movements exist—micro and macro—and both have implications for administrative practice.

Macropopulation moves relate to certain mass movements of groups of people from one section of the country to another. A current trend, for example, is from the northeastern United States down the eastern seaboard and inland to the southwest and the deep south. There are other macro movements and such trends can substantially change the character of a neighborhood or area within a short period of time. These changes may require different kinds of school response patterns, including curricular offerings and public relations programs.

Micropopulation moves are most felt in urban areas, where a change of residence involving a move of but a few blocks results in a change of schools and perhaps even school districts. There is so much of this movement that some urban classrooms reveal as much as 120 percent student turnover in a single school year. Some children's records never do catch up. Productively coping with such transiency of the student population and with the negative effect it can have on teaching and learning is one of the great challenges of an urban elementary principalship.

The implication of all of this is that the elementary principal should be spending a large portion of administrative time engaged in school-community relations activities. There will need to be a continuous information exchange and analysis of community, neighborhood, and client needs. The reader may feel that this new role of community relations specialist is overemphasized. The authors don't think so. The closest social institution to the family, to the community, both psychologically and geographically, is the elementary school. It is "right around the corner," and, because of this, the elementary school principal enjoys a rare position on the front line between the community and its social welfare delivery systems. It is a position in which the principal can perform an important coordinating function.

Thus, within the leadership dimension of the principalship are two roles: school-community relations specialist and educational engineer. One is an "outside" role; the other occurs "inside" the organization. The two are kept discrete only for purposes of discussion here because they are interrelated—one probably could not be carried out well if the other was unattended to. Moreover, these two leadership dimension roles pervade the five functions of the principalship.

SUMMARY

Five functions determine the role of the elementary school principal: school-community relations, staff personnel development, pupil personnel development, educational program development, and business and building management. Two additional dimensions of the principalship are effective management and leadership. The principal today must be an effective manager, especially in the roles of school-community relations specialist and educational engineer.

BIBLIOGRAPHY

Blake, R. R., and Mouton, Jane S. *The Managerial Grid*. Houston: Gulf Publishing Company, 1964.

Culbertson, Jack A. *et al.*, eds. *Performance Objectives for School Principals*. Berkeley, Calif.: McCutchan Publishing Co., 1974.

Drucker, Peter F. *Management: Tasks, Responsibilities, Practices*. New York: Harper and Row Publishers, 1974.

Drucker, Peter F. *The Effective Executive*. New York: Harper and Row Publishers, 1968.

English, Fenwick W. *School Organization and Management*. Worthington, Ohio: Charles A. Jones, 1975.

Fiedler, Fred E. *A Theory of Leadership Effectiveness*. New York: McGraw-Hill, 1967.

Fiedler, Fred E. *Leadership*. New York: General Learning Press, University Program Module Series, 1971.

Goldhammer, Keith *et al. Elementary School Principals and Their Schools: Beacons of Brilliance and Potholes of Pestilence*. Eugene, Oregon: Center for the Advanced Study of Educational Administration, University of Oregon, 1971.

Goldhammer, Keith, and Becker, Gerald L. "What Makes a Good Elementary School Principal." *American Education* VI, 3 (April 1970): 11–13.

Hersey, Paul, and Blanchard, Kenneth H. *Management of Organizational Behavior: Utilizing Human Resources*. 2nd ed. New York: Prentice-Hall, 1972.

Herzberg, Frederick. *Work and the Nature of Man*. New York: Workman Publishing Company, 1966.

Hines, Susan C., and McCleary, Lloyd E. "The Role of the Principal in Community Involvement." *NASSP Bulletin* 64:432 (January 1980): 67–75.

Howell, Bruce. "Profile of the Principalship." *Educational Leadership* (January 1981): 333–36.

Hughes, Larry W. "Achieving Effective Human Relations and Morale." In Culbertson *et al.*, *Performance Objectives for School Principals,* chap. 5.

Hughes, Larry W. *Critique of Lipham's Review of the Research, Administrative and Supervisory Personnel.* Atlanta: Georgia Department of Education, 1979.

Hughes, Larry W. *Informal and Formal Community Forces: External Influences on Schools and Teachers.* Morristown, N.J.: General Learning Press, 1976.

Likert, Rensis. *Motivation: The Core of Management.* New York: American Management Association, Personnel Series #155, 1953.

Likert, Rensis. *New Patterns of Management.* New York: McGraw-Hill, 1961.

Likert, Rensis, and Likert, Jane G. *New Ways of Managing Conflict.* New York: McGraw-Hill, 1976.

Likert, Rensis. *The Human Organization: Its Management and Value.* New York: McGraw-Hill, 1967.

Lipham, James M. *Review and Discussion of the Research of Educational Practices, Administrative and Supervisory Personnel.* Atlanta: Georgia Department of Education, 1979.

Lipham, James M. and Hughes, Larry W. "Administrators and Supervisors," chapter 2 in Herbert J. Walberg (ed.), *Improving Educational Standards and Production.* Berkeley, Calif.: McCutchan Publishing Co., 1982.

McGregor, Douglas. *The Human Side of the Enterprise.* New York: McGraw-Hill, 1960.

Peters, Thomas J. and Waterman, Robert H., Jr. *In Search of Excellence.* New York: Harper & Row, Publishers, 1982.

Rutter, Michael *et al. Fifteen Thousand Hours: Secondary Schools and Their Effects on Children.* Cambridge, Mass.: Harvard University Press, 1979.

Sergiovanni, Thomas, and Starratt, R. J. *Emerging Patterns of Supervision: Human Perspectives.* New York: McGraw-Hill, 1971.

Sergiovanni, Thomas, and Carver, Fred D. *The New School Executive: A Theory of Administration.* New York: Dodd Mead, 1973.

Walberg, Herbert. *Improving Educational Standards and Productivity: The Research Basis for Policy.* Berkeley, Calif.: McCutchan, 1982. (See Chapter 2, especially.)

Wynne, Edward A. *Looking at Schools, Good, Bad, and Indifferent.* Lexington, Mass.: Lexington Books, 1980.

2

The School Organization and Good Internal Communication

INTRODUCTION

Except for hermits, people are members of a variety of organizations, and for at least a portion of almost every person's life he or she is a member of an organized work group. In the process of joining an organized work group the person gives up some individual freedom, gives up some control, for at least part of the day, over how he or she will spend time. For most of us life continues as a series of interactions between ourselves and a myriad of individuals, groups, and formal organizations. We are affected in substantial ways by these interactions, and we also have an impact on the individuals and organizations with whom we come in contact.

Conditions Affecting Individual Behavior in Organizations

Several conditions affect what happens in organizations. Consider the following:

1. People work in organizations, and organizational expectations, real or perceived, affect individual behavior and beliefs.
2. At least part of an individual's energy is devoted to trying to adapt to organizational realities and expectations of superordinates, peers, and subordinates.
3. While individuals rarely have total control over their work life, they do materially affect what happens in organizations.
4. People are different: they are variously motivated, and they do not always perceive the same set of circumstances similarly.
5. People are most affected by the expectations and conditions in their immediate work group.

These conditions may be either encouraging or discouraging when one considers the need for and nature of information exchanges (communication) in order to keep the organization moving. They are encouraging because they reveal the influence the formal organization, especially that part of it that exists at the school building level—the immediate work group—has on individual behavior. This manifests itself in general conformity to the official goals of the school as these are revealed in policy statements, rules and regulations, tradition, and existing curricula. Most people try to do what is expected of them insofar as they can and still maintain an integrated personality.

The conditions may be discouraging because they also reveal that individuals have a great impact on what the organization does and determine in great part whether or not goals are reached. The wise principal recognizes the staff's need for accurate information and organizes accordingly. He or she is also aware of staff and organizational idiosyncrasies that sometimes inhibit or distort information flow. Responding to problems in an effective way requires reliable information. Fact gathering, information seeking, perception testing, all initial steps in the decision-making process, require a smooth lateral and vertical flow of information throughout an organization. Two responsibilities comprise the task of administrative leadership. One is the task of moving the organization, in this case the individual school, toward its ultimate goals. At the same time, a school principal has the responsibility of maintaining the organization so it is both efficient and effective. Neither of these responsibilities can be achieved without an effective internal communication system.

The internal communication system not only keeps the left hand aware of what the right hand is doing, but it also helps insure that both hands understand what is being done and why, and, it is hoped, keeps them in general agreement that what is being done is correct. This, of course, is the ideal and is rarely totally achieved in any complex organization, but the more nearly it is achieved, the more effective the organization will be. At the very least, personnel in the organization should not work at cross purposes out of ignorance about what they are supposed to be doing and out of ignorance about what the organization is supposed to be doing. Without adequate information, the principal and other personnel within the school are victimized when they must respond to a developing problem.

Bulletins, Briefings, and Benevolent and Brainy Benedictions

Often a school district will expend much time, effort, and dollars developing a quality external communications program that it labels public relations, but will devote relatively little attention to the nature and needs of the internal communications program. In many school systems the internal communications network is relatively unsystematized, involving often a hit-or-miss use of a ditto machine or an occasional faculty meeting. At regular intervals, perhaps, the superintendent, a member of the central office staff, or the principal will appear on closed circuit TV, radio, or the P.A. system to discuss issues of concern to the system or the building as a whole. Often that's it, and the program can simply be labeled bulletins, briefings, and benevolent and brainy benedictions. Such one-way information dissemination provides little opportunity for information exchange.

THE MULTIDIMENSIONAL ORGANIZATION

The educational organization, or for that matter any organization composed of more than two people, has a multidimensional nature. Internal communication must be examined from the standpoint of the nature of organizations and of the ways in which individuals within the organization behave and relate to one another. Without a careful study of the nature of individual behavior within the school, the internal communications effort may easily become ineffective and misdirected and largely depend upon the five "B's."

Two dimensions, or elements, of an organization can be identified: the institutional dimension and the personal, or individual, dimension. The institutional dimension of an organization is made up of the official roles occupied by individuals. These roles are the dynamic aspects of the positions, offices, and statuses within an organization. They define the official behavior of people holding these positions, offices, or statuses, positions that have, of course, certain normative obligations and responsibilities. Thus, the principal has certain responsibilities and should behave in certain ways. Similarly, a teacher, a student, a night custodian, all have certain responsibilities.

The institutional dimension of an organization can be discerned rather readily from the formal organization chart and the job descriptions of the school system. From a formal organizational point of view the responsibilities are clear, and so the organization would appear to have no difficulty in responding directly and authoritatively to problem situations. The formal organization chart suggests that each role is incumbent, each position holder devoid of individual personality. A principal is to do these things and react in certain ways; a teacher is to do these things and react in certain ways. This situation would result in a certain predictability of behaviors and reactions, provided, of course, that the individuals in the organization have the same perceptions or nearly the same perceptions about role definitions and what behaviors are appropriate for what roles.

If that were all there was to it, communication would be very easy indeed. Each person would understand what was to be done, would do it, and move on to the next task with a minimum of misunderstanding and false starts. However, official roles in a school are not filled with automatons. Roles are filled with people with individual personalities, and no two are the same. This is the point where the misunderstanding and the breakdown of communications can begin. It is in examining this that the reasons for a good internal communication program can be best illustrated. For, as noted previously, there are two dimensions to an organization. The first is the institutional dimension; the second is the personal dimension.

Personal Dimension of the School Organization

It is not enough to understand the organizational chart and the job descriptions. There must be some understanding of the nature of the individuals inhabiting the various roles or positions in an organization. The individual style each person brings to a particular role differs from the style of other individuals performing that same role. In the educational field the individual needs, desires, and ambitions of each student are considered. The good school strives mightily to deal with the learner as an individual, to understand the learner's basic drives and the reason individuals behave as they do, each as a unique entity. Schools do this in an effort to provide a more efficient and effective learning program, to help the student develop into a productive, self-satisfied being. Transfer then this knowledge about the individual learner to the personnel within the school organization: the adult worker also has needs and ambitions, and any effort to derive the greatest productivity from the individual worker must take these into consideration. Social psychologists call these traits "needs-dispositions."

In large part, an individual's needs-dispositions comprise the personality and determine how the person acts and reacts to other people and situations. They help determine what information will be accepted and what information will be rejected, how closely the person is "in tune" with the school operation, or for that matter, how closely the person is in tune with his or her own assignment within the organization. A more precise way of saying in tune is to say that the person's goals and the organizational goals are congruent. The greater the degree of congruency between person and job, and person and organization, the more effective the person will be.

It might be said then that the way to facilitate communication and provide for a productive environment is to explain precisely to each person what the specifics of the job are, lead the person to a desk in a classroom, ring a bell, and let the work begin. But, "in-tuneness" is, of course, more than this. How a person behaves, where the person thinks he or she stands in relationship to others and the organization in general, and how much he or she understands is dependent upon his own perceptual framework. People see and understand what their individual background permits them to see and understand. Once this is recognized, the internal communication program ought to begin to mature. It will become apparent that bulletins, briefings, and benevolent and brainy benedictions simply are not enough, except for low-level communication.

A great error is made by assuming that when an individual works in an organization, that individual really understands the goals of the organization, agrees with them, or for that matter, even thinks about them. The person may not join a school staff in any particular capacity because of any deep commitment to education. In fact, he or she may even be antagonistic toward education as it is being practiced there. The person may simply have wanted a job. To expect each worker within the school organization to have deeply internalized feelings about the significance of the job or the significance of the organization itself is not realistic. Zeigler has written with great insight:

> It is not merely a person's occupation which colors his attitudes, but it is his perceptions of his occupation and the extent to which the occupation is functional in maintaining an integrated personality. On the other hand, there is the question of commitment to the occupation. To some persons the occupation is a major component of their identity. Others look at the occupation in a more casual fashion, viewing it primarily as a money-making device and not so much a portion of a total lifestyle.[1]

Informal Groups

Many informal groupings of people not found on the organizational chart function within the formal framework of any school organization. These non-official groupings are characterized by a feeling of general agreement, not necessarily spoken but tacitly understood, about certain values and goals. These are groupings of people who tend to see things somewhat similarly, who meet over a cup of coffee or cigarette during work and perhaps socialize together afterward. This highly personalized system of interaction operates to modify the effect of the formal organization on individuals. The groups may or may not tend to agree with the institutional goals or the expectations of the formal organization, although overtly they may behave as if they did. Leadership within the informal organization is earned through power, personality, or prestige rather than ascribed, as in the formal organization. Further, the informal organization lies outside of the formal communications channel.

Commonly one thinks of the professional teaching staff as being the most important locus of informal groups, but informal groupings also may be found among administrators, noncertificated employees, and students. In some cases there may be a mixing of role incumbents—as in the "boiler room gang," which might include a custodian or two.

There are, then, loosely organized, but potentially influential, groups of people operating outside the formal organization of the institution. As previously indicated, these groups have their own norms, values, and needs, and individual members may perceive their functions as being somewhat different than the official organization would define them. In the negative extreme, these groups may actually operate in such a way as to inhibit the school as it moves toward its goals. The more congruence in terms of values and goals that the informal and formal organization can develop, the more successful the school will become.

One function of administrative leadership is to maintain the institution while moving it toward its goals. The principal must be aware of the function-

---

[1]Harmon Zeigler, *The Political World of the High School Teacher* (Eugene, Ore.: Center for the Advanced Study of Educational Administration, 1966), p. 3.

ing of the informal dimension and its various needs and must seek to achieve a congruence between the two. Further, a rich source of information and leadership exists in the informal dimension, a source that the perceptive principal will tap in the problem-resolution process.

Because of their nature, informal groupings do not have an intensely stable organization. There are shifts in leadership as members leave the system or the building, or as other leaders emerge. The principal must be aware of these shifts and the implication that they may have to the informal communication channels that have been set up. Informal groups are a natural part of any organization and provide for a sense of personal significance within what may be a very impersonal structure. Also, there is not only one group operating within the information structure but a number of groups. Thus, different ways of relating and dealing with these groups must be developed, depending upon the situation and the group.

Moreover, it is sometimes useful, and especially pertinent to our discussion here, to think of the educational enterprise as a combination of loosely coupled systems. Weick, in his carefully crafted analysis of organizations,[2] suggests that, rather than being composed of tightly interrelated subsystems, the elements of an educational organization (for example) are frequently only loosely tied together. By using the term "loose coupling" to describe an organization, Weick connotes that its subsystems (elements) are responsive to each other but that each still preserves its own identity and its own physical and logical separateness. Weick writes:

> . . . elements may consist of events like yesterday and tomorrow (what happened yesterday may be tightly or loosely coupled to what happens tomorrow) or hierarchical positions like top and bottom, line and staff, or administrators and teachers. Another interesting set of elements that lends itself to loose coupling imagery is means and ends. Frequently, several different means lead to the same outcome. When this happens, it can be argued that any one means is loosely coupled to the end in the sense that there are alternative pathways to achieve the same end. Other elements that might be found in loosely coupled educational systems are teachers-materials, voters-school board, administrators-classroom process-outcome, teacher-teacher, parent-teacher, and teacher-pupil.[3]

If the system is only loosely coupled, or if particular elements within the system are only loosely coupled, then the possibility of much miscommunication and distortion exists. In such a system, great care must be taken that messages are not only received, but received in the spirit intended.

How does all of this affect the development of a good internal communication system? It clearly means that principals should make use of several

---

[2]Karl E. Weick, "Educational Organizations as Loosely Coupled Systems," *Administrative Science Quarterly* 21 (March 1976): 1–19.

[3]Ibid., p. 4.

mechanisms in the communications effort. Attempting to change behavior just because it's "good for the organization" will not be a sufficient argument for many members of the staff. The development of mechanisms to involve teachers and noncertificated employees in significant tasks of a school nature that affect their job will be important to the success of a school. In other words, there must be means to provide for group attention to the problems affecting the organization. Tapping the group's intelligence will result in better problem resolution as well as engender support for the final decisions.

Certainly, bulletins, briefings, and benevolent and brainy benedictions are not enough for good communication and problem resolution. Such one-way devices do not provide an adequate opportunity to learn the reactions of the various people in the organization or to secure additional information that may materially affect problem resolution.

LEVELS OF COMMUNICATION

The discussion to this point has been treating the subject almost as if communication "A" is the same as communication "B." It is not necessary to deliver all information in person to each individual within the organization. Nor do all messages require group meetings. There are different levels of communication. Some matters can be taken care of adequately by a dittoed bulletin. Others, however, require different approaches. For lack of a better classification, the levels of communication might be called low level, middle level, and high level. The distinction among these levels is made largely on the nature of the communication, the significance of it, and the ease with which the request or the concept being explored can be understood and implemented.

Thus, a *low level* of communication covers those simple little directives such as when pay day is or when a report is due. These are simply the things that a staff member must know and can forget until the next time. Little explanation is required and the task is easily implemented.

The *middle level* of communication includes important information about the district (new policies and procedures, for example), new programs the district is involved in, the appointment of textbook adoption committees, and so on. This information requires somewhat more detail and causes a greater expenditure of energy on the part of the personnel to whom it is directed, both for comprehending the message and for implementing it.

A *high level* of communication is concerned with items of a more conceptual nature, such as major changes in direction for the district or the school, major policy changes at the school board level that would have great effect throughout the district or that deal with developing problems of some magnitude such as a dramatic change in achievement levels of students, the changing nature of the student population, and other situations that have implications for school programming and instructional procedures.

The more difficult the nature of the idea that is being conveyed, the more important it is that the sender receive a reaction from the receiver. The best communication of all is face-to-face communication, since it provides the best chance to avoid misunderstanding. One can tell by immediate action, facial expression, or response whether or not the message has been received and understood, and thus, one stands the best chance of getting the necessary feedback.

Good communication, then, requires:

1. The appropriate device.
2. A clear statement of the problem or the issue.
3. Understanding by the receiver.

Feedback

The matter of feedback deserves some attention. The informal groupings and informal communication channels in the system cannot be disregarded. Informal groupings provide the most effective way of gaining feedback and information. Of course, it is difficult for the principal to have access to or to be a member of many of the informal groups that exist within a school. This is apparent to any person who has walked unexpectedly into the teachers' lounge or interrupted the secretary pool at coffee-break time and sensed the dramatic change in the nature of the conversation. Yet, it is possible, once the existence of the informal groups has been recognized, to develop clear and open relationships with these groups, or with certain individuals within them, to secure information, and do some perception testing. It is possible to use many of these groups or leaders of the groups as sounding boards and as devices to get the word out on items of interest and concern.

Very few communication systems work as fast as the informal network in most organizations. For example, consider how long it takes for the word to get out to the affected teachers that a supervisor is in the building. The informal network can hardly be depended upon as the sole means of communication, but the principal ought to be aware of it and use it to best advantage.[4]

SUMMARY

A school organization is composed of several interacting parts and a hierarchical structure. Individuals have an impact on the work environment and the environment has an impact on individuals. Moreover, persons within the same work environment often perceive the same set of circumstances differently. In such a complex, communication problems will occur.

---

[4]A wise principal sets up a committee structure in the building to tap the insights and decision-making ability of the staff as well as to provide a means to convey messages effectively. Chapter 11 offers some specific suggestions for such a structure.

Good communication in the school organization is not an accident. It is something that only occurs with the careful attention of the principal. The communication system must be fast, reliable, and appropriate to the message being conveyed.

An organization is made up of many different kinds of people, with different backgrounds, different perceptions about their work, and different motivations. Moreover, there is an informal dimension to an organization that seldom approximates the formal organization depicted on a chart. The key to a good communication system is recognizing that complex decisions which require people to change their modes of behavior in significant ways will require much attention to communication devices that are face-to-face in nature so that clear understandings result.

SOME BASIC UNDERSTANDINGS ABOUT INTERNAL COMMUNICATION

1. We communicate for a reason: to dispense information, to promulgate a decision, to change behavior, to present an important point of view, to challenge thinking, or to raise a question. As soon as the message to be communicated has to go from one person through another to a third person, something — the spirit in which it was intended, the background of thinking involved, or even the true meaning — is probably lost in the transmission.

2. The device for communicating that is employed must be appropriate to the complexity and nature of the message one is attempting to communicate. Two-page bulletins make good filler for wastebaskets, especially if they are single spaced. Before we deplore the practice of personnel not reading the bulletins, let's admit that, typically, they are not very good literature. If it takes two pages, it probably ought to be discussed in person, at least in group meetings.

3. Quality is more important than quantity. A quality communication may be defined as one that is readily understood and understood in the spirit in which it was given.

4. The internal communications system must take into account all the people within the organization: the teachers, the administrators, the noncertificated (classified) employees, the pupils, and the board of education. The board of education, in order to make the kinds of policy decisions that will positively influence the school organization, must be kept well informed about what is going on within the organization. Every staff member has an obligation to help keep the superintendent informed so that in turn the board of education has the background needed to make good decisions.

5. There must be sensitivity to the possible reactions of others to decisions concerning which they have insufficient knowledge. Those most affected by a particular decision or communication should know why the decision was made.

6. There are many devices for insuring better understanding by people within the organization. Small group meetings, large group meetings, delivering the message in person, involvement of staff in appropriate decision making, publications ranging from bulletins to staff newsletters and on to a staff

library, as well as more common means should all be employed, but should only be specifically employed when they are the most appropriate media for communicating.

7. Even face-to-face communication does not insure understanding. Anyone who has ever taught knows this. All educators have felt frustration after thoroughly explaining something only to have someone in the back row raise a hand and ask a question that reveals that not a word was heard.

8. Good communication provides an opportunity for reaction and feedback. This is needed for two reasons: first, to be able to know whether or not what was said was understood and, second, because the reaction or feedback may indicate that some modification in the decision may be called for in the light of response.

9. In order for the communication to be effective, the receiver must pay attention, be interested in what you are saying, see some personal application to what is being said, and be willing and able to act upon what is said.

10. Finally, there must be an awareness of the informal organization and groupings within the formal structure of the organization. Organizations are made up of people whose own drives, needs, and desires modify their behavior and affect their perception. How and what they perceive affects their understanding and ability to act upon what is being communicated.

FIGURE 2-1.

BIBLIOGRAPHY

Argyris, Chris. *Integrating the Individual and the Organization.* New York: John Wiley and Sons, 1964.

Hubley, John W. "Engineer in the Boiler Room—The Role of the Principal." *NASSP Bulletin* LXII (January 1979): 6–9.

Hughes, Larry W. "Effective Human Relations and Morale." In Jack Culbertson *et al., Performance Objectives for School Principals.* Berkeley, Calif.: McCutchan Publishing Corp., 1974, chap. 5, esp. pp. 127–30.

Hughes, Larry W., and Robertson, Thomas. "Principals and the Management of Conflict." *Planning and Changing* 11, no. 1 (Spring 1980): 3–15.

Hughes, Larry W., and Achilles, Charles M. "The Supervisor as a Change Agent." *Educational Leadership* 28, no. 8 (May 1971): 840–43.

Menefee, G. R. "Communications, Decision Making, and Leadership Styles." *School Business Affairs* 44, no. 8 (August 1978): 258–59.

Sergiovanni, Thomas, and Carver, Fred D. *The New School Executive.* New York: Harper & Row Publishers, 1980, esp. chap. 12, "The School as a Political System."

Weick, Karl E. "Educational Organizations as Loosely Coupled Systems." *Administrative Science Quarterly* 21 (March 1976): 1–19.

Ziegler, Harmon. *The Political World of the High School Teacher.* Eugene, Ore.: Center for the Advanced Study of Educational Administration, 1966.

3

Students, Staff, and Administrator Rights and Responsibilities: A Legal Focus

INTRODUCTION

It is a litigious society in which we live, and in recent years this has become increasingly more the case. Schools have not been unaffected by the seemingly exponential expansion of threats to "sue." Knowledge about the laws governing human interaction, especially in the school setting, is most important for the elementary school principal.

In many states school districts, as extensions of the state, still receive protection from court action under the medieval doctrine of sovereign immunity ("The king can do no wrong"). Increasingly, however, this doctrine is being replaced. Even those states that have not totally done away with school district immunity from tort liability hold the district accountable, at least in certain instances. Principals and teachers must understand that as individuals they are seldom immune to litigation, regardless of the extent of protection their district has. Further, the growing complexity of school programs increases legal implications. Moreover, as societal attitudes change, so does the nature of many judicial interpretations.

This chapter will not attempt to replace a graduate course in school law. It cannot do so. Nor could any graduate course in school law prepare an administrator to be an attorney. But recurring legal issues and fundamental legal bases need to be addressed in a book about the principalship to provide a firm legal footing for the operation of the schools.

However, rules of law are not universally accepted. Different courts often hand down conflicting decisions regarding similar cases. Further, the interpretation of the law changes as societal attitudes change. It is important to keep abreast of these changes and of important court decisions throughout the country.[1]

Legal Structure of the Schools in the United States

By law, public school districts are state organizations, board of education members are state officers, school personnel are state employees, and school district buildings are state property. In practice, of course, the support and control of the public schools is a partnership between local, state, and federal governments. Even private and parochial schools are not totally autonomous because these school systems must meet certain state curricular and teacher certification standards. Often, too, federal regulations impinge on their operation when these schools accept financial support.

The legal framework within which school systems operate is manifest in the acts passed by federal, state, and local legislative bodies, court decisions, constitutional law, and rules and regulations enacted by regulatory and administrative bodies such as the state departments of education or health departments. A further source of legal guidelines are general opinions of various Attorneys General that stand until tested in a court of law or modified by subsequent legislative acts. Within this legal framework local administrators have latitude in the development of policies, rules, regulations, and procedures. The authority for local school board and administrative action is depicted in Figure 3-1. One extralegal impingement exists: community sanctions, attitudes, and belief structures that modify, often very directly, the development and implementation of local policies.

Limitations on local authority depend also on prevailing court philosophy in any state. In some states, the prevailing philosophy is that boards of education may adopt any reasonable policy not specifically prohibited by statute. In other states courts insist that there be specific statutory permission before a particular policy can be adopted. Generally speaking, courts have tended to uphold the rule of reason, that boards of education may adopt any reasonable policy within the law. Courts in all states do insist on strict adherence to laws concerning management of public funds, however. School boards and administrators must find clear statutory authority for the expenditure of funds derived from public revenues.

---

[1]Several services are available to the school administrator to assist in this endeavor. For example, the National Organization on Legal Problems in Education (NOLPE), 1501 West 21st Street, Topeka, Kansas 66606 distributes monthly *NOLPE Notes* to members that deal with current legal matters involving the school. Various professional principal organizations have publications containing legal information, and many of the national educational journals such as the *American School Board Journal* contain regular legal features. NOLPE promotes an interest in and an understanding of school law. In addition to meetings and membership response systems, it issues regular publications on school law subjects and serves as a clearinghouse for information on research and legal publications. It does not take official positions on policy questions but does attempt to provide broad information about current issues.

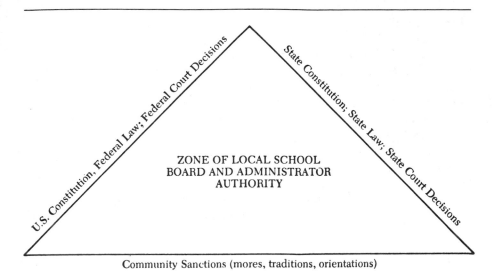

FIGURE 3-1. Circumscribed Local Authority for School Operation.

Source: Adapted from Larry W. Hughes and Robert J. Simpson, *Education and the Law in Tennessee* (Cincinnati, Ohio: W. H. Anderson Co., 1971), p. 5.

The rule of reason is relevant to principals and teachers, since it is at the school building level that the policies of the school board and the laws governing education are most often implemented. It is also at the school building level that most of the litigation involving the school system occurs. Laws and policies injudiciously applied, or incorrectly interpreted, at this level may result in children and personnel inhumanely or illegally treated. More and more frequently the result is a law suit listing principals and teachers as defendants. This chapter will focus, therefore, not on the entire spectrum of school law, but on legal issues common to the operation of a school building.

STUDENT AND STAFF RIGHTS: ESTABLISHING A FRAMEWORK

It is important to establish that although students and faculty may not always be right, they always have rights. This means that United States citizens have certain fundamental rights that cannot be abrogated by any agency, public or private. It means too, that agencies are obligated to inform employees and clients of their rights and to work diligently to insure that everyone in the organization is accorded those rights. Withholding information from anyone within and about the school organization—students, teachers, parents or classified employees—about their rights is immoral and inconsistent with the tenets upon which this country was founded; for the law insures, in short, the fairest "shake" for everyone. Attempting to keep people ignorant of the laws (and thus of their rights) violates the law.

People have no more rights today than they have ever had, but the according of these rights is under increasing review by the courts. Unfortunately, school administrators have sometimes trapped themselves into acting simultaneously as judge, jury, and prosecuting attorney, in many instances overstepping their authority and jurisdiction. Sometimes teachers, administrators, and other school employees have behaved *in loco deo* rather than *in loco parentis* and have placed themselves in untenable legal positions.[2]

Most of the individual rights enjoyed in this country derive from the Constitution of the United States, and are largely located in the first ten amendments of the Constitution, the Bill of Rights, and in some subsequent amendments, notably the Fourteenth Amendment. Basically those amendments of especial relevance to the operation of the schools are:

> *Amendment One* deals with freedom of religion and expression and rights to peaceful assembly and petition. It grants the rights of all citizens to peacefully assemble and to petition the government for redress of grievances. Amendment One has often been cited in civil rights cases involving students.
>
> *Amendment Four* focuses on the rights of persons and states that the people and property shall be protected against "unreasonable searches and seizures," meaning that appropriate warrants must precede such police action. The educational implications here affect the confidentiality of records, interrogation of pupils, and the proceedings of juvenile court.
>
> *Amendment Five* guarantees the due process of law. It says that certain rights to life, liberty, and property are inviolate and people cannot be deprived of them without due process of law.
>
> *Amendment Six* provides for judicial procedure and guarantees a speedy public trial, an impartial jury, information about the nature of the charge, confrontation by witnesses against the party, the right of the accused to obtain witnesses in his own behalf, and the right to have counsel.

----

[2]*In loco parentis*, as a legal principle, is a common-law measure of the rights and duties of school authorities relative to pupils and schools, and holds that school authorities stand in the place of the parent when a child is at school. It simply means that school personnel may establish rules and require obedience of these rules for the educational welfare of the child. Further, school personnel may inflict punishments for disobedience. The legal test is whether a reasonably knowledgeable and prudent parent would so act and the doctrine is used not only to support the rights of school personnel, but also to establish a responsibility of these same school personnel regarding such occurrences as injuries that may befall pupils. It is a presumption of the law that those having authority will exercise it properly. In claims of improper application of authority, the burden of proof falls on the person making the claim. Thus, for example, a parent who may object to a rule or to a punishment generally must prove unreasonableness.

Amendment Eight prohibits cruel and unusual punishment and excessive bail. The educational implications are clear, especially with regard to the question of corporal punishment, although undue mental anguish has also been cited as a "cruel and unusual" punishment.

Amendment Nine guarantees the "rights of the people" and states that the enumeration in the Constitution of certain rights shall not be construed to deny or discourage other rights retained by the people. This simply means that even if the Constitution is explicitly silent, it does not mean that other rights are not enjoyed.

Amendment Ten indicates that the powers that are not delegated to the United States by the Constitution nor prohibited by it to the states are reserved to the states respectively or to the people.

After the Civil War, the Fourteenth Amendment, often called the "States' Bill of Rights," was adopted. It states that "no state shall make a law which abridges the rights of citizens in the United States nor deny anyone the equal protection of the law." It states further that all persons, whether born or naturalized in the United States and subject to the jurisdiction thereof, are citizens of the United States and of the state wherein they reside. Thus, each state must guarantee the same rights to its citizens that are guaranteed by the federal Constitution. It is important to call attention to the phrase "all persons." The amendment does not say all adults; it says all persons, and that includes children.

The preceding then sets a legal framework for the discussion of student and faculty rights. In a very real sense it also sets a moral or ethical framework as well because the laws of the land reflect the morals of the land. The spirit of the law applies equally to students and nonstudents, and it does not discriminate because of age.

In general, the courts have made it clear that constitutional protections apply to students both in and out of school. Freedom of expression and other basic rights, if not always clearly defined in the schools, are well established in the law. Courts require specified procedures to safeguard those rights against the abuse of institutional authority. The matter of procedural due process, which will be discussed more completely later in this chapter, guarantees certain rights by the fair application of rules and regulations.

Some principals and teachers may argue that there have always been adequate means for dealing with student complaints and grievances, that the latch string has always been on the outside of the door, and that staff members have always been willing to listen to complaints and grievances. However, the capacity to take appropriate corrective action when such action is essential to sustain student rights is even more important than outside latch strings for, as pointed out in Tinker *v*. Des Moines School District, "Students do not surrender their rights at the school house door."[3]

---

[3]Tinker *v*. Des Moines Independent Community School District, 393 U.S. 503, 89 S. Ct. 733 (1969).

One of the major goals of school personnel should be to establish a trust based on humaneness and respect for others. A child or adult who feels unrespected and not accorded basic human rights, will not respect others. The authors especially like the court's language in the 1943 case of West Virginia *v.* Barnette[4]:

> The Fourteenth Amendment . . . is now applied to the State itself and all of its creatures—boards of education not excepted. These (i.e., boards of education) have, of course, important, delicate and highly discretionary functions, but none that they may perform except within the limits of the Bill of Rights.

Further, this same court said in what is very perceptive pedagogy:

> That they are educating the young for citizenship is reason for scrupulous protection of the constitutional freedom of the individual *if we are not to strangle the free mind at its source and teach youth to discount important principles of our government as mere platitudes.* [Emphasis supplied.]

In other words, and educators must know this is true, *responsibility cannot be learned in the absence of freedom.* Shannon puts the issue in good perspective when he writes:

> It is natural that public education would be the subject of spirited community discussion and debate, as competing values and philosophies of our polyglot society are filtered into courts of action on educational policy matters. Instead of weakness, community involvement, although sometimes rancorous and bitter, is in reality a strength of the public school system and augurs for continuing improvement in educational offerings to meet the changing demands of our changing world. As frustrating and difficult as controversy may be at times, it is a hallmark of our open and free society. Instead of rejecting it, we must learn to live with it—even in educational matters—which, in the final analysis, is clearly an area of life where reasonable opinions may differ.
>
> Finally, the wide publicity accorded student misconduct by a media bent on entertaining as well as informing people, often gives the erroneous impression that student misconduct is more prevalent than it actually is and that school authorities are inept in dealing with it. Moreover, "misconduct" is often the word used by the people as a result of media coverage, of conduct by students which the courts say is fully protected by the expanding First Amendment "free speech" right. And, "developing due process" rights characterized by elaborate hearing procedures, for students accused of misconduct which could result in their suspension or expulsion, is sometimes mistaken for authoritarian softness and permissiveness by parents whose children were never accused of serious misconduct in schools.[5]

---

[4]West Virginia *v.* Barnette, 319 U.S. 624 (1943).
[5]Thomas A. Shannon, in *Current Trends in School Law* (Topeka, Kan.: The National Organization on Legal Problems of Education, 1974), p. 5.

ISSUES OF EDUCATIONAL EQUITY

Recent years have seen increasing attention placed on the need to assure that all persons have equal access to the fruits of education irrespective of their sex, race, ethnicity, or any handicapping condition. A host of laws, often federally generated, have been promulgated and much litigation has occurred in the effort to insure equity. Of special relevance to the elementary school principal are the laws, court decisions, and educational guidelines with respect to sex discrimination, desegregation, and the provision of the least restrictive educational environment for handicapped children.

Sex Discrimination

In both academic matters and cocurricular matters the issue of sex discrimination has arisen. Although the issue of sexual discrimination in academic matters has not been a specific problem at the elementary school level, it is something about which elementary principals need be aware. More frequently in recent years, issues of sex discrimination have been located in the cocurricular realm.

In the matter of academic assignments, sexual discrimination has been found to occur most often in class assignment and admission to programs or schools. Gender has been determined to be an illegal criterion for assignment and admission. It has been held also, for example, to be a violation of the equal protection clause of the Fourteenth Amendment to use higher admission standards for females than for males for admission to an academic school. The circuit court, in Berkleman v. San Francisco Unified School District[6] said that merit is the only sound basis for admission, not such "unsupported" needs suggested by the school district officials' position that "an equal number of male and female students is an essential element in a good high school education."[7]

Nevertheless, the "separate but equal" concept with regard to schools for boys and girls is still viable where a school district (or any educational unit) can show that genuinely equal educational opportunities are provided students in these schools, when these schools are compared to all other schools or units in the system.[8] The burden of proof is, however, on the school system.

In some schools, too, females have been excluded from certain specialized vocational and prevocational courses. This practice has been challenged, and in most such cases the women were admitted to the courses before the cases came to trial. Clearly, even though there is little in the way of case law, such exclusion practices are contrary to the current thrust of the law. Unless the school administrator or the school board can show some rational basis for excluding one sex or the other from a course or program, there should be no

---

[6]501 F. 2d. 1264 (9th Cir., 1974). See also Bray v. Lee, 337 F. Supp. 034 (D.C. Mass., 1972).

[7]Ibid., at 1269.

[8]See, for example, William v. McNair, 316 F. Supp. 134 (D.C. S.C., 1970) aff'd. mem., 401 U.S. 951 (1971).

policy that would differentiate the enrollment. It is doubtful that such a basis can be developed; few human activities are physiologically determined.

Most of the litigation focusing on sex discrimination has had to do with participation in cocurricular activities, specifically participation in athletic competition. Title IX of the 1972 Education Act amendment is a buttress against sex discrimination in the cocurricular realm. Title IX established among other things that participation in organized athletic programs in the public schools must be accessible irrespective of sex.

There are two situations in which claims have arisen. The first is the failure of a school district to fund and provide a team for a specific sport for its female students, and then, while not providing a team, also prohibiting females from participating on the team it does have. The issue in these cases is not whether a girl has a constitutional right to participate in a particular sport but whether the state, having provided an athletic program, can deny an opportunity for equal participation to members of one sex. The asserted protective purpose in maintaining separate teams is frequently stated this way: girls cannot compete effectively with boys in sports because of the inherent physical differences between the sexes; thus, it is argued frequently, separate teams are reasonable and indeed even necessary. *Several courts have accepted this conclusion but have held that they could not sanction a failure to provide a separate athletic program for girls.*[9] Separate but equal athletic programs are also statutory law in section 86.41 of Title IX(B), "Administration of Athletics." Moreover, there is a provision included that states if a school district does not fund and offer separate athletic programs, it must allow members of the excluded sex to try out for the team it does have, unless the "sport involved is a contact sport."

In those instances where a girl wishes to try out for the boys' team even though there already does exist a girls' team, the courts have responded in mixed fashion. More often the courts have held that if there is a team for females, then that is the one to which girls have access, and rules prohibiting their participation on the male team are legal.[10] There have been cases, however, where exclusion has been deemed illegal even though there was also a team for females.[11]

Mainstreaming

Public schools historically have been involved in the education of handicapped youngsters, but over the last few years such activities have taken on a more precise and legally defined basis. Legislation culminating with the Education of All Handicapped Children Act of 1975 (Public Law 94-142) has mandated

---

[9]See, for example, Brenden v. Independent School District, 342 F. Supp. 1224 (D. Minn., 1972); Herver v. Meiklejon, 430 F. Supp. 164 (D. Col., 1977).

[10]See, for example, Ruman v. Eskew, 333 NE 2d. 138 (1975) and Bucha v. Illinois High School Association, 351 F. Supp. 69 (1972).

[11]See, for example, Morris v. Michigan State Board of Education, 472 F. 2d. 1207 (1973).

the provision of the "least restrictive learning environment" for handicapped children. Public Law (PL) 94-142 provides for ready access to appropriate public education for handicapped children between ages three and twenty-one and mandates the integration of these children into settings that may have been formerly limited to nonhandicapped children. The term "mainstreaming" has been applied to this practice.

PL 94-142 is buttressed by other federal laws, PL 94-143 and the earlier PL 93-112, which have established certain rights to education and fair treatment for handicapped children.[12] These rights include:

- Right to a free appropriate education at public expense, without regard to severity of handicap.
- Right to service in the least restrictive setting when the handicap requires service in something other than the normal school setting.
- Right to prior notice before any decision is made to change services given to a child.
- Right of parents to give consent before their child is evaluated, placed in a special program, or changed in placement.
- Right to full due process, including representation by legal counsel, right to confront and crossexamine school personnel, right to a verbatim transcript, right to appeal, and right to be heard by an impartial hearing officer (not a school employee).
- Right to assignment without discrimination on the basis of sex, race, or culture.
- Right to program placement without discrimination on the basis of sex, race, or culture, and to placement in a facility that is comparable to that offered to nonhandicapped clients of the system.
- Right to be served in accordance with an individual program plan that states annual goals, measurable intermediate steps, the names of persons who will provide services and their qualifications, a timetable for beginning each step in the service and its anticipated duration, a schedule for evaluating the success of the program, and the right to be transferred if the program is failing.
- Right to be protected from harm through use of unregulated experimental approaches, untrained staff, inclusion in a program with others who are physically assaultive, freedom from unreasonable corporal punishment, and freedom from work assignments without compensation.
- Right to see all records and to contest them in a hearing, with the right to place in the record information that the client feels presents a balanced picture.

---

[12]PL 94-143 is entitled the "Developmentally Disabled Assistance and Bill of Rights Act"; PL 93-112 is the "Rehabilitation Act" and was enacted in 1973.

Thus, "separate but equal" as a concept appropriate to the education of handicapped children has been found to be generally unacceptable.

The passage of PL 94-142 was the culmination of many years of litigation and legislation to protect the civil rights of children who are handicapped. The legislative act insures specified substantive and procedural provisions for handicapped children as well as an escalating funding formula to insure a free and appropriate public education for all handicapped students.

Of specific importance to school principals is that the law insists on:

1. A zero reject policy.
2. Specific due process procedures.
3. Nondiscriminatory testing.
4. A written and promulgated individual educational plan (with specific evaluation procedures about its effectiveness) for every handicapped child. This plan is to be developed jointly with parents and reviewed at least annually.
5. Provision of a least-restrictive environment.

There are several ways to meet the objectives of the act, and, while they are not mutually exclusive, each requires careful planning. Among the ways to accomplish the purposes of the act are:

1. Employ paraprofessionals to assist those regular teachers who have handicapped students.
2. Schedule special education teachers in the regular classroom to work directly with handicapped students.
3. Arrange for diagnostic-prescriptive teachers to work with regular teachers to plan instructional strategies for those handicapped children in a class. (The diagnostic-prescriptive teacher would provide no direct assistance to the student.)
4. Purchase individualized sequential materials for use by regular teachers to work with handicapped students.
5. Schedule handicapped students as needed, and arrange for a special-education teacher to be in the classroom for part of the school day.

The Individualized Education Program

For each child there must be developed a formal Individualized Educational Plan (IEP). The IEP is developed by a team including the appropriate professional educators (diagnosticians, teachers, psychologists, and principals, for example) and the child's parents. Parents must give consent before a handicapped child may be placed in a program. The IEP must contain:

1. The child's current level of performance.
2. A statement of goals and objectives.

3. The nature of the educational services to be provided.
4. The place(s) and time(s) the services will be provided.
5. The person(s) who will be working with the child.

Clearly, such a process is time consuming, expensive, and possible only with understanding, well-trained staff. (Clearly, too, such a process is consistent with good professional pedagogical practice with any child, handicapped or not!) The implications of mainstreaming for inservice-education programs is apparent.

The Desegregated School Environment

In 1954, the historic declaration was made that, with regard to race, separate schools were not equal schools.[13] For thirty years, courts, school districts, and individual schools have attempted, frequently in a hesitating manner, to remove the elements of *de jure* racial and ethnic segregation of school children. The task is not nearly complete; many issues have yet to achieve resolution or even definition. Some communities have yet to confront the problem adequately. Nevertheless:

> One thing is certain: A public school system may not elect to maintain a dual school system, and a current school board may not continue discriminatory practices initiated by previous boards. With *Brown* as a base, buttressed by subsequent court decisions and such federal legislation as the Civil Rights Act of 1964, many American school districts are required to "do something."[14]

As executive officer of the operational desegregative unit, the principal has a critical role to play in the provision of an unrestricted educational environment—and this is true whether one is discussing equity issues with regard to sex or handicap or, as in the present case, race and ethnicity. While a principal may not have participated in the preparation of pupil assignment policies or in the development of the attendance zones, there are certain activities in which he or she should engage in order to meet the spirit and intent of the law and to manage the school effectively.

Integration/Desegregation: A Distinction

There is a need to distinguish between desegregation and integration: the terms are not synonymous, even though they are related. Desegregation refers only to the deliberate physical mixing of children from different racial and ethnic groups. Integration refers to a process that results in the mutual accep-

---

[13]Brown *v.* Board of Education of Topeka, 347 U.S. 483 (1954).
[14]Larry W. Hughes, William M. Gordon, and Larry W. Hillman, *Desegregating America's Schools* (New York: Longman, Inc., 1980), p. xv

tance of, and respect for, other races and ethnic groups, and includes some level of cultural assimilation. Most social scientists argue that integration cannot occur without desegregation, however.

> In Brown *vs.* Board of Education some of the compelling arguments centered on multi-racial interaction in desegregated situations, but the Court only spoke within its jurisdiction to break down any and all governmental barriers that deprived citizens of their Fourteenth Amendment rights. Thus, the Court ordered that public schools be desegregated, that is, to proceed in the "physical mixing of races without regard to the relative status of the two groups."[15]

Thus, desegregation is the law of the land and the courts can only require that there be compliance with the law. Integration, a far more difficult process, can only result because of extralegal efforts by school and lay leaders—principals teachers, parents, and community members.

Grouping Children

Certain legal frameworks do guide principals, curriculum coordinators, counselors, and teachers, however. With regard to the grouping of children within schools, the courts have not outlawed such arrangements as ability grouping but have said·

> It goes without saying that tnere is no constitutional prohibition against an assignment of individual students to particular schools on a basis of intelligence, achievement or other attributes upon a *uniformly administered program but race must not be a factor in making the assignments.*[16] [Emphasis supplied.]

While it may appear that wide latitude exists in grouping practice, attention is called to the underlined statement in the quotation—uniformity in administration and the absence of race as a motivation. The burden of proof for these conditions is on the school. Moreover, subsequent court cases have also served to restrict grouping or tracking of students and these too have been racially motivated. The most celebrated of these cases is Hobson *v.* Hansen.[17]

In Hobson, the plaintiffs claimed that the District of Columbia school system deprived them of equal educational opportunity because of the "tracking" system then a part of the district's curricular structure. The district placed students into honors, college preparatory, general, or basic classes on the basis of their performance on scholastic-aptitude and standardized achievement tests. It was revealed that a disproportionate number of poor white and black children were in the lowest tracks and, significantly, once relegated to those

---

[15]Ibid., p. 12.

[16]Stell *v.* Savannah-Chatham County Board of Education, 333 F. 2d. 55 at 61–62 (1964).

[17]269 F. Supp. 401 (1967).

tracks, they rarely if ever moved out of them. The court found that the system violated the equal protection clause of the Fourteenth Amendment because:

> These tests are standardized primarily on and are relevant to a white middle class group [producing] inaccurate and misleading test scores when given to lower class and Negro students.[18]

Other cases followed. Hispanic youngsters were able to overturn a school district's procedures for classifying children as educable–mentally retarded by showing that there were disproportionate numbers of Hispanics in the district's special classes for children so labeled.[19] New procedures were developed as a result, including the provision of a Spanish language form of the aptitude tests used by the district.

In Larry v. Riles[20] black students alleged similar discrimination and they provided statistical evidence of a disproportionate number of blacks in educable–mentally retarded classes in a California district. The court said that where such an imbalance occurs, the school district must assume the burden of demonstrating that the testing procedures are rationally related to the separation of pupils on the basis of their abilities.

Maintaining the Equitable Environment

Regardless of the manner or the degree to which a school is desegregated, its primary mission is realized through educational programming. The focus must be on accommodating each child in a learning setting that addresses the needs of that child. If academic and social integrity are to be realized, the school program must not be influenced by predetermined attitudes about the learning, social, emotional and physical abilities of different racial and ethnic groups.

Conscious, sensitive planning can provide for an equitable learning environment. In their important book, *A Handbook for Integrated Schooling,*[21] Forehand and Ragosta establish that a well-integrated school will exhibit four features:

1. *Salience.* Successful integration is a highly salient goal for most people in effective schools, and for the most influential people in a school. Salience has both motivational and perceptual components. Motivationally, successful integration needs to be an important goal, internalized by both staff and students. It must take a high position among the myriad goals that a school must have. Perceptually, there must be a high degree of attentiveness to progress in integration and alertness to indications of success and failure.

---

[18]Ibid., at 514.
[19]Diana v. State Board of Education, Civil No. C-70-37, RFR (N.D. Calif., Feb. 5, 1970).
[20]343 F. Supp. 1306 (1972) aff'd. 502 F. 2d. 963 (9th Cir., 1974).
[21]Garlie A. Forehand and Marjorie Ragosta, *A Handbook for Integrated Schooling* (Princeton, N. J.: Educational Testing Service, 1976).

Salience implies absence of racially prejudiced behavior. The association of lack of prejudice on the part of students is one of the most pervasive findings in our study. Absence of racial prejudice on the part of the school staff is an important goal. Even if attitude change is not achieved for every staff member, a professional attitude that minimizes prejudiced behavior can be demanded. Salience also implies intention to act positively to achieve good race relations. Such intention may be motivated by a professional attitude and dedication to duty. It need not imply any particular political or ideological position.

2. *Intercultural Sensitivity.* People in effective schools are sensitive to the cultural backgrounds of the students, to the effect of backgrounds on behavior, self-concept, and aspirations, and to the need to design and carry out educational programs responsively.

3. *Interdependence.* Many respondents in effective schools often used the term "school family." It implies shared objectives, mutual concern, and mutual sensitivity. Members of a successful school family include the administration, faculty, and students. In successful schools, family feeling is regarded as desirable and rewarding.

4. *Equity.* In successful schools, the races and individual members of races are treated equitably. The term equity implies fairness and justice. It is neither synonymous with nor antithetical to equality. A school may provide equal opportunity to participate in its activities—in the sense that the activities are open to all—yet without establishing equity. If geographic location, cultural tradition, or minority status are barriers to equal participation, the mere absence of school-imposed barriers does not constitute equity. If minority students must work harder because of a heavier burden of transportation, or need to overcome negative expectations, or informal discrimination, the effect is inequity. The establishment of equity in a school requires positive action. Passively administered policies of equality are not enough.[22]

Forehand and Ragosta have also provided a diagnostic questionnaire for elementary schools to determine needed areas of improvement and to suggest corrective action. The questionnaire has eight parts:

1. The degree to which the curriculum of the school reflects multiethnicity.
2. The nature of the co-curricular activities program and the attention to the fact that many students do not live close by.
3. The way students are grouped for instruction.
4. Multiethnic teaching practices including the openness with which racial differences are treated.
5. The quality of home-school relations.
6. The nature of existing rules and regulations and the modes of disciplinary actions taken.

---

[22]Ibid., pp. 10–11.

7. The degree to which staffing patterns reflect true integration.

8. The principal's leadership behavior.[23]

Answers to questions within each category will provide the substance for necessary corrective or proactive adjustments in the operation of the school. A similar questionnaire should be distributed to students and community members, because perceptions often vary. If they do vary on any particular item or in any category, that issue will need to be addressed. Perceptions determine behavior.

This concludes the section on issues of educational equity. The remainder of this chapter focuses on important specific legal points and issues permeating the elementary-school setting.

RULES AND REGULATIONS

The efficient routine operation of any complex organization requires a well-developed, well-understood, and consistent set of rules and regulations. It is axiomatic that if staff and students are to be held accountable for certain standards, these expectations must be established and promulgated *ahead of their application* in a manner that makes them easily disseminated, learned, and understood. A principal has the right to prescribe reasonable controls for the efficient day-to-day operation of the schools, but, of course, this does not imply that the school building is a fiefdom and staff and students are serfs.

What is "reasonable"? A rule of thumb applied most frequently by the courts is, "Does the regulation enhance the education of the children, promote their interest and welfare, and is it for the common good of education?" Implicit is that the regulations be within the legal authority of the school district. Regulations beyond the province of the school board are not enforceable. A long-standing decision has held that "boards are not at liberty to adopt according to their humor regulations which have no relevance to the schools' purposes."[24] It follows that this would be no less true in the matter of rules and regulations prescribed by the principal.

Moreover, while it is sound management practice to develop procedures and guidelines that provide for consistency of school operation, the authors of this book think that the rule of parsimony should be followed. Developing

---

[23]The Forehand-Ragosta book and questionnaire was developed under a contract with the U. S. Department of Health, Education and Welfare. It is available from Educational Testing Service. A copy of the instrument may also be found in Hughes, Gordon and Hillman, *Desegregating America's Schools*, pp. 150–52.

[24]State *v.* Fond du Lac Board of Education, 63 WIS 234, 23 N.W. 102, 53 Am Rep 262 (1885).

long lists of do's and don't's in an attempt to cover every contingency can create a school climate in which the name of the game becomes beating the system, a climate in which staff and students derive a perverse joy from testing the limits. Rules and regulations that attempt to define every type of situation and recourse are not necessary. In fact, the enumeration of prohibited actions may foreclose any discretion on actions not so listed. It is better to have some general guidelines and a few specific dictums to cover the hazardous situations and common management problems than to go overboard.

The Out-of-Date Rule

Rules and regulations should be subjected to regular review to insure their continued appropriateness and efficacy. Outdated, misunderstood, inappropriate, or unnecessary rules only breed contempt for other rules. For example, a few years ago one of the authors and a colleague were members of a Southern Association of Schools evaluation team participating in a routine accreditation review of a large school.

After a morning of review activities, some of the consultants had lunch in the school cafeteria. Finding the food not quite seasoned enough for our taste, two of us looked for the salt and pepper shakers on the table. There was none. Further, as nearly as we could tell as we looked around the room, there was no salt or pepper on any of the tables. We asked a nearby student, "Where is the salt and pepper?" The student's reply was, "We don't get salt and pepper." "Why?" was our response. To this the student shrugged his shoulders.

Again and again we repeated our query to students about the location of the salt and pepper. Each time the response was "We don't get salt and pepper," and each time when we rejoined with "why," the response was nearly the same—a shrug, a glance at the ceiling, or an "I dunno." One of the students said that he had run for student council president the previous spring on a "Bring Back the Salt" ticket but had not been elected.

Having nothing to do for another half hour or so, we began to pursue this deepening mystery. Cafeteria personnel were queried about the salt and pepper. Their response was that it was a rule that students were not to receive salt and pepper, but none knew why. "Has it always been a rule," we asked. Two workers, who had indicated that they had been there for at least four years, said that to their knowledge it had always been a rule. "Does it seem to be a sensible rule?" we pursued. There was no response to this question and as we developed the issue somewhat further, it became clear that our presence was really no longer desired. The head cook was of no help, nor was the cafeteria manager, so we took our problem to the principal's office, avoiding the assistant principal because she had only been on the job for a couple of years.

The principal indicated that he thought the rule was one the cafeteria manager had issued, but confessed that he really didn't know why. We should have gone to the teacher's lunchroom, he said: "They have salt in there." "That's not the point," we replied. "We're just curious about why there is a rule against salt and pepper." At this moment a teacher who had been in the school for some time came in and, overhearing the conversation, grinned at both of us and said, "It was a punishment, because several years ago we had a rash of students unscrewing the tops of the salt and pepper shakers so that when they were used the tops would come off, dumping the contents on the food."

Further conversation determined that this had all occurred some seven or eight years previously and the rule had been invoked, presumably until just the end of the school term. Subsequent to that the principal had left and the cafeteria manager continued to apply the rule, unthinkingly, unquestioningly. So what had begun as a temporary punishment for some normal adolescent hijinks had become a school tradition summed up in the lament "We don't get any salt."

Silly? Certainly, but it is this sort of unthinking application of rules that have long since ceased to have any relevance that creates a general disrespect for rules that do have relevance. Rules and regulations that guide the school's routine operations should regularly be subjected to a review. The questions asked should be: What is this rule for? Does this rule work? Is there a better way?

Establishing Good Rules and Regulations

Three general guidelines provide good rules and regulations:

1. The principal's own good management sense will provide some insights into the kinds of rules and regulations needed to routinely guide the school. The orderly development of a school program does require certain specified times when activities are to begin, when the school lunch period will be, common standards of good conduct, and teacher responsibilities. These rules and regulations should be appropriate to the age and maturity of the children under the school's charge.

2. Rules and regulations developed for a particular elementary school, of course, should be consistent with the general policies of the school district.

3. A faculty/student advisory committee should be constituted to help identify areas needing more specific regulations and to serve as a review board for existing rules and regulations.

Neither the extreme of rules for every occasion nor its opposite, no rules at all, is sensible. Principals within the school and teachers within the classroom have the right *and the obligation* to determine reasonable policies governing the conduct of their charges, not only to maintain a proper educational climate, but also for safety. Courts have spoken to the need for rules to keep pupils from injuring themselves and have held that the absence of such rules is grounds for negligence; the failure to enforce an already existing rule also incurs a liability. When challenged in the courts, particular rules and regulations will in all probability be upheld, provided, of course, the rule is a reasonable application of an educational function and not contrary to a higher enactment by the school board or federal and state bodies.

The principal is the person most often responsible for the promulgation and enforcement of rules and regulations.

> It is he who must require that certain instruction be given in order to comply with local and state regulations. . . . Whether the principal acts in an authoritative manner, suggested by the "line" concept and makes all assignments himself, or whether he employs a cooperative plan, the legal relationships between the principal and employee are the same. Regardless of the "method" of getting things done, the principal cannot relieve himself of the legal responsibility his position entails.[25]

DUE PROCESS

The general issue addressed by due process considerations is that of the constitutional rights of personnel and students balanced against the duty of the school board to control and protect the school system and protect the rights of students to obtain an education. There are two kinds of due process: substantive and procedural.

Substantive Due Process

Substantive due process is concerned with the basic legality of a legislative enactment. School policies, rules, and regulations must stand the test of substantive due process. A person punished or denied the right to behave in some way by an existing law, rule, or regulation when that law, rule, or regulation is itself contrary to certain constitutional guarantees has legal recourse to set aside the punishment or denial and make the rule invalid. Moreover, substantive due process requires that there must be sufficient evidence or documentation of violation to warrant action by school officials or sufficient reason to believe that, if the rule is not invoked, current or subsequent acts by the parties involved will result in disruption of the educational process. The burden of proof rests with the school officials, not the transgressor.

The Tinker case is often cited in reference to presumed disruption.[26] Rules are invoked because the school principal says, in effect, "If this rule is not enforced and obeyed, the process of education in the school will be impeded." In the Tinker case, students were suspended for wearing black arm bands to school in mourning for American military personnel who had died in

[25]William E. Gauerke, *Legal and Ethical Responsibilities of School Personnel* (Englewood Cliffs, N. J.: Prentice Hall, Inc., 1959), p. 127.

[26]Tinker *v.* Des Moines Independent Community School, 393 U.S. 503, 89 S. Ct. 733 (1969). See also Burnside *v.* Byars, 363 F. 2nd 744 (5th Cir., 1966).

Vietnam, as well as to protest continued American involvement in that country. The school promulgated a rule prohibiting this, subsequent to which some students continued to wear the arm bands in open defiance. Two important legal principles of a substantive nature were applied by the Supreme Court in holding for the students: (1) There was no disruption, so therefore the presumption of the rule was false and students had the constitutional right to defy the rule; and (2) the wearing of the arm bands was analogous to free speech (a First Amendment guarantee), and the students had the right to express themselves.

· The two rules of thumb that must be applied are: (1) will the behavior cause substantial disorder to the education process or normal operation of the school? (2) will the behavior be an invasion of the rights of others? If the school principal believes the answer is yes, it must be remembered that the burden of proof rests on the principal. Courts are critical of administrator action predicated on presumption. The collection of sufficient evidence to show reason for administrative action is essential.

Guidelines to Insure Adherence to Substantive Due Process

School policies, rules and regulations, and the administrative actions enforcing these should be subjected to the following guidelines:

1. *Legality.*   Is there a basis in state and federal constitutional and legislative law for the policy, rule, or regulation? Are the constitutional rights of those for whom it was written protected?
2. *Sufficient Specificity.*   Are the conditions under which the policy, rule, or regulations will be invoked detailed? Are the terms and phraseology used definitive? Vague and unclear statements are sufficient to cause the courts to abrogate.
3. *Reason and Sensibleness.*   Does the rule or regulation really enhance the educational climate; that is, is it really necessary? Is there sufficient reason to believe that without the rule, the rights of others will be unprotected or the school will be disrupted? A rule may be declared unreasonable in and of itself *or* in its particular application
4. *Adequate Dissemination.*   Has information about the rule been distributed in such a way that persons affected can be expected to know about it, what it means, and what the penalties are?
5. *Appropriate Penalties.*   Are the punishments appropriate to the nature of the infraction? Severe penalties for minor transgressions must be avoided.[27]

---

[27]Procedures and punishment must be tailored to fit the offender and the offense. See, for example, Rhyne v. Childs, 359 F. Supp. 1085 (1973)

Procedural Due Process

Procedural due process is an orderly established process for arriving at an impartial and just settlement of a conflict between parties.[28] It entails the elements of fair warning and fair hearing.

Fair Warning. Fair warning simply means that a person must be made cognizant of the rules to follow or behavior that must be exhibited and the potential penalties for violation. The age of the person and the length of experience must be taken into consideration as well. Moreover, there must be a correlation between the penalty and the rule that has been broken.

Fair Hearing. A fair hearing is composed of the following specific aspects:

1. *The individual must be given a written statement of the charges and the nature of evidence.* This is often called "a Bill of Particulars." Clarity is very important. The accused, and in the instance of pupils, the accused's parents, must comprehend the contents of the written statement. The background and educational level of the individuals involved and the complexity of the statement should be taken into account. A personally delivered statement to the parent would provide an opportunity for clarifying charges and might be appropriate at times. The precise nature of the charges and the evidence must be incorporated in the statement. Vague rules and imprecise charges have resulted in the reversal of more school board and administrative decisions than any other defect.[29]

2. *The individual must be informed of his procedural rights.* As noted earlier in this chapter, having rights but being kept unaware of them is the same as not having rights. Individuals must be provided information specifying the appeal and defense processes available. Information such as to whom the appeal should be made, the time limit under which the appeal can be advanced, and other elements of procedural due process is necessary.

---

[28]The seriousness of transgressions ranges widely, from minor misbehavior problems of students and minor infractions of staff to major infractions capable of inflicting bodily harm or questions of incompetence and subsequent dismissal of personnel. The seriousness of the proposed penalty will determine the degree to which specific due process protections are officially and publicly accorded the person. Nevertheless, even in the instance of a minor punishment such as making a child stand in the hall for whispering in class, the teacher should mentally go over the guarantees if for no other reason than to test the fairness of the punishment. The teacher should at least be sure that the child being punished is the child who committed the offense.

[29]Full information includes an explanation of the evidence the school officials have against the student. See Goss *v.* Lopez, 419 U.S. 565 (1975) and Board of Curators of the University of Missouri *v.* Horowitz, 435 U.S. 78 (1978).

3. *Adequate time must be provided to prepare a defense.* In serious issues ordinarily a minimum of five days should be provided for an individual to prepare a defense; ten days almost certainly will sustain a court inquiry.[30]

·4. *The opportunity for formal hearing must be accorded.*[31] There are five components in the proper conduct of a formal hearing:
   a. The case must be presented to an impartial hearer. The school official bringing the charge may not also serve as hearer. The same person may not serve at once as judge, jury, and prosecuting attorney.
   b. The individual must have the opportunity to present evidence.
   c. The individual has the right to know and confront whoever brought the charges and to question that person or those persons.
   d. The individual has the right to produce witnesses and to cross-examine witnesses. The individual must have the opportunity to disprove the accusations of a hostile witness and include testimony of those who can explain the defendant's side of the issue.
   e. The individual has the right to counsel. This does not necessarily mean an attorney. It may be simply a friend, parent, or citizen on whose advice the defendant wishes to rely. It would be a foolish board of education or administrator, however, who would try to prohibit an individual from having an attorney present even though at this writing there has been no court decision mandating legal counsel at hearings such as these.

COMMON TORT LIABILITY SETTINGS

A tort is defined as *an act or an omitted act*, including breach of contract, that results in damage, injury, or loss to the injured person(s), who then may seek relief by legal action. Torts may be intentional, may result from negligence, or be caused by careless acts. School employees are liable for their individual acts of negligence[32] and for their failure to carry out prescribed duties, or the failure to carry out these duties correctly. School employees are

---

[30]Procedural due process legislation does vary from state to state and often depends on the issue. The question of a timeline for various appeals often varies and is specifically established in many laws. This is especially true in such issues as personnel terminations. It is always wise to check the specific law with the school attorney or the state code.

[31]It is important to remember that while this process takes on some of the vestments of a court of law, it is not a court of law. It simply is a provision for fair and impartial treatment. After the process is complete, the individual still has the right to take the case to court if it is felt that the act for which punishment was rendered was not a punishable one, or that the punishment was too severe. Nevertheless, according the aspects of procedural due process will be most influential with the courts. It avoids the charge of capricious action and is both legally and morally sound.

[32]Negligence is usually defined as the failure to do something that any reasonably prudent person would have done in a similar situation.

expected to behave in a reasonable manner in the discharge of their duties, avoiding acts that are capricious, arbitrary, or negligent.

Familiarization with the elements of tort liability is a must for all school employees. Tort liability suits usually demand adequate evidence of the following:

1. A prescribed or implicit duty on the part of the defendant for the care of the plaintiff.
2. An error of commission or omission by the defendant.
3. Damage, loss, or injury sustained by the plaintiff.
4. Indication of a cause-and-effect relationship between the error and the circumstance at issue.
5. Absence of contributory negligence on the part of the plaintiff.[33]

The principal who devotes some inservice training time with staff to legal aspects of the school operation will be performing an important service. The best defense against law suits is proper precaution. Principals and teachers cannot be expected to be prescient, but they should anticipate possible dangers. The discussion that follows will examine common liability settings and describe certain aspects of the legal environment.

Pupil Injuries

A school is not usually a hazardous place, but children frequently do sustain injuries in and about the school. Most of these injuries are accidental and minor, the result of normal behavior. Nevertheless, teachers and administrators do have a responsibility to provide reasonable and prudent protection for their charges and they are legally liable in tort for injuries arising from their negligence.[34] The main test of negligence is "foreseeability." That is, the behavior of an individual would be called negligent if an ordinarily prudent person would have foreseen that certain actions, or a failure to act, would lead to injury to another.

The principal is responsible for taking all steps to promote the well-being of the children within the school and to guard the welfare of the staff. There-

---

[33]Contributory negligence is determined by whether or not the party who was injured exercised the degree of caution others of the same age, sex, maturation level, and experience would have exercised under the same conditions. Obviously, more supervision would be expected of those in charge of young children; teachers and principals in the elementary school have less chance of avoiding a law suit by claiming contributory negligence than those who are charged with the supervision of older children. Nevertheless, a student who disregards or acts in direct defiance of an admonishment by a teacher or a principal would probably be held to be guilty of contributory negligence if defiance resulted in injury.

[34]Of course, not all injuries to pupils are actionable; some are simply unavoidable, the result of pure accident. Only those injuries resulting from negligence provide the injured with the right to recover. See also the meaning of contributory negligence discussed earlier.

fore, to both staff and students, the principal has a particular duty to plan and supervise to minimize the possibility of injury. At the very least, this involves supplying information to staff members about their legal responsibilities and cooperatively developing a set of rules and regulations that, if carefully followed, would result in protection for students and the elimination of negligent behavior. Pupil injuries are most likely to occur in certain settings, discussed below.

Physical Education, Field Trips, and Other Extracurricular Programs.
Field trips, other extracurricular programs, as well as the physical education curriculum itself, are inherently more hazardous than the regular academic program. They require greater supervision to avoid liability as a result of negligence, and carefully developed and well-understood written rules and regulations for their governance are important.

Adequate regulations should cover such categories as pupil conduct while a participant or spectator, medical examination for participants, medical care for sick and injured participants, transportation to and from the activity, duties of teachers and other supervisors, notification and approval in advance by parent or guardian.[35] Figures 3-2 and 3-3 depict teacher field-trip request and parent permission forms.

The Classroom. Teachers are normally in charge in the classroom and thus are most frequently held responsible for the safety of the children there. However, the principal has some responsibilities that, if not met, may result in a charge of negligent behavior. The primary responsibility of the principal with regard to classroom activities is to insure that there is a teacher or a responsible adult present at all times. Therefore, the principal should always be aware of a teacher's absence from the classroom. Failure to have a plan to provide for pupil supervision when a teacher becomes ill or is tardy to class could cause the principal to be charged with negligence if an injury resulted while the children were unsupervised. For example, a common practice is to have a check-in sheet for teachers in the morning so that the principal can know immediately of any unanticipated absence or tardiness of personnel who have responsibility for the supervision of children.

Generally speaking, however, the temporary short-term absence from the classroom by a teacher would not, in and of itself, be considered a negligent act of general supervision. If, for example, a child misbehaves and in so doing injures another child during a teacher's brief absence from the room, a court would not ordinarily find negligence, because the teacher's absence was not the proximate cause of the accident. However, in all cases, the age, matur-

---

[35]However, advance approval by a parent or guardian for participation of a child in an activity such as a field trip or an athletic event *does not* waive the right of the child to sue for damages in case the child is injured. Such a policy does perform an important function, however. It informs the parent, and the mere fact that such advance approval was required is some evidence that care was exercised by the school.

OFF-CAMPUS TRIP REQUEST

Please fill out this form and send it and its duplicates to the Director of Instruction one week prior to the date of the trip. Upon approval of the trip, the white copy will be returned to the principal to be filed, the yellow copy will be given to the supervisor, and the pink copy will be kept by the principal.

Date Submitted _____ School _____

Grade, Subject, or Organization _____

No. of students making the trip _____ Date of trip _____

Method of transportation _____ When bonded carriers are

used, give the per pupil cost _____ How will these costs be

defrayed? _____ Time of departure _____ of return _____

Destination _____

Purpose of trip (state the relationship to current study) _____

_____

What are your plans to follow up and evaluate the trip? _____

_____

Will parent permission slips be filed with the principal prior to the trip? _____
List staff members and other adults who will make the trip. _____

_____

_____

Requested By:

_____
Teacher

_____
Teacher

Approved:

_____
Principal

FIGURE 3-2.

GORDON ELEMENTARY SCHOOL

Parent Permission Slip

DATE _____

Dear Parents:
In order for your child to be allowed to go on an off-campus trip, we must have
·the following agreement signed by a parent/guardian giving permission.

Sincerely,

_____

Carlton A. Schwiebert, Principal

Please allow _____ to go with his or her group to _____
on the date set for the trip. By signing this statement I give my full permission
for my child to go on this off-campus trip.

_____   _____
             Date   Parent/Guardian

FIGURE 3-3.

ity, and intelligence of the student will bear on the question of teacher negligence in such absences. The best rule is not to leave children unattended.

Laboratories and Shops. These two instructional areas present more
hazards than any other in the school. Elementary school general science classes more and more frequently engage in experiments within the classroom,
often involving chemicals as well as common electric or gas powered laboratory equipment. Moreover, good educational practice in teaching science involves such outside classroom events as off-campus field trips and on-campus
land laboratory activities.

Similarly, greater emphasis on career education and career exploration
means that more and more elementary schools are developing prevocational
shops with at least rudimentary power equipment as well as common hand
tools. In addition, classes in home arts such as cooking and sewing continue in
popularity and require power- and hand-operated equipment.

Constant and immediate supervision is expected of teachers functioning
in these activities. Teachers must adequately instruct children in the care and
use of equipment they will be operating. If there is evidence that a child has
been permitted to use a particular tool, or perform an experiment, before
being trained and told the consequences of improper usage, negligence will be
difficult to disprove. Greater care is expected of teachers supervising children

who are exposed to dangerous equipment. Obviously too, teacher absence from a room where a class is engaged in hazardous activities, no matter how temporary, is very risky indeed.

Playgrounds. Where supervision is regular, planned, reasonable, and proper, a negligence charge in case of pupil injury on the playground is less likely. Considerations in determining the suitability of playground supervision include the kind of playground equipment in use, the size of the playground, and the number and age of the pupils to be supervised.

The courts generally appreciate the fact that a teacher is unable to keep every child within view and out of hazard at all times. Nor do they expect the teacher to be prescient. Nevertheless, negligent supervision is often held to be the proximate cause of injury. If, for example, a teacher permits a child to leave a supervised group and the child is injured in a known existing hazardous condition, then the teacher may be liable. If a teacher assigned to playground duty leaves a post for no good cause and a child is injured in a known or foreseeable dangerous condition, there may be tort liability because of negligence. Also, while teachers would not be expected to repair playground equipment, permitting pupils to use equipment known to be faulty, or beyond the maturity level of the child, could result in negligence.

The principal must organize and administer playground use and has responsibility for three major aspects. First, proper rules of behavior, consistent with good safety practices, must be developed and implemented. Second, the management system should always provide adequate adult supervision on the playground when children are present. Third, the principal must provide for frequent and regular inspection of the playground and playground equipment, reporting any hazardous conditions, apprising staff and students of these, and take action to have the condition corrected.

Regulating Student Conduct

In even the best-run schools students misbehave. There is agreement that principals and teachers may prescribe reasonable controls against the misconduct of children and many kinds of disciplinary action are available to school administrators and teachers when pupils violate school policies and rules. These include such minor punishments as short-term removal from the classroom, withholding certain privileges, detention after school, isolation from the rest of the class, being sent to the principal's office, and so on. The courts have generally upheld the right of school administrators and teachers to impose such minor punishment. Other forms of disciplinary action, however, such as suspension[36] and expulsion from school, or the use of corporal punish-

---

[36]Suspension generally is defined as dismissal from the school for a specific, although generally short-term, period of time (two or three days, or often a week). Usually the principal of the school has the authority to suspend. Expulsion is defined to mean permanent dismissal and normally is an action that can legally be taken only by the school board. There are some questions as to whether or not a pupil, otherwise within the legal age of school attendance, can be permanently excluded from a public school, although it has been established generally that for good cause the student can be permanently removed from a regular public school provided that he or she is placed in an appropriate special school.

ment are more often tested in the courts, and school administrators and teachers must take great care in the prescription of these punishments. Figure 3-4 depicts a basic information form about disciplinary action.

In any case, the question of both substantive and procedural due process is extremely important.[37] The reasonableness and legality of the rule or regulation violated must be examined with care, and the legal issue of whether or not the student has a right to a prior hearing is important.

Clearly, administrators should take care in imposing minor as well as major punishments to insure that pupils or personnel are treated fairly and not victimized by capricious or arbitrary action.

Corporal Punishment. Corporal punishment is defined as disciplinary action by the application of physical force. As a means of modifying behavior, it is probably the oldest disciplinary tool. It also may be one of the most inefficacious. More recently, acts of corporal punishment are probably the cause of more court cases than anything else.[38] However, under the legal concept *in loco parentis*,[39] the courts continue to uphold the right of teachers and principals to use "reasonable" force to insure proper conduct, or to correct improper conduct.[40]

Important guidelines, however, must be followed if the use of corporal punishment is to be adjudicated as prudent and reasonable. Corporal punishment is generally held to be prudent providing:

1. The state law and the local policy permit it.
2. The punishment takes into consideration the age, size, sex, and health of the pupil and is not excessive.
3. There is no malice, the punishment is given for corrective purposes only and is not immoderate.

---

[37]In the instance of suspension, one of the most favorable due process cases for students is Mills v. Board of Education, 348 F. Supp. 866 (1972) in which the court ordered that there must be a hearing prior to a suspension invoked for any period in excess of two days. In Goss v. Lopez, 95 S. Ct. 729 (1975) the Supreme Court ruled that basically school officials must accord students and school employees their constitutional right of due process even in routine disciplinary actions. In the Goss v. Lopez case, it held that a junior high school pupil suspended for as much as a single day is entitled to due process. Further, in Wood v. Strickland, 95 St. Ct. 992 (1975) the Supreme Court ruled that school board members and school officials can be held personally liable for pecuniary damages when students (and by logical extension one must suppose school personnel as well) are denied constitutional rights, even by accidental omission.

[38]If a teacher or a principal uses excessive force or causes untoward injury, he or she may be held liable for battery. There is often confusion among lay people about the terms assault and battery. Battery means the actual unlawful inflicting of physical violence on another. Assault is a threat to commit battery. There can be assault without battery, but battery always includes assault.

[39]See footnote 2 for a discussion of the concept of *in loco parentis*.

[40]A Supreme Court case has affirmed the right of school personnel to use corporal punishment. The Supreme Court upheld a lower court ruling that corporal punishment may be administered provided that only "reasonable force" is used and provided that pupils know beforehand that certain behavior or actions will result in physical punishment. Baker v. Owen, 385 F. Supp. 294 (1975), and Ingraham v. Wright, 430 U.S. 651 (1977).

REPORT OF DISCIPLINARY ACTION
HILLMAN JR. HIGH SCHOOL

DATE _____

STUDENT'S NAME _____ HOMEROOM ____ GRADE _____

TIME _____   SEX _____

PERSON REPORTING _____

TITLE OF PERSON REPORTING _____

NATURE OF OFFENSE:

STUDENT'S ACCOUNT:

ACTION TAKEN:

I have had a chance to tell my side _____
                                                    (student signature)

DATE OF HEARING ____ PERSON CONDUCTING HEARING _____

TIME _____ OTHER PERSON(S) PRESENT _____

INFRACTION: STATE LAW _____ SCHOOL POLICY _____

                        BOARD OF EDUCATION POLICY _____

                        CENTRAL OFFICE POLICY _____

                        TEACHER RULE _____ COMMON SENSE _____

FIGURE 3-4.

4. The pupil understands why punishment is required.

5. An appropriate instrument is used.

Sometimes courts consider other attendant circumstances such as whether there was permanent injury suffered as a result of the punishment.

To avoid legal suit and to insure the fairest treatment possible for the student, it is important for the principal and the teacher to establish reasonable rules and to make sure that the punishment for breaking these rules is suitable. It is also important to reasonably administer the rules and apply them equally to all students. It is possible to administer a reasonable rule so improperly that it becomes unreasonable. Any vindictiveness or viciousness in administering corporal punishment must be avoided. If the teacher or the principal knows that he or she is uncontrollably angry, then it is not the time to punish the child corporally, or any other way for that matter. In all cases, the purpose of punishment is for the child's benefit, not for the vindication of the school's posture.

Suspension/Expulsion. Suspension from school has been defined as a dismissal, most often by the principal, from the school for a specific, but relatively short, length of time. Expulsion means permanent or long-term dismissal from school and in most states can only be accomplished by the board of education, permanent exclusion usually being outside the authority of any school administrator. Attendance at a public school is generally viewed as a right rather than a privilege, but the enjoyment of this right is conditioned by the student's willingness to comply with reasonable regulations and requirements of the school. Violations of these may be punished by suspension or in extreme cases by permanent exclusion. Under a suspension a pupil is usually required to meet some set of conditions established by the administrator before being readmitted.

The dividing line between a short- and a long-term exclusion from school is not clearly defined, but as a result of Goss *v.* Lopez has probably been established as ten days.[41] Longer exclusions, irrespective of what they are called, will require greater attention to all the vestments of due process because they clearly bear more heavily on a student's right to an education.

In Goss *v.* Lopez the court clearly established the right of school administrators to suspend students to maintain order in the school system. However, the court did find that school officials had violated the students' constitutional right to procedural due process. In this instance, nine students were temporarily suspended from school *without a hearing,* and thus were held to be denied due process. The school board had contended that due process was not appli-

---

[41]Goss *v.* Lopez, 95S. Ct.729(1975).

cable to suspensions because there was not a "constitutional right" to public education. The court disagreed with this indicating that:

> Although Ohio may not be constitutionally obligated to establish and maintain the public school system, it has nevertheless done so and has required its children to attend. Those young people do not "shed their constitutional rights at the school house door. . . ." The authority possessed by the State to prescribe and enforce standards of conduct in its schools, although concededly very broad, must be exercised consistently with the constitutional safeguards.[42]

Second, the school board argued that even if public education was a right that was protected by due process, in this instance the due process clause should not apply because the suspensions were limited to ten days and this was not a severe nor grievous infringement on the students' right to an education. The court disagreed here also and faced the question of what kind of process is due in the instance of short-term student suspensions. The court held that only rudimentary process was required to balance student interests against the educator's need to take quick disciplinary action. The court said:

> (T)he student [must] be given a written notice of the charges against him, if he denies them, an explanation of the evidence the authorities have and an opportunity to present his side of the story. . . . There need be no delay between the time "notice" is given and the time of the hearing. In the great majority of cases the disciplinarian may informally discuss the alleged misconduct with the student minutes after it has occurred. We hold only that, in being given an opportunity to explain his version of the facts at this discussion, the student first be told what he is accused of doing and what the basis of the accusation is.[43]

This is important because it implies that while due process provisions must always be present, even in less than major punishment, the nature of the punishment and the infraction will determine the degree to which one must engage in elaborate vestments of due process. In minor infractions it would be necessary only to provide rudimentary forms of hearing. Even here, however, the important lesson is that the child to be punished must in all instances be treated fairly and that there must be clear indication of the absence of capricious action. Expulsions are a different matter. In the case of an expulsion it would seem clear that all of the vestments of due process need to be applied.

Opposition to the use of suspensions and expulsions as punishment for misconduct is growing. The authors like the following statement detailing four counterproductive effects of the exclusion of children from school:

---

[42]Ibid., p. 736.
[43]Ibid., p. 740.

While precise measurement of the psychological and educational harm done by suspension is impossible, it is clear that any exclusion from school interrupts the child's educational process. . . . It is not clear what good such punishment does. In fact, it may work against the child's improvement in at least four ways. First, it forbids the child from participating in academic work. If children with discipline problems are also weak in their studies, their missed classes, assignments and exams may doom them to fail completely. Second, suspensions merely remove troubling children. They do not set in motion diagnostic or supportive services that might uncover and remediate causes of a child's misbehavior. Thus, suspensions deny help to children. Third, suspension is a powerful label that not only stigmatizes a child while in school (or out of it), but follows the child beyond school to later academic or employments pursuits and fourth, suspensions are highly correlated with juvenile delinquency. Putting children out of school, leaving them idle with no supervision, especially when they are demonstrating they have problems, leaves children alone to cope with their future.[44]

Many schools are developing a disciplinary procedure called in-school suspension as a means of avoiding the disruption and negative effects cited above. The in-school suspension usually involves taking the student out of the regular classroom for a period of time and placing the student in another learning situation within the school building, either in an independent learning situation with supervision or in a designated special class. When this procedure is coupled with counseling by the principal, the guidance counselor, or some other clinician to diagnose and treat the problem, it is a sound practice.

Detention. It is well established that principals and teachers do have the authority to temporarily detain students from participating in extracurricular activities and even to keep children after school as a punishment, providing, of course, that the student has a way of getting home. As in other punishments, the detention must be reasonable. False imprisonment may be claimed if the principal or a teacher either wrongfully detains a student or detains a student for an unreasonable amount of time as a punishment.

In this, as in all other punishments, the main test is one of fairness. If school officials act fairly and in good faith in dealing with students, their actions will probably be upheld by the courts.

Privacy and the Confidentiality of Student Records

The question of the confidentiality and accuracy of student records is important and since the passage in August 1974 of Public Law 93-380, The Family

---

[44]Children's Defense Fund, *Children Out of School in America* (Boston: The Fund, 1974), p. 135.

Educational Rights and Privacy Act (FERPA), the issue has been legally clarified.[45] This act states that students and parents are permitted to inspect and review records and must be given a copy of any part or all of the educational
record on request. Further, it requires that in any dispute concerning the contents of a student's educational record, due process must be provided. Where
a record is found to be inaccurate, the inaccuracies must be expunged.

In essence, to protect the privacy of individuals, the act requires that the
schools and other agencies permit an individual to: determine what relevant
records are maintained in the system of records; gain access to relevant records in such a system of records and to have copies made; and to correct or
amend any relevant record.

Further, the records about an individual may not be disclosed to out-
siders except by the consent of the individual in question. The consent must be
in writing and must be *specific* in stating to whom the record may be disclosed,
which records may be disclosed, and, where applicable, the time frame during
which the records may be disclosed.

In some instances disclosures may be made without the consent of the
pupil or the pupil's parents. Information may be disclosed within the school to
teachers or guidance counselors who have a need to know, where there is a
court order, where there is required disclosure under the Freedom of Information Act, and for routine usage such as the publication of names of students
who made an honor roll or information for a directory such as class lists or
sports brochures, which might include such information as the student's name,
address, sex, or birthplace. Even in this latter instance, however, it would be
best to get prior permission through some sort of routine process.

The Family Educational Rights and Privacy Act simply legalizes what
should have been, and was in many places, common administrative practice
with regard to student records.[46] (The fact that such practice was not all that
common gave rise to the act.) It is important for schools to take voluntary ac
tion to build confidence on the part of the school constituency and to create an
atmosphere of trust. The implementation of good policies for the management
of pupil records is as good a place as any to begin to increase this confidence.

General guidelines to assist principals in developing fair policies about
student records might include the following, suggested by the Russell Sage
Foundation:[47]

---

[45]FERPA is also commonly known as the Buckley Amendment.

[46]Privacy regulations were slow in coming to school administrators. Following the passage
of FERPA in August 1974, the Department of Health, Education and Welfare was charged with
the responsibility for developing guidelines for school administrators. The complete guidelines
can be found in the *Federal Register* and have been published in two parts, the first appearing in
the March 1976 edition of the *Federal Register*, part two in the next edition.

[47]The Russell Sage Foundation has developed very helpful guidelines for the management
of pupil records: *Guidelines for the Collection, Maintenance and Dissemination of Pupil Records*.
Single copies are free from the Russell Sage Foundation, 230 Park Avenue, New York, New York
10017.

1. *Principals should develop procedures to insure that all parents and students know what kinds of information are contained in school records at a given time and are informed of their rights concerning control over the process of information collection and recording.* Schools should be diligent in the effort to provide parents with information about pupil records and this information should be in a readily understandable form.

2. *Encourage mature students and their parents to inspect the records.* As was noted in the discussion of FERPA, the rights of parents to do this are now well-established, but most parents are unaware of these rights. Increased communication and greater trust on the part of the parents might be a major benefit, especially because such a policy might provide a substantially more accurate record.

3. *Develop systematic procedures to obtain explicit and informed parental or pupil consent before information contained in school records is released to outside parties, regardless of the reasons for such release or the characteristic of the third party.* Most schools will, on occasion, give out information to law enforcement or other agencies without obtaining consent from the student or his parents. Aside from the possible legal implications of a violation of privacy, this practice can have no other effect than that of discouraging a mutually trustful relationship between the parent, the child, and the school.

SUMMARY

A good working knowledge about the legal principles governing the operation of the elementary school is an essential tool-of-the-trade for the principal. This chapter has examined the constitutional roots, case law, and legislative bases upon which the interactive relationships of pupils, teachers, parents, and principals will be legally viewed. Knowledge about the laws governing school practice is important, not just in order to keep out of court, but also to provide the kind of orderly, productive, and humane school climate essential to the furtherance of a democratic society.

BIBLIOGRAPHY

Clelland, Richard. *Civil Rights for the Handicapped.* Arlington, Va.: American Association of School Administrators, 1978.

Current Trends in School Law. Topeka, Kan.: National Organization on Legal Problems of Education, 1974.

Fischer, Louis; Schimmel, David; and Kelly, Cynthia. *Teachers and the Law.* New York: Longman, 1981.

Forehand, Garlie, and Ragosta, Marjorie. *A Handbook for Integrating Schools.* Princeton, N. J.: Educational Testing Service, 1976.

Gatti, Richard D., and Gatti, David J. *Encyclopedia Dictionary of School Law.* West Nyack, N. Y.: Parker Publishing Co., 1975.

Gauerke, William E. *Legal and Ethical Responsibilities of School Personnel.* Englewood Cliffs, N. J.: Prentice-Hall, 1959.

Gee, E. Gordon, and Sperry, David J. *Education Law and the Public Schools.* Boston: Allyn and Bacon, 1978.

Hogan, John C. *The Schools, the Courts and the Public Interest.* Lexington, Mass.: D. C. Heath, 1974.

Hooker, Clifford, ed. *The Courts and Education.* Seventy-Seventh Yearbook of the National Society for the Study of Education. Chicago: University of Chicago Press, 1978.

Hughes, Larry W. *Education and the Law in Tennessee.* Cincinnati, Ohio: W. H. Anderson Co., 1971.

Hughes, Larry W., and Gordon, William M. "Frontiers of Law. In *The Courts and Education,* Seventy-Seventh Yearbook of the National Society for the Study of Education. Chicago: University of Chicago Press, 1978. (Chapter 13)

Hughes, Larry W., and Gordon, William M. "Higher Education and the Law in the 1980's." *Journal of Teacher Education* XXXI, no. 4 (July-August 1980): 61–62.

Hughes, Larry W.; Gordon, William M.; and Hillman, Larry W. *Desegregating America's Schools.* New York: Longman, 1980, esp. Chaps. 1 and 11.

Keller, Ed. "Principal Issues in PL 94-142." *National Elementary Principal* 56 no. 4 (March-April 1977): 80–82.

Ladd, Edward T. "Regulating Student Behavior Without Ending Up in Court." *Phi Delta Kappan* 54, no. 5 (January 1973); 38–43.

Mergler, Robert. "So, Site Administrator—You Want to Mainstream." *Thrust for Educational Leadership* 9, no. 42 (November 1979): 8–9.

"Negligence—When Is the Principal Liable." From the series *A Legal Memorandum.* Reston, Va.: National Association of Secondary School Principals, January 1975. (Even though the Legal Memorandum series is published by the NASSP, many of the issues are directly applicable to the operation of elementary schools as well. A bibliography of previous issues may be secured from NASSP, 1904 Association Drive, Reston, Va. 22091.)

Nolte, M. Chester. "Legal Issues in Education." *American School Board Journal* (regular feature in this monthly journal).

Rebore, Ronald W. "Public Law 94-142 and the Building Principal." *National Association of Secondary School Principals Bulletin* 63, no. 426 (April 1979):26–30.

"Six Principals Talk About PL 94-142." *National Elementary Principal* 58, no. 1 (October 1978):21–24.

"*Student Discipline Codes: Developments, Dimensions, Directions.*" From the series *A Legal Memorandum.* Reston, Va.: National Association of Secondary School Principals, March 1981.

Student Rights Litigation Packet. Cambridge, Mass.: Center for Law and Education, 1972.

The Yearbook of School Law. Topeka, Kan.: National Organization of Legal Problems of Education (published annually since 1972).

Yarmolinsky, Adam; Liebman, Lance; and Schelling, Corinne S. *Race and Schooling in the City.* Cambridge, Mass.: Harvard University Press, 1981.

Zirkel, Perry A. *A Digest of Supreme Court Decisions Affecting Education.* Bloomington, Ind.: Phi Delta Kappa, 1978.

4

Understanding
the Community

INTRODUCTION

These are days of great societal change and an increasing awareness of the tremendous cultural diversity that characterizes most communities. There is also a growing awareness on the part of educators of the complexities of operating a responsive school system in the face of such diversity and change. Its impact is felt most intensely at the school-building level, and the person in the middle is the principal. It is the principal who usually has the most direct contact with great numbers of groups and individuals, each with a legitimate vested interest in the operation of the school. Their wants and needs vary widely, as does their understanding of the nature of the educational programs developed to meet these needs and wants. Traditional communication and response mechanisms, resting as these often do on assumptions about the immediate community to be served that are no longer true, have been shown to be relatively ineffective.

The Music Man, a popular Broadway-Hollywood musical of several years ago, opens with a group of turn-of-the-century salesmen describing their occupation while riding on a train to the next town. The refrain says that, to be a good salesman, "you gotta know the territory." No better phrase could be used to describe the most pressing need of the school principal who wants to administer a responsive school. The territory to be known shifts rapidly as neighborhoods change, as new school-attendance zones are created, as urban renewal creates a different kind of clientele or no immediate clientele at all, as schools are closed and populations combined, as ethnic and racial composition changes markedly, and as English is discovered not to be the language of a student's home. All or some of these conditions are increasingly apparent to even a casual observer.

The school and the community it serves have in many places grown increasingly psychologically distant from each other, resulting in a low-level understanding of the nature of the educational enterprise, suspicion, and often an overwhelming lack of public support in times of crisis or great need. How did this happen?

SOCIETY IN PERSPECTIVE

That societal changes over the past several decades have taken their toll can be seen by examining common relationships between school and community. One need not be a graduate sociologist to consider the impact of such phenomena as industrialization, technocracy, urbanization, and the increasing complexity of social relationships on the relationship between school and community. The increasing esotericism of professional educational practices, a concomitant of these changes, has also widened the gap of understanding between school and community. The dissolution of the small, closely knit communities of years past has made schools and the people in the area they serve strangers, each rather unsure of the other, as well as of itself or themselves. The same situation occurs in the medical profession and other welfare delivery agencies that attempt to cater to the varied, complex, and multifaceted needs of people who live in a community. The term community has come to be used in a most unsociological sense to simply mean a group of people living in close proximity and served by many of the same social and governmental agencies.

A Slowly Dying Myth

In times past two patterns were characteristic of a school's role in the community and the relationship it had with its clients. First, there was a general lack of threat and mystery about what the school was doing or was supposed to do. The ideologically unified communities of the past viewed the school primarily as an extension of the home, as an instrument for passing on the eternal verities, for teaching children how to read, write, and cipher, and for somehow inculcating into these same children the appropriate ways of behaving. Further, the financial outlay for the support of such a school was relatively small. The school itself may have been built by willing hands in the community. Out of such an environment one might have expected rather broad community cooperation and support for the local educational system.

Of course, such a bucolic wonderland probably never did adequately describe this nation, but it did describe many communities. For many educators, the state of the school-community relations program continues to be based on the notion that such a well-ordered and ideologically unified situation does exist or should exist. And that's where the trouble begins.

Ideological unity is not characteristic of very many cities and towns, and thus there is distrust, disenchantment, misconception, and a general depth of concern by many in society about school effectiveness and cost. This age is characterized generally by criticism and skepticism about public agencies and their efficiency.

The need for the development of better mechanisms to provide for effective communication between the school and the community is glaringly apparent. The principal who relies on informal relationships that may have served adequately in less complex times is operating in a precarious position indeed.

Ideological Disunity

The concept of ideological unity needs some consideration. Ideological unity in a community context refers to a community that is inherently in tune with itself, with well-understood belief structures and mores, where the eternal verities are indeed eternal and true for all. This type of community has been described by sociologists as *sacred* in orientation. It doesn't describe very many places in this country today.[1]

What does describe much of American life today is the term *secular*. A secular community struggles with a conflict in values, with old virtues viewed as hypocritical or evidence of blind conformity. People are unified largely by civil units rather than by any kinship ties. There is a great division of labor and proliferation of organizations, each with special membership and interests. Very formalized social controls are set by law and enforced by various civil agencies. Finally, secular communities create a basic anonymity to the extent that people live *in* the community without being *of* the community.

Where a community lies on the sacred-secular continuum does influence the nature of the decision process. For example, Sergiovanni and Carver have noted:

> School districts that tend toward the sacred end of the sacred-secular continuum are likely to emphasize public consensus politics that continue to characterize rural school districts in the United States. Conflict is kept from the public by working out disagreements in private. This is the natural and functional way of managing affairs because of the shared values and commitments of those in power. And, although policies, facilities, personnel, and programs change over time, they occur in such a way as to produce relatively little occasion for conflict, that is, through death, retirement, and routine updating.
>
> In a pure sacred school district, change of any type—for example, board membership, administrators, programs, school practices—is very slow to come barring highly unusual circumstances. Successful changes in the schools are minor indeed and/or are presented as logical extensions or variance of existing programs and practices.
>
> Secular communities, on the other hand, are more likely to have mechanisms that permit, even encourage conflict over major educational

---

[1]For a rather insightful view of the nature of an ideologically unified community, the reader is referred to the Broadway musical *Fiddler on the Roof*. The opening number, entitled "Tradition," describes lyrically just such a community with roles carefully spelled out and understood by one and all. The play, of course, goes on to detail the dissolution of this community because of forces within as well as without.

issues. The school board is, in part, a public forum for the discussion of major policies and decisions confronting schools. Conflict is seen as inevitable and functional in the decision-making process and, thus, does not have to occur only in private.[2]

Speaking to this same point earlier, Hughes wrote

The problem in an urbanized society such as we live in, with its evident cultural pluralism, is that various groups and individuals will reflect differing points on the sacred-secular continuum, and thus will hold different perceptions of what the institutions serving that community ought to look like. The politics of confrontation and conflict within which the school and other social institutions are caught is simply a manifestation of this.[3]

Role of the School

The mass public education system of this country is generally considered to have two primary roles: (1) to effectively and efficiently provide the important knowledge and skills needed to be a productive human being, and (2) to provide for a fluid social structure.

Attending to the demands of the first role produces about as much conflict as the second, although the conflict is often of a more specialized nature. Most citizens would agree that this is indeed the *raison d'être* for the public school system, but there is much controversy about the processes that should be used to achieve mastery of the important knowledge and skills. Further, responses to the question of what knowledge is of most use vary widely and cause misunderstanding and conflict.

The second role of the school, that of providing for a fluid social structure, is more honored in the breach than in the observance. It is generally accepted that the United States and Canada do not have the rigid class lines of many countries and that it is important to facilitate mobility up the social scale. Class lines in America do tend to be blurred. However, members of a minority group will point out that this has been primarily true only if one happened to be a white, Anglo-Saxon Protestant (WASP) or at least had an ethnic or cultural background that facilitated a one-generation amalgamation of WASP characteristics. Moreover, the many impinging negative variables mean that even if one had the appropriate ethnic characteristics, the American Dream—If one tries hard, one can succeed—becomes an impossibility for many members of the poverty-ridden social understructure.

The idea that the school's role is to provide for a fluid social structure therefore continues to be under fire and will continue to be so in the foreseeable future. The concept is generally well accepted, but aggressive efforts on

---

[2]Thomas J. Sergiovanni and Fred D. Carver, *The New School Executive* (New York: Harper and Row Publishers, 1980), p. 252.

[3]Larry W. Hughes, *Informal and Formal Community Forces: External Influences on Schools and Teachers* (Morristown, N. J.: General Learning Press, 1976), pp. 2–3.

the part of school leaders to implement the concept with busing, breakfast programs, compensatory education programs, the reorganizing of school district boundaries, bi- and trilingual instruction, among a host of policies, procedures, and processes ongoing in many schools, are met with resentment, misunderstanding, and downright hostility by many in the majority culture. Similarly, perceived or actual nonattention to inequities in school programming, organization, and instruction receive hostile reaction and frequent precipitative action by members of groups outside the mainstream.

The public school system has been viewed as an instrument of social reform for a century or more, but only in the last few decades has it overtly engaged in reform activities that have occurred mostly as a result of outside forces such as federal and state legislation, acts of the courts, or community pressures. Sadly, with some notable exceptions of course, school leaders have largely been content to avoid the issue and have provided organizational structures and response systems—PTAs, newsletters, standardized curriculum—that are somewhat out of touch with social reality and based on presumptions of ideological unity and automatic equity.

It's no wonder, then, that schools are caught in a crossfire at times, as first one group or individual and then another attempts to make the school reflect his or her beliefs about the world. Because of the nature of the public educational enterprise the school must derive its support from the outside world. People who influence policies in the community that affect the school reside in that outside world and inevitably seek ways to develop policies for the schools in conformity with their own desires and values.

Progress in education today depends in large part on the consent of parents and other citizens in the community as well as upon relationships that the school maintains with other community agencies and the government. In an economy of rising costs and an expanding sense of cultural pluralism and multiethnicity, the acquisition of additional support for the educational program, or at least the development of a firm understanding about the nature and role of education, assumes increasing importance. The problem, however, of securing adequate psychological as well as fiscal support for the schools goes well beyond the understanding of fiscal need alone. The public is interested as never before in the various dimensions of the educational system, and the demands made on individual schools are great indeed.

The school is the closest public agency to neighborhood or community residents, in both a literal and figurative sense. In geographic proximity the school is just around the corner and is the first line of communication with the area it serves. It is closer than the mayor's office, even closer in most cases than the fire station. And, the school affects the community's most prized possessions, its children and its pocketbook.

COMMUNITY INFLUENCE SYSTEMS

How are important political decisions actually made?

What kinds of people have the greatest influence on decisions? Are different kinds of decisions all made by the same people? From what strata of the community are the most influential people, the leaders, drawn?

Do leaders tend to cohere in their policies and form a sort of ruling group, or do they tend to divide, conflict, and bargain? Is the pattern of leadership, in short, oligarchical or pluralistic?

What is the relative importance of the most widely distributed political resource—the right to vote? Do leaders respond generally to the interests of a few citizens with the greatest wealth and highest status—or do they respond to the many with the largest number of votes? Are there important differences that in turn result in difference in influence?[4]

Community Power Structures

Sociologists, political scientists, and educational researchers have all examined in depth the phenomenon of power in a community. It is not necessary here to review and synthesize this research. The bibliography at the end of this chapter contains entries to assist in an examination of the concepts and constructs of community power. It does seem important, however, to briefly examine the nature of community power structure and to discuss some contrasting views about it.

Differentiated influence among community members exists. Sociologist Floyd Hunter has written:

> Power is a necessary function in society. Power is also a necessary function in a community, for it involves decision making and it also involves the function of executing determined policies or seeing to it that things get done which have been deemed necessary to be done. The social rights and prerogatives implied in power functions must be delegated to specific men to achieve social goals in any society.[5]

Power is distributed in unequal degrees throughout communities. Informal power often refers to the power of relatively few people at the top of their respective social and occupational hierarchies who have decision-making capabilities. These are often the people to see if one is interested in promoting some program in the community, for without their help any large-scale undertaking would be in some jeopardy.

Informal power must be distinguished from formal power. Formal power is manifested by the elected and appointed officers of a community—the mayor, city council, superintendent, board of education, for example. Often, members of the informal power structure neither seek nor serve in formal power positions, but they do influence in many ways the decisions of the formally constituted bodies.

---

[4]Robert Dahl, *Who Governs?* (New Haven, Conn.: Yale University Press, 1961), p. 7.

[5]Floyd Hunter, *Community Power Structure* (Chapel Hill, N. C.: University of North Carolina Press, 1953), p. 2.

Research supports the view that there are two kinds of informal community leaders: the generalist and the specialist. The influence of an informal leader designated as specialist depends upon a specific situation. The generalist, on the other hand, is a community leader who demonstrates leadership and influence in a wide variety of situations.

Two Views of Community Influence Systems

Floyd Hunter's classical Regional City study and the writings of many sociologists have led to a theory of community power structure that may be depicted by a pyramid.[6] (See Figure 4-1.) That is to say, there is a small group of key influentials at the top who interact among each other and who exert influence on an interactive second stratum composed of a larger number of individuals who, in their turn, exert influence on several other strata below them. The base of the pyramid is composed of the people in the community. Essentially, the theory is that there develops within a community and within the society a core of individuals who are all-powerful and of the generalist type. These are the individuals who make decisions of importance in all areas of the community or nation that impinge upon them or their group or affect in any way the operational sphere of their control.

A contrasting view of the nature of power structure is illustrated in the writings of Robert Dahl and other political scientists who dissent from the notion that any one person or group of persons is so powerful as to be able to exert such generalized influence on all community matters all of the time.[7] Instead, power distribution is viewed as *pluralistic* in nature with the influence of any individual or group being particularized to issues. The crowd interested in the schools, for example, is not composed of the same people who are influential in some other aspect of the community.[8]

Further, some theorists say the term "ruling elite" or "top influential" is a confused one and misleads since it is conferred upon a group with only a *high potential for control*. For example, a set of individuals in a community with control over certain resources leading to a high probability that they will agree on key political alternatives and that, if they choose to act in some specified way, those alternatives will be chosen, could be said to have a high potential for control.

But, while a group may have a high potential for control, it may not have a *high potential for unity*. Political effectiveness, or power, can be considered a product of the group's potential for control plus its potential for unity. Moreover, a group with a low potential for control but a very high potential for unity might, in the end, on any particular issue be more effective politically than the reverse. It is this latter point that may be of greatest importance to

---

[6]Ibid.

[7]Dahl, *Who Governs?*

[8]Critics of this point of view respond that the researchers simply have not looked far enough and are just describing lower-strata influentials.

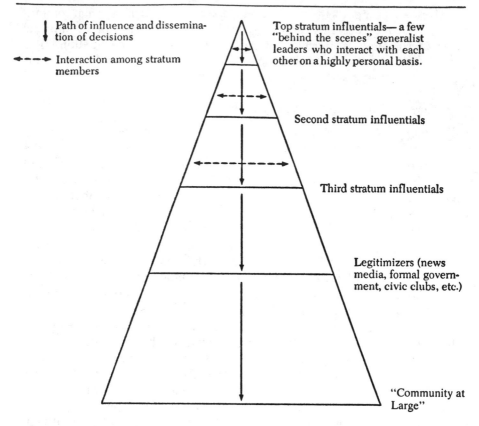

↓ Path of influence and dissemination of decisions

◄─ ─ ─► Interaction among stratum members

Top stratum influentials— a few "behind the scenes" generalist leaders who interact with each other on a highly personal basis.

Second stratum influentials

Third stratum influentials

Legitimizers (news media, formal government, civic clubs, etc.)

"Community at Large"

FIGURE 4-1. One Type of Community Influence System: The Power Pyramid.

educational leaders seeking to develop programs necessary to the total community but without support from an existing power elite.

Some members of what might be called the community understructure have shown a remarkable ability to exert influence by unifying their fellows on any given issue. Some testimony that this indeed occurs may be provided by such diverse examples as the unionization and developing political clout of migrant workers in the west; the wresting away of formal political control from whites by blacks in some areas of the country; and any number of instances where groups, not in control of any significant amount of dollar resources or the equivalent, have organized around a basic principle or cause and through adroit political maneuvering have been able to exert sufficient pressure to bring about a change.

In none of these examples could the groups exerting influence be said to have much potential for control by any standard measure. Yet, often because of a developing leadership structure, they do exhibit a potential for unity and thus represent forces for change well outside any traditionally posited oligarchic power structure. It is also important that community power structure not be viewed as static, but rather subject to great change over time. Thus, typing a power structure is analogous to taking a photograph; it is a picture of a moment in history. Movement can be expected and the direction this movement takes might even be predictable as conditions such as a changing population or changing social conditions are studied.

No one event in a community can possibly capsule the kind of organization of power that exists; few communities reflect that kind of stability. Yet, power relationships are also not totally random. Patterns of influence, while not static, are nevertheless marked with some stability, allowing a degree of predictability over a span of time.

In a pluralistic community the schools must serve many publics, each with its values and orientations. In such a setting the role of the school administrator often becomes that of mediating conflicts between various competing pressure groups. This simply means that educational administrators must be able to work successfully with many groups often pulling in conflicting directions. Among several implications the nature of power in a community may have for principals, the importance of identifying key community or neighborhood influentials and the development of informal working relations with these people cannot be overemphasized, not because these people or groups are always right, but because they usually represent the best thinking of the community and are, many times, most influenced by a rational approach to problem solving.

Out of the research of Hunter, Dahl, Agger and many other social and political scientists has come a body of knowledge about the nature of power and influence in a community. Much of this is of relevance to educators and others who work in public institutions. It is possible to conceptualize community power as one of four basic types: monolithic, factional, coalitional, and amorphous.[9] In the monolithic type of power structure one finds the "Hunter pyramid," a structure in which there is a single and often small group of individuals who make most of the important decisions in the community. The factional structure is characterized by two or more groups, each with their own constituencies and each of which vie for control of the important issues facing the community. In the coalitional type of power structure, the nature of the issues to be decided determines who works with whom in the decision-making process. Such a structure tends to be characterized by consensual decision making and is fluid in nature. The term amorphous, sometimes also labeled "inert," simply describes a community situation wherein there cannot be

---

[9]See, for example, Donald J. McCarty and Charles E. Ramsey, *The School Managers* (Westport, Conn.: Greenwood Publishing Co., 1971); John Walton, "A Systematic Survey of Community Power Research," in Michael Aiken and Paul Motts, eds., *The Structure of Community Power* (New York: Random House, 1970); and Fred D. Carver and Donald O. Crowe, "An Interdisciplinary Survey of Community Power Research," *Educational Administration Quarterly* 5 (Winter 1969): 50–65.

found any discernible or persistent pattern of groups or individuals who directly influence decision making.

The Pluralistic School Community

Confounding the problem of communicating with school patrons in a pluralistic community is that, more and more frequently, districts are reorganizing school attendance zones to achieve desegregated student bodies. Thus, as busing and noncontiguous pairings of schools occur, the neighborhood served by a school may be quite dispersed. Conventional parent and patron groups, such as booster clubs and PTAs, may be difficult to maintain because of time and distance problems. Such groups are worth the energy it takes to maintain them, however. Beyond this, it is apparent that a considerable portion of the administrative effort will be required to work with existing community groups in the various neighborhoods from which students come, as well as to develop schoolwide advisory groups with cross-sectional representation.

Neighborhood Influence Systems

Neighborhoods also have influence systems and these may be especially important in the principal's sphere of interaction. As was noted earlier, the individual school building remains, in most communities, the closest public agency, certainly in terms of geographic proximity. Thus, it is handy, if nothing else, to members of the immediate neighborhood. In a very real sense it is also in an excellent position to feel the pulse of the surrounding area.[10]

As urban and suburban communities have become more and more complex and power sources have become diffused, neighborhood influence systems have become increasingly important at least partly because of a perceived lack of responsiveness of certain community welfare delivery systems such as schools. More often such influence systems also reflect racial or ethnic homogeneity. Individual schools may serve as effective mechanisms to receive information from and to dispense information to neighborhood leadership. Research suggests that an individual community member's decision to support or not support any particular community issue is more often than not based on the influence of friends and neighbors rather than on the presence of any outside objective data. It would seem, therefore, that the perceptive school principal should become familiar with the leadership structure of the neighborhood the individual school may serve.

Every social group has a leadership structure that, with some diligence, can be identified. The principal who wants to begin a new kind of dialogue with the immediate community will do well to engage in this endeavor, for what is true of community power structure generally—that it represents some

---

[10]An especially good reference for working within neighborhood social structures is Donald J. and Rachel B. Warren, "Six Kinds of Neighborhoods," *Psychology Today* 9, no. 1 (June 1975): 74–80.

of the best thinking of the community—will also be true of neighborhood influence systems.[11]

Several years ago during the early part of the Johnson Administration the Community Action Programs (CAP) were implemented. Some readers may remember that an important aspect of CAP was the initial constitution of a local policy-making and decision-making body that had under the law the task of governance of the several programs. The provision establishing the governing board of the Community Action Program required that there be representation of substantial numbers of those people who were to be helped by the programs. That is, the policy and advising board would be composed of a large number of the poor. "But, who?" was the question most often raised in local government circles and among those charged with getting the programs going. At first in many communities no one knew just how to go about *locating* individuals who might be interested in serving on such advisory boards. Surprisingly to many, however, they discovered that there was indeed a leadership structure among the understructure and it could be rather readily identified, often through reputational means by surveying the storefront churches, the local welfare agencies, the less well-known social clubs, the membership of small union locals, among any number of other somewhat formal sources. Not very helpful were such agencies as PTA/PTO, the well-known churches, and the well-known civic clubs. There is a lesson here for the principal who wishes to engage in a new kind of relationship with the community, especially if that community is characterized by heterogeneity in racial, ethnic, or social makeup. Further, a neighborhood leadership structure may not be composed of or contain very many people who are also parents of children attending the schools.

The major point is that the old mechanisms may not suffice for a school administrator interested in developing effective school-community relations programs based on mutual trust and a willingness to examine issues of mutual concern. Traditional community groups often do not have a membership comprised of anything approximating the real nature of the community or the neighborhood served by the schools, and there may exist, well outside these more conservative groups, a leadership structure that has not yet been recognized but that has important things to say to the schools. School administrators should not engage in self-delusion about the nature of the leadership pattern in the neighborhood the school serves. An examination of the membership rolls of the local formal parent-teacher organization and a comparison of cer-

---

[11]It is often not easy to initiate this dialogue because the principal may be viewed with suspicion and distrust by various community members. Vidich and Bensman cite several studies which indicate that the school administrator or any professional educator who is removed from direct contact with children and parents is considered the "alien expert" who "knows the ways and laws of the world and who uses this knowledge to shape the community as it bears on him and his ends which are necessarily in the *selfish interest* of education." [Emphasis supplied.] Vidich and Bensman, *Small Town in Mass Society* (Princeton, N.J.: Princeton University Press, 1968), p. 195.

tain characteristics of these people with general demographic characteristics of the student body of the school may reveal that certain people are missing. If different kinds of people are missing, one can be sure that many key neighborhood influentials are not being reached by school messages. Principals, like most of the rest of us, are most comfortable when surrounded by persons who reflect a background similar to their own. Principals tend to be most comfortable when speaking with other professionals. This fact alone, then, may suggest a careful analysis of the procedures currently being used to tap community leadership sources.

Community Groups. The most intense memberships are held in groups that could be classified as *Blut und Bod,* those groups with kinship and territorial bonds rooted in certain ethnic or racial ties.

For example, Bernard has written,

> A common language, a common dietary, a common neighborhood, common experience with outsiders, a common history, make people feel more comfortable with one another, more at ease. They understand one another, they read one another; they get one another's messages. They feel they can count on one another for support. They constitute an in group; everyone else is an out group.
>
> The bonds that hold people together also separate them from others; invisible lines are drawn to protect the boundaries between them and outsiders.[12]

People in the community are also often members of an array of different formal and informal groups that may impinge upon the schools. They are members of clubs and associations as well as other more general self-help groups such as the American Indian Movement, the League of United Latin American Citizens, the Congress of Racial Equality, or a group such as the DAR or the "moral majority," for example. All of these organizations will demand loyalty from their membership and may oppose certain school system procedures and policies. Membership in what may at times be adversary groups may be the source of much community-school conflict.

> In sum, then, characteristic of our complex society are communities which are more generally reflective of cultural pluralism. The fact is that many people in the community will not derive their normative behavior from white, middle-class heritage—and by extension, of course, neither will the student body; nor the teaching staff. Responses to traditional control and decision systems in the school and the community may vary from hostile acquiescence to open challenge. Teachers and administrators must learn to cope with this great diversity.[13]

---

[12]Jesse Bernard, *American Community Behavior* (New York: Holt, Rinehart and Winston, 1965), p. 358.

[13]Hughes, *Informal and Formal Community Forces,* p. 19.

It is apparent, then, that school leaders need to identify the influential people and groups in the community or neighborhood. Power structure and influence systems vary from community to community and neighborhood to neighborhood. Assuming that all influentials in a particular power system feel similarly about school issues and that there is always unanimity is unwise. There is an indeterminacy and amorphousness about power structure and influence systems, but the degree to which various leaders in a community are able to agree on a direction education ought to take and the degree to which they are able to accept certain principles and guidelines that school leaders determine, in great part, will determine the extent of reform, modification, and growth of the educational institution in the community.

There are many instruments available to assist school leaders in gauging the nature of interest in the schools, the degree of educational enlightenment, and the nature, extent, and identification of influential people and groups in the community. The school administrator should subject the area that the school serves to a community analysis not only to develop good public relations strategies but, more important, to utilize the resources and problem-solving ability manifest in neighborhood or community influentials, thus providing a foundation for cooperative development and growth of both school and community.

Pressure Groups. No discussion of community influence systems would be complete without some discussion about the nature of pressure groups. Pressure groups must be distinguished from a normal community decision system because of the somewhat temporal nature of their activities and their tendency to form and reform around single issues or causes, or because of a specific decision made by the school leadership.

Pressure groups should not be dismissed lightly because they have been a source of great disruption in many communities as well as a source of productive change. When one thinks of the term "pressure group," it is difficult to put it in a noninflammatory context. Immediately thoughts of book burnings, witch hunts, placard-carrying demonstrators, impassioned pleas from the pulpit or the podium come to mind. One also gets the picture of school boards and superintendents hastily capitulating to the onslaught of such charges that the "schools are Godless," that the English department is assigning lascivious literature, that sex education should not be taught in the schools, among a host of similar kinds of charges, emotion-ridden in context and within which rational thinking often goes out the window.

Conflict is not inevitable, but it is frequent in any society. Conflict is not necessarily disruptive or negative. In fact, it is often out of conflict that greater understanding results, provided the situation is characterized by positive acts of openness, a willingness to compromise, and well-understood procedures for resolution.

Negotiating with Pressure Groups

From time to time, all school administrators will be confronted with requests from organized groups of people who represent a particular point of view about a school-related issue. Frequently, such pressure groups begin their inquiry at the individual school level in the principal's office. The issues may run the gamut, from complaints about teachers, textbooks, or specific courses of study to alleged institutional racism and demands for more equitable staffing or pupil personnel decisions. Often these are legitimate concerns, and they must always be dealt with sensitively and sensibly. The following guidelines may help the besieged principal:

1. An early identification should be made of the group that is in opposition or is likely to be in opposition to certain school programs. Who are they, and more important, who are their leaders?

2. Can the group and its leaders be talked to? Once the opposing group and the leader(s) of that group have been identified, it is appropriate to contact them for a closed-door session to explore the elements of the issue. The principal may gain some more definitive notion of just what it is that is troubling the group. This meeting or series of meetings may develop ways, if the cause is legitimate, for the school to help the group achieve its goals. It may require great insight to find out what the real issue is, because stated "reasons" for opposition to this or that school issue are often at variance with the real causative factors. It is important to know what the real reasons are if the group is to be dealt with effectively and if subsequent negotiations are to be successful. (At this point, it is also important to apprise the central office of the potential hostile situation and to seek counsel.)

3. Following these informal meetings, it is important to reach a decision. Some important points must be determined at this time, including the question about how strong the opposition really is. Do they have a good chance to beat the school in its present position? Most important, do they have a good solid point on which to differ with the school? It is at this time that the principal must decide whether or not the issue will be fought on the basis of the initial position of both sides or whether some areas of accord are possible. Before a decision is made to fight it out, there is usually an alternative.

4. Is there room for compromise? The political system under which we operate functions on compromise. Politics is the delicate art of compromise. Professional educators view themselves as experts who know what is needed for good education, but it is within this context that educational administrators often show a lack of political sophistication. The greater good sometimes demands compromise solutions where desirable changes can be achieved without compromising principles or without loss of integrity.

Of course compromising may not be necessary. Perhaps simply sitting down with members of the pressure group and explaining the school's position and the facts may dissuade the group from further action. Administrators who have engaged in potential community-conflict situations over the years would suggest that compromise through negotiations may be the more likely result. The pressure group's motives may be highly complex. Its needs and goals are every bit as important to its membership as the needs and goals of the particular administrator or school system in question.

In any effort to influence or achieve compromise, timing is important. One really can't wait until the organized campaign is underway to effect compromises or modify points of view. The time to influence a pressure group is before the particular group has launched its initial fusillade and before the school or the administrator is totally committed to a position. Common sense says that it is increasingly difficult, if not impossible, to change someone or some group when there will be much loss of face, real or imagined, by doing so.

5. Seek help from other community members. Assuming that all efforts to appease the opposition are unsuccessful, what does the administrator try next? The first step is to find out who is on the school's side, or who it appears ought to be on the school's side. Some community analysis can be conducted even at this stage and may prove fruitful. Who besides the school really stands to lose? School principals should not forget about other less-organized neighborhood groups of people who, though they seemingly have a low potential for power, might have a high potential for unity on the particular issues and who could be called upon for counsel and other help.

In all situations, it is crucial to determine what the real goal is and what results or gains can be expected from the achievement of that goal. In other words, is the school's position or is the school administrator's position on the issue tenable? If so, evidence must be presented to substantiate why it is tenable. Many school administrators have ended up in hot water because of a refusal to negotiate or compromise or because of a determination to stick to their guns on irrelevant points of contention. Further, it must be remembered that it is clearly the right of citizens to protest when they feel that the school is failing to accomplish the right thing. It is a wise school administrator who looks to community opinion as an invaluable source of information about the quality of decisions made at the school.

Evaluating the Legitimacy of the Critic. Members of the community, of course, have the right and obligation to legitimately question and criticize the schools, although defining the word "legitimate" in this context is difficult. One of the best benchmarks for judging legitimacy is observing the behavior exhibited by the particular group. Is it willing to meet with appropriate educational system personnel out of the harsh glare of TV lights or without benefit of newspaper rhetoric? Is it considerate of the other sides of the issue? Is criticism mostly characterized by reason and rationality, or does it seem mostly emotional in nature?

To help judge the legitimacy question Raywid has advanced six rules of evidence:[14]

1. Does the critic generalize from only one or a few situations to make all-encompassing statements?
2. Does the critic accept demonstrable facts? As Raywid indicates, "one cannot deny [the existence of facts] merely because he simply would prefer things to be otherwise."
3. Does the critic recognize and tentatively accept what is less certain but is nevertheless indicated by the weight of present evidence?
4. Does the critic accept the rules of logical inference? The critic must not fail to examine other possible explanations for a condition before arriving at his conclusion.
5. Is the critic honest, or does he distort the evidence?
6. Does the critic have the ability to distinguish between evidence and emotion?

To this point we have discussed pressure groups in such a manner as to suggest that conflict is inevitable. Conflict is not inevitable but is frequent in any society. Conflict is not necessarily disruptive or negative, and often greater understanding results from conflict situations, provided the situation is characterized by positive acts of openness, a willingness to compromise, and well-understood procedures for resolution.

NEED FOR WELL-DEVELOPED POLICIES

If conflict can be expected on educational issues, if total ideological unity is not characteristic of very many complex communities, and if criticism can be expected as a part of the normal life of the administrator of any public institution, what can be done to modify the divisive effects of such actions and instead capitalize on the rich diversity of views and opinion to improve the schools? Foremost would be to provide a broad set of policies, both at the school-district level as well as at the school-building level, that establish a framework within which diverging views can be heard in a regular and systematic manner. Such a framework provides, in effect, procedural due process whereby dissidents factions in a community can formally register their views.

Figure 4-2 is a sample form that some districts provide to those individuals who are objecting to the use of certain educational material. Such a complaint form could be adapted to other issues and, if used judiciously, provide a vehicle for citizens to make their views known in a rational and systematic way. It can help insure due process.

---

[14]Mary Ann Raywid, *The Ax Grinders* (New York: Macmillan Co., 1963).

CITIZEN'S REQUEST FOR RECONSIDERATION OF
EDUCATIONAL MEDIA

Title of media _____

    Type of media: (circle)

      Book   Film   Filmstrip   Recording _____

                                              (other)

    Author/artist/composer/other   _____

    Publisher/producer (if known) _____

Request initiated by _____ Phone _____

Address _____

Complainant represents _____

    _____ Self

    _____ (Name of organization) _____

    _____ (Identify other group) _____

1. After having read/viewed/listened to the item in question, to what do you object and why? (Please be specific; cite pages, frame, other) _____
_____

2. What do you believe is the theme of this item? _____
_____

3. What do you feel might be the result of students reading/viewing/listening to this item? _____
_____

4. For what age group would you recommend this item? _____
_____

5. Other comments _____
_____

_____   _____

    Date   Signature of Complainant

ORS: 11/23/70

FIGURE 4-2.

Using Review Boards. Individual principals would be wise also to establish some kind of review body on whom the principal could rely for advice, counsel, and the development of criteria for judging potentially controversial instructional materials. Help is available to such a professional review body from such agencies as the National Council for Teachers of Social Studies or the National Council for Teachers of English, as well as other sources.

The importance of involving a wide array of appropriate personnel in the development of policies to anticipate problems is important because it provides the basis for information sharing and good decision making. Principals cannot be expected to know everything. No principal should expect to be able to respond instantaneously to a critic. The advice and counsel of the school staff, as well as the community, and the development of broadly based policies and policy review boards are needed to provide for effective decision making and intelligent responses to questions that may issue from the community.

SUMMARY

The focus of this chapter has been to examine the nature of the communities served by a school. There are a multiplicity of social forces that interact with and act upon the schools. Neighborhood influence systems, pressure groups and the differing characteristics of power structures impinge on the life of the elementary school principal. The need to be sensitive to the outside demands and to analyze the very nature of the school community is apparent. The successful school administrator develops a wide range of response patterns, due-process mechanisms, and information-seeking devices so that the school can be at once responsive but also true to its obligation to serve all of the people.

BIBLIOGRAPHY

Agger, Robert; Swanson, Bert E.; and Goldrich, Daniel. *The Rulers and the Ruled: Political Power and Importance in American Communities.* New York: John Wiley and Sons, 1964.

Brandt, Richard M. et al. *Cultural Pluralism and Social Change.* Syracuse, N. Y.: National Dissemination Center, School of Education, Syracuse University, 1977.

Carver, Fred D., and Crowe, Donald O. "An Interdisciplinary Framework for the Study of Community Power." *Educational Administration Quarterly* 5 (Winter 1969): 50–65.

Goldstein, William. "The 'Now When I Was in School' System." *NASSP Bulletin* 64, no. 432 (January 1980): 44–47.

Hines, Susan C., and McCleary, Lloyd E. "The Role of the Principal in Community Involvement." *NASSP Bulletin* 64, no. 432 (January 1980): 67–75.

Hughes, Larry W. *Informal and Formal Community Forces: External Influences on Schools and Teachers.* Morristown, N. J.: General Learning Press, 1976.

Hughes, Larry W.; Gordon, William M.; and Hillman, Larry W. *Desegregating America's Schools.* New York: Longman, Inc., 1980, esp. chaps. 10 and 11.

Lipsky, Morris. "Toward a Theory of Street Level Bureaucracy." In W. D. Hawley *et al.,* eds. *Theoretical Perspectives on Urban Politics.* Englewood Cliffs, N. J.: Prentice-Hall, 1976, pp. 196–213.

Mann, Dale. *The Politics of Administrative Representation.* Lexington, Mass.: Lexington Books, Inc., 1976.

McCarty, Donald J., and Ramsey, Charles E. *The School Managers.* Westport, Conn.: Greenwood Publishing Corporation, 1971).

Scribner, Jay, ed. *The Politics of Education*. Seventy-Sixth Yearbook
    of the National Society for the Study of Education, Part II.
    Chicago: University of Chicago Press, 1977.
Sergiovanni, Thomas J., and Carver, Fred D. *The New School Execu-
    tive*. New York: Harper and Row Publishers, 1980, esp. chap. 13.
Vidich, Arthur J., and Bensman, Joseph. *Small Town and Mass Soci-
    ety*. Princeton, N. J.: Princeton University Press, 1968.
Walton, John. "A Systematic Survey of Community Power Research."
    In Michael Aiken and Paul Mott, eds. *The Structure of Community
    Power*. New York: Random House, 1970, pp. 443–64.
Warren, Donald J., and Warren, Rachel B. "Six Kinds of Neighbor-
    hoods." *Psychology Today* (June 1975): 74–80.
Wayson, William W. "Power, Power, Who's Got the Power." *National
    Elementary Principal* 58 (March 1979): 12–20.

PART TWO

Administrative Tasks and Functions

Several chapters comprise Part Two, each of which describes a task area or functional aspect of the principalship. Guidelines for action as well as underlying principles are contained in each chapter. The purposes of this part of the book are to provide insights about the responsibilities that accrue to the principal, describe successful practices, and offer suggestions for implementation in a variety of school settings.

Five functional aspects are treated in the following order: curricular and instructional development; staff selection, evaluation, and development, including a chapter on negotiations; financial and building management; and public relations. The effort is to stimulate creative thinking about these task areas rather than prescribe a single approach. Where appropriate, however, prescriptive material does appear.

5

Guidelines and Goals
for Planning
School Programs

INTRODUCTION

Schools really can make a difference in the achievement levels of
students, but a school is as good or bad, as creative or sterile, as the person
who serves as the head of that school. The key factor in making good schools
work is the "principal principle."

What do effective principals do?

> Principals of effective schools are strong instructional leaders who know
> how to manage time and money effectively. . . . they concentrate on prior-
> ity goals . . . they set as their main goal the acquisition of basic skills. . . .
> effective principals have high expectations for all students and they will en-
> list the support of others in meeting common goals.[1]

This chapter and the next deal with the leadership role and the necessary
conceptual knowledge a principal must have of the curricular and instructional
program of the school. The principal is the one person in a school who can
oversee the entire program because of his or her interest in the success of the
entire school and all of its parts. Therefore, the principal is in the best position
to provide the necessary sense of direction to the various aspects of a school.
Research has shown that the most effective principals have a clear sense of purpose and priorities and are able to enlist the support of others toward these
ends.

Many of the problems of direction within a school organization are very
subtle, will be difficult to solve, and require great conceptual and technical

---

[1] *Good Schools—What Makes Them Work* (National School Public Relations Association,
1980).

FIGURE 5-1. The Six Interrelated Program Organization Components.

knowledge of curriculum, instruction, and learning. The principal must have the necessary understanding to find proper and just solutions to these problems and many others like them.

Interdependence of the School's Organizational Components

The school program is organized into a series of interrelated organizational components. Each of these components is dependent upon and influences the others. One component, for example, is the curricular organization of the school. Other components include instructional processes, practices in grouping children, the organization and utilization of staff, the scheduling of learning time, and the organization and use of the facility. Decisions about each of these six components must be made for every school, and they *must* be made under the leadership of the principal. If not, special interest groups may attempt to organize the school for their own needs and preferences.

Three factors must be considered in making decisions about the six program organization components: compatibility, balance, and flexibility.

PROGRAM COMPATIBILITY

The interdependence of program components demands that attention be paid to all six areas when a change is proposed for any one. The situation is analogous to a six-piece jigsaw puzzle. If the shape of one piece is altered, the puzzle can be made complete again only if the shapes of the adjacent pieces are also altered.

For example, if a decision is made to individualize the instructional program, attention must be given to the alteration of student group patterns and staff organization as they will be affected by the decision to individualize. Curriculum, scheduling, and facility utilization will probably be affected also.

Mistakes are frequently made in implementing innovations for organizational components because adequate attention has not been given to program component compatibility. Many of the efforts to implement ideas such as team teaching were unsuccessful because of this lack of proper attention to compatibility with the other organizational components. Somewhere in the organization the decision was made to be innovative and utilize a new staffing pattern called team teaching. Being basically conservative in nature and not wanting to change the program too radically, planners limited the change to that one component. No changes were made in instruction or scheduling or student grouping, and as a result, the innovative idea was not effective and gradually faded away. School organization components are closely interdependent and must be considered in concert with one another.

ORGANIZATIONAL BALANCE

The second major concern that a principal must have for the organizational program components is that of balance—how much of each component is needed. Concern for this point is particularly important when contemplating a change or implementing an innovation.

A case in point is the technique of individualized instruction. Two excellent aids in individualized instruction have been the use of learning packages and the use of independent study. Both are good ideas, but either done to excess is doomed. Children can be papered and penciled to boredom with the overuse of learning packages even if the packages are good ones. The same is true of too much independent study. Used with discretion, independent study is an excellent tool, but overdone, as was necessary in some of the "unscheduled time blocks" of the early modular schedules, independent study was disastrous.

Any good innovative idea carried to an extreme or emphasized out of balance with its counterparts is not good. Instructional patterns, curriculum, student grouping, staffing, scheduling, and facility utilization must be in balance.

ORGANIZATIONAL FLEXIBILITY

Adults, as well as children, usually like order, uniformity, consistency, and simplicity. Therefore, the attempt is often made to organize schools along pure, simple lines. The more alternatives built into a system, the more complex it becomes and the more difficult to implement. However, the varying needs of learners require flexibility. The school principal must be willing to overcome some of the desire for simplicity and ease of operation and recognize that a good instructional program is indeed complex and must be flexible.

How often has a lesson that is still going strong been interrupted as the bell rings, or a field trip turned down because of the inability to schedule it into the everyday time tables? What about the student who needs additional work or reading skill development but must go on to a social studies lesson with the rest of the group? The inability to adjust for each of these things is really the result of a lack of adequate flexibility in arranging organizational components of a school. The organizational components should be arranged to allow the administrators and staff to vary them or adapt them to a particular need, preferably without reconstructing the entire schedule of the school.

The principal's role in program organization is that of providing balance between and among the various interests of a school. No aspect of the school should be allowed to become out of balance with the other components. The principal also insures the compatibility of the several organizational components by not letting new ideas be thrust upon the school without considering the school's overall goals and the necessary adjustments in the total program that will result from changes. The principal must insure program flexibility, allowing and encouraging desired changes and adjustments in the program to take place by encouraging an openness to planned change and reducing rigidity in the school's organization.

SETTING PROGRAM GOALS

The goals of a school should relate to social expectations, wants and needs, and the individual differences of children. How does one organize such a program in a school?

The structure of a school program requires that specific thought be given to each of several organizational components of the program: (1) curricular organization, (2) instructional processes, (3) student grouping practices, (4) staff organization, (5) the scheduling of learning time, and (6) facility utilization and design. While the six components can be separated for discussion purposes, the program that results for any particular school must give detailed attention to both the contribution that each component makes to the achievement of the goals and objectives of the school as well as the development of each component in such a way that it is compatible with the other five components. For example, a goal statement may speak of meeting the individual needs of each child. From this goal an individualized instructional format might be selected. This instructional format must then be supported with a student grouping plan, staffing plan, and schedule. In turn, if the staffing selection proposes team teaching, the facility utilization design should provide appropriate work spaces for teaching teams.

The organizational components are not equally important and should not be considered as equals; nor are they independent entities. Decisions regarding the organization of the curriculum and instructional program should be made first. These must logically be based on the goals and objectives for the school. The other four components serve the first two.

Goal Determination

What are the goals of the school, how are they determined, and by whom? Are they determined by teachers, administrators, students, or the community?

In reality each of these groups contributes either directly or indirectly to the establishment of goals. The principal has the opportunity to bring these goals and objectives into focus where they can be considered in a rational manner. Of course, they can remain a somewhat vague set of assumptions upon which school decisions are based. The problem with leaving goals vague is that many important decisions relating to the organizational structure of a school rest upon these goals. To leave them as vague, unfocused assumptions does not provide a sufficient foundation upon which to base decisions. The following guidelines can be helpful in determining goals and objectives:

1. Relevance of the statement of philosophy to the larger purpose of the American democratic commitment.
2. Attention to intellectual, democratic, moral, and social values, basic to satisfying the needs of the individual and his culture.
3. Recognition of individual differences.
4. The special characteristics and unique needs of secondary school children.
5. Concern for the nature of knowledge and for the nature of the learning process as they apply to learners and their total development.
6. Consistency of philosophy with actual practice.
7. Identification of the roles and relationships expected of the community, the student, the teacher, and the administration in the educational process of the school.
8. The role of the secondary school program of the school district and the importance of the articulation with other elements of the overall educational program.
9. The responsibility for making a determination as to a desirable balance among activities designed to develop a cognitive, affective, and psychomotor demands.
10. The relationship of the school and all other educational learning centers.
11. The responsibility of the school toward social and economic change.
12. The accountability of the school to the community it serves.[2]

---

[2]*Elementary School Evaluative Criteria,* National Study of School Evaluation, A Guide for School Improvement (Arlington, Va., 1973), pp. 39–40.

Goal statements generated from these points can be commonly applied to curriculum development projects to determine what is to be taught in the school. The application of these goal categories to the development of the school curriculum is a necessary step. Moreover, these goal categories need to be applied to the other facets of the school's organization as well. For example, using the first goal category, that of establishing goals consistent with democratic ideals, a curriculum goal relating to democratic ideals might be fulfilled through some aspect of the social studies curriculum. On the other hand, another objective consistent with democratic ideals might be the creation of independent learners capable of continuing their learning in a systematic way after leaving school. The objective probably will be best approached through one of the organizational components such as instruction or scheduling. Here, through independent study techniques, the skill of becoming an independent learner could be practiced and applied directly to the democratic-ideals goal.

DEVELOPING APPROPRIATE OBJECTIVES

. Once goals have been agreed on, the task becomes one of determining how well the goals are being met. Discrepancy analysis or needs assessment can be carried out to see which goals are being least successfully achieved. This then becomes the basis for an improvement plan.

Goal statements should provide a sense of direction for the school, but they often do not provide a specific target to be achieved within a given time period. For that reason, goals often need to be spelled out in the form of specific achievable objectives. Here are three goal statements from an elementary school, each with a set of specific objectives developed by the faculty for achievement this year.

ELEMENTARY SCHOOL GOALS AND OBJECTIVES

Goal I. To provide the opportunity to acquire the basic skills of reading, writing, listening, speaking, and calculating necessary to be a productive member of society.

> *Objective 1.* To implement and evaluate the mathematics curriculum developed by our system for grades kindergarten through six.
>
> *Objective 2.* To continue the Holt Reading series and Management Program in grades one through four and implement this program in grade five.
>
> *Objective 3.* To implement the adopted Holt science text in grades one through six.
>
> *Objective 4.* To continue use of the adopted Ginn social studies text in grades one through six.

Objective 5. To implement the system's standardized testing program.

Objective 6. Kindergarten and junior primary instruction will complement the programs used in grades one through six.

Goal II. To encourage responsibility for one's own actions and encourage respect for the rights and property of others.

Objective 1. To continue to stress school discipline and enforce stated school rules.

Objective 2. To provide opportunities for students to develop skills necessary for good interpersonal relationships, positive self-concepts, self-discipline, and motivation.

Objective 3. To hold students responsible for the return, repair, or replacement of lost or damaged school materials or property.

Objective 4. To encourage the use of praise to reinforce proper behavior and identify expectations for irresponsible behavior.

Goal III. To provide the opportunity for the individual to continue to grow intellectually, aesthetically, physically, and emotionally.

Objective 1. To attempt to provide programs in all the above areas that allow children to continue to grow.

Objective 2. To continue to provide guidance services.

Objective 3. To encourage the administration and the school board to provide specialized personnel adequate to meet minimum state standards in the following areas: music for sixty minutes per week and art for sixty minutes per week.

Objective 4. To encourage the administration and the school board to provide one full-time specialized physical education teacher for each school.

Objective 5. To implement Public Law 94-142.

Objectives represent the basis for a plan of improvement. They should be written for a specific time period; in many cases a year is appropriate. They should be written in a form that will allow the results to be observable or measurable.

Objectives should be written with major participation by the faculty. If teams or departments are operating, they can form a basic working unit to develop objectives from the needs assessment; then representatives from each team can review and modify the statements to develop a schoolwide list. Team objectives are also desirable.

Attention can be focused on the objectives in several ways: objectives can be made the focus of staff and inservice meetings, or team and school objectives can become part of the staff evaluation plan for the school when an evaluation-by-objectives model, such as the one discussed in Chapter 14, is used.

SUMMARY

The goals of the school are statements of intent or direction for the organization. They are important to the organization because every objective and every action should be planned to move the organization toward the goals. It is important that all members of the staff and school community be cognizant of the goals, and it is preferable that they have all had a hand in their development or modification. Goal understanding on the part of the members of an organization is a sound basis for their coordinated action in moving the organization in the desired direction.

The principal has the responsibility to provide the leadership to the faculty and the community for the development of these educational goals and objectives, to keep the current goals and objectives constantly in front of the staff in order to maintain direction, and to see that goals are frequently reviewed and revised when desirable.

BIBLIOGRAPHY

English, F., and Kaufman, R. *Needs Assessment: A Focus for Curriculum Development.* Washington, D. C.: Association for Supervision and Curriculum Development, 1975.

Kaufman, R. "Possible Taxonomy of Needs Assessment." *Educational Technology* 17, no. 11 (November 1977): 60–64.

National School Public Relations Association. *Good Schools—What Makes Them Work.* 1980.

Northern California Program Development Center, and Phi Delta Kappa, Commission on Educational Planning. *Educational Goals and Objectives: A Model Program for Community and Professional Involvement.* Bloomington, Ind.: Phi Delta Kappa, 1972.

Rose, B. Keith et al. *Educational Goals and Objectives: A Model Program for Community and Professional Involvement. Administrator's Manual.* Bloomington, Ind.: Phi Delta Kappa, Commission on Educational Planning, 1972.

Stake, R., and Gooler, D. "Measuring Educational Priorities." *Educational Technology* 11, no. 9 (September 1971): 44–48.

Witkin, B. "Needs Assessment Kits, Models, and Tools." *Educational Technology* 17, no. 11 (November 1977): 5–18.

6

Individual Differences
and Student Grouping

INTRODUCTION

The concept of individualized instruction has reached prominence in the past few years. Underlying all of the efforts to provide greater individualization is the knowledge that children grow and develop at different rates.

What is the nature of the child? What differences count when organizing a school? Differences can be found in children's abilities, height, weight, age, sex, interests, needs, ethnic background, learning styles, achievement, and personalities. But before determining which differences matter in school organization, we should consider what these differences really are. Obviously, as children mature, differences increase. Many characteristics can be measured against accepted fixed scales and spoken of in fairly concrete terms. Items such as sex or ethnic background remain fixed and can usually be described in specific terms, also. However, factors such as ability, interests, needs, learning style, and personality are far more difficult to assess, for they are far more complex, varied, and changeable. As a result, our efforts to classify people become more dependent on other constructs for definition and therefore less exact. For example, rarely will a single continuum suffice in a description of ability. Ability to do what? To be meaningful, ability descriptions must also be scaled in some way. Ability compared to what or to whom? Ability to do something or do something better than someone else? Comparative information, then, is necessary in studying or determining differences in abilities because of the abstract nature of terms such as ability.

Achievement vs. Ability Differences

One reason for looking at individual differences is to determine the conditions they may set for organization. Individual differences obviously affect the way instruction and curriculum are organized. Contributing to these organizational decisions will be decisions relating to grouping children. Achievement is most often used as a basis for predicting ability. As a result, the two terms become inappropriately interchanged. Achievement can be measured with a fairly high degree of accuracy, but translating achievement into ability is fraught with dangers because of our inability always to know of, or adequately place in the formula, those factors contributing to a student's opportunity to achieve.

For example, a child may have the ability to be an excellent fisherman, but if he or she has never been fishing, future performance is uncertain. Thus, to take past achievements in fishing as a predictor of future success would be erroneous. More thought about the conditions or circumstances under which past achievement occurred needs to take place before making instructional decisions.

If one is not going to look at ability but rather at achievement as a determinant for organizing children for learning, what kind of differences should one expect to find in a school population? Studies done at the University of Minnesota in the early 1940s established a simple rule of thumb to indicate an achievement range.[1] The rule is that "the achievement range of an age group of children is equal to two-thirds of their chronological age." A group of six-year-old children will have an achievement range of four years; a group of nine year olds will have an achievement range of six years. In other words, the slowest nine year old will be approximately equal to an an average six year old (three years below) and the fastest nine year old will be approximately equal to an average twelve year old (three years above). Figure 6-1 illustrates the formula for school-age children. Note particularly the overlap of achievement over any three-year age span. A group of six year olds, a group of seven year olds, and a group of eight year olds have a broad range of achievements in common. The extremes contribute only fractional difference across the several years. One could rightly question the need for age-level grouping if its major basis is achievement differences.

DIFFERENCES IN LEARNING STYLES

A second factor in individual differences that merits attention for organizational progress is learning styles. How do children learn best? An identification of how children learn has tremendous implications for how we teach. If there are different learning styles, different teaching styles should be developed when instruction is organized.

There are a number of existing theoretical models that may be used for assessing learning styles. Learning styles can best be assessed by ongoing informal observation of student-teacher interaction using one or more of these models. It is generally a good idea for teachers to record their perception of students as an aid in planning instruction or in grouping.

---

[1]Walter W. Cook and Theodore Clymer, "Acceleration and Retardation," in Nelson B. Henry, ed., *Individualized Instruction, 1962 Yearbook of the National Society for the Study of Education* (Chicago: NSSE, 1962), pp. 179–208.

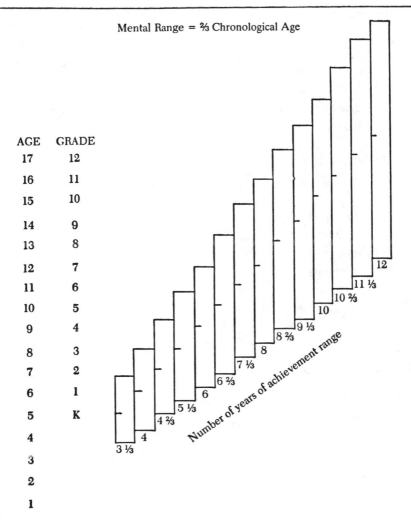

FIGURE 6-1. Achievement Formula for School-age Children.

Tempo Models

Does the student work:

1. Slowly, cautiously, and accurately
2. Slowly and inaccurately
3. Quickly with good quality
4. Just to get the assignment over with
5. At a variable rate
6. At the same speed all the time

Independence in Work

Does the student need:

1. A minimum of teacher help
2. Help at the beginning
3. Intermediate help
4. Constant assistance[2]

Thinking and Problem Solving

Does the student approach the learning task:

1. From beginning to end
2. From an overview before proceeding
3. From the specific to the general
4. From the general to the specific
5. From personal and concrete experience
6. From a nonpersonal and abstract viewpoint[3]

This last model is similar to the 1972 model of Gregerc, which discusses a way of processing information from the random to the sequential, in four learning styles. (See Figure 6-2.)

	Concrete	Abstract
Sequential	1 CS	2 AS
Random	3 CR	4 AR

FIGURE 6-2. Four Learning Styles.

---

[2]Aida Shanisky, "Individual Differences in Learning Styles in Learning Performance and Individual Differences," in Len Sperry, ed. *Essays and Readings* (Glenview, Ill: Scott Foresman and Co., 1972), p. 122.
[3]Ibid., p. 318.

LEARNING INTERESTS

Student interests represent another area of important individual differences. Many factors from a child's life affect interests in school. Only a portion of a child's interests are created within the school environment; the balance are generated from the home environment, the community, and differences in children's basic nature.

The activity curriculum of John Dewey's day was organized around interests, or "impulses" as he called them. Dewey identified four such impulses: (1) the social impulse shown by a child's desire to share experiences with others; (2) the constructive impulse manifested at first in play, in the rhythmic movement in makebelieve and then in more advanced forms in the shaping of raw materials into useful objects; (3) the impulse to investigate and experiment, to find out things; and (4) the expressive or artistic impulse that seems to be a refinement and further expression of the communicative and constructive interests.[4]

John Dewey referred to students' interest as uninvested capital. Dewey, of course, was looking to the strong motivating force that interests can contribute to learning. This motivation can be further supported by some of the more recent work of Taylor[5], who in studying human talents has identified six talents that he believes are significant in our culture: (1) academic, (2) creative (productive), (3) evaluative (decision making or wisdom), (4) planning, (5) forecasting, and (6) communicating. Studying these talent areas, Taylor found that people were more self-directive (motivated) in the areas of their greatest talent. Interest, therefore, seemed to be positively correlated with talent.

Significant implications for Taylor's work exist in viewing individual differences in relation to interests if these talents are distributed evenly across a population but unevenly in relationship with one another. In other words, a high rank academically says nothing about one's creative ability. In fact, when a population is considered across all six variables, 90 percent of the people will be above average in something. In any one area, of course, by definition only 50 percent can be above average. A close tie, therefore, can be seen among interests, motivation, and talents, with definite implications for curriculum and instructional organization.

STUDENT GROWTH AND MATURITY

Any discussion of individual differences must obviously pay heed to effects of maturation on changes in student interests and needs. Several notions in particular are significant when considering the organization of a

---

[4]John Dewey, *The School and Society* (Chicago: University of Chicago Press, 1900), chapter II.

[5]Calvin Taylor, "Talents—Waving Good-bye to the Average Man," *Pace Magazine* (June 1969).

school. The first is that all children do not mature at the same rate. The difference in maturation of boys and girls is quite obvious both physically and mentally. The same variation in size, mental capacity, interests, and needs also exists within children of the same sex at a given age, only to be in a different balance or relationship after several more years of maturation. These differences, of course, should have a bearing on instructional techniques and curriculum offerings, as well as on ways of grouping students.

As children mature, their interests and needs as well as their mental capacities expand and change. Interests begin to broaden as they come into contact with more and more of the world. Curiosities continue to expand. Needs change and children's requirements for safety, security, love, affection, and self-esteem take on new dimensions. The source of need fulfillment transfers successively from the home and parents to the teacher and then to peers, first of the same sex and finally to a peer of the opposite sex.

Quite often in organizing schools we tend to resist responding to these basic drives. The child who seeks attention, the child who needs a friend, the child who comes to school hungry, the child who needs status often cannot find solace in school because the adults there feel that since fulfilling these needs is not listed anywhere in the curriculum outline or specifically mentioned in someone's lesson plan, they are inappropriate concerns of the school.

Psychologists believe that every human being has needs that are constantly seeking fulfillment. Some theorists suggest that these needs can be classified into categories such as physiological (food, warmth), safety and security (safety from bodily or mental harm now and in the immediate future), love and belonging (a need to be wanted, appreciated, and understood and a sense of being part of a group), self-esteem (a sense of self-worth, a good self-concept) and, finally, a need for self-actualization (the opportunity to be or become what one wants to be or become). Some psychologists believe there is an ascending order to these needs and that basic needs (those first on the list) must be satisfied before an individual will consider higher-order needs. In other words, needs for food or warmth (physical) must be met before needs for safety and security, which in turn must be fulfilled before a concern for love and belonging surface. Need fulfillment also operates on several wave lengths. Hunger, obviously, is a recurring need that demands satisfaction several times daily. Other needs, once fulfilled, may sustain themselves for an extended period of time without reinforcement.

Several important lessons can be found in the application of needs theory to school organization. Most desired educational outcomes occur in the realm of the higher-order needs of self-esteem and self-actualization. If lower-order needs must be satisfied before higher-order needs, then as educators we must create an environment that satisfies the physiological, safety and security, and love and belonging needs of the student. The hungry, the fearful or insecure, and the left-out will all experience a great reduction in learning if those needs are not fulfilled.

Second, since a need creates a drive or motivation on the part of the individual, planners should create learning environments that emphasize rewards of love and belonging, self-esteem and self-actualization. Group learning, praise for achievement, opportunity for self-direction can all be directed to achieve both personal and school goals. Finally, knowing that needs change as children mature, we can design curriculum using needs theory. The curricular organization, through the establishment of course sequences, has become more responsive to changes in mental capacity, but in the area of matching school organization to student interests, the school has been only partially successful.

For example, the graded curriculum represents an effort to adapt the content to the levels of student capacity. It is possible to look at various curriculum materials and make a fair judgment of their appropriate intended maturity level through the degree of difficulty of the materials. On the other hand, instruction tends to look very much alike from the lower elementary grades through college. The way children are grouped, the way school staffs are organized, the way facilities are used look very much the same at all grade levels. It would seem that if varying interests and needs motivation of students were being considered, differences would be apparent. Our lack of adequate attention to school program organization and to developing needs and interests to motivate students may be partly behind the year-to-year increased disenchantment with school on the part of children. If the activities and outcomes educators have planned for schools are not congruent with the needs and interests of the students, the increasing disinterest on their part is only natural and leads to a greater turning away to activities outside those planned by the school. The problem of lack of congruence between school programs and student interests and needs is illustrated by Figure 6-3. Circle A represents the

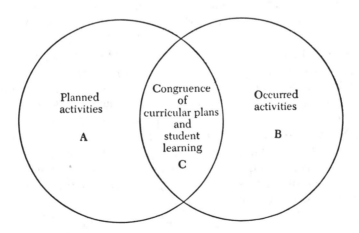

FIGURE 6-3. Planned versus Occurred Student Activity.

planned activities and outcomes of the school such as social studies, language arts, math, science, health, physical education, music, and art. Circle B represents those things that actually occur for children through their interaction with the school environment such as frogs, rubber bands, paper airplanes, bicycles, girls, boys, stories, graffiti on restroom walls, fights on the playground, motorcycles, hot rods, sex, drugs, questions about what they are going to do when they finish school, and so on and so on. Area C represents the area of congruence or the area in which what was planned actually occurred.

A school with a program highly attuned to students' needs, interests, and differences will have a high percentage of congruence between Area A and B, resulting in a large Area C. This congruence will probably not exist for the school that pays little attention to these factors.

Recent research on academic learning time by William Fisher has shown that more time on task produces more achievement. This also supports the idea of the importance of the congruence between occurred and planned activities.

It is important to give adequate attention to individual differences and varying maturity rates and levels and to recognize that student interests and needs are broadly based. The organization of a school program must account for these needs, interests, and capabilities in all their diversity and provide learning experiences that will motivate all students.

GROUPING STUDENTS

Instruction in any normal school setting requires numerous decisions about the grouping of children. Basically, these decisions will relate to three variables: group size, group composition, and group tenure. The basic purpose of grouping students is to bring about the highest quantity and quality of instruction possible. Grouping practices should be consistent with curricular decisions and should be compatible with each student's needs and interests. These lofty goals must be tempered by two factors. The first is the complexity of the individual learner. The second factor is the practical consideration of the cost of a particular organization design in comparison to its related effectiveness. For example, group size usually suggests certain staffing patterns that can be converted into dollar costs. A school might conclude that a staffing ratio of three-to-one would give the best quality and quantity of learning per student but that it would be too expensive. Instead, grouping designs must consider more economical staffing ratios, most likely in the range of fifteen to thirty students per one staff member.

Group Size

Research studies indicate that the quantity of learning does not improve each time the size of a class is reduced by one.[6] Reducing class size from thirty to

---

[6]Martin N. Olson, "Ways to Achieve Quality in School Classrooms: Some Definitive Answers," *Phi Delta Kappan* (September 1971):63–65.

twenty-nine and then again from twenty-nine to twenty-eight probably will not result in any observable increase in learning on the part of students. On the other hand, significant behavior changes do occur in the classroom when student/teacher ratios are reduced from a high of thirty-five or forty to one to about twenty-five to one. If the ratio is larger than twenty-five to one (assuming little or no assistance from aides and volunteers), teachers seldom vary their instruction or accommodate to various learning styles within the group. The reason may be that attempting to individualize instruction with a large group is so overwhelming that experience suggests that it is better to try to keep the children together for most of the learning activities and teach to the mean. When ratios fall below twenty-five to one, teachers seem to provide more individualized instructional styles.

Furthermore, as group size drops to fifteen and lower, cross-member interaction and discussion greatly increase because it is possible for every member to participate in discussions. Finally, when the ratio is reduced to five to one or fewer, a tutorial style of instruction begins to emerge, with teachers assigning work to children on a one-to-one basis. Followup and evaluation are conducted in a similar style.

Two meta-analyses of class-size research by Gene V. Glass and Mary Lee Smith, published by the Far West Laboratory, have been widely interpreted as providing convincing evidence that smaller classes are better than larger ones. The basic finding of analyses on class size indicated that smaller classes resulted in increased achievement. However, the study showed that in classes ranging from twenty to forty pupils, class size made little difference in achievement. The major benefits from reduced class size were obtained as size was reduced below twenty pupils.[7]

The Educational Research Service (ERS), somewhat alarmed at some of the conclusions of the Glass-Smith studies, published a response and further explanation in 1980, stating "The conclusions from these meta-analyses only confuse the class size issue; . . . What is needed are practical guidelines for flexible class size policy. Flexibility allows decision makers to vary the size of classes to fit the needs of pupils, teachers, and diverse school situations."

ERS had previously found that smaller classes can have a positive influence on pupils in the early primary grades (achievement in reading and mathematics) and also on low-achieving and economically or socially disadvantaged students. However, few pupil benefits can be expected from reducing class size if teachers continue to use the same teaching methods that they used in larger classes.[8]

---

[7]Gene V. Glass and Mary Lee Smith, "Meta-Analysis of Research in the Relationships of Class-Size and Achievement," in *The Class Size and Instruction Project*, Leonard S. Cahen, principal investigator (San Francisco, Calif.: Far West Laboratory for Educational Research and Development, September 1978).

[8]*Class Size: A Summary of Research* (Arlington, Va.: Educational Research Service, 1978).

Administrative Decision Making about Group Size

In the past administrators have used group size as a constant and made instructional decisions based on group size. However, instructional decisions should be dominant, and decisions regarding group size should be secondary in nature. Therefore, if the instructional decision demands a tutorial approach, a staffing ratio of five to one would be both effective and efficient. For purposes of group discussion and maximum interaction among all members or for intensive skill work, a group size of fifteen is about the maximum. If the instructional demand on teachers includes individualization of instruction, a ratio of not more than twenty-five to one apparently is needed. Finally, if instructional plans require the presentation of basically the same material to all members of a group with the need for only one-way communication, a group of any size is appropriate. The limiting factors become those of space and the number of children. Further discussion of variability or flexibility in group size requires a discussion of variations in staff utilization.

Group Composition

What should be the basis for organizing children into groups? Obviously efficient instruction requires groups. The question of group composition has intrigued educators for years. This section will deal first with some of the more controversial grouping practices such as homogeneous ability grouping and retention and their accompanying problems. Then, on a more positive note, alternative grouping patterns based on interest, age, skill, and achievement as well as group flexibility and tenure will be discussed.

Ability Grouping. A common practice is to organize or group students on the basis of their supposed ability, creating a tracking system with a two-, three- or four-group continuum consisting of the high-ability, average-ability, and low-ability students. The basic assumption underlying this pattern of student organization is that by subdividing children from the extremely broad ability continuum found in any normal school population, teachers will better be able to focus instruction on the needs of the children in any particular group. Thus, ability groups supposedly narrow the range of abilities within any group and make it more possible for the teacher to organize and prepare materials for a narrower range of abilities.

Factors used to determine group composition have included achievement test scores, I.Q. scores, previous grades, and teacher opinion. Serious problems develop when any of these criteria or combinations are used as the basis of organizing students on a permanent basis or for long periods of time. This method of grouping is usually not very effective. A previous chapter included a lengthy discussion of individual learner differences in such areas as achievement, interest, and learning styles. Differences exist from child to child on each of these variables. The pattern for each child is different. No common denominator can be found for long-term grouping across disciplines or even within disciplines. For example, interest can greatly change productivity within a discipline, overriding previous supposed ability measurements.

Children can be successfully grouped according to one factor to obtain a degree of homogeneity, but the group remains heterogeneous on all other aspects of curriculum and instruction. For example, homogeneity in mathematics can be obtained by placing in a group all children who know their multiplication tables through twelve, but they remain a heterogeneous group for the rest of the curriculum, including other areas of mathematics.

When the descriptors of homogeneity are based on previous math achievement, an I.Q. test score, or all previous grades, almost all useful definition of homogeneity is lost, for in almost any specific skill or knowledge some children placed in the lowest group on one basis will exceed the knowledge level of other children placed in the highest group on another. Therefore, homogeneous grouping as a broad-based or permanent grouping design simply does not work, and the homogeneity is a figment of the imagination of the staff. (See Figure 6-4.)

Many teachers and administrators have argued strenuously that ability grouping does work and that definite differences exist among students. Of course, differences can be seen, but the point is that the overlap in abilities is far greater from group to group than most of us imagine, and, most importantly, homogeneous grouping overlooks the individual child.

Several attitudinal factors must also be considered in a discussion of homogeneous grouping. The phenomenon of the self-fulfilling prophecy enters into the ultimate outcomes of ability grouping. This prophecy says that children become what we say they are or what they think they are.[9] Research about self-concept has shown that children's own attitude toward themselves as a person and their assessment of their own abilities represent major factors in their ultimate success or failure in school. Teacher attitudes as well as the student's self-concept contribute greatly to the child's ultimate success or failure in school. The placement of a child in a group on the basis of perceived ability can seem to prove itself correct by adjustments in productivity on the part of the child that in fact take place as a result of the placement, thus fulfilling the prophecy. Over the past forty years numerous research studies have considered ability grouping. A massive review of many of these studies was reported in 1973 with the following conclusions:[10]

---

[9]A study by Rosenthal investigated the concept of the self-fulfilling prophecy and found that teacher attitudes and expectations about a child do have a direct bearing on the child's performance. Robert Rosenthal and Lenore Jacobson, *Pygmalion in the Classroom* (New York: Holt, Rinehart, and Winston, 1968).

[10]Dominick Esposito, "Homogeneous and Heterogeneous Ability Grouping," *AERA Journal* (Spring 1973):163–79.

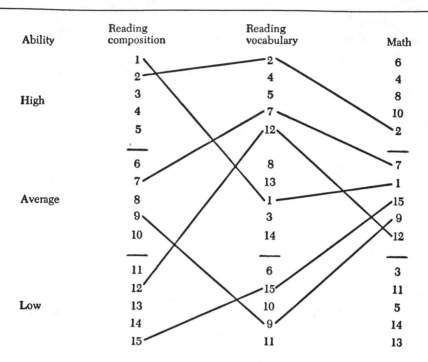

FIGURE 6-4. Homogeneous Grouping—Student Rankings.

1. Homogeneous ability grouping as currently practiced shows no consistent positive values for helping students generally, or particular groups of students, to achieve more scholastically or to experience more effective learning conditions. Among the studies showing significant effects, evidence of slight gains favoring high ability students is more than offset by evidence of unfavorable effects on the learning of students of average and below average ability, particularly the latter.

2. The findings regarding the impact of homogeneous ability grouping on affective development are essentially unfavorable. Whatever the practice does to build or inflate the self-esteem of children in the high ability groups is counterbalanced by evidence of the unfavorable effects of stigmatizing those placed in average and below average ability groups as inferior and incapable of learning.

3. Homogeneous ability grouping, by design, is a separative educational policy, made ostensibly according to test performance ability but practically according to socio-economic status and, to a lesser but still observable degree, according to ethnic status.

4. In cases where homogeneous or heterogeneous ability grouping is related to improved scholastic performance, the curriculum is subject to substantial modification of teaching methods, materials and other variables that are intrinsic to the teaching-learning process, and that, therefore, may well be the causative factors related to academic development

wholly apart from ability grouping per se. Similarly, with respect to social development, evidence that points to variables other than ability grouping tends to relate substantially to personal growth or lack of growth.

Retention

One form of ability grouping that is often overlooked is the result of the retention policies operating in many school districts. Retention places a child with a less intellectually and socially mature group based on the child's demonstrated ability or achievement. Therefore, it is actually an instance of ability grouping—adjusting the placement of the child to fit a curriculum and instructional level thought more appropriate, rather than bringing the appropriate curriculum and instructional level to the child.

Retention is as ineffective an approach to the grouping of children as the previously discussed method. A poorly achieving fourth grader is not more like third graders. That student is still more like his or her peers and will be more successful with them than if retained and placed with a younger group of children. At any grade level the achievement range will spread over a number of grade levels. The Cook studies of the early 1940s concluded that:

> When pupils in the lower 10 percent of the classes are failed because of low achievement, they do not become better adjusted educationally or socially in the retarded position. The available evidence indicates that, on the average, they achieve as much or more by being given more regular promotions.

The study goes on to point out that:

> When attempts are made to reduce the range of abilities and achievement in a school by retarding slow learning pupils and accelerating fast learning pupils, there is an increase in the proportion of slow learning pupils in each grade. Average grade achievement is lowered.

The study concluded, somewhat tongue-in-cheek, that:

> If the major concern of the teachers is to maintain grade level standards, the most effective way of increasing achievement standards in a school is to retard the bright and accelerate the dull pupils.[11]

Appropriate Bases for Grouping

Groups are necessary for school organization, but retention and homogeneous ability grouping as semipermanent forms of student organization are not effec-

---

[11]Walter W. Cook, "Effective Ways of Doing It," *Individualized Instruction, 1962 Yearbook of the National Society for the Study of Education*, ed. Nelson B. Henry (Chicago: NSSE, 1962), chap. 3.

tive. What should be the basis for grouping? The following principles and techniques for organizing students are sound:

1. Grouping can be used on any known common factor found among students.

2. The homogeneity of a group of students is improved directly in ratio to the specificity of the grouping criterion. In other words, the more factors you include in your grouping criteria, the less you will be able to discriminate among children.

3. The ensuing curriculum and instruction can assume commonality among students only according to the single factor used as a basis for the grouping. On all other factors the group must be considered to be heterogeneous.

4. Most grouping criteria, if they are fairly specific, are valid only for a short period of time. As learning takes place, children who were grouped to learn a specific skill need to be regrouped for other skills. Children who have been grouped on the basis of interest must be regrouped when either that interest area is completed or the student's interests change.

5. Age is not necessarily a factor in grouping. In other words, children of various ages may be grouped together if some other appropriate criterion is being used; single-skill development, for example.

6. No grouping practice should damage the self-concept of a child or create stereotypes in the eyes of other students or teachers toward particular children.

7. In most instructional settings a variety of grouping criteria should be used and integrated into the various parts of the school day.

With these criteria in mind, a tremendous variety of grouping bases is available. Possible designs include the following:

Heterogeneous Grouping. A heterogeneous group is a group created to represent a cross section of the available student population. Planned heterogeneity is not the same as that which may occur by simply placing together an available group of children. Many factors within a school can indirectly affect. the availability of children for heterogeneous groups. Care must be taken if true heterogeneity is sought to insure the distribution of children in some uniform fashion across the various groups being created. By definition, unlimited heterogeneity would even include a proportionate number of children from each age group within the school. In other words, if the school consisted of grades one through six, the group would consist of children from each of those age categories.

Age Grouping. Children of a particular age or range of ages are placed into a single group. The group may still be heterogeneous in all other factors except age.

Multi-age Grouping. A common practice is to not limit age groupings to a one-year span but to group children over a two- or three-year span. Therefore, children between five and seven, six and eight, ten and twelve, or fifteen and eighteen are eligible for membership in particular groups.

Interest Grouping. This technique brings students directly into the decisions regarding grouping. Based on individual interests, the child selects the group according to whatever criteria have been established for group organization. Learning centers at the elementary level and minicourses at the secondary level would be compatible curriculum components to accompany interest grouping.

Skill Grouping. Children are grouped on the basis of possessing or not possessing particular skills that are usually quite narrowly defined. Skill grouping is often used in conjunction with a curricular area of a skills nature that lends itself to a detailed continuum of learning with a logical sequence and order. By diagnosing previous student skill acquisition, a current skills placement can be identified for each student. A choice of several appropriate learning activities then is available. Instructional modules are usually short, requiring from one to five hours of student and teacher time. Students needing a particular skill are placed together in a group for instruction on that particular skill. When the skill has been learned, a new group is found for them. The new group may consist of the same children or new children, depending on the progress of the other children in the group and the availability of other children for inclusion in the new skill area. Reading and mathematics represent two elementary subject areas where such groups have been organized. With available diagnostic instruments, children can be accurately placed and organized into groups where similar needs exist. The major problem with skill grouping is that a relatively large group of approximately 100 children is usually desirable as a base group from which to create the skill groups. This allows for the creation of skill groups large enough for efficient use of teacher time but limited to a relatively narrow range on the skills continuum.

Achievement Grouping. Achievement grouping is similar to skill grouping but is somewhat less specific, covering a wider range of previous learning. It is based on demonstrated achievement, not predicted ability. It should be as narrowly defined as possible, rarely expanding outside of a single discipline and preferably representing a subset within a discipline. For example, an achievement group might be established within language arts on the basis of previous demonstrated competence in composition writing. The same grouping should not be used for spelling, grammar, reading, or literary analysis. Each of these would need their own achievement groups. Within the area of composition, a whole series of subskills could be defined for the further breakdown of groups into skill groups. Achievement groups are usually used where minute skill details cannot be adequately diagnosed, are not needed for intended instruction, or would create groups too small for efficient instruction. Achievement groups are based on previously demonstrated achievement. Achievement should not be confused with ability, a prediction of potential rather than a measure of past achievement.

Group Flexibility

How long should an established group remain intact? When groups are reorganized, how extensive should that reorganization be? At what level within the organization should decisions for group reorganization take place? These questions relate directly to the ultimate flexibility that can be obtained for grouping within any school organization.

Groups should remain intact until they have accomplished their skills objective. Once the original purpose for the grouping has been achieved, the group must be reorganized. This may be after one hour of instruction in a skills group, or it might be after three years together as a heterogeneous, multi-age group. Skill groups, interest groups, and achievement groups should be designed so they can be reorganized daily if necessary.

Problems of Regrouping. The need for frequent regrouping in the school presents several problems in school organization. First, it is impractical to refer all grouping decisions to the principal since the quantity and frequency of needed grouping decisions would overwhelm that office. More significant, most of the information needed for intelligent grouping decisions is found at the teacher-student level.

To give teachers and students an opportunity to make flexible grouping decisions, a school is best organized into learning communities consisting of two or more teachers, their students, and an extended time block. With this arrangement students and teachers can group students. The unit design for school organization with a team of teachers, aides, and a group of 75 to 150 students is a good example of this organization.[12]

A number of tools are available to aid learning communities in the mechanical details of internal team grouping. Skill continua and diagnostic tests are available in many subject areas to aid in the placement of students. Some instructional systems include tools such as key sort cards, similar to the Wisconsin Design for Reading Skill Development,[13] that allow rapid grouping and regrouping of students on a daily basis if necessary. (See Figure 6-5.)

The important concept here is that the principal has passed on power of decision making regarding grouping directly to the teachers. Once the components of the learning community have been designated, the principal's role be-

---

[12]*IGE Unit Operations and Roles* (Institute for Development of Educational Activities, 1970).

[13]Board of Regents, *Wisconsin Design for Reading Skills Development* (Madison, Wisc.: Board of Regents, University of Wisconsin System, 1972–73).

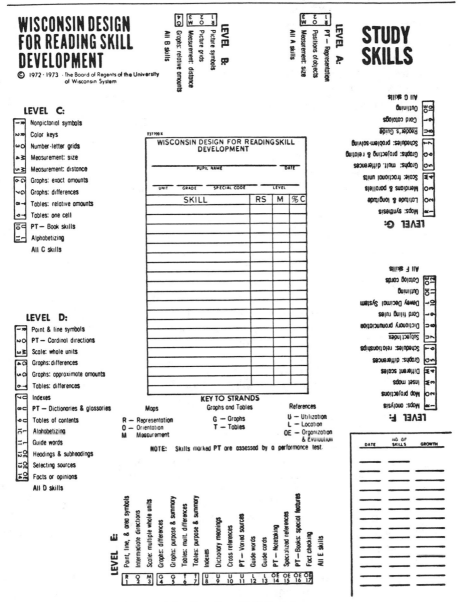

FIGURE 6-5. Grouping Tool for Reading Skill Development.

comes one of giving advice to the teams for internal grouping decisions. The teachers, in turn, then organize the groups or may pass directly on to the students many grouping decisions based on interest. Students can group themselves according to whatever ground rules are established by the learning community team. The student-selected learning center is a good illustration of this technique.

Grouping Guidelines

Student grouping is necessary for all school organization. (1) For purposes of assigning students to individual teachers or teams, a heterogeneous or mixed grouping plan is usually best. (2) Homogeneous grouping should take place in the classroom and be done by teachers. The basis for internal class grouping can be interest, achievement, skills, age, or designed heterogeneity.

(3) Homogeneous grouping should be kept flexible with several different grouping patterns used each day. All homogeneous groups are usually of short duration. Flexibility is necessary because of the changing nature of groups and the problems of negative student self-concept or poor teacher attitudes that can develop from rigid homogeneous grouping patterns.

(4) Homogeneous groups should not be used for more than one-half of each school day.

BIBLIOGRAPHY

Board of Regents. *Wisconsin Design for Reading Skills Development.* Madison, Wisc.: University of Wisconsin System, 1972–73.

Cook, Walter. "Effective Ways of Doing It." In *Individualized Instruction, Yearbook of the National Society for the Study of Education.* Chicago: NSSE, 1962, chap. 3.

Dunn, Rita, and Dunn, Kenneth. "Learning Styles, Teaching Styles: Finding the Best Fit." *NASSP Bulletin* 59 (October 1975). A presentation of current kinds of programs with their philosophies and the skills that students need to function successfully within each program. It also describes various learning styles and accompanying skills, including instructional program in traditional classrooms, instructional program in individualized classrooms, and instructional program in alternative programs. Also discussed are the emotional, sociological, and physical elements of varying learning styles.

Esposito, Dominick. "Homogeneous and Heterogeneous Ability Grouping." *AERA Journal* (Spring 1973):163–79.

Goodland, John I., and Anderson, Robert H. *The Nongraded Elementary School.* New York: Harcourt, Brace and World, 1959.

Hoen, Robert T. "An Evaluation of Multi-Age Classes at Carnarvon School 1971–1972." *ERIC* (June 30, 1972), ED 076 649.

IGE Unit Operations and Roles. Institute for Development of Educational Activities. Dayton, Ohio, 1970.

Martin, Lyn S., and Pavan, Barbara N. "Current Research on Open Space, Nongraded, Vertical Grouping and Team Teaching." *Phi Delta Kappan* 57 (January 1976):310–15.

Mitchell, Joy, and Zoffness, Richard. "Elementary Pupils Favor a Multiage Class." *Education* 91 (Fall 1971):270–73.

Neill, Shirley. "Self-Starting School: Multi-Age Grouping Program." *American Education* 11 (October 1975):25–29.

Olson, Martin N. "Ways to Achieve Quality in School Classrooms: Some Definitive Answers." *Phi Delta Kappan* (September 1971):63–65.

Rosenthal, Robert, and Jacobson, Lenore. *Pygmalion in the Classroom.* New York: Holt, Rinehart and Winston, 1968.

Wiles, Hilda L. "Multi-Age Team Teaching Program." *Educational Leadership* 29 (January 1972):305–8.

7

Organizing the Elementary School Curriculum

INTRODUCTION

Several years ago one of the authors was working as a consultant with the faculty of a middle school in a curriculum development project. The teachers were proposing a curriculum that he felt was somewhat narrow. In order to point out to them that the children's interests went far beyond the curriculum offerings, he asked to work with seven or eight of their children for an hour or so. After a familiarization period, these seven or eight children from grade six were asked what they would like to have in their curriculum that was not now included. Their answers were serious and thoughtful, but quite divergent from the standard "three R's".

One little girl from a poor home asked to learn how to cook because she had to fix dinner for herself and her younger brother and sister each evening while her mother worked. Another child, with a most serious face under a shock of red hair, wanted to learn to fish. In response to some apparent amusement on my face the child explained. Most of his friends, apparently, had accompanied their fathers on fishing excursions, but this lad had no father and had never been fishing but wanted desperately to learn. Now it's a matter of opinion whether cooking or fishing should be in an elementary school curriculum, but the interest and need apparently were there.

In contrast, recent years have brought about a resurgence of emphasis on basic skills, state-mandated proficiency tests, and skills continua. Politicians campaign for a "no-frills curriculum," often accompanied by severe budget restrictions which result in cuts in other programs, including music, art, guidance and other areas that are not considered to be part of the three R's.

How is school curriculum to be organized? Our analysis of curriculum usually defines both a vertical and horizontal dimension. The vertical dimension considers what content is to be presented or what objectives are to be met at a particular maturity level with sequence as an important aspect of the vertical dimension. The horizontal dimension focuses on the array of subjects or concepts available or taught to a student or group of students simultaneously.

The graded curriculum of many of our schools has both a vertical and horizontal dimension. The vertical organization of the math program of an elementary school utilizes graded math texts based on knowledge about what an average child at a particular grade level is ready to learn. The horizontal dimension of the graded mathematics curriculum includes as much information regarding topics such as numeration, fractions, addition, and subtraction as a child can assimilate at a particular time. As specialization develops at the high school level, this horizontal dimension becomes vertical, with the offerings of subjects such as algebra I, geometry, algebra II, and trigonometry sequenced through the four years of high school.

The horizontal dimension of curriculum usually includes all the subjects available to a student at a given time. When a student participates daily or weekly in social studies, English, science, mathematics, health, art, music, and physical education, the student participates in the horizontal dimension of the curriculum. The horizontal structure of most of our schools is relatively uniform, and curricular areas are almost standard among schools and among grade levels. The horizontal balance remains about the same from year to year, providing students with equal doses of each subject area. Schools that are departmentalized, such as some upper elementary and junior high schools, have an additional problem with horizontal organization. The departmentalization creates *compartmentalization,* and the several disciplines being taught are not well-coordinated or -integrated for the student but are taught as totally separate and unrelated bodies of knowledge.

CURRICULAR FLEXIBILITY

If individual differences are to be recognized, both the vertical and horizontal dimension of the curriculum require flexibility. Figure 7-1 illustrates the three different rates of learning. Since most children vary from the norm, the curriculum needs to be organized to allow each child to progress individually, as shown by lines A, B, and C.

The organization must allow both child B and child C access to appropriate information as it is sequenced according to the difficulty of concepts and materials. The achievement of the student over time will depend, therefore, on the capability of the student to learn and the time committed to that subject.

In subjects such as reading and mathematics, where we traditionally have assumed that all basic skills are taught in the elementary school, we must now recognize that, because of their slow maturation rates, a large portion of our children have in fact not learned these basic skills to a satisfactory level in each grade. Therefore, these subjects must be continued through the middle school years and on into high school.

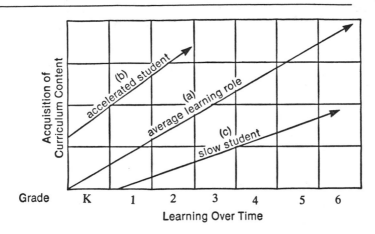

FIGURE 7-1. Impact of Individual Differences in Rate of Learning.

Varying Curricular Emphasis

Curricular emphasis can also be varied by the flexible use of time. The distribution of time over the curriculum does not necessarily need to be equal. One student might spend five hours a week in language arts, one hour in science, three hours in social studies, ten hours in music, and three hours in physical education. Another student might spend ten hours in language arts, three hours in science, one hour in social studies, two hours in music, and five hours in physical education.

In order to accomplish curriculum variation, schools require a greater variety of curricular offerings. Also, because of the varying rates of progress caused by either differences in ability or in time commitment, a major portion of any skill-sequenced curriculum must be available for instruction at any time. Variations in curriculum should also be available to fulfill student needs and interests.

CURRICULAR CONTINUITY

How much freedom should a student have to pursue needs and interests when curriculum selection is determined? Should a student have unlimited choice or should he or she be guided according to some plan? How can the school program curricular opportunities for the student who can move rapidly up a vertical skill sequence ladder, for the student who progresses at a slower rate, for the student who wants or needs an extremely broad range of content areas, or for the student who must concentrate on basic skills? In the past we have not differentiated for individual students but have provided a very basic curriculum for everyone, allowing for little variation.

This traditional curriculum is shown in Figure 7-2. The same basic subjects are included in each year of a child's education.

Kindergarten							
1	L	S	M	S	A	M	P.
2	A	O	A	C	R	U	E.
3	N	C	T	I	T	S	
4	G	I	H	E		I	
5	U	A		N		C	
6	A	L		C			
7	G			E			
8	E	S					
9		T					
10	A	U					
11	R	D					
12	T	I					
	S	E					
		S					

FIGURE 7-2. The Traditional Curriculum.

A Curricular Model

Consideration of needs and interests of students throughout the curriculum should accommodate different maturity levels. Furthermore, curriculum must be divided into priorities with different weightings for each subject. Equal amounts of all curricular areas are not necessarily appropriate for each year. For example, basic skills in communication and computation are obviously needed in the early years of education. As a child matures and as interests broaden, the curriculum of the school should expand along with the child. By the middle of the elementary school years, the curiosity of most children is very broad in scope, and a child may participate in thirty or forty different curriculum areas over the course of the year. Obviously, if the child participates in many different activities, covering any in depth is unlikely.

The pattern of curricular choices can be somewhat different for each child. For example, during one week a particular child may select sewing, reading, the study of insects, listening to records, spelling, and math. A second child may select topics on the basis of what friends select because of a real need to belong to a specific group. Two weeks later the pattern for both children might be different. This normal variation of curricular patterns among children raises the important question of what areas of learning are common to all children.

Organizing curriculum around areas of importance rather than considering all curricular areas equally offers one solution. In this way, varying emphasis can be placed on different areas as appropriate during each segment of a student's school career. One well-accepted model clusters curriculum into four major areas:

1. Basic skills
2. Common learnings
3. Exploratory areas
4. Specialization

Figure 7-3 shows the type of subjects to be included in each area.

Our culture demands that children learn certain basic skills. Included are skills in communication and computation and a knowledge of basic health care, including physical education. American society also requires basic familiarity with other more general areas, such as the knowledge of democracy and the way it works. A school can provide this information in many different ways. A real danger exists in curricular organization in regard to what to include as required common learning. It is easy to include so many topics that all of the available school time is utilized to teach this information and no discretionary time remains for exploratory and student-selected curriculum. Thus, areas of common learning must be kept to a bare minimum if other concepts are to have room in the program. The interrelationship of basic skills and

Basic skills	*Common learning*
Reading	Health
Arithmetic	Social studies
Psycho-motor skills	Science
	Language

Exploratory	*Specialization*
Social sciences	College prep
Science	Computer science
Art	Drafting
Music	Commercial foods
Mathematics	Distributive education
Typing	Horticulture
etc.	etc.

FIGURE 7-3. Major Curriculum Clusters.

common learnings and exploratory or student-selected activities can be diagrammed as in Figure 7-4.

Initially schools concentrate on basic skills development. This work consumes most of a child's time during the early years of school, gradually diminishing as a percentage of the total time spent on learning as other things are added to the program. Common learning curriculum may begin in small amounts during the child's early mastery of basic skills and increase as skills are learned. The exploratory or student-selected aspect of the curriculum should continue to broaden as a child matures. The curriculum will reach its greatest breadth at a point approximately midway through the school career when it is made up of many varied and diverse parts, including many of the student's own choosing.

The time involvement of the child in the several parts of the curriculum is varied. The school year contains a predetermined amount of time. The time during the early primary years has depth or concentration only in basic skills, with a relatively narrow scope of curriculum.

By the time the child has reached the midschool point, time can be spent on more curricular areas. In other words, with so many curricular selections available during those middle years, students will spend less time on a particular subject. A child will be expected to learn a little about many things rather than a lot about a few things.

By considering the natural motivation of the child, this expanding curricular organization better meets his or her growing curiosity during the elementary and middle school or junior high school days. In high school the needs and interest of students begin to change. They begin to make

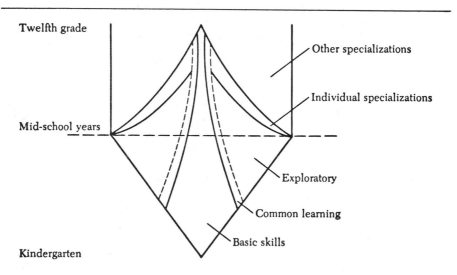

FIGURE 7-4. Interrelationships in the Curriculum.

tentative decisions relating to life as an adult. Puberty brings about emotional and psychological changes. The organization of the school system should take this into account. These changes have particular implications for curricular organization.

The interests and needs of children collectively continue to remain very broad and diverse, requiring a continued wide range of curricular offerings. On the other hand, the interests and needs of a particular child usually narrow as future life goals are sorted out. The curriculum of the school must allow students to begin to narrow their own curriculum into a specialization when they reach a maturity level that calls for it. The implications here for a flexible and active guidance program are also apparent.

During high school the individual child begins to devote more and more time and thus, curricular scope, to an area of *individual specialization* as shown in Figure 7-4. Specialization gradually replaces the exploratory phase of a student's curriculum. This individual specialization may be the move into a specific vocational program of one type or another. It may mean preparation for a particular vocation requiring continuation into a specific college program, or it may simply mean a decision to go to college.

INDIVIDUAL VERTICAL CURRICULAR SELECTION

The consideration of how much time an individual child should spend in the various aspects of the curriculum is not adequately illustrated in the model. Knowing that children do not all mature at the same rate in their capabilities, interests, and needs, some way of showing time dimensions that allow for differing maturation rates is needed. Consideration must also be given to priorities for time.

The amount of "academic learning time" that a student spends on a particular subject or skill area has a tremendous effect on the academic achievement of the student in that area. A most powerful tool in increasing achievement in a given subject is to increase the academic learning time (ALT) in that subject for the child. This does not mean, however, that more time be assigned to that subject but rather that the time spent in academic learning be increased by the available time being used more efficiently. It can also be enhanced by students engaging in learning activities where they experience a high success rate.[1]

For example, if a particular child is not progressing in reading skill development at a rate comparable to the majority of children that age, the child should probably spend a great proportion of time in basic skills. The question then is what should give way? The choices probably rest between common learnings and exploratory activities.

---

[1]Charles Fisher, Richard Marliave, and Nikola N. Filby, "Improved Teaching by Increasing Academic Learning Time," *Educational Leadership* 37, no. 1, (October 1979): 52–54.

At first glance it would seem that exploratory activities should probably give way to common learnings. But should they? Many children need strong motivation during the middle elementary years to keep up their interest in school. If exploratory activities are diminished for an increased skills emphasis, all may be lost. On the other hand, if the common-learnings area is reduced, the interest in the exploratory areas might save the day (or the year), allowing a return to common learnings later on. One might even consider the content of the common-learnings areas as appropriate material for instruction in basic skills, providing a double-barreled program with the emphasis on the skills rather than on the common learning content.

SPECIAL PROGRAMS FOR SPECIAL STUDENTS

Gifted Students

Exploratory areas are one of the best opportunities to provide supplementary activities to gifted students and still have them participate with all children in the majority of curricular areas. Special programs in natural science, microcomputer science, mathematics, and so on can be made available on an interest basis or on a selective-qualification basis while still providing other programs for all children.

Handicapped Students

In a similar fashion students with one or more handicapping conditions also need the opportunity for exploratory opportunities. Often when these students have difficulty acquiring basic skills, opportunity for exploration gets a low priority and is replaced by additional basic-skill activities. This presents a real dilemma in that well-taught exploratory activities often are children's major motivators in their entire school program. Thus the reduction in exploratory activities reduces the motivation that is so desperately needed for learning the basic skills.

Curricular breadth at various school levels can be illustrated in different ways. Two illustrations, one from the elementary and one from middle-school levels, are shown in Figures 7-5 and 7-6. The list in Figure 7-5 is from a primary grades classroom. This curriculum is taught through learning centers with daily skill group instruction in reading and mathematics.

The illustration in Figure 7-6 is from a middle school covering grades five through eight. During these years curriculum offerings must be broadest. Exploratory labs are offered to students twice each week, and each child selects two. Every nine weeks a new series of labs is offered, and students assist in determining topics.

Name_____   △ Two each day
Date_____

CENTERS	Mon.	Extra	Tues.	Extra	Wed.	Extra	Thurs.	Extra	Fri.	Extra
△ 1. Spelling										
△ 2. Math										
△ 3. Handwriting										
△ 4. English										
△ 5. Reading Center										
△ 6. Science										
△ 7. Creative Writing										
△ 8. Counting										
△ 9. Health										
△ 10. Phonics										
△ 11. Current Events										
△ 12. SRA										
13. Read for Fun										
14. Music										
15. Art										
16. Library										
17. Take-a-part										
18. Wendy House										
19. Math Games										
20. Sewing										
21. Listening for Fun										

FIGURE 7-5. Breadth of Curriculum in the Primary Grades.

SUMMARY

A variety of curricular concepts have been outlined in this chapter. In summary, they are as follows:

1. Curriculum has a vertical dimension, which is the sequencing of a particular discipline over time.

2. Curriculum has a horizontal dimension. It includes the several components of a discipline that are taught at the same time or the combination of the several disciplines that are included for a student at a particular point in time.

3. Curriculum should be organized flexibly so that students can move to a sequence of learning experiences at different rates (vertically).

First Hour Labs	Second Hour Labs
America's Summer Sport—Baseball	America's Summer Sport—Baseball
Basket Weaving	Cheerleader Tryouts
Chess	Chess
Chorus	Chorus
Creative Weaving	Crewel and Needlepoint
Crewel and Needlepoint	Drawing and Sketching
Embroidery	Environmental Crafts—Recycled Arts
Environmental Crafts—Recycled Arts	Good Grooming
Good Grooming	Heroes and Heroines in American History
Hiking	Hiking
4-H Club	Middle School Journalism
Model Building	Model Building
Outdoor Games	Newspaper
Picture Creativity	Outdoor Games
Putting It All Together	Picture Creativity
Rhymes and Things	Plant Power
Rock-Hounding	Putting It All Together
Rocketry	Rock-Hounding
Running and Standing Broad Jump	Rocketry
Safety and First Aid	Running and Standing Broad Jump
Science Fiction and Mystery	Safety and First Aid
Science Investigations	Say It in Spanish
Sculpture and Modeling	Science Investigation
Short Stories	Sculpture and Modeling
Softball	Short Stories
Typing II	Soccer
Volleyball	Softball
What Makes You Tick	What Makes You Tick

FIGURE 7-6. Breadth of Exploratory Curriculum in Grades Five through Eight.

4. Curriculum should be organized so that more or less time can be spent by a particular student in certain aspects of the curriculum as needed (horizontally).

5. Curriculum should be organized flexibly to provide open access to meet the various needs and interests of children (exploratory, electives, specialization).

6. Curriculum should be organized so that all subjects are taught to some degree each year through high school (common learning, basic skills).

7. Improving academic learning time is of critical importance to ensure that basic areas of the curriculum are given adequate attention.

8. Exploratory areas offer a way to provide more flexibility and open access to programs for special students.

BIBLIOGRAPHY

Alkin, Marvin C. "Evaluating 'Curriculum' and 'Instruction.'" *Curriculum Theory Network* 4, no. 1 (1973–74): 43–51, EJ 097 886.

Banks, James A. "Ethnic Studies as a Process of Curriculum Reform." Paper presented at the Anti-Defamation League of B'nai B'rith Conference on Cultural Pluralism. Tarrytown, N. Y., April 1975, ED 110 377.

Borden, Christopher III. "Back to Basics?—Back is Here." *Educational Horizons* 58, no. 2 (1979–80): 85–88.

Brokes, A. L., and Jenks, C. L. *Planning for Program Implementation—A Process Guide. Instructional Planning Series.* San Francisco: Far West Laboratory for Educational Research and Development, 1975, ED 102 741.

Davis, O. L. Jr., ed. *Perspectives on Curriculum Development, 1776–1976.* Washington, D. C.: Association for Supervision and Curriculum Development, 1976, ED 119 341.

Deming, Basil S. and Phillips, James A., Jr. "Systematic Curriculum Evaluation: A Means and Methodology." *Theory Into Practice* 13, no. 1 (February 1974): 41–45, EJ 095 544.

Garber, John B. "2 × 4 × 6 × 9 = ? What is the Role of the Community in the Curriculum?" *Community Education Journal* 4, no. 3 (May–June 1974): 27–29, EJ 096 090.

Klein, M. Frances; Tye, Kenneth A.; and Goodlad, John I. "Perspectives of Curriculum." Paper presented at American Educational Research Association annual meeting. Washington, D. C., April 1975, ED 103 959.

Knoop, Robert, and O'Reilly, Robert. *Participative Decision Making in Curriculum.* Educational Resources Information Center, 1975, ED 102 684.

Kowalski, Theodore J. "The Principal's Role in Curriculum Development: What are the Barriers?" *Contemporary Education* 50, no. 3 (Spring, 1979): 159–61.

Piemonte, Charles. "The Crusade for Problem Solving: An Interdisciplinary Effort." *Curriculum Review* 20, no. 3 (1981): 220–23.

Schaffarzick, Jon, and Hampson, David H., eds. *Strategies for Curriculum Development.* Berkeley, Calif.: McCutchan Publishing Corp., 1975, ED 114 936.

Sturges, A. W. "Certification of Curriculum Workers: Where Do We Stand?" *Educational Leadership* 32, no. 6 (March 1975): 398–400, EJ 125 025.

Texas Association for Supervision and Curriculum Development. *School Curriculum Design for the 1980's. The Possibilities for Tomorrow's School: A Proposed Program for the 1980's.* Austin, Tex.: 1974, ED 098 660.

Unruh, Glenys G. *Responsive Curriculum Development. Theory and Action.* Berkeley, Calif.: McCutchan Publishing Corp., 1975, ED 114 935.

Wise, Robert I. "The Use of Objectives in Curriculum Planning: A Critique of Planning by Objectives." Paper presented at American Educational Research Association annual meeting. Washington, D. C., April 1975, EO 103 956.

8

Organizing Elementary School Instruction

INTRODUCTION

If curriculum can be defined most simply as *what* is taught in the school, then instruction is *how* it is taught—the methods and techniques that aid students in their learning. The emphasis in instruction is on learning and not on teaching, but obviously both are significant.

Instruction is the lifeblood of a school. It is the process by which content or curriculum is transported to the student. Instruction, however, requires a learner who gains insight, acquires information, and forms values not only from the context of the curriculum but also through the processes by which the content is presented, or the instruction. The entire learning environment of the school, therefore, constantly provides content for learning. This entwining of curriculum and instruction requires school administrators to look very carefully not only at *what* they teach in the schools but at *how* they teach it, for the medium is truly the message.

Consideration of instruction as the process of providing content to the learner presents several major problems to the thoughtful organizer of the school program. These can best be presented as four questions:

1. What instructional processes should be used?
2. How do these processes accommodate individual differences?
3. What curricular overtones will be created by specific instructional styles?
4. What are the implications of these instructional processes for the other organizational components of a school?

Answers to these questions are not necessarily required, but principals should be aware of the implications of each.

Instructional Processes

Instruction can take place according to different formats. Types of instruction can be divided into several basic categories:

1. Lecture presentation or demonstration
2. Discussion
3. Laboratory
   a. Group or individual
   b. Independent study

Each category presents a different mode for student learning. The purpose of instruction and the expected outcomes should be major factors in determining which instructional type should be used. For example, if the purpose of instruction is to introduce or present an overview of a topic, a lecture presentation to a large group might be best. On the other hand, if the anticipated outcome is the modification of values, then an instructional format that directly involves the learner, such as a laboratory or discussion, would be more effective. Figure 8-1 presents the major purposes of different categories

---

CATEGORIES OF INSTRUCTION AND MAJOR PURPOSES

I.   *Presentation*
Build concepts through information
Stimulate inquiry
Enrich course
Relate course to reality
Make assignments

Usually most efficient and
effective in large groups.

II.   *Discussion*
Raise questions
Report experience
Discuss ideas
Generalize
Form opinions
Plan independent study

Usually most efficient
and effective in small
groups (7–15 persons).

III.   *Laboratory*

Individual Study		*Independent Study*
Student	Build concepts and	Student
performed	principles through	directed
directed	action and viewing	planned
Teacher	Practice skills	performed
directed	Apply ideas	evaluated
planned	Develop investigative	Teacher
evaluated	skills	advised
managed	Develop problem-solving	
	techniques	
	Develop evaluation skills	

These activities may be small-group (2 or more) or individual in nature. These activities can be either scheduled or unscheduled.

FIGURE 8-1.

---

of instruction. Note that each category also has certain group-size recommendations.

ALLOWANCE FOR INDIVIDUAL DIFFERENCES

The question of how these processes allow for individual differences must be viewed from three different perspectives:

1. Instructional process as applied to student ability
2. Instructional process as applied to different individual learning styles
3. Instructional process as applied to individual human or psychological needs

Earlier we considered factors regarding the nature of the learner, such as the range of student achievement levels as well as the variation in talent or ability levels within each child. The complexity of the variations among and within children show the futility of efforts to provide any type of permanent or semipermanent grouping of children for instruction based on ability or achievement. The variation in talents would require many groups, and they would need constant reorganizing. While certain kinds of learning groups are necessary, they must be kept flexible in order to provide for individual differences within the group. In order to do this the entire curriculum needed by the slowest to the most advanced student must be available.

The problem of instruction is further complicated by the differing student curriculum needs discussed above.

The flexibility required to achieve the extent of individualization of instruction necessary to meet the high degree of differences within any group of children will demand techniques different from those most often used in traditional classrooms. For example, recent research by the Far West Laboratory for Educational Research and Development[1] has found that in skill development, a high student success rate is of critical importance in maximizing learning. In other words a student must be provided materials and instruction at a level with which he or she can achieve success in approximately 80 percent of the child's efforts. Other research by the same group shows that for students who are externally as opposed to internally motivated, direct instruction is more effective than large amounts of working alone at their desks or other independent learning activities. The dilemma, therefore, still exists as to how to provide direct skill instruction on narrowly defined instructional levels and also take into account the variables of achievement differences and learning styles.

The implications for staffing and scheduling now become more obvious. No matter what the organizational design, it is apparent that within any class-

---

[1]*Studies on Teacher Evaluation,* Technical Reports, Far West Laboratory for Educational Research and Development, 1978–80.

room a great variety of instructional activities must be going on simultaneously in order to begin to meet the demands of individual differences. However, the differences in learning styles as described by French[2] in addition to the relationship of instruction technique to intended outcomes should prevent one from thinking that individualized instruction always means independent work. Our knowledge of human needs indicates that more often than not, small group activities will best meet security and belonging needs as well as those associated with self-esteem.

OVERTONES OF INSTRUCTION

Most experienced educators will say that they can go into a classroom and after only a few minutes have a very good feel for the amount of learning that is taking place in that room. What are they feeling? How can they make such a quick judgment? Words such as warmth, busyness, and climate are usually part of their answers. Numerous studies have tried to determine the implications of teacher behavior for student learning and attitude development. The organization of instruction as well as the behavior of individual teachers affects what is actually learned in a school. For example, a child will learn independent-study skills only if given numerous opportunities to practice them. A child will learn how to think and discuss in a group situation only if given numerous opportunities to practice discussion. Some of the more recent studies on nonverbal teaching behavior also show that teachers increasingly direct student learning simply by their support or rejection of certain actions.

INSTRUCTIONAL IMPLICATIONS FOR PROGRAM ORGANIZATION

In a system of instruction where a great variety of activities are going on simultaneously and where many independent activities occur, special care should be taken for the actual progress and development of the individual child. A real danger exists that teachers may become so busy running a complex individualized system that they lose sight of the individual child in the process.

Even a school that is doing all the right things to create a properly individualized instructional system can create a serious problem if individual children are neglected in the process. The next section focuses on ways to keep individual learner needs foremost.

INDIVIDUALIZED SYSTEMS OF INSTRUCTION

Schools must give adequate attention to placing individual students into the best learning environment for their motivation and success. That

---

[2]Russell L. French, "Teaching Strategies and Learning Processes," *Educational Considerations* (Fall 1975): 27–28.

placement should be done on an individual basis with a design for utilizing teacher time and talents in order to better implement what must be done. The Individually Prescribed Instructional (IPI) model for individualized instruction is an appropriate example.

The IPI model divides teacher responsibility into the following functions:

Specifying learning goals
Assessing pupil achievement of learning goals
Diagnosing learner characteristics
Planning long- and short-term programs with pupils
Guiding pupils in learning tasks
Evaluating the learner
Directing off-task pupil behavior
Employing team work with colleagues
Enhancing the learner's development

This list assumes some form of team approach. Figure 8-2 illustrates through a flow chart these teacher functions, their order, and their relationship to one another.

The model depicts a teacher role that has been modified significantly from the traditional. Nowhere in the model does there appear a function for the teacher to be a fountain of all knowledge that must be passed on to the children. Rather, teaching is replaced with the word guide, placing a greater responsibility for progress on the learner.

On the other hand, the teacher's role in the IPI model does take in a number of functions that would often lie dormant in more traditional styles. The model suggests that learning goals must be worked out in greater detail for an individualized program. In order for a child to develop a sense of self-di-

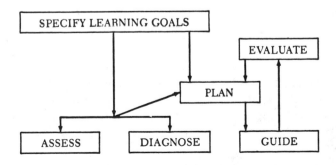

FIGURE 8-2. Teacher Functions in Individually Prescribed Instruction.

rection, he or she needs a fairly specific idea where the lesson is going. In the traditional classroom where the teacher provides fairly detailed step-by-step directions for all students, outlined goals and objectives are not necessary. However, goals must be well laid out for the individualized classroom in order to have self-directed students.

In order to specify goals and a plan for a particular student, teachers must assess and diagnose learning needs and interests. Where assessment points up serious discrepancies, teachers can prepare a more detailed diagnosis of probable learning disabilities. In cases where student interest or previous exposure to a subject is to be the basis for the selection of learning activities, an interview can be an assessment tool.

Planning is a direct outgrowth of assessment and diagnosis and should be done in conjunction with the student and reviewed and revised frequently. The frequency of revision will depend somewhat on the age and maturity of the student. Out of the planning should come a variety of learning goals for the particular student as well as a set of activities to aid in achieving these goals. The student's activities may be the same as those of many of the other children, or they may be unique.

Once the student's immediate plan is complete, the next step for the teacher is to help the student initiate the plan and provide the appropriate learning environment and activities. Some of this environment will be in the form of teacher-organized but self-instructional materials and activities. The amount of teacher time spent on directed group teaching will remain high, but the time will be spent with different groups of students. Some students will have increased amounts of time for independent activities.

Evaluation has unique characteristics in an individualized system. With individual student pacing as well as different learning goals, evaluation no longer can be a uniform function. There can be no more identical spelling tests every Friday morning for all. Instead, tests can be given to students who have indicated they are ready or when the teacher thinks they should be prepared. Teachers, of course, are at liberty to schedule an exam, but the decision will be based on knowledge of the individual student's progress and not on class administrative convenience or group pacing.

INSTRUCTIONAL TOOLS FOR INDIVIDUALIZATION

What are the specific tools for operating instructional programs? We have emphasized individualized instruction and the need to provide a variety of self-instructional activities for students in order to make such a system functional. The next question is how to organize or create materials for self-instruction. Must each teacher develop materials? Are good commercially prepared materials available?

Excellent commercial materials are now available for individualized systems and more are becoming available each year. In areas such as reading and math, schools can purchase an entire system for a wide range of student achievement levels. Other material can be organized and coordinated for instruction by the teacher using that material. Teachers, of course, should also continue to use their own material.

The real problem, however, is organizing materials in a systematic way so they are adequately available to students when they need them, adequately self-instructional so that teacher time can be appropriately balanced, and adequately organized to assure proper instructional sequencing, recording, and evaluation. Today microcomputers can be a great aid to managing individualized instruction.

Several techniques have been developed in recent years to achieve these goals. Among them are learning packages, learning centers, and individual study contracts. Each represents a way of matching instructional goals to appropriate materials, resources, and activities. An evaluation system completes the instructional cycle.

Learning Packages

Simply stated, a learning package is a prepackaged self-instructional lesson. It includes:

1. A statement of purpose
2. A specific goal or objective
3. A list of resources or activities designed to aid the student in achieving the stated objectives
4. A form of evaluation to allow the student and the teacher to determine if the instructional goal has been achieved

The basic purpose of the learning package is to organize an instructional module or lesson in such a way as to make it as self-instructional as possible, thus providing individualized instruction in the classroom. The teacher's role in this kind of learning activity is to assign, or help the student select, a particular set of learning packages and to help explain anything in the learning package that is not understood. This is done either on an individual basis or with several students with similar problems. Learning packages are designed to be self-instructional in order to provide necessary teacher freedom as well as flexibility for individualized instruction.

Learning Centers

A learning center is also a lesson or series of lessons organized around a concept or theme and presented as self-instructional. Learning centers are also goal directed, utilize multiple resources, and are multimedium, as are learning packages. Learning centers are basically places where children learn by doing. Task cards provide preorganized instruction allowing the student to proceed independently. Learning centers may be used as a support mechanism following directed instruction, or instruction can actually be initiated through the center as the beginning point.

Entire classrooms may be organized around as many as fifteen or twenty different learning centers. A list of centers that might be appropriate for elementary classrooms follows:

Learning Centers

research	social studies	take-apart center
current events	games	reading
creative writing	spelling	mathematics
science	Wendy House	fun center
music-listening	dramatics	talk center
art	dance	quiet
recreational reading	craft	cooking
typing	hobby	sewing
handwriting	health	nature trail
computers	physical education	farm

When many learning centers are used, the entire class area is used for centers. Study space is provided in each center to serve the other learning needs of the classroom. The only other seating may be a small area used for small-group instruction.

Independent-Study Contracts

Independent study basically provides adequate instructional flexibility for the student when selecting learning experiences pertinent to individual needs and interests. Independent-study contracts are particularly useful as a means of providing curricular enrichment for gifted students. From the point of view of student development, their overall purpose is to individualize instruction and develop an independent, self-sufficient learner. Self-sufficiency in this case can mean venturesomeness, resourcefulness and organization, interdependence (as opposed to independence), goal direction, full involvement, and personal stability. These attributes can be initiated through independent learning-center activity and carried forward through learning packages requiring greater self-direction than the centers. Ultimately, the goal of developing the independent purposeful learner must be to take the student and the instructor-advisor to more independent learning than the center or package can provide. Here the independent-study contract enhances the development of the student's skills.

While independent study can occur within the classroom, usually it takes place elsewhere. The student determines a plan of study with guidance from a faculty advisor or someone with the needed specialty designated by an advisor. Independent study places the major responsibility for learning directly in the hands of the student.

A contract form should be developed to aid the student in the selection, formation, organization, implementation, and evaluation of independent study projects. The contract may be simple in format but should include sections on:

1. An overview of independent study
2. Independent study application forms, including a place for advisor and parent approval
3. Specification of weekly conferences, use of facilities, and schedule revisions, as well as a scheduled outline of the proposed exploration
4. A statement of goals and the times they are to be met
5. Criteria for grading and the expectations of the advisor
6. Independent study student log with daily entries
7. Student evaluation form
8. Advisor evaluation form

To implement an independent-study program the school should provide adequately staffed and equipped learning spaces, appropriate for independent study. These spaces should reflect the needs and interests of students in their educational development and must be part of a network of learning areas that include the library. The school also should provide an active support system for independent study that would include a faculty member with overall responsibility for the program and that would be supported by the rest of the faculty.

External Independent Study

Numerous schools are developing more and more external education programs that create learning experiences well outside the school grounds. The independent-study contract becomes a valuable tool for coordinating such external education programs. Schools such as the St. Paul Open School in St. Paul, Minnesota have as many as 25 percent of their students out of the building on any given day. In such external projects, students may accompany a doctor on rounds, view a lawyer in court, observe a construction project, or investigate city government. All of these activities can be organized for meaningful learning activities through independent-study contracts.

SUMMARY

An individualized system of instruction requires a new role for most teachers. Extensive preparation is needed to develop a variety of learning goals, objectives, and activities, so that an individualized plan can be developed for each child. The teacher's role in the classroom in addition to direct instruction must include management and guidance of students through a variety of activities such as learning packages or learning centers that have been prepared in advance of the class session.

The principal must have an understanding of individualized instruction and exhibit an expectation of such instruction from the teachers rather than an expectation for large-group, teacher-presentation recitation style. Elementary school instruction should include a number of processes including presentation, demonstration, discussion, and individual and independent study. Instruction must take into account individual differences such as ability and learning style. If a great variety of activities are to operate in a classroom simultaneously, a number of these activities must be independent student learning activities.

BIBLIOGRAPHY

Barth, Roland. "Assumptions about Learning and Knowledge." *Phi Delta Kappan* 53 (October 1971): 98–99.

Beginning Teacher Evaluation Study. Far West Laboratory for Educational Research and Development, 1978.

Coppedge, Lloyd L. "Characteristics of Individualized Instruction." *Clearing House* 48 (January 1974): 272–77.

Davidson, Helen H., and Lang, Gerhard. "Children's Perceptions of Their Teacher's Feeling Toward Them Related to Self-Perception, School Achievement, and Behavior." *Journal of Experimental Education* 29 (December 1960): 107–18.

Duchastel, Phillipe C., and Merrill, Paul F. "Effects of Behavioral Objectives on Learning: A Review of Empirical Studies." *Review of Educational Research* 43 (May 1973): 53–69.

Gilstrap, Robert L., and Martin, William R. *Current Strategies for Teachers: A Resource for Personalizing Instruction.* Pacific Palisades, Calif.: Goodyear, 1975. A resource book providing twelve strategies for personalized instruction: lecture, discussion, drill and practice, independent study, group investigation, laboratory, discovery, learning center, simulation, behavior modification, performance-based learning activities package, and do-look-learn.

Gronlund, Norma E. *Individualizing Classroom Instruction.* New York: Macmillan, 1974.

Henderson, Judith E., and Lanier, Perry E. "What Teachers Need to Know and Teach (for Survival on the Planet)." *Journal of Teacher Education* 24 (Spring 1973): 4–16.

Individually Prescribed Instruction. Philadelphia: Research for Better Schools, Inc., undated (promotional literature).

Kraener, James D. "Individualized Education: Some Implications for Media." *Programmed Learning and Educational Technology* 10 (September 1973): 342–46. A description of goal setting at McMaster University Faculty of Medicine.

Powell, Marjorie. "New Evidence for Old Truth." *Educational Leadership* 37, no. 1 (October 1979): 49–51.

Stuckley, Michael H., and O'Dell, Robert T. "The Open Learning Model Using Computer Instruction." *Educational Technology* 26 (February 1976): 39–42.

Ubben, Gerald. "The Role of the Learning Package in an Individualized Instruction Program." *Journal of Secondary Education* 46 (May 1972): 206–9.

9

Using Student Records
and Reporting to Parents

INTRODUCTION

The elementary school should retain a comprehensive file of records on each student for guidance and direction of student learning and for maintenance of historical records. However, record maintenance can easily get out of hand. If records are not kept up to date, vital information can be lost; if not occasionally purged, files can become full of inappropriate material. If record forms are not carefully controlled, redundancy in data collection can develop and information retrieval become all but impossible.

In late 1974, the passage of the Family Education Rights and Privacy Act, popularly known as the Buckley Amendment,[1] focused the attention of the education community on student records. This legislation forced school administrators to look at the information collected in permanent record folders. Much of the material was not needed and often was inappropriate for a permanent file. Particularly dangerous for permanent historical records was the inclusion of comments by teachers that may have been relevant when contributed but which quickly lost their meaning or were later shown to be inaccurate.[2]

GUIDELINES FOR STUDENT RECORDS

The Russell Sage Foundation has proposed that student records be kept in three categories: 1) permanent records that follow the child through

---

[1]Guidelines for parental access to records can be found in Chapter 3.

[2]For example, one young man applying for jobs found himself rejected time and time again for no apparent reason. In this particular instance, the entire cumulative record card from his school career appeared in his employment file. Ultimately, upon review and investigation, he discovered that eight years earlier, when he was in the fourth grade, a teacher had entered a remark on that card that said "shows some homosexual tendencies." This kind of information obviously should never have entered the record, particularly a record that was going to exist for more than a year or so.

his or her entire school career and become the school archives; 2) semipermanent records that remain on file while the student is enrolled in that building and are destroyed upon the student's promotion or transfer; 3) temporary records that at the end of the year are destroyed or promoted to semipermanent records.[3] Permanent records include basic identifying data, statements of academic work completed, opinions concerning the quality of academic work, and attendance data. Semipermanent records include diagnostic information such as standardized intelligence tests, aptitude tests, interest inventories, health data, family background, teacher and counselor assessments, and behavior patterns. Temporary records concern immediate learning or behavior situations and include reports by teachers, a counselor, parents, or classroom test results.

All three classes of material should be maintained in common files for access by authorized school employees. Professionals working with students on an active basis also should maintain personal files and records that would include professional notes maintained by the counselor and classroom records maintained by the teacher on projects, homework, and examinations.

At the end of each school year, temporary files should be purged. Anything that would assist the school the following year in properly diagnosing the child's needs and in giving guidance should be reclassified and filed with the semipermanent records. The rest should be destroyed.

Procedures for Developing New Record Forms

Often the principal has the responsibility for developing new record forms or revising existing forms. The following are good guidelines to follow in record development:

1. Records should be designed to promote the welfare of the student.
2. Those who keep and use records should have a voice in creating the form and governing their use within the law.
3. Record forms should be readily accessible to those who are authorized to have access to them but also should be protected to give individuals the privacy granted to them under the law.
4. Efforts should be made to limit the number of new forms generated and to consolidate or eliminate forms whenever possible.
5. Electronic data files should be used whenever feasible in order to allow easy updating of records as well as ease in the generation of reports.

Record Maintenance

The task of recording information can be overwhelming. However, good organization can simplify much of this task. Cumulative record cards can facilitate rapid but accurate information transfer. Where feasible, electronic data processing should be used. All cards should be designed to accept the gummed

---

[3]Russell Sage Foundation, *Guidelines for the Collection, Maintenance and Dissemination of Pupil Records,* Report of a Conference on the Ethical and Legal Aspects of School Recordkeeping (Sterling Forest, N. Y., 1969).

labels from computers that are available for almost all standardized machine-scored tests on the market today. A well-organized cumulative record card that has labeled boxes of the appropriate size printed on the card, as well as extra spaces, will save time in transferring scores. Schools that use electronic data processing for grade reporting should use a gummed label to transfer annual grades and attendance information to the cumulative record card.

Other registration material should be organized so that a minimum of handwriting or typing needs to be done. For example, the single sheet personnel data form shown in Figure 9-1 can be maintained as part of the personal record and easily updated. It also carries all of the information in a more usable fashion than the more traditional printed file folder that schools often have used.

Microcomputers have made possible the keeping of low-cost, electronic record systems at the building level that were not feasible a short while ago. Microcomputers such as the TRS-80, Apple II, and Commodore Pet, as well as many others, have adequate memory, storage, and speed, and a reasonable cost when used on a daily basis in schools for record keeping.

Records that must be retrieved frequently or that need to be organized differently for different people are the most logical records to store on a school computer. Prepared programs called data-based management systems can be tailored by a nonprogrammer to fit the recordkeeping format used in a particular school. For example, the forms in Figures 9-2 and 9-3 can be adapted easily to a computer screen by the novice.

The advantages of computerization are several:

1. Many forms repeat the same information over and over again. For records maintained electronically, the information has to be entered only once and can be automatically transferred to each new form.
2. Changes can easily be made and the record updated when students' addresses, phone numbers, or occupations change.
3. Partial records can be sorted and printed, providing important information to particular people who need it. For example, each homeroom teacher can be given a list of names, phone numbers, addresses, parents' names, and test scores for each child in their room.
4. Lists of children organized by bus load, by test scores, or by other recorded factors can be generated.
5. Statistical analyses can be carried out regarding such things as student attendance, grades, and achievement test scores. These can be done without retyping the information.

Most computer stores and computer salespeople can provide information regarding the purchase of software that will carry out these functions. In addition, many educational agencies provide consultant assistance and advice in the purchase of microcomputer systems.

Sample Records

Sample records are often useful to school staff when they are developing new ones. The following collection of sample records is organized into the three categories suggested by the Russell Sage Foundation. Permanent record information that will follow a child through the entire school career and beyond is found in the Personal Data Sheet (Figure 9-1), the Elementary Transcript (Figure 9-2), the Health Record (Figure 9-3), and the Standardized Test Record (Figure 9-4). Semipermanent information, which should be maintained during the years the child is a student in the respective school, is illustrated by the Student Medical Examination form (Figure 9-5), the Release of Information form (Figure 9-6), and the Family Educational Rights and Privacy Act form (Figure 9-7). Temporary information that should be reviewed at the end of each year includes any problem letters sent home (Figure 9-8), a Request for Modified Physical Education Program (Figure 9-9), a Student Transfer form (Figure 9-10), and the Pupil Transfer Record (Figure 9-11).

Cumulative Record
Preliminary Form*

HILLMAN COUNTY SCHOOLS
PERSONAL DATA SHEET

REGISTRATION (To be completed by parent or teacher):
School _____, Hillman County, Kentucky
Pupil's Name _____
                    (Last)   (First)   (Middle)
White ___ Black ___ Other ___ Sex ___ Birth Date _____
                                        (Month) (Date) (Year)
Place of Birth: City _____ County _____ State _____
Source From Which Birth Information Is Obtained:
    Birth Certificate (Number) _____ Bible _____
    Insurance Policy (Number) _____ Other (Explain) _____
Place of Residence _____
                    (Number, Street, P.O. Box, or Route No.) (City) (Telephone)
    Lives With Both Parents: Yes___ No___ ; If Not, Relationship To Guardian ____
Number of Brothers _____   Number of Sisters _____

IN CASE OF ACCIDENT OR ILLNESS AT SCHOOL:
Physician's Name _____   Telephone _____
Hospital's Name _____   Telephone _____
Father (Or Guardian) _____
                    (Name)   (Occupation)   (Employer)

_____
        (Work Telephone)   (Church Preference-Member)   (Health)
Mother _____
                    (Name)   (Occupation)   (Employer)

_____
        (Work Telephone)   (Church Preference-Member)   (Health)

Person To Call If Parents Are Not Available _____ Telephone _____

* To be used when enrolling new pupils.

FIGURE 9-1.

Elementary Transcript
Cumulative Record (Revised 1984)

1. BACKGROUND INFORMATION

Hillman County, Kentucky **SCHOOL** _____

NAME _____
(Last) (First) (Middle)

RACE _____ SEX _____ PLACE OF BIRTH _____
(City) (County) (State)

DATE OF BIRTH ___/___/___
(M) (D) (Y)

DATE OF
ENTRANCE ___/___/___
(M) (D) (Y)

DEPARTURE ___/___/___
(M) (D) (Y)

PUPIL LIVES WITH	AUTHORITY FOR BIRTH DATE	NAME	OCCUPATION
Parent ( ) Guardian ( ) Other ( )	Birth Certificate ( ) Family Bible ( ) Parent's Statement ( )	Parent Guardian	

2. SCHOLASTIC AND ATTENDANCE RECORDS

ATTENDANCE

School Year	Grade/Year	Days Present	Days Absent		

ELEMENTARY SCHOLASTIC RECORD

Write in grade code: _____

Grade/Year	Date Entered	Citizenship	Reading	English	Spelling	Writing	Mathematics	Science	Vocal Music	Instrumental Music	Art	Health	Physical Education	Promotion

SCHOOL	TEACHER

FIGURE 9-2a.

139

3. DEVELOPMENTAL HISTORY

PERTINENT HEALTH INFORMATION: _____

_____

COGNITIVE DOMAIN: Achievement in Tool Subjects: _____

_____

ACHIEVEMENT IN ART, MUSIC AND PHYSICAL EDUCATION: _____

_____

AFFECTIVE DOMAIN: Indications of Personal Maturing: _____

_____

_____

4. MOST RECENT STANDARDIZED TEST SCORES

Name of Text	Form	Level	Date	Grade	(Write in subtest titles)							

_____   _____
Principal's Signature   Teacher's Signature

FIGURE 9-2b.

Cumulative Record: Part IV Health Record

Name _____ (Last) _____ (First) _____ (Middle) _____ Birthdate _____ School _____

1. Physical Examination

Grade		Height & Weight						
Date	Age	Inches	Lbs.					
Nutrition								
Skin								
Lymph Nodes								
Thyroid								
Eyes								
Ears								
Nose								
Teeth								
Oral Hygiene								
Tonsils								
Heart								
Lungs								
Abdomen								
Orthopedic								
Posture								
Speech								

CODE: O=satisfactory. 1, 2, 3=slightly, moderately, markedly unsatisfactory. X=needs medical dental attention. —(dash)=no information obtained. OO=correction made.

2. Other Physical Tests (possibly at grades 1, 4, 7, and high school)

	Hearing		Vision	Visual Acuity		Plus Lens	Muscle Imbalance	Refer
Date	Results		G. Date	Near Point	Far Point			Y N.
	R L							
	R L							
	R L							
	R L							
	R L							
	R L							
	R L							
	R L							

OI=Both eyes, P=Pass, Plus Lens=Farsighted Test

Notes on Above Tests

3. Immunizations & Clinical Tests

	Date	Date	Date	Date
D.-P.-T.				
Mumps				
Polio				
Tetanus				
Measles				
Rubella				
TB Test				
Diabetes				

—Diphtheria-Pertussis (whooping cough)-Tetanus

4. Disease Record

	Date	Year
Chickenpox		
Diphtheria		
Frequent Colds		
Rubella		
Mumps		
Pneumonia		
Polio		
Red Measles		
Rheumatic Fever		
Strep Infections		
Whooping Cough		
Typhoid Fever		

5. In emergency, choice of

	Telephone
Physician	
Hospital	
Ambulance	

Person to call if parents are not available:

Name _____

Name _____

6. Homebound Program

From	To	Reason

7. Hospital Program

From	To	Reason	Date

FIGURE 9-3a.

141

8. NOTES AND SIGNIFICANT FACTS (group therapy experiences, psychotherapy, services from agencies, vocational rehabilitation, medication, treatment, illness, accidents, operations, health status at end of school year). (The information on this page should be considered semipermanent and not transferred to another building.)

Date	

FIGURE 9-3b.

Cumulative Record: Part V Standardized Test Record

Name _____ Birthdate _____ Sex _____ School _____ Hillman County, Kentucky

METROPOLITAN READINESS TEST	
(Give 1 only)	
Date	
Total Score	
%ile Rank	
Letter Rating	

INTELLIGENCE TESTS

Name of Test	Date	Level	Form	Chron. Age	Mental Age	I.Q.	Comments

ACHIEVEMENT TESTS (on Print-outs)

FIGURE 9-4a.

DIFFERENTIAL APTITUDE TESTS

Date	Form	Verbal Reas.		Numer. Abil.		Abst. Reas.		Space Rela.		Mech. Reas.		Clerical S/A		LU-I: Spell.		LU-II: Sent.	
		Raw Score	%ile	Raw Score	%ile	Raw Score	%ile	Raw Score	%ile	Raw Score	%ile	Raw Score	%ile	Raw Score	%ile	Raw Score	%ile

KUDER PREFERENCE RECORD PERCENTILE RANK

Date	Level	Outdoor	Mechanical	Computational	Scientific	Persuasive	Artistic	Literary	Musical	Social Service	Clerical

METROPOLITAN HIGH SCHOOL ACHIEVEMENT TEST BATTERY

Date	Form	Gr.		Read.	Spell.	Lang.	Lang. St. Sk.	Soc. St. St. Sk.	Soc. St. Voc.	Soc. St. Inf.	Math. Comp. & Conc.	Math. Anal. Prob. Solv.	Sci. Conc. Underst.	Sci. Inf.
			St. Sc.											
			%ile											
			Sta.											
			St. Sc.											
			%ile											
			Sta.											
			St. Sc.											
			%ile											
			Sta.											

ADDITIONAL TESTS

Name	Form	Level	Date

FIGURE 9-4b.

HILLMAN COUNTY SCHOOLS
STUDENT MEDICAL EXAMINATION FORM

Name _____ Birthdate _____

Address _____ School _____

REQUIRED IMMUNIZATIONS
(Complete section A *or* B.)

A. Specify dates.

DPT	Polio (Sabin Trivalent)	Rubeola (Red Measles)
1. _____	1. _____	_____
2. _____	2. _____	
3. _____	3. _____	Rubella (German Measles)
B. _____	B. _____	
B. _____	B. _____	_____

If dates cannot be specified, please indicate if, in your opinion, this child is immunized by signing the following section.

B. It is my opinion that the above-named child is completely immunized against diphtheria, measles, poliomyelitis, rubella, tetanus, and whooping cough and is in compliance with Kentucky state laws governing immunizations of school children.

_____ Date_____ Signature of Physician

PHYSICAL EXAMINATION

Pertinent past medical history _____
_____
_____

Remarks regarding physical condition or recommendations for care of child
_____
_____
_____

I certify that I have examined the above-named child and found his/her physical condition to be suitable for participation in school activities including physical education.

_____ Date _____ Signature of Physician

FIGURE 9-5a.

To Whom It May Concern:

In order to assist you in complying with the *Rules, Regulations, and Minimum Standards* — 1984–85 and the Department of Public Health regarding immunization and physical examination of school children, we have prepared the following information for you.

Please read this in its entirety and submit the completed form to the school at the beginning of next school year.

I. **REQUIREMENT STATE BOARD OF EDUCATION**

"There shall be a complete medical examination of every child entering school for the first time with pertinent immunizations given at this time."

"This applies to nursery school, kindergarten as well as first grade and other pupils for whom there is no health record."

II. **REQUIREMENT DEPARTMENT OF PUBLIC HEALTH**

"No child shall be permitted to enroll in any nursery school, kindergarten, or first grade of any grade school until proof of immunization against diphtheria, measles (rubeola), poliomyelitis, tetanus, whooping cough and rubella (german measles) is presented to the admissions office of the school (unless otherwise exempted as provided by law) and it shall be the duty of the school authorities to enforce the provisions of this regulation."

III. This completed form will become a part of each child's permanent record and should be presented at the school upon entry.

FIGURE 9-5b.

HILLMAN COUNTY SCHOOLS
RELEASE OF INFORMATION FROM STUDENT'S SCHOOL RECORD

I hereby authorize _____ School to release all school records and information on

_____
(student's name)

to the agencies and institutions checked below:

☐ schools to which the student has applied for transfer or enrollment

☐ prospective employers to whom the student has given permission to obtain information

☐ insurance companies to which student has applied for a good student or driver education discount

☐ others _____

Notice: I understand that I have the right to request a copy of this student's record and to have it interpreted to me by a qualified member of the school staff by appointment.

Date signed _____
For student under age 18: Parent sign _____
Student age 18 and above: Student sign _____
Student's sex _____ Date of birth _____

(*Note to school personnel: Keep this form in student's record folder. Back of form may be used, at your option, to keep a log of records sent.*)

FIGURE 9-6a.

LOG OF RECORDS SENT
(optional)

Student's Name_____

	Date Sent	Place to which sent	Notes
1			
2			
3			
4			
5			
6			
7			
8			
9			
10			
11			
12			
13			
14			
15			
16			
17			
18			
19			
20			

FIGURE 9-6b.

THE FAMILY EDUCATIONAL RIGHTS AND PRIVACY ACT

Date _____

On this date I/we saw my/our child's, _____ ,
                                              name
CR_2 at Hillman Middle School in the presence of _____ ,
                                                          name
teacher, who interpreted the educational data in this file.

_____
Parent's Signature

FIGURE 9-7.

Original to parent
Duplicate to principal

DEMONT ELEMENTARY SCHOOL
Robertsville Road
Hillman, Kentucky

Date

Dear Parents,

In our continuing efforts to establish a better learning atmosphere at DeMont School, we would like to bring to your attention a problem that we are experiencing.

Our problem is _____

_____

_____

_____

_____

We would certainly appreciate any assistance and support that you can give us in helping with this situation. Call us here at school if you feel the need.

Homeroom Teacher

FIGURE 9-8.

HILLMAN COUNTY SCHOOLS
REQUEST FORM FOR MODIFIED PHYSICAL EDUCATION PROGRAM

1. *TO THE ATTENDING PHYSICIAN:*

   The student whose name appears below is requesting, through his parents, a modified physical education program. Such request will only be honored by the instructor when the information has been completed and signed by you, the attending physician, and returned to the school.

   Rules, Regulations, and Minimum Standards of the State Board of Education, July 1976, states the following: "The physical education program shall be modified for pupils who have physical disabilities, provided it is recommended in a written statement by a physician. The statement of the physician shall show the type of disability, the probable duration of the disability, and a recommended activity program."

2. *TO BE COMPLETED BY STUDENT AND PARENT:*

   Name of Student _____ Sex _____
   School Attending _____ Grade _____
   Name of Physical Education Instructor _____

3. *TO BE COMPLETED BY PHYSICIAN:*

   It is desired to keep all students in contact with regular physical education classes where possible. Please indicate which of the following groups of activity would be best suited for your patient. If any group other than GROUP A is indicated, please give your estimate of the length of time this student should remain in this modified program.

_____ GROUP A — No excuse indicated
_____ GROUP B — Omit shower bath; Length of time
_____ GROUP C — I have checked below the activities in which _____
                       can participate: (name)

_____ Angling	_____ Fun Games	_____ Speedball
_____ Apparatus work	(Relays)	_____ Stunts and
_____ Archery	_____ Golf	Tumbling
_____ Badminton	_____ Horseshoes	_____ Swimming
_____ Basketball	_____ Movement	_____ Table Tennis
_____ Bicycling	_____ Paddleball	_____ Tennis
_____ Bowling	_____ Rhythmical	(Floor Tennis)
_____ Calisthenics	Activities	_____ Track and Field
_____ Croquet	_____ Roller Skating	_____ Volleyball
_____ Fencing	_____ Rope Jumping	_____ Walking
_____ Field Hockey	_____ Shuffle Board	_____ Weight Lifting
_____ Fitness Testing	_____ Soccer	_____ Wrestling
_____ Flag Football	_____ Softball	_____ Others

Duration of Exemption

Remarks:

_____ GROUP D — Omit all participation in physical activity–substituting activities such as scorer, referee, monitor, clerical duties, or related written assignments

_____ GROUP E — Other recommendations by physician:

                     Please indicate briefly the nature and duration of the student's disability if classified in other than GROUP **A.**

_____   _____

DATE   PHYSICIAN'S SIGNATURE

COMMENTS BY INSTRUCTOR:

_____

                       Instructor's Signature

PROCEDURE FOR USE OF THE MEDICAL EXCUSE FORM

1. The student asking to be excused from Physical Education will be given the form to be filled out properly and signed by the parent and attending physi-
·cian. When completed it is to be returned to the instructor in charge.

2. The instructor will assign the student to activities based upon the physician's recommendation. The instructor will then sign on the reverse side and make any necessary comments in the space provided.
3. Each instructor will send the Medical Reports received from his respective students to the office of the principal for permanent filing.
4. A record of the Medical Report will be kept in the instructor's file and one sent to the Physical Education Coordinator.
5. All information on these Medical Report forms should be kept confidential. The completed forms should not be left lying out in the open for anyone to see!
6. With this plan functioning properly, there should be an accurate accounting for all Medical Report forms with the instructor, the Physical Education Coordinator's office, and the Principal's office at any given time.

FIGURE 9-9.

STUDENT TRANSFER

DEMONT MIDDLE SCHOOL
Route 20, Gray Hendrix Road
Hillman, Kentucky

*Name*_____ *Homeroom Teacher*_____

*Date of Withdrawal*_____ *Date of Birth*_____

*Reason for Withdrawal*_____

*Transfer to*_____ Days Belonging_____

Days Present   _____

Days Absent   _____

*Grade*_____ *School Insurance* _____

Subjects	Books Checked in	Subject Grades	Teacher's Signature
1. Language Arts			
2. Social Studies			
3. Science			
4. Math			
5. Librarian's Signature			

GRADING CODE:
SP, EP, AP, MP, UP
SP = Superior Progress
EP = Excellent Progress
AP = Average Progress
MP = Minimal Progress
UP = Unsatisfactory Progress

_____
Teacher's Signature

STUDENT *MUST* RETURN BOTH COPIES TO OFFICE

FIGURE 9-10.

PUPIL TRANSFER RECORD
HILLMAN COUNTY BOARD OF EDUCATION

Name of Pupil _____ Sex _____

Home Address _____

Date of Birth _____

Name of Parent or Guardian _____

School Attended _____ School Address _____

Date of Last Attendance _____ Days Present ____ Days Absent _____

Pupil Placement and Progress*   Comments

Reading _____ Grade Level _____
                (Name of Text)

Spelling _____ Grade Level _____
                (Name of Text)

Math _____ Grade Level _____
                (Name of Text)

Check specialists with whom child is now working:
    Speech _____ Sight _____ Other _____

                                    _____
                                    (Signature of Homeroom Teacher)

* If test results and other pertinent information are desired, the school principal
should make a request in writing.

FIGURE 9-11.

REPORTING TO PARENTS

The purpose of a good parent reporting system is the development of a positive communication link between the teacher, parent, and child regarding the child's education. A variety of methods can be used for such reporting, including report cards, parent-teacher conferences, personal phone calls, school or teacher team newsletters, student papers, and "gripe" sessions.

Report Cards

Report cards are a controversial topic in many schools. They are usually demanded by parents, feared by children, and considered inadequate by many educators. Attempts to improve the report card by using something other than the traditional A, B, C grades have met resistance from parents.

If the purpose of a parent reporting system is to develop an effective communication link, and the parents highly value written reports, then the school should use some form of written report card. A written report alone is not adequate, however, and a personal communication link, such as the parent-teacher conference, should be added.

To effectively report a child's progress, a report card should provide three kinds of information. First, it should estimate the child's overall ability compared to other children the same age. This can be done through standardized tests and a teacher's judgment of the child's ability based on diagnosis and observations. The report card shown in Figure 9-12 has a column to indicate whether the child's performance has been above grade level, on grade level, or below grade level.

PARENT COMMENTS AND SIGNATURE

First Report Period:

_____
Signature

Second Report Period:

_____
Signature

Third Report Period:

_____
Signature

EXPLANATION OF SYMBOLS

A √ In appropriate column indicates:

PROGRESS CODE:

EP   Excellent Individual Performance
        with Outstanding Effort
AP   Average Individual Performance
        with Adequate Effort
MP   Minimal Individual Performance
        with Little Effort
UP   Unsatisfactory Performance
        (No apparent learning —
        Conference is requested)

LEVEL: (As determined by teacher assessment)

+   Above Grade Level
=   On Grade Level
—   Below Grade Level

CONDUCT:

O   Outstanding Citizenship
S   Satisfactory Behavior
U   Unsatisfactory Behavior
        (Conference is requested)

This pupil is assigned to _____
for the coming school year.

_____
Principal

ATTENDANCE: Days Present
                        Days Absent

FIGURE 9-12a. Sample report card.

PUPIL NAME

LANGUAGE — TEACHER — GRADE (EP AP MP UP) — LEVEL (+ = -) — CONDUCT (O S U) — COMMENTS — 1 2 3 4

READING — TEACHER — GRADE (EP AP MP UP) — LEVEL (+ = -) — CONDUCT (O S U) — COMMENTS — 1 2 3 4

SOCIAL STUDIES — TEACHER — GRADE (EP AP MP UP) — LEVEL (+ = -) — CONDUCT (O S U) — COMMENTS — 1 2 3 4

MATHEMATICS — TEACHER — GRADE (EP AP MP UP) — LEVEL (+ = -) — CONDUCT (O S U) — COMMENTS — 1 2 3 4

SCIENCE — TEACHER — GRADE (EP AP MP UP) — LEVEL (+ = -) — CONDUCT (O S U) — COMMENTS — 1 2 3 4

HEALTH — TEACHER — GRADE (EP AP MP UP) — LEVEL (+ = -) — CONDUCT (O S U) — COMMENTS — 1 2 3 4

ART — TEACHER — GRADE (EP AP MP UP) — CONDUCT (O S U) — COMMENTS — 1 2 3 4

MUSIC — TEACHER — GRADE (EP AP MP UP) — CONDUCT (O S U) — COMMENTS — 1 2 3 4

INST MUSIC — TEACHER — GRADE (EP AP MP UP) — CONDUCT (O S U) — COMMENTS — 1 2 3 4

PHY ED — TEACHER — GRADE (EP AP MP UP) — CONDUCT (O S U) — COMMENTS — 1 2 3 4

CAREER EXPL — TEACHER — GRADE (EP AP MP UP) — CONDUCT (O S U) — COMMENTS — 1 2 3 4

— TEACHER — GRADE (EP AP MP UP) — CONDUCT (O S U) — COMMENTS — 1 2 3 4

FIGURE 9-12b.

153

Second, the report card should indicate the child's individual progress, based on estimated ability, to measure the child's achievement in the classroom since the last marking period. This statement is not a comparison to other children but the teacher's estimate of whether or not the child is achieving as much as possible. The sample report card uses an EP (exceptional progress), AP (average progress), MP (minimum progress), and UP (unsatisfactory progress) code on achievement.

Finally, the report card describes the child's conduct in school. Conduct may be rated with a check mark to indicate satisfactory behavior or with a code that indicates outstanding citizenship, satisfactory behavior, or unsatisfactory behavior.

Recording the relationship between the child's ability and his or her achievement is extremely important. The sample report card shown in Figure 9-12 provides a means for making finer judgments about the child's progress than more simply constructed report cards. For example, to illustrate the extremes, a child of high ability who is simply coasting along in school may do as well as many other children, but certainly not be working up to ability. A plus mark in level, indicating ability above the average, would accompany a minimum progress grade (MP), indicating a lack of achievement in relation to potential. On the other hand, a child with poor aptitude who had been trying exceptionally hard to make good progress would receive a minus for level but possibly an exceptional progress (EP) for a subject grade. The level indicator should be relatively stable over time, while the achievement grade may change.

It is often desirable to provide additional details to parents concerning a child's progress in school. In subject areas such as reading and mathematics that have been placed on a skills continuum, very specific information can be provided to the parent regarding both the level on which a child is working as well as progress in the number of skills completed. The form illustrated in Figure 9-13 can supplement a grade card. It should be based on a locally adopted skills continuum. The lettered levels each represent approximately one year's work with the bracket showing the typical span of work for children at each grade level.

Letter Grades vs. Other Symbols. Many educators prefer the use of symbols other than the traditional A, B, and C to report student progress. Codes such as those shown in Figure 9-12 illustrate alternatives. The major rationale for moving away from traditional letter grades is often an effort to make parents more conscious of the meaning of particular symbols. When one compares the many and varied ways children learn and the complexities of the learning process, the attempt to sum up growth by using the barest symbol of the English language—a single letter—borders on the absurd. Symbols other than A, B, C are most often used when schools want to reflect something other than a comparison to a strict grade-level standard or a comparison of one child to another. At the elementary school level, particularly, a grading system other than the traditional A, B, and C is desirable. A word of caution, how-

MATHEMATICS SUPPLEMENT   Student _____

Hillman County Middle School Report Card   Grade _____

19_____   *Please Note Reverse Side*

GRADE	6		7		8
LEVELS	F	G	H	I
Number of required skills	46	37	44	33
Number Mastered	8 10 49			
Number of enrichment skills	15	14	12	11
Number mastered	2 1 3 0			
GRADING PERIOD: The first column of each level indicates student placement at beginning of school year.	First Second Third Fourth	First Second Third Fourth	First Second Third Fourth	First Second Third Fourth

In Hillman County Schools the mathematics continuum represents an individualized, continuous progress approach in mathematics education. For the purpose of determining "on," "below," or "above" grade level, continuum levels have been grouped according to what might be expected for each grade, i.e. levels F–G for grade 6; levels G–H for grade 7; levels H–I for grade 8. The "overlapping" of levels is to be expected in a continuous progress program.

This chart indicates your child's placement within the continuum. It shows the accumulated number of skills your child has mastered thus far out of the total number of required and enrichment skills at each continuum level. The first grading period also shows the number of skills your child had mastered before the current school year began.

FIGURE 9-13.

ever, is in order. Any move to convert a grading system from one presently accepted by a community to any other design should be done cautiously and with a great deal of parent involvement, both in the development of the system as well as in its implementation.

Parent-Teacher Conferences

Parent-teacher conferences offer a major advantage over most written reports sent home in that they make possible two-way and three-way communication. More information can be shared with the parent in a fifteen- to thirty-minute face-to-face discussion than can be provided in a written report only. The parent can also provide insights into the child's behavior. If the child is present for at least part of the conference, the sometimes different interpretations of reality between home and school can be bridged.

Organizing for the Conference. A parent-teacher conference can be effective only if the teacher has spent adequate time organizing for the meeting.[4] Students should participate in a preconference planning session with the teacher, and the student should be asked to participate in the conference in some manner, depending upon age and ability.[5]

The following agenda is appropriate to use for a conference approximately thirty minutes in length.[6]

1. *A get-acquainted period.* To many parents, the school may be a forbidding place and the teacher a powerful authority figure. A friendly casual discussion, a cup of coffee, and a smile may be needed to open communication lines with the parent. The conference should take place in the child's classroom; this is what the parent wants to see. The conference should be conducted away from the teacher's desk in a comfortable spot. It is important to have adult-sized furniture. Information from tests and opinions gathered from other staff members should be available. Examples of student work should be collected and the student's goals reviewed.

2. *Review the classroom and program with the parent.* Discuss how the room is arranged, point out children's work that is being displayed, and show where their child sits. In general terms review the activities that are presently underway. If the child is present at the conference, this is a good time for participation.

3. *Discuss the child's basic ability in the several subject areas as perceived by the teacher.* The child's most successful areas should be identified and appropriate praise given. Trouble spots should also be identified and analyzed. Kindness and candor should characterize this part of the session.

4. *Outline the goals and activities available to the child.* This discussion should cover academic, personal, as well as social goals and activities and should conclude with an identification of the particular goals and objectives appropriate to the child. This is also a good time for the child's involvement in the presentation.

5. *Report on the achievement of goals and objectives.* What has the child accomplished in school so far this year? Examples of student's work saved by the teacher should be used to illustrate achievement. Again, this would be an appropriate place for the child to report accomplishments to parents.

---

[4]In order to maintain top efficiency under normal circumstances, each conference should be the responsibility of only one teacher. This is true even in a team situation where the advisor should assume that role.

[5]Teachers who involve students directly in conferences with their parents have found this to be a very rewarding technique.

[6]An excellent source of materials, including a sample parent-teacher conference packet, can be found in Larry W. Hughes, *Informal and Formal Community Forces: External Influences on Schools and Teachers* (Morristown, N. J.: General Learning Press, 1976), appendix, "Field Work Materials: Parent-Teacher Conference Packet," pp. 40–43.

6. *Identify goals and objectives for future.* These should be discussed by the teacher and student prior to the conference and, depending on the degree of individualization within the school, should be tailored to the particular needs of the child.

7. *Conference close.* At the end of the conference, it would be appropriate to excuse the student to permit confidential comments by either the teacher or the parents.

Scheduling Parent-Teacher Conferences. Parent-teacher conferences must be scheduled to give teachers adequate time to prepare and reflect upon each child as an individual. They should *not* be tightly clustered over a few days as a replacement for the report card. Rather, they should be used as a supplemental communication to the report card and should be scheduled throughout the semester. If every teacher schedules three conferences per week October through December and again February through April, each set of parents can be reached twice during the year and the jamming-up of conferences will not occur. In addition, if there is only one conference on any given day, the conference schedule can be flexible enough to accommodate most parents.

Tips for Improving Parent Participation. Some schools do not have a high degree of parent participation in school conferences. The schools that have worked hard at solving the problem of parent participation have been rewarded by the increasing popularity of conferences and by improved school-home communication. The following practices seem to be related to successful conferences:

1. Offer scheduling options for parents, recognizing the need to hold some conferences in the evening. (See Figure 9-14.)

2. Arrange for daycare or baby-sitting services for parents during conference time.

3. Schedule conferences approximately one week ahead and follow up with a phone call or note home the day preceding the conference.

4. If the neighborhood or community seems composed of reluctant parents who have negative images of the school, use praise calls several weeks preceding the conference request.[7]

---

[7]A praise call works like this. On a given day, the teacher selects two children to watch closely and during the day identifies several things they have done of a noteworthy nature. That evening, around the dinner hour, the teacher calls each child's home to comment on the pleasure of having the child in school this year, and mentions the things of a complimentary nature noted that day. If the home does not have a telephone, a similar effect can be achieved with a note home. The underlying theory is that schools have built negative images in their communities and with many parents. The only contact the school often has with the home is when there is trouble. As a result, parents learn to dislike the school (possibly even remembering negative things from their own school days) and when asked to come to school for a conference, exhibit avoidance behavior. Praise calls have been shown to build positive school images quickly.

DEMONT ELEMENTARY SCHOOL
Robertsville Road
Hillman, Kentucky

Dear _____

    Each year I schedule two conferences with parents to discuss their child's progress in school. I would like to meet with you next week on _____

                                              day   date

at _____ to review _____ work this year.
     time   child's name

    If this conference is scheduled during school hours, I will ask your child to be present for the conference also. If we schedule this conference before or after school, please bring your child.

    If it is not convenient for you to be here at my suggested time next week, please call the school at 966–3284 for another appointment.

Sincerely,

(Signed) _____

P.S.   If you work during the day and prefer an evening appointment, I can schedule one.

FIGURE 9-14. Invitation to Parent-Teacher Conference.

---

5. Schedule several evenings during the semester for conferences with parents who work during the day. Make this a schoolwide activity and never one for an individual teacher or team on a particular night, both for safety reasons as well as for efficiency in communications.

6. If a parent has several children in school, coordinate appointments on the same day so that the parent makes only one trip.

7. Extremely reluctant parents can possibly be reached if the teacher takes a child home after school and is introduced by the child.[8]

These techniques suggest that much effort on the part of the school personnel is necessary to achieve a high level of success with parent-teacher conferences, but such conferences do represent effective ways of improving school-home relationships. Teachers and principals must become more aware of the importance of this connection for effective education.[9]

---

[8]Several precautions must be identified if teachers are to take children home. Be sure your teachers are adequately covered by liability insurance. In most states their personal automobile insurance is adequate for an occasional trip. But check! Secondly, it is usually wise not to go to the door with the child but give the child time to invite the parent out. Thirdly, in many neighborhoods, one teacher should not go alone but should go only accompanied by another adult.

[9]See Chapter 20 for a detailed analysis of community involvement.

SUMMARY

Maintaining quality record systems is an important administrative function for every school, both for guidance and direction of school programs and maintenance of historical records.

Major concerns in record maintenance include clear, concise record forms; regular updating and purging of record data; adherence to federal and state guidelines and to directives regarding records and their access.

Reporting to parents is a significant obligation of the school. Reporting should be considered by educators as an opportunity to develop an effective communication link with the home. Common reporting media include report cards, phone calls, and parent-teacher-student conferences. All three forms should probably be used.

Report cards need to reflect, in addition to grade-level comparative information, a child's progress based on ability and conduct information. Direct contact with parents through parent-teacher conferences offers the opportunity for two-way communication and should be used at least once each year.

BIBLIOGRAPHY

Borislow, Bernard. "Self-evaluation and Academic Achievement." *Journal of Counseling Psychology* 9 (Fall 1962): 246–54.

Coombs, Robert B. "Student Achievement Through Individualization." *American Biology Teacher* 37 (March 1975): 171–73.

Ediger, Marlow. "Reporting Pupil Progress: Alternatives to Grading." *Educational Leadership* 32 (January 1975): 265–67. A discussion of student-teacher conferences and observation as a means of gathering valuable data for the assessment of learning.

Evans, David N. "Standards are Needed for Criterion Referenced Tests." *Educational Leadership* 32 (January 1975): 268–70.

Hartman, Catherine L. "Describing Behavior: Search for an Alternative to Grading." *Educational Leadership* 32 (January 1975): 274–77. Each educator must have clear beliefs and objectives and must be able to plan teaching procedures and evaluation methods congruent with those objectives. An example of such a practice is given.

Hess, Hanna S. *The Third Side of the Desk.* New York: Scribners, 1973.

Hughes, Larry W. *Informal and Formal Community Forces, External Influences on School and Teachers.* Morristown, N. J.: General Learning Press, 1976.

Sartore, Richard L. "Grading: A Searching Look." *Educational Leadership* 32 (January 1975): 261–64.

Simon, Sidney; Kirshenbaum, Howard; and Napier, Rodney. "The Day the Consultant Looked at Our Grading System." *Phi Delta Kappan* 51 (May 1970): 476–79.

Stoops, Emery, et al. *Handbook of Educational Administration.* Boston: Allyn and Bacon, 1975, esp. pp. 574–78.

Warren, Donald I., and Warren, Rachel B. "Six Kinds of Neighborhoods." *Psychology Today* 9, no. 1 (June 1975): pp. 74–80.

10

Creating a Positive Learning Climate: Student Services and Student Control

INTRODUCTION

Many things go on in a school that are not in the curriculum. The needs of children are varied and only partly addressed by the formalized set of classroom or cocurricular activities.

Students may be said to have four interacting selves: an intellectual self (an inquiring mind in need of systematic development); a physical self (a developing body); an emotional self (a psychological dimension); and a social self (a need to be accepted in groups of interacting humans). All of these selves come to school with the student and affect individual growth. If the only self educators had to be concerned about was the intellectual self, it would be a much simpler professional world, but this is not possible. The interaction of each of the other three selves precludes ignoring any one. Reams have been written about the nature of human nature and specifically about the nature of and reasons for learner behavior. What makes students act as they do? What turns students "on"? What turns students "off"? Professional educational and psychological literature abounds with research and conceptual treatment of the subject. Yet we really don't seem to know much about why some schools have a student body that evidences productive learning; why students in other schools manifest dissonance and disruption, others are deceptively quiescent, and still others are openly hostile, if not aggressively so. Of one thing we can be certain: students do affect, sometimes in dramatic ways, the climate of a school.

The real or perceived normative behavior of a student body will determine reward or punishment practices, teacher and administrator attitudes and behaviors, and even teacher and administrator attrition rates. Some schools in a community may be classified as "tough" schools; others as "good places to work"; most often the reference is to normative student behavior patterns. In all of this it is easy to forget that, normative behaviors and "mass actions" to the contrary, a student body is composed of many bodies and, while certain groups may determine in great part the "accepted" behavior, the student who walks through the door of the principal's office is an individual complex of forces that may or may not epitomize the student body.

This chapter focuses on student behavior patterns and mechanisms for helping students be successful. It includes a discussion of the positive control of student behavior, counseling programs, and other pupil personnel services. Perhaps we know a lot about young people in general, but we really don't know much about each young person who makes up the school population. That is why generalizations and the general application of rules and punishments are often uneasy ones and why principals and teachers must reserve judgment about the cause (and effect) of the behavior of individual youngsters.

MAINTAINING POSITIVE STUDENT CONTROL

In Gallup poll after Gallup poll, discipline is reported to be one of the top five problems facing the public schools.[1] What is meant by discipline as a problem in the school varies with each respondent, but it can be generally summed up as the control of student (mis)behavior.

In its charge to principals, one school district stated the principal's responsibilities with respect to creating a positive learning climate as follows:

> It is recognized that there are no short cuts or easy-to-follow rules for establishing and maintaining discipline in a school. Discipline is based on the overall school purposes and program. A strong instructional program geared to individual student needs is the foundation for good discipline.
>
> The primary task of the principal is to establish a proper learning environment, one which affords the opportunity for both students and teachers to successfully engage in the teaching-learning process. The central position which the principal occupies in the school requires that he be aware of disciplinary problems and appropriate disciplinary procedures. Ideally, his awareness of potential problem areas affords him the opportunity to prepare more effectively to deal with problems as they arise.
>
> Schools should be dedicated to the twofold task of helping students understand that (1) every human being inherently possesses dignity and worth and (2) inalienable rights are accompanied by inescapable responsibilities. Such responsibilities, however, cannot be learned in the absence

---

[1]For the past several years George Gallup, in cooperation with the Kettering Foundation, has surveyed the public about their attitudes toward public schools. These surveys are reported in the September issues of *Phi Delta Kappan*.

of freedom. *Children generally learn better from what educators demon-strate than from what they advocate.* [Emphasis supplied.]

When it is obvious to students that administrators are responsive to the serious concerns of young people, the school administration and staff can focus upon preventive discipline rather than punitive discipline.[2]

Development of a Preventive Program

The principal of a school has a particular responsibility to lead the staff in de-veloping school policies to control student behavior. This does not mean that the principal personally should write the policy but that the principal should set up procedures by which the staff can establish a behavior philosophy, dis-ciplinary procedures to be followed, and techniques for corrective action.

Fundamental to an orderly learning climate is a collection of well-under-stood, appropriate, and consistently applied rules and procedures. Once the rules are in place there are two equally important conditions that must be met:

1. The rules must be promulgated in a manner that insures understand-ing by all affected.
2. There must be regular and systematic evaluation of the need for and efficiency of the existing rules. Times change, needs change, and re-sponse patterns change. Therefore, it is important that rules be examined in view of whether or not they continue to serve their pur-pose in an efficient and effective manner.[3]

A good policy statement should include a referral system where teachers know under what circumstances they should ask for assistance, and of whom, and a statement of who accepts responsibility for the youngster's behavior after the referral. (If the school is operating on a team arrangement, teacher to team to principal is a good order to follow.) For example, a teacher should refer a student for discipline when the situation has gone beyond the teacher's reasonable ability to handle it. At that point, the problem is turned over en-tirely to the referral agent, and changes and modifications in teacher-assigned punishment can be made and understood without undermining the teacher's authority.

All extreme discipline cases should require the involvement of a second professional. This person should give advice and present a level head in treat-ing the problem as well as provide the legal protection of a witness.

An adequate followthrough reporting system must exist so that all staff members involved will be aware of any action taken. Any policy developed at the building level must follow the policies established by state rules and regu-lations and local board of education policies.[4]

---

[2]Memphis City Schools, *Helpful Hints for Discipline* (Memphis, Tenn.: Department of Pupil Services, undated, pp. 4–5).

[3]See Chapter 3 for an extensive discussion of rules and regulations and procedural due pro-cess as these relate to a positive learning climate.

[4]Chapter 3 contains a more complete discussion of these issues.

Good student behavior in the school comes as a result of adequate supervision and the use of good student management techniques. There are certain areas of the building and school grounds, for example, that require appropriate supervision to maintain a good preventive program. Guidelines drawn up by teachers themselves often offer the best solution, both in ensuring that all such areas are supervised as well as providing teacher cooperation in carrying out the plan.

"Time-Out" Areas and In-School Suspensions

The separation of children with behavior problems from other children often functions as a mild form of corrective behavior. Within the classroom the teacher may have an isolation booth or an area apart from the other children that minimizes contact, preferably visually as well as physically, and is used as a temporary abode for the child who is exhibiting inappropriate behavior.

For more serious cases requiring a possible out-of-school suspension, many schools are having much success with the "in-school suspension." This entails setting up an adequately supervised isolation area within the school where the child will work during the suspension. When both parents work, the in-school suspension seems to offer a good solution. It certainly is more educationally sound.

Ten Steps to Help Students Achieve Good Behavior

From time to time almost every teacher and administrator has a series of minor disciplinary encounters in their interaction with children. In the great majority of cases a stern look, a reprimand, a suggestion for other behavior solves the problem and life goes on. Every so often, however, a child just does not respond to the normal repertoire of behavior controlling techniques. Nothing seems to work. Finally out of exasperation the teacher sends the child to the office. Some teachers seem to run out of ammunition much sooner than others, but eventually almost all teachers encounter an unmanageable child. The following ten steps for coping with serious behavior problems have been successful in dealing with those difficult cases:[5]

1. Analyze your behavior in relation to the student in question. What have you been doing to control the child's behavior?
2. Stop doing what you have been doing. If you have a problem with the student, obviously what you have been doing doesn't work.
3. Decide to do each day one thing on your own initiative that you haven't done in the past that you believe the student will see as a friendly gesture from you. A compliment or special attention or a special privilege will do.

---

[5]William Glasser, "Disciplining Children in School," *Principal's Audio Journal* I, nos. 9 and 10 (September-October 1974).

4. Ask the child very directly to stop doing what is bothering you. This will work only if coupled with steps 1–3. This may end your problem but if not, proceed to step 5.

5. Ask the child, "What are you doing, and is it against the rules?" If the child says that it is not against the rules or that the rules don't matter, you should describe the behavior and indicate that it *is* against the rules. Say this calmly. If the problem persists, proceed to step 6.

6. Tell the youngster to stop the behavior now and to see you for a conference at a designated time and place later that day to talk over the problem. In the conference, review what you've done and said. Ask, "What did you do that was against the rules?" "Did it help you?" Then you may add, "Can we make a plan to improve your behavior?" Assist the youngster in developing such a plan and continue the regular routine. If step 6 does not work at first, keep repeating it. Accept no excuses and administer no punitive punishment. The next four steps will use step 6 as their foundation.

7. If the child is belligerent or extremely upset, send the child to a time-out area in a corner of the room away from the other children. Make it a comfortable, pleasant, but separate area where the child can hear and see but not participate. The child stays there until calmed down and then returns to the group after a conference.

8. A child who will not sit still or calm down should be sent to a place established by the school, such as the principal's, nurse's or counselor's office, to sit outside and away from the teacher's classroom. When the child has become calm, the principal, nurse, or counselor should take over and go back through step 6.

9. Assign a tolerance day with the parents. Send the child home with the understanding that parents will keep the child home for the day without punishment and send the child back the next morning. The principal then again holds a conference. If the parents are not at home, an in-school suspension could be used.

10. Call on community resources when school resources have been exhausted. Resources to consider might include a guidance center, a psychiatric clinic or, in extreme cases, a juvenile court. Thereafter it should be an outside school volunteer, Big Brother or someone that can provide the child with an hour or two per day in a non-failure activity.

The good behavior of students is necessary before an instructional program can be fully effective. Discipline, however, is not always easy to maintain. Environmental factors outside the school's control have a major effect on the behavior of children in school, as well as the climate created by staff in the school.

There are, however, a number of functions well within the control of the school administrator that can contribute mightily to a positive learning climate. Disorder and lack of control in schools are frequently a result of the existence of large, impersonal masses of students. Students' feelings of alienation and teachers' feelings of helplessness must be recognized and addressed

1. Be visible. Often the principal's presence in the halls, cafeteria, or playground serves as a deterrent to misbehavior and gives the teachers a feeling of support.
2. Develop school discipline policies consistent with school board policies and make sure that parents, teachers, and pupils are familiar with them. This may be done through a school handbook.
3. Base all rules and regulations upon whether or not the educative process is disturbed rather than on whether or not the educator is disturbed.
4. Require teachers to keep records of recurrent misbehavior. A simple card file will suffice for this.
5. Encourage teachers and parents to make the initial attempt to solve problems.
6. Emphasize the responsibility that parents have in regard to their child's behavior.
7. Let minor infractions be handled by the teacher, recognizing that some teachers need more help than others with discipline.
8. Ask teachers to submit a disciplinary report along with the request for help from the principal. That is, teachers should report what happened; who did what to whom, and why.
9. Use some convenient method to inform teachers of the disposition of referred discipline problems.
10. Encourage teachers to assume responsibility for school discipline. A word from a teacher to students running or scuffling is often a sufficient deterrent.
11. Identify trouble spots such as restrooms, halls, and the cafeteria, and assign faculty members to be there at specified times.

FIGURE 10-1. Maintaining Control: Tips for Elementary School Principals.

by the administration through reorganization of the school into smaller learning communities.

A large percentage of severe discipline problems are caused by a small percentage of the students. Special facilities and methods are needed to handle the more severe disruptive behavior of children if these cannot be handled effectively in the classroom. Much alienation and misbehavior is caused by a curriculum that is irrelevant and inappropriate for many students. A curriculum that is appropriate and relevant to the students' life can do much to improve behavior.

The principal's own behavior and activities will help set the tone. A principal who helps teachers develop good discipline practices, a principal who maintains direct contact with students, and a principal who is visible are all critical to a good learning climate. Attention to the list of procedures in Figure 10-1 will establish a positive framework.

THE COUNSELING PROGRAM

What is usually meant by student advisement and guidance? Traditionally, the guidance program is assigned to a particular person called a guidance counselor within the school who is given the responsibility for everything that deals with psychological services, testing, and student programs. Elementary schools that have been able to afford an elementary guidance counselor have found that they perform roles very much like that of their high school counterpart. In many cases, however, the advisement and guidance needs of elementary school children require a different professional role and pattern or organization.

To properly analyze the function of elementary guidance, one must first look at the needs of the elementary student. The age range, from kindergarten to junior high or middle-school entry, means that the needs will indeed be diverse. Included in such a list of younger student needs are:

1. A surrogate parent
2. A friend
3. A personal counselor for problems of family, peer, and teacher relationships
4. An academic counselor to oversee and direct the student's learning in a personal way
5. A liaison with the home to share the school's perception of the child in the area of academic counseling as well as to receive information about the child and to cooperatively set goals for the child

Most educators would readily agree that an elementary school should meet these needs but that this cannot be done by one person called a guidance counselor. The question then becomes, "How can these needs be met?"

Student advisement and guidance in the elementary school should remain the function of the classroom teacher. The basic advisement and guidance functions for a particular child should be in the hands of a single professional in order for someone to have a picture of the whole child. The main problem the classroom teacher faces in organizing an effective student advisement program is usually one of time. There are ways to gain time for student counseling, however. Organizing activities and dividing some of the responsibilities with other appropriate personnel will assist teachers in this endeavor.

Advisor-Advisee Systems

A system of teacher-child advisement on a regular basis has successfully combated the problem of child identification in an individual classroom. Each teacher assumes responsibility for the curricular decisions and learning goals for a particular group of children. The ratio of students to advisor is based on the total student-staff ratio in the school. Some schools involve every professional staff member in the school, including the principal, librarian, and specialists. Involving everyone reduces the ratio and also involves every staff member in a specific instructional role.

The advisor is responsible for meeting with the entire group of children at least once a week and with each child individually at least once every other week. Individual conferences are scheduled on an appointment basis during times convenient to both the advisor and the student. These conferences should average about ten to fifteen minutes. Commonly used times are before school, during instructional breaks common to both the student and the advisor during the day, or immediately after school. For example, an advisor having twenty-five students must see an average of three per day to complete the cycle each week. It is a good idea for an advisor to attempt to see all students in four days, leaving the fifth day each week for makeup appointments.

To a certain extent the specific function of the advisor depends on the rest of the organization of the school program. In a traditional elementary school, the teacher in a self-contained classroom performs this advisor role automatically. In a school with a team organization or in a school where students have more than one teacher, such as one with traditional middle school staffing patterns, the advisor role has several possibilities. A basic contact on the faculty can help the student with any personal problems, making referrals to a counselor or other appropriate person. The advisor's main role is to review with the student the learning progress in various subjects, to help in setting goals, and to recommend to the student and teachers any program modifications required as a result of the review.

In schools that have team teaching, flexible schedules, or individualized instructional and curricular programs, the job of the advisor can be all-powerful. The extreme flexibility of thoroughly individualized programs requires control functions. Someone must plan with the child a curriculum and its accompanying instructional format. In programs that allow a high degree of scheduling flexibility, the individual student will make scheduling decisions daily or at least weekly. The advisor's role is to provide competent professional assistance to the student in making these choices. The power of the advisor is further strengthened with control of all curricular and instructional decisions.

The rationale underlying this transfer of power from the teacher to the advisor is that the advisor has a better opportunity to observe the whole child than the individual staff members in the various contact subjects and that the advisor can take a more neutral position as to the importance of one subject over another for that particular child. In this model, the advisor has the power to remove a student from a particular part of the curriculum and place the student in another, to recommend a different instructional format for a student, or to reschedule the student in some other way. These changes should of course be done in concert with the teachers in that child's school program. This achieves a very direct and immediate link between the student and the student's program. It provides the flexibility that is necessary, particularly in an individualized situation.

An advisor-advisee model such as the one just described obviously requires a time commitment of every staff member, usually one hour or more per day. Schools that are effectively using such a system seem to feel that the ten or fifteen minutes devoted to each individual are worth ten to fifteen hours of group instruction in increased motivation for that child.

Developmental Guidance and Counseling

The three basic development activities include group guidance, individual student counseling, and parent conferences.

Group guidance activities may be varied, but underlying them should be the advisor's responsibility to aid students develop good peer relationships, good interpersonal problem-solving skills, and a good learning-community climate. Group process methods such as Glasser's class meetings[6] or the group guidance activity in the Magic Circle[7] material are appropriate activities.

Individual counseling accomplishes two purposes. First, it provides the opportunity for each student to interact with the advisor as a friend and confidant. Second, it provides frequent program planning and evaluation. At least biweekly conferences are necessary, and they should function as the main stage for academic planning. A teacher describes such a conference as follows:

> For each of my students, I have a file folder in a box next to my desk. Every paper completed by that student is placed in that folder, and it has been appropriately graded or reviewed, and remains there until the night before our scheduled appointment. Each night I take home the 3 folders of the students I plan to see the next day and regroup and review their papers according to subjects. I also review my notes from earlier conferences with each child and look at the goals we had established in previous weeks. I then write down tentative goals that I have in mind for the student for the next two week period. The next day when that student comes to my desk for his conference, I review with him his schedule of activities and the amount of time that he has spent on each subject area. We then go over his papers and I ask if he is having any particular problems. I will note for him problems I have identified from my review. Next, we look to see whether previously set goals have been achieved and begin our discussion of which goals and learning activities should come next. I prefer that each of my students set goals for himself rather than for me to always have to suggest them. We each write down the goals agreed upon and identify some of the activities to be done toward each. As might be expected most are continuations of previously laid plans, but if new interests or needs have developed, these are to be included. Finally, a cover letter is stapled to the entire 2-weeks collection of papers to be taken home to the parent. (Figure 10-2 is an example of a letter such as the one referred to above.)

Some teachers prefer to use a form on which to set and record goals that can also be shared with parents or at least made a part of the student's yearly diagnostic file. An example of such a form is shown in Figure 10-3.

A conference with parents gives teachers an opportunity to hear from parents about their child and to share information with the parent.

---

[6]William Glasser, *Schools Without Failure* (New York: Harper and Row Publishers, 1968).
[7]Human Development Training Institute, Inc., *Magic Circle Human Development Program* (La Mesa, Calif.: Human Development Training Institute, Inc., 1976).

DeMont Elementary School

Dear Parent:
Here are the papers completed by your child during the past two weeks. I have reviewed with _____ and we have made plans for the next set of
(name)
activities.
Although not all items in the packet have correction marks, the general concepts have been reviewed.
If you have any particular questions, please call me at school (966–2704) and leave a message for me to return your call.

Mr. Dietz
Blue Bird Community

FIGURE 10-2.

Selection of an Advisor

The effective advisor must be able to communicate with each child on a friendly, personal basis. Thus, a good personality match between advisor and student is desirable. This can be achieved if several advisors are available. Alternative advisors exist when the school operates on a team or expanded-team basis. After staff and students have become acquainted in the fall, the team can assign to each of its members an appropriate number of advisees, keeping in mind the needs of each individual student and which team member might best meet those needs. One approach that has worked particularly well is for students to select advisors.

Another organizational technique that greatly aids the effectiveness of the advisement program is multi-age grouping, which places children with a particular team for two or three years, enabling a child to keep the same advisor during that entire period. This long-term arrangement gives the teacher a much better opportunity to become acquainted with each child and to apply that knowledge over an extended period.

An excellent opportunity to reduce the student-teacher ratio can be created by using the expanded-team concept for student guidance. This concept calls for participation in the guidance program by professionals within the school not ordinarily assigned to teams for purposes of instruction. Included would be teacher specialists, resource teachers, the librarian, and the

ADVISEMENT CONFERENCE

Student Name _____   Term _____

Advisor _____   Date _____

A. Goals set by student and teacher
B. Adjustments and accomplishments toward previously set goals
C. Additional teacher comments
D. Additional student comments
E. Next conference date _____

FIGURE 10-3.

principal.[8] By expanding each team with one additional professional for purposes of guidance, each regular teacher's advisement load can be reduced by five or six students.

If persons outside the team act as advisors, they must have adequate time. This includes time for individual as well as group activities with the children as well as some planning time with the team in order to coordinate adequately with team instructional operations.

Tips for Establishing a Good Advisement Program

Try for maximum flexibility in advisor assignments so that more than one teacher could logically be assigned as a child's advisor. Keep the advisor-student ratio as low as possible. The concept of using all professionals in the school as advisors helps. Have advisors schedule meetings regularly with advisees, both on a group as well as individual basis. Figure 10-4 shows four different types of advisor-advisee activities, with their group and individual application. It assumes each advisor has twenty-four children. The total weekly commitment by the advisor to individual conferences is approximately four hours per week during the school day and two hours after school. Group guidance activities can be built into the regular school schedule, requiring approximately thirty minutes each day for a total of two and one-half hours each week.

---

[8]This offers a good opportunity for the principal to have a direct one-to-one relationship with a group of children without having to be tied permanently to an instructional responsibility. It gives that kind of contact that a principal often needs to keep in touch with the real world of teaching.

	Academic	Personal Development	Parent Reports	Administrative
Individual Applications	Diagnostic prescriptive Goal setting evaluation 1 15-minute conference every two weeks	Counseling as needed Average of 10 additional minutes every four weeks per child	Pupil Teacher Parent } Conferences Phone contact 1 30-minute conference each semester plus 30 minutes planning time for each conference 2 conferences per week (2 hours) beginning after first six weeks of school	*Unscheduled*
	3 hours per week total	1 hour per week total		
6 hours per week (4 during school day, 2 after school)				
Group Applications	Standardized tests Orientation of advisor-advisee relationship General goal setting	Group process problem-solving class meetings	Parent orientation	Administrative announcements, records completion, attendance
	(2 30-minute periods per week) 1 hour per week	(2 30-minute periods per week) 1 hour per week	(1 1-hour after school or evening session each semester)	(1 30-minute period per week)
2⅔ hours per week in school				

FIGURE 10-4. Guidance Activities and Suggested Average Times Needed.

STUDENT ADVISEMENT SCHEDULE

Week 1 of a two-week cycle
15 minutes each conference

8:00 Early bus arrivals ...	Susan D.	Pat M.	Pete H.	Elizabeth S.	Makeup
8:30	Classes begin				
	Lunch and Playground				
12:15 Walkers	Henry D.	Daryl P.	Ellen T.	Shirley B.	Makeup
3:00	Classes end				
3:10 Late bus departures.	Larry Z.	Brenda M.	Bill T.	Earl H.	Makeup

FIGURE 10-5.

Teachers should schedule individual conferences as well as group activities in advance. If time is not set aside, conferences tend to be easily forgotten in the press of time. A regular appointment calendar on a two-week rotation should be established, and each child should know the designated time in advance.

A teacher with an advisee load of twenty-four students should plan to see approximately three advisees each day, leaving Fridays open for makeup appointments. Most appointments can be scheduled during noninstructional hours, either immediately before or after school, or during a noon-break recess period.

Each advisor should collect and file information about each child in a systematic manner. Diagnostic information collected from the student and parents, personal data sheets, interest information recorded by the teacher, learning style observations, as well as reports on academic progress are all appropriate. Forms such as those shown in Figures 10-6 and 10-7 offer systematic ways to gather such data.

The Role of the Guidance Counselor

An individual trained as a guidance counselor has a particularly important role to play in the advisement structure of an elementary school. The elementary school guidance counselor could assume five different responsibilities.

1. In order to keep close touch with the program, become attached to a team and assume an advisor responsibility along with the other specialists within the school.

STUDENT EXPERIENCE RECORD   Name_____

Instructions: List experience, date and period of time.

READING LANGUAGE ARTS	MATH	SCIENCE	SOCIAL STUDIES	MUSIC	ART	PE
		Example: 5–78 3rd grade completed. Science fair project on leaf classification 2 months study.		*Example:* 3–78 participated in spring musical production — USA song solo.		

FIGURE 10-6.

OBSERVATION AIDE

Name of Child	Behavior Exhibited	Creative	Name of Friends	Interests	Clues to Sensory

FIGURE 10-7.

174

2. Function as a school referral agent to handle problems identified by the teacher advisor and team. A major role for the guidance counselor is doing the diagnostic work the teacher cannot do.
3. Administer and supervise the advisement program.
4. Provide and direct staff development activities in the techniques of advisement for both group guidance functions and individual diagnostic work. A major portion of the guidance counselor's time should be spent directly on staff development activities.
5. Assist the teachers in establishing and maintaining a good record system.

In sum, the role of the guidance counselor in the school should be one of accepting student referrals, conducting staff development activities, and providing overall supervision for the advisement program. If no guidance counselor position exists, the program becomes another one of the many responsibilities of the principal.

Pupil-Personnel Referral Services

Most school systems provide a complement of specialists to meet needs beyond those that can be met by the regular school staff. Each school should have someone designated to coordinate special service needs of the school. A guidance counselor is an appropriate referral agent initially to determine the need as well as to identify the proper source for available services. If a guidance counselor is not available, this responsibility falls on the principal and the classroom teachers.

A good pupil-personnel service program does not attempt to replace the need for teacher interest in the development of each of the selves of students. Pupil-personnel services are meant simply to augment the role of the teacher through the delivery of expert technical and professional services where needed.

Thus, pupil-personnel services include all of those special classroom supportive services outside of the curricular and cocurricular offerings that impinge upon the maturation of the four selves of the student. The pupil-personnel-services professional becomes a member of the instructional team, providing technical services and additional professional insight in the diagnosis, prescription, and treatment of individual learner difficulties as well as in the design of balanced programs for all learners.

Each school should prepare a list of available services and people to contact for those services so that teachers will know who to contact for particular problems. It is often appropriate to share this list with parents. Included on such a list should be guidance, special education, and attendance counselors; the school psychologist; special education resource teachers; pathologists; homebound teachers; and reading specialists. An example of such a list provided for an elementary school staff is shown in Figure 10-8.

PUPIL-SERVICES PERSONNEL AVAILABLE AT WASHINGTON SCHOOL

1. *Washington Guidance Counselor* Mr. Richard Johnson is a full-time staff member at Washington offering counseling, testing, and referral help to parents and students. Telephone 699–3194.

2. *School Psychologist* Dr. Fred West is available to all Washington parents and students. His services are available by referral through the Pupil Services Department. Telephone 699–2860.

3. *Special Education Counselor* Mrs. Janice Collins is the school counselor responsible for coordinating placement and for assisting parents and students in the hearing disability classes. Telephone 699–2860.

4. *Special Education Teacher* Mr. John Fredricks is a full-time Washington staff member who teaches students experiencing learning problems.

5. *School Pathologist* Miss Gladys Haines is a full-time Washington staff member. She is responsible for diagnosis and treatment of speech and hearing problems in our school.

6. *Homebound Teacher* Mrs. May Bell Anderson is available at the physician's request to every pupil who is unable to attend school for a period of four weeks or longer. Requests are made through Pupil Personnel Department.

7. *Diagnostic Center.* This center is being operated by Mrs. Betty Larson to fully diagnose and prescribe educational programs for students experiencing problems in school. Contact your school counselor.

8. *Home-School Coordinator* Miss Phyllis Lamar serves as liaison between the home and school. Telephone 699–2860.

9. *Attendance Counselor* Mr. Pete Smith coordinates all attendance and data processing. He is responsible for attendance problems, juvenile court contacts, enrollment projections, report cards, secondary and junior high scheduling, and processing of test data. Telephone 699–1658.

10. *Reading Specialist.* Washington School has 1½ reading teachers who work with students needing extra help with their reading. The teachers are Mrs. Helen Davis and Mrs. Mary Pearson.

FIGURE 10-8.

SUMMARY

This chapter has focused on three elements of a good learning climate: student behavior, counseling activities, and pupil-personnel support services. Basic to a well-functioning school is an understood framework of rules and regulations so that students and teachers know what is expected of them. Each school should develop a discipline philosophy and policy acceptable to the staff, administration, and community, outlining the basic procedures to be followed when behavior problems occur. A good discipline policy will outline the basic steps to be used in severe discipline cases, indicating the referral procedures for the involvement of other professionals.

Moreover, students have special needs that can only be attended to by an effective counseling program. The elementary school counseling program must be a total school program. The classroom teacher is responsible for most day-to-day counseling. A structured program including both individual and group counseling should be built into the schedule. The guidance counselor in the school administers the teacher-counseling program and coordinates referral services and staff development as they relate to the guidance program.

Still other specialized services characterize the good school system. Most frequently, these are housed in a central office and provided districtwide.

In a sense, with respect to the delivery of these other pupil-personnel services, the principal is a person in the middle—not as a gatekeeper but rather as a facilitator. While an organizational structure is frequently developed to deliver many of the pupil-personnel services, it is still incumbent on the principal to take the lead in the orderly provision of these services to teachers and students in the school building.

BIBLIOGRAPHY

Anderson, G. J., and Wahlberg, H. J. "Learning Environments." In H. J. Wahlberg, ed., *Evaluating Educational Performance*. Berkeley, Calif.: McCutchan Publishing Corp., 1974.

Brookover, W. J. "Elementary School Social Climate and School Achievement." *American Educational Research Journal* 15 (1978): 301–18.

Canter, Lee. *Assertive Discipline*. Los Angeles, Calif.: Canter and Associates, 1976.

Curwin, Richard L., and Mendler, Allen N. *The Discipline Book: A Complete Guide to School and Classroom Management*. Reston, Va.: Reston Publishing Co., 1980, esp. chap. 13.

Duke, Daniel L. "School Discipline Policy in the 1980's." *Education Digest* XLVI, no. 6 (February 1981): 6–9.

Elardo, Richard. "Behavior Modification in an Elementary School: Problems and Issues." *Phi Delta Kappan* 59, no. 5 (January 1978): 334–38.

Englander, Meryl E. "The Courts Mandate to Parents, Local Authorities and the Profession." *Phi Delta Kappan* 59, no. 8 (April 1978): 529–32.

Foster, Herbert. *Ribbin and Jivin and Playing the Dozens*. Boston: Ballenger Press, 1974.

Glasser, William. *Schools Without Failure*. New York: Harper and Row Publishers, 1968.

Glasser, William. "Disorders in Our Schools: Causes and Remedies." *Phi Delta Kappan* 59, no. 5 (January 1978): 331–33.

Hubel, Keigh; Tillquist, Paul; Riedel, Robert; and Myrbach, Charles. *The Teacher/Advisor System*. Dubuque, Iowa: Kendall Hunt Publishing Co., 1974.

Mosley, Charles E. *Behavior Modification: Discipline in Urban Schools, STEM XII.* Houston: University of Houston/Houston Independent School District Substitute Teacher Education Program, 1980. (Available from the University of Houston College of Education.)

Rogers, Carl. *Freedom to Learn.* Columbus, Ohio: Charles E. Merrill, 1969.

Wynne, Edward A. *Looking at Schools: Good, Bad, and Indifferent.* Boston: Lexington Books, 1980.

11

Effective Staff Organization

INTRODUCTION

One of the greatest responsibilities assigned to a principal is organizing and assigning staff in the school. Included in normal staffing responsibilities is the deployment of all employees and volunteer workers to the instructional program and service functions of the school. Often, central office administrators and supervisors have a hand in these assignments, but the basic responsibility usually rests with the principal.

Inherent in any good staffing design is optimal utilization of staff. Staff planning must take into account the present needs and functions of the members of the organization as well as the school's long-range goals and plans that might modify hiring practices in the future.

Traditionally, staffing has been by simple unit-classroom analysis, that is, one teacher, one group of students, one room, sometimes one instructional format, and sometimes one subject. Staffing plans have been built and modified from year to year using this basic classroom unit. Such a procedure is very restrictive, particularly when used in conjunction with some of the curricular, instructional, and grouping ideas presented in previous chapters.

Staffing Analysis

There are three basic dimensions to staffing: single-to-multiple staff assignments, generalized or specialized curricular assignments, and division of teaching functions.

Single-to-multiple staff assignments describe the number and kinds of people that are to work together in the organization. Such assignments might require a single staff member or multiple staffing arrangements. The simplest is the single teacher. The complexity of staffing patterns can be increased by adding teacher aides or forming a collegial team arrangement with coequals.

179

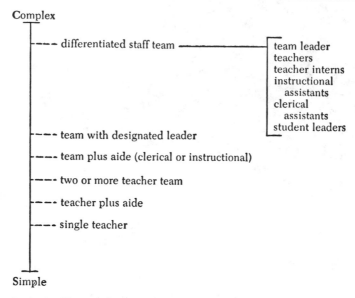

FIGURE 11-1. Staffing Assignments—Simple to Complex.

Finally, assignments might fulfill a differentiated staffing pattern that includes several teaching levels such as master teacher, teacher, teacher intern, as well as several classifications of support personnel such as instructional aide, clerk, student aides, or volunteers. (See Figure 11-1.)

The continuum of generalized and specialized assignments relates teacher assignments to the curricular and instructional program of the school. A generalized assignment requires one teacher to teach many subjects, the extreme being the one-room schoolhouse where the teacher has responsibility for all grades as well. Specialization is introduced through the gradual narrowing of the grade span and content areas for which a teacher has responsibility. Instead of teaching a dozen or more subjects as is commonly done in elementary schools, a teacher would share the age span and instructional load with other teachers and would be responsible for preparation in a few subjects or a fused curricular area such as social studies or language arts. The extreme of specialization is responsibility for a single subject offering within the school for a homogeneously grouped class. These last two specialization categories have led to a departmentalized form of staffing within the school. (See Figure 11-2.)

The relationships of staffing to curriculum and staffing to instruction can be analyzed by considering the two-dimensional relationship of single teachers to teaching teams as well as the relationship of generalized curricular assignments to specialization. As a result of this analysis, four major staffing relationships emerge: (a) the one-teacher unit in a self-contained classroom with

Generalization				Specialization
All subjects Multi-age	All subjects except P.E. music art	Teach only L.A. S.S. Sci. or Math	Teach only L.A.	Teach only Reading or P.E. or Science

FIGURE 11-2.

responsibility for all subjects; (b) the one-teacher unit with subject specialization, usually referred to as departmentalization; (c) a teaching team with subject area specialization, referred to as a disciplinary team; and (d) a team with responsibility for all subjects, referred to as an interdisciplinary team. These four staffing relationships are illustrated by the four quadrants of Figure 11-3.

None of these four categories is mutually exclusive, and many variations are possible with slight alterations in either the staffing or curricular dimension, including heterogeneous or homogeneous student grouping. Using the four lettered quadrants of Figure 11-3, several common staffing patterns can be described as follows:

1. A + B requires a one-teacher unit for most curricular areas plus specialists also operating in a one-unit fashion for subject areas such as music, art, and physical education.
2. C/D requires an interdisciplinary team, with teacher specialization of subjects within the team, and a common group of students.
3. C/D + B requires an interdisciplinary team as above with the addition of self-contained subject specialists for the other parts of the curriculum, such as art, music, and physical education.

As can be seen, an almost endless variety of combinations is possible, depending on the particular desires and needs within a given school.

The third staffing dimension, instructional functions, can be added for further analysis to any of the designs, particularly a team dimension, permitting specialization in the planning, teaching, guiding, diagnosing, materials preparation, and supervising dimensions. The teaching functions of planning, teaching, guiding, evaluating, developing materials, diagnosing, and supervising represent another way of analyzing the differentiation between specialization and generalization. A teacher may fulfill the functions for a particular

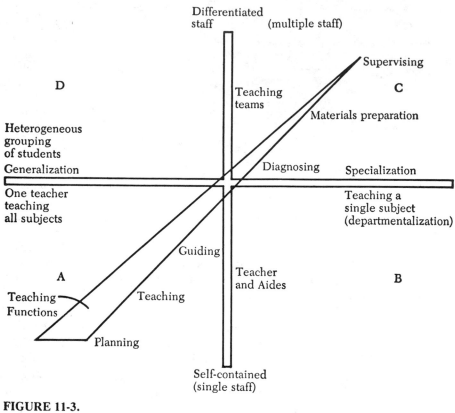

FIGURE 11-3.

subject or all subjects, or, in concert with other staff members, may carry out increased or reduced responsibilities within these functions. A teacher working alone obviously must always do them all. However, when teachers work within a team arrangement, one member of the team might be responsible for planning and coordinating the reading program, while several other teachers might carry out the plan and assume direct teaching responsibility for reading, while yet another staff member or aide may provide only general supervision of children related to reading. This dimension of staffing must be considered as a major factor in determining team working relationships. (See Figure 11-3.) Each of these functions must be performed by someone no matter what the staffing pattern.

    Teaching function analysis is useful when designing staffing patterns other than the single-unit system. Teachers are not equally talented at planning, teaching, guiding, evaluating, diagnosing, developing materials, or supervising children, nor do they have the time to do a good job in each of these areas for the entire curriculum. These functions present a way of subdividing responsibilities when multi-unit or team approaches are used in organizing schools.

Considerations for Selecting Particular Staffing Models

Since such a wide variety of staffing patterns is possible, how can anyone determine what is best in a particular situation? The following discussion may be helpful in making such a determination.

Generalization versus Specialization. The question of generalization or specialization has gone on for many years under the guise of discussions relating to self-contained versus departmentalized school arrangements in the one-teacher unit classroom. The major argument for generalization has been that one teacher who operates the entire curriculum has ample opportunity for contact with each child across a broad segment of school life. The teacher gets to know a child extremely well over an extended period of time and thus can consider the child in a broad range of social as well as academic settings. The teacher in this situation is aware of the child's development in all subjects. If the child is having difficulty in a particular subject, the teacher may be able to determine the source of difficulty from knowledge about the child's development in other subjects. The major problem of the self-contained, all-subject classroom has been the burden placed on the teacher for preparation in such a broad range of subjects. It can be overwhelming and ultimately prevent the teacher from adequately preparing in all but a very limited number of subjects.

This problem leads directly to the argument favoring specialization. A teacher with the responsibility of preparing for a reduced number of subjects can do a much more thorough job and can come to the classroom much better prepared. This is particularly important as children become older and require more knowledge from the teacher. The major weakness of specialization is that a teacher is aware of only a limited portion of the curriculum and is knowledgeable about a child's growth and learning only in that portion of the curriculum and thus is not in a good position to judge total learning. If the child is having difficulty in social studies, the teacher may not be aware that the child also has a serious reading problem that may be the underlying cause of the difficulty. A further criticism of specialization is that it forces the teacher to work with a much larger number of children during the day, again reducing the contact with each individual child. Both the arguments for and against specialization and generalization are logical. The best solution probably lies somewhere between the two extremes or may be most effectively resolved with the inclusion of some kind of team teaching.

Single Staff versus Multiple Staff. Team teaching has been used with varying degrees of success in schools for years. Persuasive arguments can be given both for and against it. Reasons favoring self-contained classrooms are as follows:

1. Teacher training and experience traditionally has been for the self-contained classroom. Many teachers favor it because they know it best.

2. Buildings are designed for self-contained classrooms, not for team arrangements, and they simply do not lend themselves to team teaching.
3. Teachers, when placed on teams, develop difficulties in interpersonal relationships because of different personalities, teaching styles, or philosophies.
4. Team teaching requires a great deal of additional time on the part of the teacher in planning that could be devoted to children or to preparation of lessons in the self-contained classroom.

Arguments in favor of team teaching are that:

1. A teaching team provides variation for the children as they have contact with a set of teachers.
2. Teacher productivity generally increases under a team arrangement since teachers tend to support each other in the achievement of goals.
3. Flexibility of grouping becomes possible and building-level scheduling can be greatly simplified when teachers are working together in a team.
4. The advantages of both specialization and generalization can be obtained when teachers specialize in either or both the curricular and instructional dimension within the team and still have the opportunity to observe the whole child as that child works with the team over the major portion of the day.
5. Individualized instruction can more easily be attained with the team of teachers sharing the variety of instructional tasks necessary to successfully implement an individualized program.

DISCIPLINARY VERSUS INTERDISCIPLINARY TEAM DESIGN

Interdisciplinary teams of the "D" or "D/C" type (Figure 11-3) seem to be the most functional. This type of team can function as a unit, sharing in assuming the responsibility for the majority of the education of a group of children. This factor of team responsibility for a group of children is the secret of success of a dynamic staff organization. Instead of only one teacher being totally responsible for a child, or a group of teachers each being independently responsible for only one discipline, the team collectively is responsible and accountable for the progress of each child. As a result, the best aspects of the self-contained classroom are retained, along with the strengths of teacher specialization.

Two major problems occur with the creation of disciplinary or C-type teams. They require many students to satisfy the hour-by-hour demand on the team. For example, a team of four social studies teachers could teach from 100 to 120 students per hour for each hour that it operated. This requires not only a fairly large school to supply adequate numbers of students but would place very stringent demands on scheduling.

Disciplinary teams have more difficulty with interpersonal relationships than interdisciplinary teams. When two or more teachers within a given discipline are placed together, the potential for disagreement increases, since the opportunity for philosophic and teaching style conflicts is greatest when people have virtually identical assignments. In addition, one teacher's desire for domination may conflict with the attitudes of other members of the team. Interdisciplinary teaming does not face this problem, because each teacher has a given area of specialization within the team. Other members of the team do not come into direct conflict over that assignment.

Team Compatibility. Efforts should be made to provide as much team compatibility as possible when teams are initially organized as well as when making additions or replacements. Some of the items to consider in determining team compatibility are as follows:

1. Do the members have similar teaching philosophies and styles?
2. Do they have similar work habits? Do they come to work early or stay late, have a clean room or a messy room, follow a fairly rigid schedule or are somewhat irregular in scheduling?
3. Do they fit together with an appropriate combination of curricular and instructional interests and talents?

When formulating teams, the overriding consideration should probably be the individual acceptance by each teacher of the particular staffing and instructional model to be used in the school. This acceptance, of course, can be greatly enhanced by involving the staff in the initial determination of the model. Personnel not accepting the model should be allowed to make other arrangements. Transfers now will greatly ease implementation later. If no other schools in the system can take transfers, dissatisfied staff members will have to be accommodated into the new system. The choices of what to do with them are really three:

1. The teams can be balanced by assigning dissatisfied members equally among the teams, hoping to reduce their impact or convert them through involvement. However, experience has shown that this is generally a bad practice. The adage "One rotten apple can spoil the whole bushel" holds true.
2. These members of the staff can be grouped together on teams to concentrate their influence in a limited area, hopefully reducing their impact on the entire school. This allows the principal to maintain, at least on paper, a uniform staffing pattern throughout the school. This is a good workable solution.

3. A school can have some teams as well as self-contained classrooms, allowing those unwilling to try a team arrangement to continue to operate in the traditional way.

This latter approach has often been found to be most desirable. Its major advantage is that it creates an alternative to the team situation not only for the teachers but also for the students and their parents, some of whom may prefer, at least initially, a self-contained situation.

TEAM PLANNING

One of the most crucial factors in a successful team operation is adequate planning time and efficient utilization of that time. If at all possible, team planning should occur during the regular school day. Planning should be regularly scheduled; at least two hours per week are needed in a minimum of one-hour blocks. Each team meeting should have an agenda, prepared by the team and distributed in advance, and each meeting should have a designated chairman. A secretary for the team should keep minutes of the meeting.

Building an agenda for team meetings needs to be an opportunity for all team members to share in the planning for the team. One good way is to place an agenda planning sheet in a central location, for the team to list items they wish to discuss at the next scheduled meeting. Some principals have the teams prepare their agenda on a spirit-master so that copies can be quickly reproduced and distributed to team members, as well as other key people such as the librarian, special education teacher, or the principal, who may want to attend the team meeting. Figure 11-4 is an example of a form to be used for agenda building.

A variety of different planning tasks of both a long- and short-term nature needs to be carried out by each team. Effective use of planning time can usually be enhanced by focusing on a particular purpose during a meeting. The following five types of planning meetings are suggested with recommendations regarding frequency.

(1) Goal-setting Meeting. One goal-setting meeting should be held each semester to look at the philosophy of the school, the curriculum guidelines existing for its direction, and the identification of goals for the particular group of students for whom the team is responsible. These goals would be long-range in nature and would be things to work toward over a semester or year.

(2) Design Meeting. A design meeting is a planning meeting to select instructional topics and develop instructional units. Principles and objectives as well as general ideas for the unit are considered. After the topic has been

TEAM_____   DATE OF MEETING_____

I. *STUDENTS*

Name	Person presenting	Concern	Est. time needed
_____	_____	_____	_____
_____	_____	_____	_____
_____	_____	_____	_____
_____	_____	_____	_____
_____	_____	_____	_____

II. *PROGRAM DEVELOPMENT*

Area	Person presenting	Est. time needed
_____	_____	_____
_____	_____	_____
_____	_____	_____
_____	_____	_____
_____	_____	_____

III. *STAFF DEVELOPMENT*

Area	Person presenting	Est. time needed
_____	_____	_____
_____	_____	_____
_____	_____	_____
_____	_____	_____

IV. *ADMINISTRATIVE*

Area	Person presenting	Est. time needed
_____	_____	_____
_____	_____	_____
_____	_____	_____
_____	_____	_____
_____	_____	_____

FIGURE 11-4. Form for Agenda Building.

selected, one team member is usually assigned the responsibility for drafting the unit. When the draft is ready, the team modifies and builds on the design. Specific objectives are listed, overall responsibility for each member of the team is outlined, and the calendar of events is developed with specific target dates. Methods of student evaluation are also planned. One of these meetings is necessary for each new unit, and a minimum of one each quarter or marking period is essential.

(3) Grouping or Scheduling Meeting. This planning meeting outlines activities for the next week or two, defining specific instructional plans, organizing students into appropriate groups, and constructing the weekly calendar and daily schedule. One of these meetings is needed at least once every two weeks, if not weekly.

(4) Situational Meeting. This meeting focuses on individual children. Various children within the group are discussed by the various members of the team to coordinate information and develop plans for learning activities for that child. The teacher advisor for the particular child has the responsibility of

---

Two team meetings should be held each week.

Prior to school year	• Goal setting for the semester
	• Design of units for the first grading period
	• Initial grouping and scheduling of students assigned to team
Week 1	• Situational meeting
	• Grouping and scheduling meeting
Week 2	• Situational meeting
	• Grouping and scheduling meeting
Week 3	• Situational meeting
	• Grouping and scheduling
Week 4	• Situational meeting
	• Design meeting—plans for the next period meeting
Week 5	• Situational meeting
	• Design meeting
Week 6	• Situational meeting
	• Evaluation meeting (of teaching)
Week 7 (repeats Week 1)	• Situational meeting
	• Grouping and scheduling meeting

FIGURE 11-5. Schedule of Team Meetings.

---

carrying out team decisions. These meetings should probably be held each week, with each teacher advisor determining which children need to be discussed by the team.

(5) **Evaluation Meeting.** The major focus of this meeting should be the evaluation of the instructional program and units. Questions to be asked are: Did we achieve our goals? What were our strengths? What were our shortcomings? How well did we function together as a team? One of these meetings should be held each quarter immediately after the close of the quarter or immediately after the completion of a major unit.

(6) **Team Meeting Schedule.** Assuming a planning schedule that allows for two planning meetings per team each week in a six-week instructional period, a schedule of team meetings for the period might look as shown in Figure 11-5.

Extra grouping and scheduling meetings as well as situational meetings are scheduled early in the year to work through changes in enrollments and to place children better as more data are available.

DIFFERENT STAFFING PATTERNS

Different staffing patterns are possible for any situation, from the traditional self-contained classroom to a variety of team and differentiated staffing models. Given a basic student population of 600 for an elementary school, as shown in Figure 11-6, the following examples illustrate several basic staffing designs.

5-year-olds	75
6-year-olds	80
7-year-olds	95
8-year-olds	85
9-year-olds	100
10-year-olds	90
11-year-olds	75
TOTAL	600

FIGURE 11-6. Grade Distribution of Student Population.

Grade	Students	Teachers	Class Size
K	75	3	25
1	80	3	26–27
2	95	3 or 4	31–32 or 23–24
3	85	3	28–29
4	100	3 or 4	33–34 or 25
5	90	3	30
6	75	3	25

Staff Teachers		21 or 23	
	Plus	1 Principal	
		1 Librarian	

	Staff Totals	23	overall ratio 1–26.1
		25	overall ratio 1–24.0

FIGURE 11-7. Staffing Assignments for Self-Contained Classrooms.

Traditional Self-Contained Classrooms

A traditional staffing pattern with total reliance on self-contained classrooms based on a student-teacher ratio for each classroom of approximately thirty-to-one is shown in Figure 11-7. As is often the case, tough dollar decisions determine when to exceed the thirty-pupils-per-classroom figure and when to hire additional staff to reduce the ratio. For a totally self-contained program, the only additional support staff would be the principal and possibly a librarian.

Teachers Plus Specialists

Usually, a school prefers specialists in certain areas such as special education, art, music, and physical education. Figure 11-8 illustrates a specialist staffing pattern with two special education teachers each taking a class load of ten to fifteen students, thus reducing class size by approximately one or two students in each room. The art, music, and physical education specialists, on the other hand, either come into the classroom with the regular teacher once or twice a week or take the children from the regular teacher for several periods each week, giving the regular teacher a break. The total staff size is increased by the number of specialists added, increasing the total staff in this example to twenty-eight or thirty.

Team Teaching

Teaching teams can easily be implemented as an alternate pattern to those just outlined using the same number of students and staff positions. (See Figure

Grade	Students	Staff Team	
K	75	3	
1	80	3	
2	95	3 or 4	
3	85	3	Sp. Ed. 1
4	100	3 or 4	
5	90	3	
6	75	3	Sp. Ed. 1
Specialists	Art, Librarian, Music, P.E.	4	
Principal		1	

	Staff Totals	28 overall ratio 1–21.4
		30 overall ratio 1–20.0

FIGURE 11-8. Staffing for Grade-Level Teams.

11-8.) Each team consists of three or four teachers in grade-level arrangements. The special education teachers attach themselves to either the primary or intermediate teams, dividing their time among the several groups. The art, music, and physical education specialists and the librarian form a team also for staff organization. Advantages as well as disadvantages of team organization have been discussed earlier.

Team Teaching with Aides

Grade-level teaching teams can be enhanced if each team adds a teacher aide. In many communities, aides can be hired for a minimum wage, or in some cases volunteers can be used to support the team. The cooperative organization of a team approach permits sharing students. Teachers often prefer to employ aides rather than additional teachers to reduce class size. If, as shown in Figure 11-8, grades two and four could function with three-teacher teams instead of four, the salary dollars saved could pay the salary for eight aides (part-time if necessary), one for each of the school's teams. (See Figure 11-9.)

Teams, Aides, and Multi-Age Grouping

One of the problems still not adequately resolved in the illustrations used thus far is the unequal size of classes from grade to grade. In most schools children are unequally distributed across the grades.

The utilization of multi-age grouping in conjunction with a team staffing pattern can resolve this problem of unequal class size. Multi-aging simply means placing children of more than one age in one group for purposes of instruction. It represents a move on the generalization-specialization continuum towards generalization and greater heterogeneity of student grouping. The

Grade	Level	Teams		
		teachers		aides
K	75	3		+ aide
1	80	3	Sp. Ed. 1	+ aide
2	95	3		+ aide
3	85	3		+ aide
4	100	3		+ aide
5	90	3	Sp. Ed. 1	+ aide
6	75	3		+ aide
Specialists, art, music, P.E., librarian		4		+ aide
Principal		1		
	Staff totals	28		8 aides

overall staffing ratio 1–16.7

Eight aides can be hired for the salary of two teachers.

FIGURE 11-9.   Grade-Level Teams with Aides.

age span may be two or more years, but three years seems to be a fairly common age cluster. By overlapping the ages from unit to unit, each learning community served by a team of teachers can be held to a prescribed size. For example, in the case of the previously used illustration, children could be grouped as shown in Figure 11-10 into five units of 120 students each. Teaching staff to support these five groups would be deployed as shown in Figure 11-11. The organizational pattern illustrated in Figure 11-12 results in the same staff requirements but distributes responsibilities more evenly. This type of team organization, coupled with multi-age grouping, allows for an extremely even distribution of students. Even when the enrollment numbers vary greatly or when staffing ratios are unfavorable, balance can be provided, ensuring uniform availability of instructional services.

Grade	Available Children	Unit 1	Unit 2	Unit 3	Unit 4	Unit 5
K	75	40	35			
1	80	40	40			
2	95	40	45	10		
3	85			60	25	
4	100			50	35	15
5	90				60	30
6	75					75
		120	120	120	120	120

FIGURE 11-10.   Multi-Age Grouping of Children.

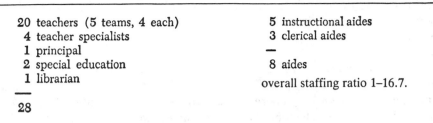

20 teachers (5 teams, 4 each)   5 instructional aides
4 teacher specialists   3 clerical aides
1 principal   —
2 special education   8 aides
1 librarian   overall staffing ratio 1–16.7.

28

FIGURE 11-11. Staff Utilization in a Team Organization.

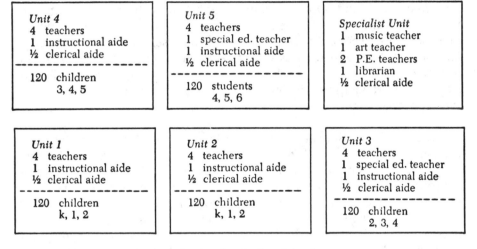

FIGURE 11-12. A Multi-Unit Design for Staff and Students.

Utilization of Staff Specialists

The addition of specialists for special education, reading, math, learning disabilities, physical education, art, and music has been a mixed blessing in our schools. Most schools have desperately needed the extra help but have not been able to make maximum use of the talents specialists can provide.

Part of the problem of using specialists arises from single-classroom organization. The specialist in a "pull-out" program is a fifth wheel and often is never fully integrated into the program. Specialists often have been set apart in little rooms by themselves to call children out of regular classrooms, disrupting the regular program for the child as well as using their own time very inefficiently.

A team organization leads to a variety of ways to use specialists. In some cases, specialists can best be utilized by dividing their time into fractional units and assigning them to teams for each unit. Following are three examples of how a team organization can utilize the services of specialists or the services provided by special programs.

School One: Resource Teachers. A school organized in a multi-unit fashion similar to the school just discussed was allocated two additional reading and math positions out of federal funds. One was for remedial reading and the other, mathematics. The school decided to integrate these positions fully into the teams so that no specialist would work with more than one team. In order to do this, the specialist positions were divided into fractional units and student loads were adjusted accordingly. Instead of hiring new people for these positions, interested faculty from the existing staff were identified and given the special training necessary for the new assignments. The two positions were divided into four units of time and distributed among the existing staff. Each team was assigned a one-fourth-time reading specialist and a one-fourth-time math specialist. The released staffing money was used to hire two more regular teachers. Specialist services were integrated into each team to make the available instruction relate closely to the organized program. Federal guidelines were met by assigning designated students to these specialists for the appropriate times.

School Two: Special Education Mainstreaming. In order better to mainstream the exceptional children within this school, also organized according to a multi-unit pattern, these children were assigned on an age basis to the appropriate learning community. The two special education teachers for the exceptional children in this school worked together as a team with the instructional teams in the school. They attended team planning meetings when appropriate and scheduled their visit to coincide with the skill-grouped reading program of the team. During the reading schedule they became part of the team and took the exceptional children into expanded reading groups, thus bolstering the reading staff. The children of this school never identified and labeled these two specialists as special education teachers, even though they spent almost all of their time with certain children. A way to save time for the special education staff is to place all the exceptional children into two or three learning communities, reducing the number of different teams with which specialists must work.

School Three: Art, Music, and Physical Education Specialists. In the third school the art, music, and physical education specialists served two major functions: (1) They served as student advisors along with each of the other four teachers on the team to which they were assigned. They did this during the early minutes of the school day, the noon hour, and the last thirty minutes of the afternoon. (2) During an approximately two-and-one-half-hour block in the morning and again each afternoon, two physical education teachers, an art teacher, and a music teacher worked on a unit rotating basis, taking one-half of the children from two of the units for instruction in their specialities. Thus, for two and one-half hours once or twice a week, each team had a block of time with only half of the children and could concentrate on small group instruction activities.

Team Integration

A multi-unit design results in the formation of a series of learning communities consisting of three to five teachers and aides, students, and a curriculum. This design must be able to allow effective individualization of instruction and enhance the implementation of the curriculum. This can be accomplished more successfully by a team design than by single-unit classrooms, but only with proper planning.

The full integration of the team's instructional program is the key to its success. All teachers must share in organizing the curriculum, preferably with an interdisciplinary approach with each teacher carrying a specific independent assignment. The teachers must share the children and together discuss their problems. Specialization in curriculum can be used to reduce the planning required of any particular teacher, but not to the extent that it causes departmentalization of the curriculum. Figure 11-13 illustrates how one learning-community staff divided the workload after much discussion and planning. All of the children were organized into twelve skill groups for reading and eight for math. Thus, each of the four regular teachers had three reading skill groups and two math skill groups. In addition, each teacher took several other curricular responsibilities for learning-center development as well as for direct instruction. Each team member also assumed some administrative responsibility. The physical education teacher worked directly with the team only part of each day. Each week a schedule was planned.

Teacher A	Teacher B	Teacher C	Teacher D	P.E. Specialist
25 advisees team leader advisement coordinator	25 advisees reading coordinator	25 advisees math coordinator	25 advisees learning center coordinator	20 advisees
reading (3) math (2) writing crafts language	reading (3) math (2) science spelling learning center	reading (3) math (2) social studies library learning center	reading (3) math (2) science health	

FIGURE 11-13. Learning-community Staff Assignments.

Schoolwide Staffing

A principal has several schoolwide staffing functions. Gone is the day when the principal could make major instructional and curricular decisions for a school without the direct involvement of the staff. This is true because in many cases, teachers are more knowledgeable than the principal regarding particular problems as well as possible solutions, and because curricular and instructional decisions affect the teachers most directly. Good organizational theory has shown that people have greater commitment to decisions in which they are involved.

Participatory Management. An excellent way to involve the faculty is through the formation of a faculty council to improve the school's curricular and instructional program. If the school has a multi-unit learning community design, this faculty council should be made up of the head of each learning community and the principal.

Matrix Management. In a similar fashion to the advisory council, special coordinating committees to deal with curricular areas such as reading, math, social studies, or any area that requires cross-unit coordination should be appointed. These committees may be permanent or temporary in nature, depending on the assignment.

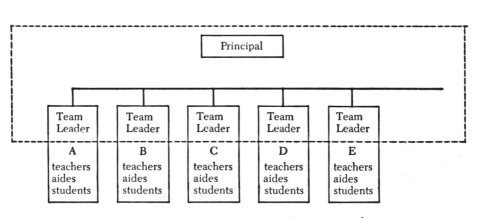

The staff within the dotted line makes up the Principal's Advisory Council.

FIGURE 11-14. Principal's Advisory Council.

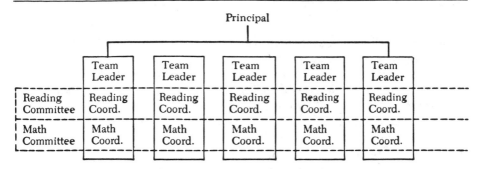

FIGURE 11-15. Multi-Unit Curricular Coordinating Committees Matrix Management.

If a multi-unit staffing design is used, these committees can best be formed with one teacher from each team. (See Figure 11-15.) The curriculum committee thus formed provides representation from each of the teams as well as communication back to each team. Each staff member also shares in the schoolwide efforts to provide continuity and thrust to the curricular and instructional program. The major line of responsibility (vertical) in the matrix still rests with each team. The curriculum committees (horizontal) function only to coordinate the overall school program.

If a school maintains a more traditional staffing pattern, these school-wide staffing designs can still be used. There will be some loss of representation, however. In any case, staffing must be viewed in the context of the total mission of the school.

PARAPROFESSIONALS

Many tasks performed every day in the elementary school do not require professional training. Some tasks relate directly to improving instruction, while others are noninstructional in nature. The move toward individualized instruction, the multiple-activity classroom, and the many additional services of a food, health, or welfare nature that are provided in schools increase the demand for nonprofessional employees.

In some schools clerical and instructional aides have performed these functions. Other communities, without funds for aides, have used volunteers.[1] Paid or volunteer aides can be a great asset to the school, but schools must properly select and train these aides to avoid problems.

---

[1] An excellent source of the information and ideas for volunteer aide programs can be found in the publications of the National School Volunteer Program, 300 North Washington Street, Alexandria, Va. 22314.

Types of Aides

There are two kinds of aides: the instructional or classroom aide, and the clerical or support aide. Instructional aides usually work directly with a classroom teacher or team and assist in instructing children under the direction of a teacher or team. In addition, they fulfill a variety of clerical, support, and supervisory tasks assigned by the teacher or team. A clerical or support aide usually does not work directly in a classroom but in the office, clinic, school store, library, or resource room.

Whether the aides are paid or volunteers, the aide program must provide a sound orientation and training period as well as careful appraisal of special talents and abilities possessed by the aides.

A first step in the utilization of any special nonprofessional in the school is the approval of the central office and board of education for such a program. This is obviously necessary if the aides are to be paid, but it is also very important when volunteers are used. There are many legal ramifications of such a program, and a policy regarding the aide program should be developed in each school district and ought to include recruitment, selection, orientation, and training.

Recruitment and Selection of Aides

Aides can be drawn from the entire community. If most aide positions are established on a part-time basis—three to twenty hours per week—the potential available work force is very large. Available persons might include college students, high school students, housewives, retirees, and men or women who work evening shifts. Professional people may also often be available as resource people and for short special assignments.

Recruitment can occur through newspaper articles, letters to parents, the PTA, church announcements, telephone, or any other contacts available. After an aide program has been initiated, a television news story on the aide program followed by a call for assistance may be an effective recruitment device.[2]

Each aide should be interviewed before acceptance into the program. In the initial interview, the principal should attempt to gauge the individual's motivations, assess potential contributions, and decide the kind of responsibility the person can most effectively assume. Factors that should be considered during an interview include educational background, the use of language, appearance, poise and personality, interest in children, willingness and ability to

---

[2]One of the more successful recruitment ideas is the establishment of a volunteer-operated daycare center for the children of the volunteer mothers. The daycare center is extremely appealing to mothers who are home with small children, and the opportunity to get out and relate to other children and adults brings them to the school to volunteer. A free lunch for retirement volunteers also works extremely well.

follow directions, special interests, abilities, and training, past employment, general health (a physical examination should be required), and the aide's home situation. By far the most overriding consideration is the aide's dedication to the welfare of children and a willingness to commit time and energy on their behalf.

The interview serves to inform the aide of the goals of the school and helps the aide decide if the school is a desirable place to work. The interview also can be used to determine whether a volunteer would work well directly with children. If not, the aide can receive other kinds of assignments, provided of course the person has the appropriate technical skills.

Orientation and Training Program. Each aide should attend at least one formal orientation session. Additional sessions can be scheduled as the year progresses and as needs arise. Aides should be familiar with basic principles before they begin work. They must understand lines of authority within the school and must know where to turn in a conflict situation. An introduction to administrative and supervisory personnel will smooth relationships and give aides an understanding of who to contact if a problem arises.

Aides must realize that they have undertaken an important service with a fixed schedule, specific demands, and supervision of some activities. They should understand that the school expects a high quality of effort, reliability, and cooperation. They must learn to be friendly, tactful, helpful, and fair to all students. They must be instructed not to discuss children with parents and not to divulge any information from private records to anyone. They should be aware that disciplinary action is the responsibility of the teacher only, and that the teacher handles all parental problems.

A third phase of the training program for aides should involve a discussion of the psychological aspects of their work. This discussion should cover general characteristics of children and the implications of working with them, along with their physical, social, mental, and emotional attributes. It should focus on the procedures and attitudes that are conducive to the best psychological atmosphere and climate within the classroom. This phase of the program should help aides learn the general approach to children used by the staff.

The final phase of an aide program is continuous. It constitutes participation in the daily activities and operation of the school and is truly on-the-job training. In addition, instructional aides should participate as much as possible in teacher inservice training. The training program for clerical and support aides is similar to that of the instructional aides but also includes specific training in regard to clerical duties.

Creating a Supportive Atmosphere for the Aides

Aides, as well as teachers, must have a warm working climate within the school. They need a gathering place and time for a coffee break as well as the opportunity to share activities and responsibilities. An advisement committee of aides should meet with the principal on a regular basis to discuss improving the role of the aide within the school. Schedules for aides should be made as flexible as possible to accommodate outside responsibilities.

Administration of the Aide Program

If the aide program consists largely of volunteers, day-by-day scheduling becomes an important task. A principal does not have time to manage this on a daily basis and can use aides to administer the work program.[3]

Liability Implications for Aides

One particular caution needs to be raised regarding the use of aides: the legal question of tort liability. Training aides for the jobs they hold is important.

Specific supervisory training as well as the development of clearly defined supervisory policies, including lines of authority and responsibilities, are recommended. A training program for aides should consider techniques of supervising children, what to do in a variety of situations, how to handle the children who need disciplining, and how to handle emergency situations. If each aide, whether paid or voluntary, receives this training, the potential for a negligence charge stemming from a personal injury situation will be greatly reduced. Some states require liability insurance for aides. Education associations usually provide this insurance in those states requiring it.

SUMMARY

Three dimensions of staffing were considered in this chapter: the teacher's involvement with the curriculum as either a generalist or a specialist, the teacher's interaction with other school personnel functioning either as an individual or as a member of a team, and the various teaching functions that must be carried out as part of the act of teaching. These three dimensions interact and should be reviewed collectively when organizing a school staff. When teachers work independently, decisions about curricular responsibilities and teaching function are limited. When teachers are organized into teams, many more staffing options are available. The multi-unit pattern for staffing, curricular organization, and student grouping makes maximum use of staffing potential.

The concepts of participatory management with the use of a principal's advisory council and curriculum committees can greatly strengthen decision making and faculty participation.

---

[3]In one case observed recently, several women who wished to work in the program but were unable to leave the home because of health reasons were used to place the calls each evening to the homes of the other volunteer aides reminding them of their hours of employment for the next day.

Paraprofessionals can be used to augment a school's staff by performing tasks that do not require the professional skills of the teacher but that do demand the attention of an adult. These people may be paid staff or volunteers. In either case it is important to provide the aides with adequate orientation and training to maximize their use in the schools.

BIBLIOGRAPHY

Castetter, William B. *The Personnel Function in Educational Administration.* New York: Macmillan, 1971.

Hughes, Larry W. *Education and the Law in Tennessee.* Cincinnati, Ohio: W. H. Anderson Co., 1971, esp. chap. 10.

Joyce, Bruce, and Well, Marsha. *Models of Teaching.* Englewood Cliffs, N. J.: Prentice-Hall, 1972.

Martin, Lyn S., and Pavan, Barbara N. "Current Research on Open Space, Nongraded, Vertical Grouping and Team Teaching." *Phi Delta Kappan* 57 (January 1976): 310–15.

Marx, Leo. "Can We Create Together What We Can't Create Alone?" *Change* (Summer 1975): 38–43.

Petrie, Hugh G. "Do You See What I See? The Epistemology of Interdisciplinary Inquiry." *Educational Research* 5 (February 1976): 9–14.

Sorenson, Juanita S.; Poole, Max; and Joyal, Lloyd H. *The Unit Leader and Individually Guided Education.* Reading, Mass.: Addison-Wesley, 1976.

Stoops, Emery, et al. *Handbook of Educational Administration.* Boston: Allyn and Bacon, 1975, esp. chap. 24.

Templeton, Ian. "Differentiated Staffing." *NAESP School Leadership Digest Series* 8 (1974), *ERIC*, ED 095 608.

Zahorik, John A. "Teacher Planning Models." *Educational Leadership* 33 (November 1975): 134–40.

12

Scheduling Staff
and Students

INTRODUCTION

The school schedule is considered by many to be the command performance of the principal. It is here that the ability to conceptualize, to organize, and to carry out detailed planning is most visible. If well done, the schedule will strongly support the instructional and curricular program of the school. On the other hand, if poorly designed, the schedule will be a roadblock to a balanced curriculum and instructional flexibility.

Scheduling can be defined as the plan to bring together people, materials, and curriculum at a designated time and place for the purpose of instruction. Its basic purpose is to coordinate the requirements laid down by previously reached decisions regarding curriculum, instruction, grouping, and staffing.

Several important concepts in scheduling should be reviewed before actually beginning the construction of a schedule. These include the flexibility, simplicity, and complexity of the schedule, the decision level at which schedule changes are made, and the timeliness of the schedule. Other concepts to consider are: previously made decisions concerning the design of curriculum and instruction, staffing and grouping patterns, and space availability and utilization.

Schedule Flexibility

The schedule should have either the potential of being legitimately changed with great frequency or the internal elasticity of meeting a variety of curricular and instructional requests within its regular structure. For example, the teacher who would like to take a group of children on a half-day field trip should be able to do so without disrupting the entire school schedule. Or, the group that needs an extra hour to complete a project should be able to have that hour with an easy adjustment in the schedule.

Simplicity and Complexity

The schedule needs simplicity to prevent interdependence of the components of the schedule, so that the modification of one component does not require the modification of several others. Complexity, on the other hand, is also needed in order to meet the demands of individual differences of students. To meet individual differences, intricate schedule designs need to be constructed. This seemingly creates a paradox. An analogy that seems fitting to describe this relationship is found in the new modularized television sets. The complexity of their circuitry is an amazing example of modern-day technology, but, on the other hand, this complex design is constructed in such a way that if a failure occurs, a circuit module can be removed and replaced very quickly without having to disassemble the entire set once the trouble spot has been identified. So it is with this: a good schedule must permit the complex construction required for individual differences while maintaining simplicity to allow easy changes.

Timeliness of Scheduling Decisions

Timeliness is part of flexibility. Schedules must be designed so that daily and weekly instructional and curricular needs can be met as they occur.

Decision Level

The decision level is the point in the hierarchy of an organization where decisions are made. A basic rule for good decision making in most organizations is that decisions should be made at the lowest level within the organization where adequate information exists for that decision. The application of this rule to scheduling suggests that students and teachers should have maximum involvement in scheduling decisions. At the building level, scheduling should be kept as simple as possible so that the various components can be changed without disrupting the entire school. Also, each building should have maximum control over its schedule and not be frequently subject to the schedules of other schools in the school system. Some traditional areas of conflict such as coordinating bus schedules between schools or scheduling shared teacher specialists require higher-level decisions.

The major conflicts will arise over making up specialists' schedules within the school, in coordinating special areas such as gymnasiums and music rooms, and in scheduling schoolwide programs such as lunch.

SCHEDULING TECHNIQUES

There are several approaches to achieving a good schedule. One of the best is to provide relatively large blocks of time unencumbered by outside influences to teams of teachers and groups of students so they can develop a

Morning	Team Scheduled Block	Team Scheduled Block	T.S.B. P. E. MUSIC	P.E. MUSIC T.S.B.
	LUNCH	LUNCH	LUNCH	LUNCH
Afternoon	Team Scheduled Block P. E. MUSIC	P. E. MUSIC Team Scheduled Block	Team Scheduled Block	Team Scheduled Block

FIGURE 12-1. Block Schedule.

detailed daily schedule to meet curricular and instructional needs. Such a schedule would only have to accommodate special activities such as lunch, physical education, or music. (See Figure 12-1).

Inside these large blocks of time the team of teachers and students plans all of the learning activities. These internal schedules can differ from one day to the next as plans are made by the team reflecting the instructional format, curriculum, groupings, and staffing assignments. Because each of these instructional blocks stands alone, changes within them do not affect the remainder of the school.

Figure 12-2 illustrates a simple form of scheduling within the block of time that can be used by a team of five teachers following a basic rotating design. In this schedule, each teacher has access to each group of children operating in a semidepartmentalized school-within-a-school design. The

	Group A	B	C	D
Block of time	R	SS	SS	M
	SS	SC	M	R
	SC	M	R	SS
	L	L	L	L
	M	R	SS	SC
	P.E.	P.E.	Music Alternate Days	

R Reading
SS Social Studies   Four teachers responsible for
SC Science   groups A–D
L Lunch
M Math

FIGURE 12-2. Block-of-time Rotating Schedule.

schedule does not meet all of the curricular, instructional, and grouping recommendations made in the previous chapter, but it also does not preclude further development to meet the additional criteria. The team has a high degree of autonomy to plan their schedule as they see fit and can modify it as frequently as every day if they choose.

Numerous schedule variations can be created from this basic design. It offers an excellent opportunity to create groups that vary in size as well as the ability to group students according to a variety of special interests and skills patterns.

A team might create small groups for reading instruction by assigning children to instructional groups on a skills basis. Each team member can teach a small group of children by sharing activities and placing children in several different learning activities. To have reading groups of a reasonable size, three teachers of a four-member team can each take ten children in their reading group while the fourth teacher supervises the other children in some form of teacher-planned self-instructional activity. (See Figure 12-3.) Sharing responsibility among teachers within a schedule permits the group variation necessary for good instruction. During additional periods, the schedule can shift so that each teacher has supervisory as well as reading instructions duty. (See Figure 12-4.) An instructional aide could also assist in supervising learning centers and independent study activities, while the rest of the staff directs reading instruction.

Grouping patterns can remain flexible. As the team's planning develops, the internal schedule can change as frequently as needed. Variations for math; the addition of science, or social studies, or language arts activities, including independent study work, and the scheduling of field trips can be built in and designed by teachers without requesting approval from an outside authority. Only when special teachers, facilities, and services for these activities are needed must the team consult and coordinate with the principal at the building level.

Ultimately, how the block schedule is to be used depends on the decisions regarding curriculum, instruction, grouping, and staffing. If teachers are organized in teams, the curriculum has a broad base of subjects, the instructional program is individualized, and the grouping is designed to allow change frequently, the schedule must be designed to be able to accommodate those needs with ease.

	Teacher A	Teacher B	Teacher C	Teacher D
9–9:30	Reading Group 1 10 children	Reading Group 2 10 children	Reading Group 3 10 children	90 children learning centers

FIGURE 12-3. Staffing for Small Skill Groups.

	Teacher A	Teacher B	Teacher C	Teacher D	Aide
9:30–10	R–4 10 children	R–5 10 children	Learning centers 90 children	R–6 10 children	Learning centers
10–10:30	R–7	Learning centers (90)	R–8	R–9	Learning centers
10:30–11	Learning centers (90)	R–10	R–11	R–12	Learning centers

Twelve groups, including those in Figure 12-3 — thirty minutes directed instruction of each group.

FIGURE 12-4. Reading Skill Group Schedule.

SAMPLE SCHEDULE

A sample internal block schedule is shown in Figure 12-5. It is designed to meet the time needs based on the following major tenets:

1. A flexible curriculum (different subjects in different amounts for different students)
2. Individualized instruction (use of learning centers, small skill groups, independent study, and student interest groups)
3. Varied and flexible grouping (skill groups of ten to fifteen for reading and math instruction, interest groups with student advisor direction for learning centers, large heterogeneous grouping for directed instruction, e.g., in science, social studies, and health)
4. Organization of the staff, a team of five teachers and an aide, in a learning community

This schedule is not to be permanent. The reading and math schedules are fairly constant for the teachers each day, but the groups change for the children as they learn their skills and are regrouped in both math and reading.

The schedules for the other subjects change frequently as instruction is planned and group sizes are determined. Students use learning centers in a similar fashion to the old seat-work concept when they have no scheduled group activity. A typical student's schedule corresponding to the above-described teachers' schedule might look like Figure 12-6.

	Teacher A	Teacher B	Teacher C	Teacher D	Teacher E	Aide
8:00			PREPARATION FOR DAY AND FINAL TEAM COORDINATION			
8:30	Children Arrive Group Advisement					Lunch Count Attendance
9:00	Reading 1 (10)	Reading 2 (10)	Social Studies Large Group (50)	Science (50)	Learning Centers (30)	Science
9:30	Writing (25)	Learning Centers (95)	Reading 3 (10)	Reading 4 (10)	Reading 5 (10)	Learning Centers
10:00	Reading 6 (10)	Reading 7 (10)	Social Studies Large Group (50)	Science (50)	Learning Centers (30)	Science
10:30	Writing (25)	Learning Centers (95)	Reading 8 (10)	Reading 9 (10)	Reading 10 (10)	Learning Centers
11:00	Reading 11 (10)	Reading 12 (10)	Social Studies Large Group (50)	Social Studies Large Group (50)	Learning Centers (30)	Science
11:30	Writing (25)	Learning Centers (95)	Reading 13 (10)	Reading 14 (10)	Reading 15 (10)	Learning Centers
12:00	Lunch (duty free)	Lunch (duty free)	Lunch (duty free)	Lunch Supervision	Lunch Supervision	Supervision
12:30	Playground	Playground	Playground	Lunch (duty free)	Lunch (duty free)	Lunch (duty free)
1:00	Math 1 (15)	Math 2 (15)	Math 3 (15)	Health (25)	Learning Centers (80)	Learning Centers
1:30	Learning Centers (55)	Spelling (15)	Learning Centers (50)	Math 4 (15)	Math 5 (15)	Learning Centers
2:00	Math 6 (15)	Math 7 (15)	Math 8 (15)	Health (25)	Learning Centers (80)	Learning Centers
2:30	Learning Centers (55)	Spelling (15)	Learning Centers (50)	Math 9 (15)	Math 10 (15)	Learning Centers
3:00	Group Advisement Cleanup					
3:30	Dismissal	Dismissal	Dismissal	Dismissal	Room Supervision	Bus Load
4:00			PREPARATION TIME			

The number in parentheses indicates the number of children for that activity. Learning Centers are supervised by the teacher indicated but all teachers contribute to their preparation.

FIGURE 12-5. Sample Daily Schedule.

208

8:15 a.m.	Arrive at school
8:30 a.m.	Group advisement, Teacher **A**
9:00 a.m.	SS Teacher **C**
9:30 a.m.	Reading, Teacher **D**
10:00 a.m.	L C, Teacher **E**
10:30 a.m.	Writing, Teacher **A**
11:00 a.m.	Science, Teacher **D**
11:30 a.m.	L C, Teacher **B**
12:00 a.m.	Lunch
12:30 p.m.	Playground
1:00 p.m.	Health, Teacher **D**
1:30 p.m.	Math, Teacher **D**
2:00 p.m.	L C, Teacher **E**
2:30 p.m.	L C, Teacher **C**
3:00 p.m.	Group advisement, Teacher **A**
3:30 p.m.	Go home

FIGURE 12-6. Student's Daily Schedule.

A child's daily schedule is based on skill groups. Since children are grouped in the morning on a skills basis for reading, reading then becomes the grouping basis to direct children to all other subjects during the morning. In the afternoon the math groups become the organizational block in which children are directed to the other group activities. This provides homogeneous grouping according to skills in reading and math and heterogeneous grouping in all other subject areas. The only exception to this rule occurs when children are allowed to group themselves on an interest basis for other activities while not in reading or math.

The schedule can be simplified or made more complex as the situation changes. Skill in scheduling evolves with practice and time. Adequate team planning is an essential component to making the schedule function properly.

TEAM PLANNING TIME

One of the most important features of any schedule involving team teaching is the provision of adequate team planning time. Every teacher should have a minimum of five hours each week for planning and materials preparation. Much of this time must be in common with other members of the team. Teachers usually prefer to arrange this time in several large blocks rather than divide it into many small segments. Teachers and aides can occasionally alternate supervision, giving each team member some time for planning or materials preparation. However, extended planning sessions where all team members are present is also a must.

Team planning time can usually be best arranged on a schoolwide basis using parallel scheduling. Parallel scheduling provides large blocks of planning time through the use of specialists. The staff must include three or four full-

	Monday	Tuesday	Wednesday	Thursday	Friday
Morning	Specialists Replace Team A	Replace Team C	Replace Team E or Specialist Planning	Replace Team B	Replace Team D
Afternoon	Replace Team B	Replace Team D	Replace Team A	Replace Team C	Replace Team E or Specialist Planning*

*In a five-team school the specialists use an extended duty-free lunch for planning.

FIGURE 12-7. Team Weekly Parallel Schedule.

time specialists such as music teachers, art teachers, and physical education teachers. These teachers are scheduled in a design paralleling that of the regular teaching staff so the specialists can replace each of the regular teaching team members, freeing them from all of the children in their learning community for a given block of time. The specialists then work in rotation with these children from one team for a period of one or more hours. (See Figure 12-7.) Specialists can handle additional children if there are more specialists available or if an aide can work with a specialist and increase group size. The specialists work with each group of children so that, within a one- or two-day period, they replace each team (the team organization used here is the one shown in Figure 12-3).

These examples of schedules are meant only to be suggestions to generate ideas. Many variations can be developed from these different models. Each school and each team must develop a schedule of their own, tailored to meet their individual needs. It is important to let the schedule follow the demands of the curricular and instructional program and the student grouping and staffing patterns and not allow the schedule to dictate the rest of the program.

MIDDLE-SCHOOL SCHEDULES

Middle schools have unique problems in scheduling teachers and students. If staff members hold only secondary teachers' certification, they are limited in the number of subjects they may teach. Also, since the material being taught becomes more complicated in the higher grades, more daily preparation time by the teachers is necessary. This is difficult if each teacher is responsible for a large number of subjects. On the student side, the range of differences in abilities during the middle-school years becomes greater and greater (see Figure 6-1), suggesting the need for more skilled grouping.

The block schedule shown in Figure 12-1 is probably the best design for a schoolwide schedule in the middle school, along with the following ideas to be used for the internal team schedule.

Achievement grouping is recommended for use in reading and math instruction because of the relatively large span of abilities in the middle school. In addition, the fact that curriculum tends to be organized according to skill levels in these two subjects makes them the best candidates for this technique. Most other areas of the curriculum should use heterogeneous grouping, in that the overuse of ability grouping is more damaging to students than beneficial (if too much is used, it negatively affects student self-concepts, peer roles, and teacher attitudes).

Homogeneous grouping is more successful in improving learning when the curriculum is modified for the homogeneous grouping, i.e., when reading and math skills learning continues. When homogeneous grouping is used, the criteria for grouping must specifically match the curricular area, e. g., total reading scores for reading groups; math scores for math groups. Grouping on the basis of things like an I. Q. score is much too general and should not be used.

It is almost impossible from a scheduling standpoint to group more than two subjects if each teacher teaches a separate subject. The schedule shown in Figure 12-8 will allow homogeneous grouping in reading with good flexibility in assigning and moving students, because all four teachers will be teaching reading at the same time.

The math teacher can homogeneously group children during periods 2 through 5 into four or eight levels for mathematics. However, this schedule may fail to meet the specification of heterogeneity for social studies, science, and language arts because the math grouping will spill over into these subjects; the good math students will stay together in science, period 3; social studies, period 4; and language arts, period 5.

The problem with homogeneous grouping, carrying over in an undesirable manner, can be corrected, however. In order to meet the correct specifications, a matrix must be designed that will undo the grouping created by a subject such as math that runs parallel to social studies, science, and language arts. The matrix must reassign the math groups to bring about the desired heterogeneity. This can be done by assigning each of the math classes a series of scheduling numbers and placing children in groups of four or five (called modules.)

These subgroups for the math grouping can then be dispersed through the other classes in an orderly manner.

The first column (math) of Figure 12-9 assigns each succeeding group of five math students a number. The top five math students are assigned number 1. The lowest five math students are given number 24. This number assigned to them in math class is then used to disperse them, thus creating heterogeneous grouping in the other three subjects.

Teacher Period	A	B	C	D
1	Reading Groups A–E	Reading Groups B–F	Reading Groups C–G	Reading Groups D–H
2	Math 1	Science	Social Studies	Language Arts
3	Math 2	Science	Social Studies	Language Arts
4	Math 3	Science	Social Studies	Language Arts
5	Math 4	Science	Social Studies	Language Arts

FIGURE 12-8. Middle-School Team Schedule.

A schedule for a four-teacher middle-school team might carry the following specifications. Many variations of these assignments are possible, however.

all teachers teach reading—reading is divided into eight skill levels

one teacher teaches math—math is divided into four or more skill levels

one teacher teaches social studies ⎤ these classes are to be grouped
one teacher teaches science ⎟ heterogeneously and not reflect
one teacher teaches language arts ⎦ either the math or reading
⠀⠀⠀⠀⠀⠀⠀⠀⠀⠀⠀⠀⠀⠀⠀⠀⠀⠀⠀⠀⠀⠀⠀⠀grouping

Home Base: Heterogeneous groups   2 subjects each teacher
Reading: Skill groups — 8 groups
Math: Skill groups — each math module contains 5 students — 120 total
Other Subject: Heterogeneous groups

Teacher Period	Home base heterogeneous	Home base heterogeneous	Home base heterogeneous	Home base heterogeneous
1	(Heterogeneous groups are created by rank ordering on reading scores with each home base receiving every fourth card.)			
2	Reading skill groups A,E	Reading skill groups B,F	Reading skill groups C,G	Reading skill groups D,H
3	Math homogeneous groups 1　　4 2　　5 3　　6	Language Arts 7　　16 10　　19 13　　22	Science 8　　17 11　　20 14　　23	Social Studies 9　　18 12　　21 15　　24
4	Math 7　　10 8　　11 9　　12	Language Arts 15　　24 18　　3 21　　6	Science 13　　22 16　　1 19　　4	Social Studies 14　　23 17　　2 20　　5
5	Math 13　　16 14　　17 15　　18	Language Arts 20　　5 23　　8 2　　11	Science 21　　6 24　　9 3　　12	Social Studies 19　　4 22　　7 1　　10
6	Math 19　　22 20　　23 21　　24	Language Arts 1　　12 4　　15 9　　17	Science 2　　10 5　　14 7　　18	Social Studies 3　　11 6　　13 8　　16

7, 8 Lunch-activity period — Art — Music — PE — Health — Guidance — etc.

FIGURE 12-9. Middle-School Team Schedule—Four-Teacher Team.

SUMMARY

Scheduling has as its basic purpose the bringing together of curriculum, staff, and students for the purpose of instruction. It must be kept flexible, allowing for changes in group size and instructional time. Schedules must also provide for adequate staff planning and allow major scheduling decisions to be made by the team. Block-of-time schedules assigned to the team and parallel scheduling for team planning offer good solutions to scheduling demands.

BIBLIOGRAPHY

Hillson, Mourie, and Bongo, Joseph. *Continuous Progress Education: A Practical Approach.* Palo Alto, Calif.: Science Research Associates, 1971.

Ubben, Gerald C. "A Fluid Block Schedule." *NASSP Bulletin* 60, no. 397 (February 1976): 104–11.

13

Staffing the School: Recruitment, Selection, and Termination

INTRODUCTION

Recruitment and selection policies of local schools vary. The principal's involvement in the recruitment and selection process will depend on local district practice and policy. Central office personnel often assume the initial responsibility for the recruitment and screening of applicants for teaching positions. The principal should maintain a major role in the process and aggressively pursue it, if necessary. Central offices, often as a means of expediency and sometimes as a policy of control, tend to limit the input of principals and staff in the selection process. If the principal is to be held in any way accountable for the quality of instruction in his or her building, he or she must have a major voice in the selection of personnel.

RECRUITMENT

The major recruitment efforts of the principal begin with good position and person descriptions. Figures 13-1 and 13-2 depict sample position and person descriptions. If the principal finds it difficult to locate appropriate candidates, central office personnel should be contacted to review the recruitment process. For example, if the principal, in an effort to diversify the staff, has asked for a teacher from somewhere other than the local college and the personnel office has not posted vacancies at other colleges, the recruitment drive will be ineffective. The principal is responsible for seeing that recruitment policies are broad enough to meet personnel needs.

Lakeview Schools
219 Lakeview Ave.
Lake City

PERSON DESCRIPTION

Position: Elementary Teacher.
Sex: Prefer male.
Teaching Experience Necessary: None.
Training Requirements: BS; prefer graduates from other than local college.
Certification: Elementary, K–3.
Teaching Strength: Strong reading training, interest in social studies.
Other Skills: Prefer someone with training or experience with team teaching or I.G.E.
Other Interests: Prefer someone with avocational interests that would appeal to young boys such as camping, hiking, model airplane making, and so on.

FIGURE 13-1.

Lakeview Schools
219 Lakeview Ave.
Lake City

POSITION DESCRIPTION

Position Title: Teacher (team) grade level Elementary 1 – 3.
Purpose of Position: To plan, organize, and instruct primary children.
Starting Date:
Salary Range: Beginning teacher, B.S. – $13,000
　　　　　　　　　　　　　M.S. – $15,000
Principal Duties: The teacher will be a member of a four-teacher team working with six- to eight-year-old children. Instruction is organized on an interdisciplinary basis with cooperative planning units. The team has four assigned classrooms and schedules children in a flexible manner into these spaces. Major instructional responsibilities will include reading and mathematics as well as participation in the integration of other subjects.

Performance Responsibilities:

I. Instructional Skills

A. Knowledge and Training
1. Is academically competent in assigned teaching areas.
2. Keeps abreast of new findings and current trends in the field.
3. Remains open-minded and willing to grow and change.
4. Provides opportunities for all students to experience success.

B. Classroom Environment and Management
1. Maintains a classroom environment conducive to learning (by using special interest areas, learning centers, units, themes, furniture arrangements, proper lighting, heating, ventilation, and structured rules and regulations understood and accepted by all).
2. Monitors individual pupil progress and adapts the pace of instruction accordingly.
3. Uses democratic procedures that show consideration for the rights of others.

C. Methods and Techniques
1. Uses a variety of stimulating instructional techniques (such as the lecture method, demonstration, self-directed activities, both small and large group activities (drill and rote activities), and community resources, audiovisual aids and individualized programs).
2. Demonstrates and fosters the growth of communication skills.
3. Presents subject matter in a functional manner.
4. Makes homework assignments for meaningful instructional purposes.

D. Planning
1. Establishes short- and long-range goals with well-defined objectives and identifies appropriate procedures to accomplish them. (Example: A minimum competency and curriculum guide.)
2. Provides opportunities for all students to experience success.
3. Has a well-defined alternative plan for substitute teachers.

E. Evaluation
1. Provides feedback to students on their accomplishments and progress with positive and effective reinforcements.
2. Uses instruments based on activity, objective, or goal-oriented criteria.
3. Guides students toward self-motivation, self-evaluation, and self-direction.

II. Student Attitudes and Performance

A. Demonstrates consistency, firmness and impartiality in dealing with students in a professional manner

B. Appreciates individuality.

C. Shows positive attitudes toward students by helping all children experience success, possibly through the use of tutorial and counseling activities.

D. Promotes desirable standards of work and behavior within the classroom.

III. Personal Qualities

A. Demonstrates a positive and enthusiastic attitude and a genuine interest in students, colleagues, curriculum, and the education field in general.

B. Recognizes and capitalizes on his or her own assets, thereby projecting a good model for students in dress, demeanor, and speech.

C. Is able to profit from constructive criticism.

D. Shows qualities that reflect the importance of punctuality, efficiency, dependability, accuracy, and congeniality.

IV. Professional Growth and Development
   A. Participates in enrichment activities, including such activities as study in his or her field and/or travel.
   B. Actively pursues avenues of personal and professional growth through workshops, classes, professional organizations, and seminars.
   C. Establishes personal goals for professional development.
V. Teacher Relationships
   A. Teacher-Parent
      1. Establishes an effective line of communication between home and school via notes, conferences, written reports, work samples, telephone conversations, and meetings of groups such as the PTO that stress discussion of students' strengths and weaknesses.
      2. Encourages parents to form a partnership with the teacher in the total education of their child—mentally, emotionally, physically, and spiritually.
   B. Teacher-Community
      1. Works effectively with legitimate community organizations and identifies and utilizes community resources to augment the educational opportunities of the children.
      2. Projects a positive image of the total school program to your community; liaison function is served.
   C. Teacher-Teacher
      1. Cooperates fully with colleagues in shared responsibilities.
      2. Shows tolerance for peer differences.
      3. Shares experiences, ideas, and knowledge with peers.
      4. Communicates effectively with other teachers who have shared or will share the same students for the purpose of developing smooth continuity between grade levels and subject matter.
   D. Teacher-Administrator-Supervisor
      1. Understands and adheres to the chain of command.
      2. Participates in decision making when appropriate.
      3. Demonstrates cooperation in performing both classroom and extra duties.
      4. Seeks advice and counsel when needed.
      5. Forms a partnership to develop good public relations in the school district.
   E. Teacher-Student
      1. Recognizes the uniqueness of all students.
      2. Guides and encourages students in a friendly, constructive, and impartial manner.
      3. Initiates procedures that will invite regular feedback for students.
      4. Maintains a classroom atmosphere conducive to mutual respect, one that adequately establishes appropriate roles.

FIGURE 13-2.

The selection of personnel should be a cooperative effort between the district personnel office and the local school. The central-office role is to screen applicants and then to send those best matching the position descriptions to the principal for final selection. In some large school districts, a personnel office may employ teachers unassigned to specific buildings, but even in this case, the building principal should have the final decision regarding who works in the building.

FEDERAL REGULATIONS TO PREVENT DISCRIMINATION OF EMPLOYMENT

Care must always be taken to abide by the federal laws regarding recruitment and selection of staff. The Civil Rights Act of 1964 and the Equal Employment Opportunity Act of 1972 make it unlawful to discriminate on the basis of race, color, religion, sex, or national origin.

EEOC Regulations

It is unlawful to ask about the following on either a written application or during an interview.

1. Complexion or color of skin.
2. Applicant's religious denomination, affiliation, church, parish, pastor, or religious holidays observed.
3. Applicant's sex, marital status, name or other information about spouse, or ages of children if any.
4. Whether applicant has a disability or has been treated for any of certain diseases; (however, you may ask if the applicant has any physical impairments that would affect the ability to perform the job for which the applicant has applied).
5. If the applicant has ever been arrested. (You may ask if the applicant has been convicted of a crime.)
6. Any previous name that the applicant has used. (You may ask if he or she worked for your organization under a different name, i.e. a maiden name.)
7. Birthplace or birthplace of applicant's parents or spouse; birthdate or certificate or naturalization papers, and so on.
8. Require the applicant's photograph before hiring.
9. Whether the applicant or a relative is a citizen of a foreign country. (You may ask if the applicant is a U. S. citizen, intends to become one, or has a legal right to be in the United States.)
10. The applicant's native language. (You may ask which languages the applicant speaks and writes.)
11. Questions or information about the applicant's relatives. (Prior to employment, you may not even ask the name of a person to contact in case of emergency.)

12. The clubs, societies, and lodges to which the applicant belongs. (You may ask the applicant to list organizations he or she believes to be pertinent to the job.)

After the individual has been employed, many of these items of information can then legally be asked on an employee information form but cannot appear or be asked on an application or during an interview.

THE SELECTION PROCESS

The selection process has several steps. The first is application clarification. Prior to an interview, the principal should carefully review the candidate's application file, comparing the application with the personal description. Few candidates will possess all the qualifications that have been specified, but the principal should try to find candidates with most of them.[1]

The second step in the selection process should be a discrepancy analysis of the application materials. Applicants present themselves in the best manner possible, minimizing weak points. One technique used to uncover discrepancies is to search the file for missing information. Common problem areas are efforts to conceal unfavorable past activities by excluding dates and not listing appropriate reference sources. Other things to check for include health and legal problems.

The reviewer should look particularly at references from previous employers to make sure each employment situation is represented. Read between the lines on health records. Look for gaps in employment or school records. The interviewer can request more detailed explanations concerning those areas where possible discrepancies have been identified. Most often, candidates will give perfectly acceptable explanations regarding the discrepancies, but occasionally interviews uncover serious problems by a discrepancy review.

If the job candidate has had previous teaching experience and is one of the final candidates being considered for the position, a personal telephone contact with the previous principal or some other school administrator who is acquainted with the candidate is usually helpful. Often, interviewers can obtain more information during a phone call than from a written reference.

The Job Interview

The job interview has several basic functions. It provides an opportunity for the candidate to clarify any apparent discrepancies found in the written job application. The job interview, however, goes beyond the written application by

---

[1]Gerald C. Ubben, "Selecting Personnel," *Principal's Audio Journal* 1 (December 1974). Cassette Services, St. Paul, Virginia.

allowing the principal to gather information in greater depth than can be obtained from written materials only.

Another purpose of the interview is to gain insights into the personality and interpersonal skills of the applicant. Teaching is a "people" business, and teachers must be able to relate well to other adults and children. Research has shown that good verbal skills are particularly significant in determining the quality of a teacher. These skills can best be assessed through an interview.

If the interview can be arranged in the school where employment is to take place, it is helpful to involve teachers from the staff in the interview process. Department heads particularly should play a major role in interviewing prospective teachers for their departments. Teaching teams should always have the opportunity to interview a prospective new teacher in order to focus on personality match and compatibility of educational philosophy and to discuss how the current staff functions. Whenever possible, an employment recommendation should be based on group interaction with the principal and the existing staff.

Finally, in an interview a candidate must receive, as well as give, information. Two decisions must be made before employment can take place: your decision to employ the candidate and the candidate's decision to work in your school. The candidate needs a good information base from which to make this decision. This offering of information to the candidate should include an expansion of the position description providing more detail about the organization and philosophy of the school and the kinds of children who attend. Also, the specific assignment as well as the working conditions should be outlined. If the candidate is not from a local area, a brief orientation to the community might be helpful. Many principals or recruiting officers prepare a brief slide presentation on their community.

At the close of the interview, the principal should outline the next steps. If a decision has been made not to employ, the individual should know. The principal should indicate whether more candidates are to be interviewed before the final decision and should state an approximate date for the final decision. The candidate should also know the principal's authority is simply to recommend to the central office. In addition, contract information and such specifics as when the school year begins, what the individual might do in the meantime to prepare, and when the new employee might expect to receive the first paycheck should also be discussed.

The selection process does not end there but should continue through the first several years of employment until the recommendation for permanent employment tenure.

EMPLOYEE PROBATIONARY STATUS

The selection process for staff continues through the probationary phase. Most states have a one-to-three-year probationary period during which

the employee is on a continuing contract before receiving tenured employment. During this period, the principal and department head must reaffirm
the original decision to employ a particular staff member. Usually the contract
renews automatically around April 15 unless notification is given to the
teacher for nonrenewal. Through the continuation of the orientation phase and
evaluation of instructional competence, which is discussed in more detail in a
subsequent chapter, the emphasis for staff development is upon improving the
quality of teaching. The selection process is usually considered complete only
when tenure is granted. During this probationary period, the principal must
consider the possibility of termination or nonrenewal of the contract when
there is reason to suspect that the original selection was not wise.

TEACHER TENURE

One of the most misunderstood concerns in education is tenure.[2] It
is not, as often believed, a guarantee of a job from which dismissal is all but
impossible. Rather, in most states, tenure is simply a statement of the guarantee of due process assuring exercise of academic freedom for the teacher by allowing dismissal only for specific causes listed in the tenure law. Tenure does
not guarantee the right to a job. If the job is abolished or a teacher is found to
be incompetent, insubordinate, or guilty of a variety of socially unacceptable
behaviors, that teacher can be dismissed, with proper due process.

In the last few years, federal courts have broadened their decisions regarding due process and human rights to the point that due-process guarantees, including many of the guarantees found in the tenure laws, have been
extended to most employees. As a result probationary teachers are now guaranteed many of the same due-process rights afforded tenured teachers in the
past.[3]

INVOLUNTARY TERMINATION

An extremely poor or incompetent teacher should never be kept
on the staff of a school simply because dismissal is difficult. The law establishes definite rights for employer and employee. Procedural due process is
guaranteed, but due process does not mean that teachers cannot be dismissed.
What it does mean is that teachers have specific rights, such as the right to a

---

[2]A good discussion of the future of tenure can be found in Larry W. Hughes and William
M. Gordon, "Frontiers of Law," *The Courts and Education*, 77th Yearbook of the National Society for the Study of Education, ed. Clifford Hooker (Chicago: University of Chicago Press, 1978),
final chapter.

[3]See Chapter 5 for information about the steps in procedural due process.

hearing, the right to be treated in a fair and nondiscriminatory fashion, and the right to require that just cause be shown for a dismissal action. The law may be more specific about the causes and process of dismissal for teachers under tenure, but dismissal can still be accomplished.

Every dismissal action should be carried out on the assumption that it will ultimately go to court. This attitude is the best way to prevent court action. Rarely will an attorney engaged by a dismissed teacher or provided by a teacher association take a case to court if the school district has prepared its action carefully. When the courts reject the dismissal and order reinstatement of a teacher, it is most often because of improper procedure on the part of the school district and less likely directly due to teacher behavior.

Preparation for Dismissal

Dismissal decisions should not be made quickly. A tentative decision not to rehire a first-year teacher for the following year should be contemplated three to four months before the deadline for contract renewal. For a tenured teacher, often two or three years are needed to build a case defensible in court to reverse earlier recommendations that were positive enough to have resulted in tenure, even though the recommendations may have been a mistake. Unfortunately, poor personnel records and poor evaluation procedures are common in school districts.

The defense attorney will often demand to see the entire personnel file for a teacher being dismissed. If positive evaluations have been given in the past, even though they were unjustified, a greater collection of data of a negative nature is required to offset them. Evidence that the teacher received specific notice of inadequacy and was offered help is important.

In a hearing, the courts will try to answer the following questions: Was procedural due process used? Is the evidence appropriate and supportive of the case? Was the employee discriminated against? Were efforts made to help the employee? Did the employee have prior knowledge that his or her work was unsatisfactory? Was the employee provided time and the opportunity to improve or correct whatever deficiencies existed?

Due Process

Teachers must be given timely notice of the decision not to rehire. If contract renewal comes on April 15, with a two-week hearing notice deadline, employees should be notified by April 1. A certified letter is the best way of assuring a record of such notification. Employees must be informed that they have the opportunity for and the right to a hearing. The hearing time, date, and place should be stated in the letter. If the teacher is tenured, the letter should also include the specific causes or charges for dismissal. Recent due-process decisions from the courts in some cases make it highly advisable to provide this opportunity for a hearing to nontenured teachers as well as to those who have tenure.[4,5,6]

Appropriateness of Evidence

Evidence should be firsthand, factual, and documented accurately with appropriate dates. If the offense is cumulative in nature, the collection of data should also be cumulative. Descriptive notes of supervisory meetings and conferences, for example, expressing agreed-upon outcomes and a statement describing the extent of the implementation or the lack thereof on the part of the teacher should be included. The statements should be objective. Rather than stating "This teacher did a poor job of teaching today," the note should state that in presenting a lesson on the Civil War the teacher did not hold the interest of the class, the students did not understand the lesson as presented, and the class became unruly while under the teacher's direction. Include the date; the time; the events that led up to the conference, such as the previous involvement of a supervisor; and any immediate followup action that was taken. A note might simply read, "Mr. Smith arrived at school at 8:30 on December 2, 3, and 4. His designated time of arrival is 8:00. He has been notified of this deficiency." This is not a judgmental statement but a simple statement of fact. Such items, properly collected, can be used to support a claim of incompetence, neglect of duty, or insubordination. The important thing to remember is to record facts, not opinions, and to do this in a timely fashion.

---

[4]See Chapter 5, especially the reference to Illinois Education Association v. Board of Education, 320 N.E. 2nd 240 (Ill. App. 1974).

[5]Cases Related to Due Process—Teacher Dismissal

a. Board of Regents v. Roth, 92 S. Ct. 2701 (1972) and Perry v. Sunderman, 928 Ct. 2694 (1972). These are the precedent-setting cases regarding due process just as Brown v. Board of Education set the precedent for discrimination cases.

b. Paul v. Davis 424 U.S. 693 (1976); Bishop v. Wood 246 U.S. 341 (1976); and Meachum v. Fano 427 U.S. 215 (1970).

c. 7th Cir., the Court of Appeals in Confederation of Police v. City of Chicago 547 F. 2d 375 (1977).

d. Codd v. Velger 97 S. Ct. 882 (1977).

e. Arnet v. Kennedy 416 U.S. 134 (1974).

f. Peacock v. Board of Regents 510 F 2d 1324 (9th Cir.)

g. Withrow v. Larken (421 U.S. 35, 1975).

h. Hortonville 96S Ct. 2308.

i. Mt. Healthy City School District v. Doyle 97 S. Ct. 568 (1977).

[6]While most state tenure laws and continuing contract laws in and of themselves do not require a hearing for nontenured staff, the federal Constitution and the Civil Rights Act of 1964 might. According to a series of court decisions over recent years, a teacher is considered to have certain rights under the First and Fourteenth Amendments to the Constitution. While nonrenewal of a contract does not require a hearing, dismissal does. If a denial-of-freedom-of-speech claim is made, a hearing is advisable, and if the case is receiving much publicity so as to endanger the individual's opportunity for other employment, a hearing should be held. Also, if discrimination is charged, a hearing should be held. If an opportunity for a hearing is not granted, the teacher may later file a complaint charging violation of due process.

Equal Rights

Was the employee treated in a fair and nondiscriminatory manner? Was anything done to or for this employee that was not done or available to other employees? Was the assignment unfair? Was the teacher asked to do more or less than the rest of the staff? Was supervision uniform? A grossly unequal schedule for supervision, for example, can be construed to be harassment. When problems arise, however, it is not unreasonable for supervision to increase as long as the time sequence can be demonstrated. Supervisory appointments and documentation included only in the file of the teacher being dismissed with no evidence of supervision included in the files of the other members of the staff, however, will often be looked upon as discriminatory action by the courts.

Were Efforts Made to Help the Teacher? The courts will want to know what was done to make this individual an effective employee. Was adequate supervision of a helping nature developed? Was adequate time given for the improvement effort? If not, the courts may not uphold the dismissal action but may reinstate the employee, suggesting that the supervisory staff provide assistance.

Most often, when the principal is well prepared and has central-office support, teacher dismissal, while serious, will take place quietly. A teacher who knows that school officials are well prepared most often will not request a hearing and will simply resign. Most cases resulting in the failure to dismiss are a result of poor preparation and improper procedure on the part of the school district. See Figure 13-3 for a flowchart for employee dismissal procedures.

Reduction in Force

Loss of enrollments and reductions in funding in recent years have forced many school systems to reduce the number of staff members employed. Often the policies directing these staff reductions are outside the authority of the principal to control but rather are determined by school board policy or by teacher master contract. There are, however, a number of measures a principal can take when it appears that a reduction in force (RIF) is approaching.

1. If as much as two years are available before RIF there is still time to do the thorough job of staff evaluation that should have been done all along. This may provide an opportunity to eliminate the weaker members of the staff if the principal has gathered adequate evidence and documentation to actually show them to be the weaker.

2. If policies or regulations prescribe that reductions in force are to be made by position; that is, that a given position is eliminated and the person holding that position is the one who must leave, then the principal can have some control over who goes by seeing that that person had previously been placed in the position most likely to be eliminated. This position might be a

Begin here

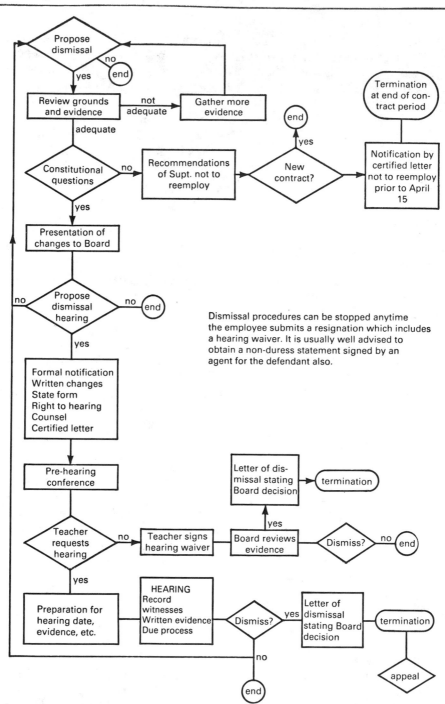

FIGURE 13-3. Steps in Dismissal Procedures.

split third- and fourth-grade post or an additional section of first grade, or whatever.

3. Teachers who are most likely to be affected by a reduction in force should at least informally be given as much warning as possible regarding the likelihood of their being "RIFed." This not only allows these individuals to begin making plans for other employment; it also increases the morale of the remaining staff members by reducing the rumors about who is going to be losing their jobs.

4. Encouraging the retirement of eligible members of the staff in order for others to keep their positions is another way a RIF can be made less destructive.

5. Job sharing is another idea that has met with much success when teaching positions have had to be reduced. Rather than one member of a staff losing his or her position, two staff members each assume a half-time assignment sharing a classroom, with one working the morning and the other the afternoon. Often the benefit to the school district is greater than that of having one full-time teacher because of additional time that is available for preparation and the reduction in fatigue that occurs.

VOLUNTARY TERMINATIONS

Each year staff members will resign from a school for a variety of reasons: retirement, transfers, better jobs, starting a family, going back to school, and incompetence. In every case the principal should hold a termination interview before that person departs. Several basic purposes exist for such an interview. Of primary concern is the help the school might offer the individual in adjusting to a new life situation.

Second, the interview should be an opportunity to investigate the perceptions of the departing employee regarding the operation of the school. At times principals have difficulty getting good information about the operation of the school and the existing climate within the staff. Often, departing employees will be very candid about their perceptions concerning existing problems. They may even identify some previously hidden reason for leaving.

Finally, the interview can be useful in identifying prospects for substitute, part-time, volunteer, and future employment when the departing employee is planning to remain within the community. Retired teachers, or those who are staying home to rear a family, are particularly good candidates for part-time employment or volunteer positions.

SUMMARY

The search for and the employment of new staff members is one of the most important tasks of a school administrator. The process begins with the determination of staff needs, including recruitment, selection, orientation, and staff development, and culminates with the placement of the employee on tenure.

Termination of employees, voluntarily or involuntarily, will occur in most schools each year. The principal needs to conduct exit interviews with all terminating employees. Involuntary termination is usually a difficult, but sometimes necessary, task. An important point in staff dismissal is following due process and insuring that the employee's rights have not been violated.

BIBLIOGRAPHY

Beach, Dale S. *Personnel: The Management of People at Work,* 2nd ed. New York: MacMillan, 1970.

Bishop, Leslee J. *Staff Development and Instructional Improvement.* Boston: Allyn and Bacon, Inc., 1976.

Bolton, Dale L. *Selection and Evaluation of Teachers.* Berkeley, Calif.: McCutchan Publishing Corp., 1973.

Castetter, William B. *The Personnel Function in Educational Administration.* New York: MacMillan, 1976.

Crowe, Robert L. "The Computer and Personnel Selection." *School Management* 16 (August 1972): 40.

Dipboye, Robert L.; Avery, Richard D.; and Terpstra, David E. "Sex and Physical Attractiveness of Raters and Applicants as Determined by Resume Evaluations." *Journal of Applied Psychology* 62 (June 1977): 288–94.

Drake, Frances S. "The Interviewer and His Art." *The Personnel Man and His Job.* New York: American Management Association, 1962.

"Evaluating School Personnel." *National Elementary Principal* 52 (February 1973): 12–100. The entire volume is devoted to evaluating personnel.

Flippo, Edwin B. *Principles of Personnel Management.* New York: McGraw-Hill, 1971.

Hooker, Clifford, ed. *The Courts and Education, 77th Yearbook of the National Society for the Study of Education.* Chicago: University of Chicago Press, 1978, esp. the chapter entitled, "Frontiers of Law."

Hughes, Larry W., and Ubben, Gerald C. *The Elementary Principal's Handbook: A Guide to Effective Action.* Boston: Allyn and Bacon, 1978.

Hyman, Ronald T. *School Administrator's Handbook of Teacher Supervision and Evaluation Methods.* Englewood Cliffs, N. J.: Prentice-Hall, Inc., 1975.

McKenna, Bernard H., and McKenna, Charles D. "How to Interview Teachers." *American School Board Journal,* 155 (June 1968): 8–9.

Redfern, George B. *How to Appraise Teaching Performance.* Columbus, Ohio: School Management Institute, Inc., 1963.

14

The Principal as
Supervisor and Evaluator

INTRODUCTION

Staff development and evaluation are essential activities of the elementary school principal. Just as a teacher manages student learning by using a diagnostic prescriptive model, so can the principal direct staff development using staff evaluation as a diagnostic tool and an evaluation-by-objectives approach as a prescriptive tool. For proper staff development and evaluation the principal must take an initiating, rather than reacting role, and the comprehensive plan for staff evaluation must be based on a sound rationale.

Staff evaluation has two basic purposes: (1) to improve the performance and provide direction for the continued development of present staff; and (2) to provide a sound basis for personnel decisions such as awarding of tenure, promotions, transfers, or dismissals.

These two purposes create a dilemma for many administrators, even though both support quality education. Staff improvement is largely a helping relationship most effectively carried out when built on trust between the teacher and the principal. Personnel decisions are judgmental in nature and can cause teacher apprehension.

Characteristics of a Good Evaluation Plan

A desirable evaluation model should include the following specific characteristics:

1. The opportunity for teachers to establish individual goals or job targets based on individual needs as well as schoolwide goals for total staff development.
2. Participation by both the individual and the supervisor in setting goals with a provision for input from other appropriate groups.

3. A plan to identify activities by which goals or targets might be reached.

4. A list of instruments to be used for data collection, including observation guides, checklists, and survey forms.

5. Data collection on teacher performance from appropriate information sources, including students, parents, administrators, peers, and self.

6. A uniform means of summarizing, analyzing, and interpreting observation data.

7. A means of providing evaluative feedback directly to the teacher or through the immediate supervisor or principal.

8. A means of recording evaluative information to be used for personnel decisions.

9. A means of using evaluative information for individual staff development as the basis for setting new job targets.

10. A means of collecting evaluative data as the basis for planning building-level or district-level staff development activities.

ATTRIBUTES OF AN EVALUATION MODEL

Each school district should develop a set of suitable evaluation procedures. A staff evaluation plan should include the following basic considerations as desired attributes of an evaluation system.

1. *Development of a Positive Teacher Attitude.* Every evaluation plan should make a strong effort to create a positive teacher attitude. Teachers should want and anticipate evaluation because of the insights they will gain.

2. *Multiple Performance Perceptions.* The data collection phase of evaluation should include the gathering of information about teacher performance from all appropriate sources such as students, parents, administrators, and other community representatives with a legitimate contribution.

3. *Teacher Participation.* Teachers should take part in the development or selection of observation instruments, checklists, and summary sheets that make up the evaluation package so that they will know the criteria and process by which they are being judged.

4. *Comprehensiveness.* The evaluation process must be comprehensive, reflecting all aspects of the daily working environment of the staff. When an evaluation component reviews only a portion of work responsibility, it should be kept in proper perspective in relation to the total work load.

5. *Stated Philosophy and Objectives.* The evaluation process should be based on local philosophy and objectives. Individual evaluations should be designed to consider the particular goals and objectives of

the staff member while keeping in mind the overall goals of the school.

6. *Self-improvement Focus.* The evaluation process must recognize that from the vantage point of staff development the end product is one of self-improvement.

7. *Validity and Reliability.* The evaluation design must emphasize the truly significant aspects of job performance and measure them with a high degree of accuracy and consistency. The use of multiple perceptions by one or more evaluators usually improves validity and reliability.

8. *Good Use of Time.* The evaluation procedure must not take too much time but should take enough time to ensure justness and fairness.

9. *Benefits.* The evaluation system must improve staff performance in order to justify the cost of its operation.

These nine considerations provide the underpinning for the development of an evaluation plan. Based on these considerations, a number of different evaluation processes are possible.

THE STAFF EVALUATION CYCLE

Staff evaluation and development is a cyclical process. Staff evaluation leads to a staff development prescription that is checked once again through evaluation.

Seven basic steps in the evaluation cycle focus on the ultimate purpose of improving instruction. The cycle begins when the teacher and principal plan goals and targets for the year and include other people in the evaluation process during the year. (See Figure 14-1.) The seven steps of the evaluation cycle are as follows:

1. Identify and integrate individual and institutional goals.
2. Select specific objectives or activities for observation.
3. Determine the observation method, time, and place.
4. Observe and collect data.
5. Analyze data and provide feedback.
6. Summarize and interpret collective observational data.
7. Report evaluation results, target achievement, and make recommendations for individual and staff development at annual conference.

The Identification and Integration of Individual and Institutional Goals

Goal Identification (Step 1). To maximize improvement of instruction, a necessary first step in the evaluation of instruction is goal identification. A

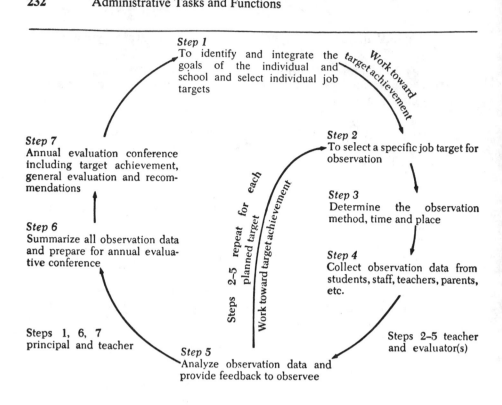

FIGURE 14-1. Staff Evaluation and Development Cycle.

principal should meet with each staff member yearly to select goals and specify job targets for that year.[1] The goal selected by the teacher should come from stated school goals as well as perceived individual needs.

The school goals selected by the teacher can come from numerous sources including accrediting-association studies, a packaged program such as Individually Guided Education[2] that includes a list of thirty-five goals, or simply from a local assessment. No matter what its source, each school should have a list of school goals, and this list should be the basis for individual teacher planning and goal setting for personal improvement. The kinds of goals that come from a schoolwide assessment process are often broadly stated and must usually be restated as a series of specific objectives.

---

[1]A goal is something to strive toward, while a job target is a specific objective to be met.

[2]Individually Guided Education is a model elementary school design focusing on individualized instruction and team teaching, disseminated by the Institute for the Development of Educational Activities, Kettering Foundation, Dayton, Ohio.

A general checklist of overall performance categories for individual needs can be reviewed by both principal and teacher. This list, however, is never the only source of information for individual goal setting. In the goal-setting conference, the principal should aid the teacher in identifying personal problem areas and should be prepared to discuss and identify specific targets for improvement.

Setting Job Targets. After identifying appropriate goals, specific job targets should be designated for each goal. A planning document such as the one shown in Figure 14-2 can be most helpful in this process.

Probably the most difficult technical task in setting goals is translating general goals into specific job targets. This task is very similar to organizing instruction for the classroom. For example, appropriate goals might be as follows:

> *Goal I:* To individualize instruction more effectively.
>
> *Goal II:* To organize instruction to include greater student participation in learning activities.

These goals are very general in nature, and while they provide a sense of direction for the teacher, they are not specific enough to direct action.

A variety of targets must be developed to fit each goal. For example, appropriate targets for goal I might be as follows:

> *Target IA:* To build and use three good learning centers for a fall science unit.
>
> *Target IB:* To develop and use a skills grouping plan for reading skills instruction.

Targets should be written as behaviorally stated objectives. These targets provide the teacher with something specific to work toward and accomplish. It is also appropriate to identify dates for the completion of targets.

Activities. Activities or tasks must be carried out to meet a target successfully. For example, meeting target IA might depend on the following activities:

> *Activity IA1:* Read the book *Learning Centers* by John I. Thomas.
>
> *Activity IA2:* Take a summer course on learning center construction.
>
> *Activity IA3:* Build a practice learning center, ask a colleague for an opinion and try it out on the children.
>
> *Activity IA4:* Attend an inservice workshop on learning-center construction.

These activities should give a teacher the basic skills necessary to fulfill the target of building and using learning centers for the science unit. The activities

EVALUATION FORM FOR TEACHERS

Purposes

The purpose of teacher evaluation is to improve the quality of teaching through an evaluative process that (1) recognizes strengths, (2) encourages professional growth and improved competency, (3) identifies areas of weakness and provides specific plans for teacher improvement through cooperative effort on the part of the teacher and the evaluator(s), and (4) provides a fair and just means for retaining or terminating the services of personnel.

One copy to be completed by teacher and principal at Goals and Target Conference. Each should give prior thought to possible entries.

Name _____   Experience: 1st yr.

School _____   2nd yr.

Assignment _____   3rd yr.

Date of Initial Conference _____   4–10 yr.

11–20 yr.

over 20 yr.

Goals, Targets, and Activities for Professional Growth:
(Use separate sheet for each goal.)

Goals, Targets, and Activities for Personal Professional Growth:
(Use separate sheet for each goal.)

Goal I _____
_____
_____

Target IA _____

date _____ / _____

Activity IA1 _____
_____
_____

Activity IA2 _____
_____
_____

Activity IA3 _____
_____

Target IB _____
date _____ / _____
    Activity IB1 _____
    _____
    _____

    Activity IB2 _____
    _____
    _____

    Activity IB3 _____
    _____
    _____

Target IC _____
date _____ / _____
    Activity IC1 _____
    _____
    _____

    Activity IC2 _____
    _____
    _____

    Activity IC3 _____
    _____
    _____

FIGURE 14-2.

are not the significant items; completion of the target is because it indicates movement toward the goal of improved individualized instruction.

This initial step in the evaluation cycle is extremely important. It provides direction, focus, continuity, and purpose to the entire evaluation process. Through this process, each individual within the school organization receives a specific charge that sets direction. The principal's involvement in setting goals and targets for each teacher keeps the staff moving in the same direction, while the involvement of the teachers allows the evaluation cycle to become an individual self-improvement process.

The planning schedule of the evaluation process is completed with the scheduling of the activities and the selection of dates for the completion of the various targets. Figure 14-3 illustrates an evaluation-cycle time schedule. Upon completion of the planning document the staff members proceed to initiate the plan, carrying out the activities as outlined. The process of clinical supervision is often used for this. As the first target date approaches, the teacher

CALENDAR FOR EVALUATION CYCLE

By June or end of September for new staff (principal and teachers):
Plan goals, targets, and activities (Step 1)
(This can be an extension of the Annual Evaluation Conference for returning staff.)

By end of November (teachers and evaluators):
Achieve at least one job target using a preobservation, observation, and post-observation conference (Steps 2-5)

By end of January (teachers and evaluators):
Achievement of additional job targets (Steps 2-5)

By March 1 (teachers and evaluators):
Achievement of additional job targets and submission of all evaluative data to principal (Steps 2-5 for Step 6)

By March 15 (principal and nontenured teachers):
Completion of all annual evaluation conferences with nontenured teachers. All appropriate evaluation forms and recommendations forwarded to personnel office (Steps 6 and 7)

By April 1 (principal and teachers):
Completion of all other annual evaluation conferences where transfer or termination is to be recommended. All appropriate evaluation forms and recommendations forwarded to personnel office (Steps 6 and 7)

April 15 (principal and teachers):
Completion of all other annual evaluation conferences for all tenured staff. All appropriate forms and recommendations forwarded to the personnel office (Steps 6 and 7)

End of the school year (principal and teachers):
Planning conferences to set goals, targets, and activities for returning staff (Step 1)

FIGURE 14-3.

plans for an evaluation of that target, beginning with a preobservation conference.

Clinical Supervision. Steps 2 through 5 of the evaluation model draw from the concept of clinical supervision. This is basically a four-step process of (1) selecting a specific purpose for an observation; (2) learning from the teacher what specifically is planned for the lesson to be observed; (3) making the observation, looking specifically for those areas agreed upon in the preobservation conference; and (4) feeding back to the teacher what was observed in relation to the plans the teacher had described.

Preobservation Conference

The preobservation conference has two basic purposes: (1) selecting a particular topic for observation and (2) planning the details of the observation.

Target Selection (Step 2). A teacher's job targets are usually too many or too varied to be observed and evaluated properly all at one time. Individual job targets should be selected one at a time for observation and evaluation.

Planning the Observation (Step 3). Once the particular target has been selected, plans should be made for data collection regarding its achievement.

Observers. A preobservation conference should include the teacher to be evaluated and those responsible for data collection. The principal should *not* attempt to conduct all observations personally. Sometimes the principal is an appropriate data collector, but students, other teachers, parents, and other supervisors are also available. Numerous research findings support the position that others besides a principal who come in contact with the teacher at work can make valid and reliable judgments about that work.[3] Also, good data collection for evaluation takes time, usually more time than most principals have available.

Observation Tools. A variety of observation instruments are available or can be created for various types of data collection for teacher evaluation. Elementary students, for example, can provide data on certain types of teacher behavior through the use of the smiley-face questionnaire. (See Figure 14-4.) During the actual observation students might be questioned about their degree of involvement in planning, and samples of student-planned activities could be collected. Some of the responses can be recorded directly by the students if they are mature enough.

Time and Place. The time and place for the observation also need to be arranged during the preobservation conference.

Steps 2 and 3 determine the specific target to be observed, the method by which data will be gathered, the time(s) data collection will be done, and those who will do it.

Collection of Observation Data (Step 4). Data collection is simply the carrying out of the plan outlined in Step 3.

Observations need not be long, particularly if the job target is narrow in scope. Making separate observation cycles for different job targets is often better than trying to combine a whole series of observations into one command performance. Fifteen minutes is usually adequate time to observe one technique or activity. The observation should take place at a scheduled time and place and should maintain as normal an atmosphere as possible so the data will be reliable.

Postobservation Conference (Step 5). The observer should report and analyze the observation and provide feedback to the person observed.

---

[3]An excellent reference for client-centered evaluations is the publication of the Educational Research Service, *The Evaluatee Evaluates the Evaluator* (Washington, D.C.: American Association of School Administrators and Research Division, NEA, No. 5, 1970).

ELEMENTARY STUDENT CLASSROOM
ATMOSPHERE EVALUATION FORM

Categories of the Evaluation

    This evaluation was designed to evaluate the role of the teacher in setting a classroom atmosphere in which the child feels important and has an active part. It was designed to check those areas that make a child either like or dislike the classroom. The statements cover these categories:

   I.   STUDENTS' ATTITUDE TOWARD TEACHER: Statements 1, 4, 10, 13, 25.

  II.   TEACHER'S ATTITUDE TOWARD STUDENTS AS PERCEIVED BY THE STUDENTS: Statements 7, 17, 19, 22.

  III.   TEACHER'S INTEREST IN STUDENTS' OUT-OF-SCHOOL LIFE: Statements 2, 8, 15.

  IV.   TEACHER'S ROLE IN CREATING STUDENT PARTICIPATION IN CLASS: Statements 9, 14, 16.

  V.   TEACHER'S INTEREST IN STUDENTS' PROBLEMS: Statements 3, 6, 18, 20.

  VI.   TEACHER'S FAIRNESS IN DEALING WITH STUDENTS: Statements 12, 21, 23.

  VII.   TEACHER'S AWARENESS OF THE CLASSROOM ENVIRONMENT: Statements 5, 11, 24.

ELEMENTARY STUDENT CLASSROOM
ATMOSPHERE EVALUATION FORM

Fill in the face

1.   When my teacher helps me with my work, I feel . . .

2. When I talk to my teacher about my family, she looks . . .

3. When my teacher is busy and I raise my hand to tell her about a problem, she looks . . .

4. When my teacher talks to the class, it makes me feel . . .

5. When I walk into my classroom and look around, I feel . . .

6. When I do not understand something and I ask my teacher about it, she looks . . .

7. When I talk to my teacher about my work, she looks . . .

8. When I talk to my teacher about what I do at home, she looks . . .

9. When I have a good idea and I tell my teacher about it, she looks . . .

10. When my teacher talks to me, I feel . . .

11. When I tell my friends how my classroom looks, I feel . . .

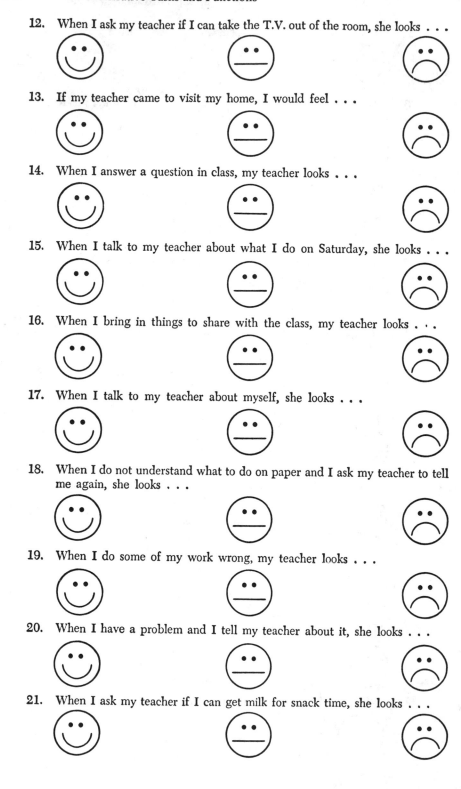

12. When I ask my teacher if I can take the T.V. out of the room, she looks . . .

13. If my teacher came to visit my home, I would feel . . .

14. When I answer a question in class, my teacher looks . . .

15. When I talk to my teacher about what I do on Saturday, she looks . . .

16. When I bring in things to share with the class, my teacher looks . . .

17. When I talk to my teacher about myself, she looks . . .

18. When I do not understand what to do on paper and I ask my teacher to tell me again, she looks . . .

19. When I do some of my work wrong, my teacher looks . . .

20. When I have a problem and I tell my teacher about it, she looks . . .

21. When I ask my teacher if I can get milk for snack time, she looks . . .

22. When I do good work, my teacher looks . . .

23. When I ask my teacher if I can take the lunch report to the office, she looks . . .

24. When I look at the walls and bulletin board in my classroom, I feel . . .

25. If I had my teacher next year, I would feel . . .

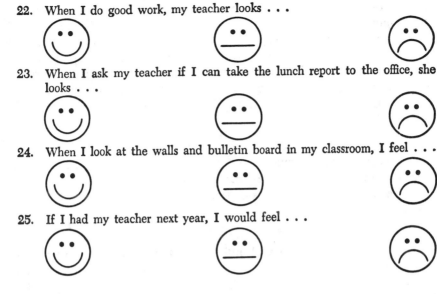

FIGURE 14-4.

The postobservation conference should be conducted by the person in charge of data collection. In some cases it will be the principal; often it will be another teacher. Information gathered from students or parents is returned to the principal or other designated person. Confidentiality of responses should be maintained.

Feedback on direct observation as well as other recorded data should be provided to a teacher the same day as the observation or at least within a day or so. This immediacy will be helpful to both the observer and the observed. The results of the observation should be filed with the principal for the annual review and report.

The postobservation conference should include a review of the target or goal, a review of the activities leading up to the observation, and a description of the data collection itself. Postobservation conferences should take a positive direction. Praise goes much further in bringing about improved performance than criticism. Often it is wise to have the person observed describe their perceptions of the observation period or their expectations of the results of the questionnaire first. Most people are more critical of themselves than others will be, and self-criticism is usually the least destructive criticism for an individual.

If the self-criticism is close to being accurate, then the evaluator can say little of a negative nature. Remember, one of the first attributes listed for the evaluation model was that teachers should have a positive attitude toward evaluation. Negative criticism can destroy positive attitudes or prevent their development.

A positive note on which to end postobservation conferences is asking the person observed to indicate how the observation cycle helped them. After they have responded, it is appropriate for the evaluator, teachers, principal, or supervisor to share with them any new insights gained by functioning as the evaluator.

A Cyclical Process (Steps 2–5). Steps 2 through 5 of the evaluation cycle may be repeated numerous times during the year for different job targets or for repeated evaluations of a particular job target. The relationship of the steps to each other over time is illustrated in Figure 14-3. Steps 1, 6, and 7 are usually done only once each year.

Preparation of the Annual Individual Evaluation Report (Step 6). At the end of each annual evaluation cycle, and in time to meet the legal deadlines for contract renewal or termination, the evaluative data gathered during the year should be summarized. Each teacher should be sure that all the necessary data collection has been done for each target established. The actual task of analyzing and summarizing the evaluative data belongs to the principal.

Each set of goals and targets should be evaluated for the degree of achievement. The principal should not expect teachers to meet all targets, however. Teachers should work toward goals through the completion of set targets, but if they must achieve all targets each year, teachers will very quickly learn to set only achievable targets and will never reach out to challenging ones. Therefore, some targets may not have been reached. Each case, of course, must be judged on its individual merits.

Comments should be written about each job target and its degree of achievement. Recommendations should be considered as proposals for job targets for the following year. This evaluative summation can be recorded on a form similar to the one on which job goals, targets, and activities were entered earlier. (See Figure 14-2.)

The principal should prepare a general overall performance evaluation at this time, reviewing the normal expectations of the teachers within the organization. Such items as meeting certification requirements, following general rules and regulations of the school district, teacher effectiveness, personal characteristics, management of students, and effectiveness in working with others may be included. The overall performance evaluation should only indicate whether a teacher is performing satisfactorily or not in each of these categories. An unsatisfactory rating, however, requires an explanation. Figure 14-5 illustrates a checklist evaluation form for teachers. This summarized performance evaluation should be shared with the teacher along with the recommendations developed in Step 7.

CHECKLIST EVALUATION FORM FOR TEACHERS–FORM TC

One copy is to be completed by the teacher and one by the principal evaluator.

Check the appropriate response under each statement. List any areas of strength you want to point out under each statement. If your response is "unsatisfactory" for any statement, substantiate the response and give recommendations for improvement.

1. The teacher is meeting the *Rules, Regulations, and Minimum Standards* of the State Board of Education:

   Satisfactory ☐   Unsatisfactory ☐

2. The teacher is meeting the policies, procedures, rules, and regulations of the Hillman County Schools Handbook:

   Satisfactory ☐   Unsatisfactory ☐

3. The teacher's effectiveness in working with students is:

   Satisfactory ☐   Unsatisfactory ☐

4. The teacher's personal characteristics are:

   Satisfactory ☐   Unsatisfactory ☐

5. The teacher's student management is:

   Satisfactory ☐   Unsatisfactory ☐

6. The teacher's effectiveness in working with others is:

   Satisfactory ☐   Unsatisfactory ☐

7. The teacher's professional ethics are:

   Satisfactory ☐   Unsatisfactory ☐

243

Form TC   Page 2
RECOMMENDATIONS: This teacher is recommended for (check appropriate boxes):

1. ☐   Continuation in his or her present position at this school.

2. ☐   Transfer to another position in this school system.

3. ☐   Termination of employment with appropriate notice according to the Conditions of Employment (contract).

4. ☐   Tenure in this system.

We discussed the above report in a conference

(date) _____

Signed _____ Teacher

Signed _____ Principal

FIGURE 14-5.

ANNUAL EVALUATION CONFERENCE AND RECOMMENDATIONS

The annual evaluation conference, held usually in March or April with each teacher, includes three distinct tasks:

1. A review of the year's targets and the determination of the degree to which they have been achieved, using a form such as the one shown in Figure 14-2.
2. A summary evaluation by the principal of each teacher's overall performance, using a summary checklist similar to the one shown in Figure 14-5.
3. Recommendations for future targets for staff development.

Recommendations for staff development should take two forms. The first is the identification of a proposed set of individual targets or goals as recommended improvement points for the next cycle of staff evaluation. These recommendations become the basis for generating new goals.

The second major thrust focuses on staff development on a schoolwide basis. Gathering the criticisms and target recommendations for teachers in a school portrays a particular pattern of staff training needs. This is a most useful planning tool for outlining group staff development activities. (See Figure 14-6.) If, for example, a staff needs profile indicates a need for learning-center development or improvement, it would be helpful to organize a collective improvement program in that specific target area.

 • A collective staff development program can also be used on a school-district level if similar evaluation programs are used in each individual building. The more teachers available for the various parts of a planned, personalized inservice program, the greater will be its efficiency and effectiveness.

SUMMARY

The evaluation plan outlined in this chapter has two major components that operate on an annual cycle. One component consists of an annual review that pulls together the evaluative data for a particular teacher, summarizes those data with the teacher (Step 6), and recommends appropriate goals to be included in next year's agreement. In addition, it notes those recommendations for input into the school staff development program (Step 7). The annual evaluation conference ends with the beginning of the new cycle

Teachers	Group Interaction	Learning Centers	Small Group Instruction	Discipline	Record Keeping	Reading Skills Instruction	Team Skills	Other
Abbott, C.		X	X	X		X	X	X
Carson, B.			X	X	X			X
Dole, J.	X	X		X			X	X
Goff, R.	X	X			X			X
Harris, S.		X	X	X		X	X	X
Henderson, F.	X	X		X		X		X
Jones, B.	X	X		X			X	X
Nance, D.		X	X	X	X			X
Poriera, A.	X		X				X	X
Smith, L.		X			X	X		X
Wall, S.		X	X				X	X

FIGURE 14-6. Staff Development Needs Survey.

and the development of a new set of goals and targets based on the individual needs of the teacher, as well as schoolwide goals.

The second major component of the evaluation cycle consists of the identification of particular targets and activities for immediate attention (Step 2), the planning of the particular observation (Step 3), the actual observation and data collection (Step 4), and finally the postobservation conference where feedback is provided to the teacher on performance (Step 5). Steps 2 through 5 can be repeated numerous times during the year for the various goals and targets selected by the teacher in preparation for the annual evaluation conference.

BIBLIOGRAPHY

Abramson, Paul. "When Teachers Evaluate Each Other." *Scholastic Teacher* 43 (September 1972): 26–28.

Amidon, Edmund J.; Kiss, Kathleen M.; and Palisi, Anthony. "Group Supervision." *National Elementary Principal* 45 (April 1966): 54–58.

Bishop, Leslee J. *Staff Development and Instructional Improvement.* Boston: Allyn and Bacon, 1976.

Bolton, Dale L. *Selection and Evaluation of Teachers.* Berkeley, Calif.: McCutchan Publishing Corp., 1973.

Cogan, Morris L. *Clinical Supervision.* Boston: Houghton Mifflin, 1973.

Delano, June S. "In-Service for Change." *Educational Leadership* 32 (1975): 520–23.

Educational Research Service. *Evaluating Teaching Performance.* Washington, D. C.: American Association of School Administrators and Research Division, NEA, 3 (1969); 3 (1972).

Goldhammer, Robert. *Clinical Supervision.* New York: Holt, Rinehart and Winston, 1969.

Green, Jay E. *School Personnel Administration.* New York: Chilton Book Co., 1971.

Harris, Ben M. "Supervision Competence and Strategies for Improving Instruction." *Educational Leadership* 33 (February 1976): 332–35.

Krajewski, Robert J. *Journal of Research and Development in Education* 9 (Winter 1976).

Lane, Willard, et al. *Foundation of Educational Administration: A Behavioral Analysis.* New York: Macmillan, 1967, esp. chaps. 11 and 13.

Mosher, Ralph L., and Purpel, David E. *Supervision: The Reluctant Profession.* Boston: Houghton Mifflin, 1972.

Newton, Robert R. "Three Dilemmas of Supervision." *NASSP Bulletin* 56 (December 1972): 52–64.

Reeves, Billy B. "To Change . . . To Grow . . . /I/D/E/A/'s Clinical Training Workshops." *Educational Leadership* 31 (March 1974): 541–44.

Rosenshine, Barak. "Evaluation of Classroom Instruction." *Review of Educational Research* 40 (April 1970): 279–300.

Sergiovanni, Thomas J. "Human Resources Supervision." *Professional Supervision for Professional Teachers*. Washington, D. C.: Association for Supervision and Curriculum Development, 1975, pp. 9–31.

Sergiovanni, Thomas J., and Starratt, Robert J. *Emerging Patterns of Supervision: Human Perspectives*. New York: McGraw-Hill, 1971.

Stoops, Emery, et al. *Handbook of Educational Administration*. Boston: Allyn and Bacon, 1975, esp. chap. 27.

Trusty, Francis M. *Administering Human Resources*, Berkeley, Calif.: McCutchan Publishing Corp., 1971.

Tuckman, Bruce Wayne. "Feedback on the Change Process." *Phi Delta Kappan* 57 (January 1976): 341–44.

15

Staff Development

INTRODUCTION

Teachers often view staff development or inservice training more negatively than almost any other part of the school program. Recent studies in several states have shown that as many as three-fourths of today's teachers believe that many inservice activities are not relevant to any of their felt needs; over two-thirds of the teachers questioned did not like to attend inservice sessions.[1]

There are many reasons for this dissatisfaction: some of the most frequently mentioned are poor planning and organization, activities that are unrelated to the teachers' day-to-day problems, lack of teacher involvement in planning, inadequate needs assessment, and unclear objectives. One problem of staff development rests in the attitude of administrators or in the way administrators plan inservice activities. They organize the program and then "lay it on" the teachers as if staff development were something you "do to teachers." Staff development must be exciting and motivating to the people involved if it is going to be effective. This can happen only if there is positive acceptance of the planned activities; this can be greatly enhanced if there is direct teacher participation and involvement at all levels of the staff development program.

Another problem of staff development has been its traditional districtwide focus, distant from the needs of teachers and administrators in their own schools. In a recent review of many inservice programs, the Rand Corporation found inservice plans that were conceived, developed, and implemented at the building level were better accepted and more effective than those that operated at the district level.[2]

[1]Jack L. Brimm and Daniel Tollett, "How Do Teachers Feel About In-Service Education?" *Educational Leadership 31* (March 1974): 521–25.

[2]Paul Berman and Milbrey Wallin McLaughlin, *Federal Program Supporting Educational Change VIII: Implementing and Sustaining Innovations* (Santa Monica, Calif.: RAND Corporation, May 1978, pp. v–x).

The Rand study also found that the most successful training was "concrete, ongoing and teacher specific, giving teachers hands-on training and access to assistance they needed when they needed it." This is also substantiated in the research of Lawrence,[3] who found that the more successful inservice programs were those in which teachers helped each other. More success was also reported when the principal helped conduct the program as well.

Finally, we have not organized inservice education with the techniques that we expect teachers to use in the classroom. Most inservice programs do not have well-planned goals and objectives, and little long-range planning exists. Coordination is poor between school goals and inservice goals, and options for individualized learning are not considered relative to the needs of the learner. Inservice programs are often the "sit up and listen" type, with little opportunity for active involvement or concrete experience. These are important learning techniques for adults as well as children.

The Lawrence study also indicated that major change almost always required changes in attitudes and motivation in addition to the development of new techniques. Often without these attitude changes, good ideas were not effectively implemented. This point can be illustrated by the teacher who was overheard to say, when notified of a meeting, "Why should I go to another inservice meeting when I already know how to do a much better job of teaching than I'm presently doing?"

The problems identified thus far in this chapter point out the major difficulties with present staff development programs and indicate the direction in which a good staff development program should move.

Purposes of Staff Development

Staff development should be viewed as a means of providing a common direction and focus for the improvement of the entire school rather than as a means of upgrading the skills of individual teachers. Most of us think we are pretty good just the way we are and tend to resist "correction." Much inservice training is perceived this way. However, when the focus is on improving the school and participation can assist in achieving school goals, then the threat to the individual teacher is removed. The individual's skill development will occur as a material part of the learning necessary to achieve the school goals, because it provides a rationale for teachers to help each other. That is not to say that individual improvement should not be planned as part of the inservice program. The focus, however, should be on schoolwide improvement.

---

[3]Gordon, Lawrence, *Patterns of Effective In-Service Education: State of the Art Summary of Research and Materials and Procedures for Changing Teacher Behavior for In-Service Education* (Tallahassee, Fla.: Division of Elementary and Secondary Education, Florida State Dept. of Education, 1974), ED 176 424.

Characteristics of a Good Staff Development Plan

Based on the research and studies just discussed, the following list of characteristics forms a good basis around which to plan staff development activities.

1. The involvement of the principal
2. The involvement of a faculty planning committee
3. Communication with the district office, supervisors, and administrators
4. Concrete, teacher-specific, job-related activities
5. School-goal–oriented with specific objectives
6. Long-range plans rather than single-shot objectives
7. Provision for options and choice of activities
8. Frequent internal staffing of activities instead of the use of outside consultants
9. Many small-group or team-oriented activities
10. An orientation to the individual level of the improvement plan and to the individual job targets of the teachers
11. Timeliness—inservice education scheduled when teachers need it and want it

PLANNING FOR STAFF DEVELOPMENT

Maximum opportunity for involvement is the key to success when planning for staff development. Initial planning should be done by the principal, aided by a faculty planning committee such as the principal's advisory council mentioned in Chapter 11. This group should organize to obtain input from the entire faculty to develop a needs assessment. For example, brainstorming with teachers divided into groups of four to six works well to generate ideas for staff development activities.

Sources for Staff Development Ideas

Ideas for inclusion in the needs assessment should come from several different sources. Figure 15-1 shows the contribution of school goals and staff evaluation to a staff development needs assessment. The figure also illustrates the relationship among district, building, and individual staff development activities. Previously established school goals should be a major source of input. (Developing school goals should have preceded this. Chapter 5 provided much information on school goal development.) One focus of the planning can be "How can we through our staff development activities better reach our school goals?"

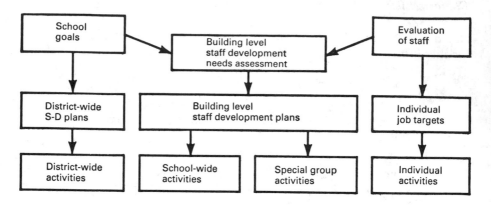

FIGURE 15-1. Planning for Staff Development.

In a similar manner, summary data taken from the staff evaluation documents should contribute to the needs assessment. (Chapter 14 showed how to organize these data.)

Another source of input is material on teaching responsibilities taken from job descriptions such as those shown in Chapter 13 or from lists of major categories of teaching responsibilities as shown in Figure 15-2. These lists can help organize participants' thinking for suggestions of specific items to include in the needs assessment list.

Finally, the major curriculum areas of the school should be reviewed for ideas. Lists of student competencies or expectations for learning can provide a focus for new areas of learning for teachers.

PLANNING MODEL

Planning for staff development should involve in an orderly manner the entire staff and should provide for a maximum sharing of ideas. The following model shows an excellent step-by-step staff development plan.

Planning Steps

Phase I

Step 1. The principal along with the advisory council should bring together the goal and evaluation documents and develop plans for a meeting of the entire staff to brainstorm topics to be included on a needs assessment instrument.

1. Assessing and diagnosing
2. Planning instruction and learning activities
3. Conducting instruction
4. Managing student behavior
5. Managing the school environment and resources
6. Evaluating instruction
7. Working in a school-community context
8. Working with other staff members (teammates, administrators, teacher aides, parent volunteers, special education personnel, and so on.)
9. Evaluating self

FIGURE 15-2. Major Areas of Teaching Responsibility.

Step 2. Organize the staff into small mixed groups (not by team, grade level, or department), assigning each group school goals, evaluation results, job responsibility lists, or student competency lists as a basis for brainstorming ideas for staff development activities. Have each group review their list and reduce it to the ten best ideas.

Step 3. Next ask each group to suggest colleagues or other resource persons who can conduct training sessions. Many experienced and talented teachers have developed effective methods and techniques. The school's own local talent should be identified first, before outside people are suggested.

Step 4. At the second meeting with teachers, now organized by work groups (teams, grade groups, or department), provide each faculty member with the list of suggestions from the brainstorming session and have them indicate with an *S* their top two choices for the school; with a *T* their top two choices for their team, department, or grade-level group; and with a *P* their top two personal choices, keeping in mind the general school goals and staff evaluations for the year. While each teacher's recommendations should be his or her own, discussion should also take place, particularly for the team's choices. Additional recommendations for trainers should also be requested for their priority areas.

Step 5. The principal's advisory committee should tabulate the results. From among the favored choices, the schoolwide selections for staff development should be made and reported to the faculty, as well as staff development recommendations for individual teams or grades.

Phase II

For each staff development activity a projected plan is prepared including:

1. The topic of the inservice session
2. Specific objectives to be attained

3. Dates and places
4. Session trainers or consultants
5. Outcomes to be evaluated

Figure 15-3 shows a completed project plan. The planning for the schoolwide activities should be done by the principal's advisory council. Each team, grade-level group, or department should complete similar planning for those staff development activities that are unique to their group. Staff development activities specifically for individuals usually reflect the job targets from the staff evaluation system and are organized in a similar fashion.

Each group should suggest to the principal the trainers or consultants whom they would like to ask for help. Naturally, having money above the regular budget available for staff development allows for more flexibility in carrying out an effective program. The funds can come from local operating accounts, federal programs, pilot project grants, or special allocations through the district office. It is a mistake, however, to feel that money is the decisive

---

TOPIC: Training and planning for an improved math program
SPECIFIC OBJECTIVES:
1. To identify methods of assessing children's math skills.
2. To identify or develop a math inventory to use with each child.
3. To learn methods for teaching students to work independently with math texts.
4. To develop a filing system for math materials based on a skills continuum.

DATES AND PLACES: Meetings will be held October 14, October 28, November 11, November 25, December 2, and two days each in both January and February.
CONSULTANTS:
1. October 14—Objective 1: Mary Jones from the intermediate school.
2. October 28—Objective 2: Dr. Paul Burns, University of Tennessee.
3. November 11—Objective 3: Mary Jones.
4. November 25—Our team is going to the intermediate school to see their filing system for math skills.
5. December 2—We plan to work on our own to begin to put our math files together.

OUTCOMES: We plan to evaluate our progress:
1. By presenting a description of the ways we are assessing math skills.
2. By presenting a copy of a completed math inventory for each of our children.
3. By asking the principal and math supervisor to come to our rooms and observe the degree to which our children are working independently in their math books.
4. By displaying the completed math skills file.

FIGURE 15-3. Illustration of a Staff Development Specification.

---

factor for a successful school-based staff development program. Competent faculty members from your own staff should almost always be your first choice for consultants. They can often be of the greatest assistance anyway. Regional service centers and state departments of education often have personnel available to help with teacher training. Universities often provide assistance on a low-cost basis to local schools, and many professors will give assistance for the opportunity to work in a school. As can be seen, even though a school does not have a big budget for its staff development program, a quality program can be developed.

Implementation

Each team or work group should submit to the principal their staff development plan in similar fashion to the one shown in Figure 15-3. With the assistance of the advisory council these plans should be reviewed and approved, with appropriate action taken to ensure implementation. In a similar fashion, the schoolwide staff development plan prepared by the principal's advisory council should be implemented, with the principal assisting with the logistics. It is also the principal's task to oversee the entire staff development program, making sure that the assessed needs of the teachers are being met.

Evaluation

Both the principal and the advisory council should assume responsibility for an ongoing evaluation of the program. The principal should definitely plan to participate in some capacity in all schoolwide inservice programs and should occasionally drop in to the team sessions. This will not only allow the principal to keep sight of the progress of staff development but will also show the high interest level on the part of the principal that the research indicates is so critical to the success of a staff development program.

Each staff development plan such as the one illustrated in Figure 15-3 should include an evaluation component. Many of the evaluation plans require the presence of the principal in order to complete them. As part of that evaluation process the larger picture should always be kept in mind by trying to answer the following questions:

1. What can the staff do better now than they could before they took this training?
2. What are our students able to do now that they were unable to do before the staff took this training?

By scrutinizing each objective, the staff can review the training areas and decide whether they need to continue in the current area of staff development or move on to another area. While the planning for staff development often is initiated at the beginning of the school year, the process of meeting objectives, assessing progress, and establishing new objectives is ongoing and continuous.

The ultimate goal of the program is student achievement, but many factors affect this. Teacher skill improvement, the focus of the staff development program itself, is measured by self-evaluation and demonstration of increased competency as seen by the principal, supervisors, and the community.

ORIENTATION OF NEW STAFF

The basic purpose of orientation is to provide new staff members a rapid adjustment to their new position and an early integration into the working environment. The main focus of orientation should be on instruction, operating procedures, and interpersonal relationships. Orientation of new staff can be divided into three basic phases and should begin shortly after the decision to employ. Phase one is based on the assumption that the new employee will have been under contract for a month or so before the beginning of the school term.

Phase One

Phase one should be initiated with a welcome-aboard letter from the principal and an invitation to visit the school before the start of school, if convenient. Pertinent information regarding the teacher's specific assignment should be provided as soon as it is available. A second letter to the new teacher should include items such as a staff policy manual or handbook, last year's faculty roster or, better yet, a yearbook that includes teachers' pictures. This will aid the new teacher in getting acquainted.

If a summer visit to the school is arranged, the new teacher should be provided with teacher editions of major texts that will be used. Teachers have more leisure time to review materials in the summer than after the school year begins. If new teachers are not going to visit the school during the summer because of distance or other commitments, they should be sent the material anyway. Providing advance information is one of the most productive ways of helping a new teacher get off to a good start.

Phase Two

Phase two begins with the preschool teacher conference and lasts into the first week of the school term. Now that the entire staff is present, the first priority should be developing good interpersonal relationships. Many of the questions and concerns of the new staff member can be handled informally if people are acquainted. Even returning staff members may need some help in redeveloping an effective working relationship. Two good opening group activities to aid in orientation as well as the renewal of acquaintances are useful.

Pairs and Squares. Everyone identifies the person in the room they know the least well. When everyone is paired up with another person, each partner takes three minutes for an introduction. After the six-minute interchange is completed, step two begins. Each pair is instructed to look around, find another pair of staff members whom they know least well, and join them to create a new group of four. Each person introduces the new friend, taking one minute for each introduction. This second phase takes approximately four or five minutes. The entire exercise takes only about fifteen minutes. If the group is large, it can form groups of eight and repeat the introductions.

Getting to Know You. The second game organizes staff members into groups of four to six members. Again, those who know each other least well should be grouped together, mixing new members of the faculty with returning staff members. One member of each team is appointed timekeeper. Each member of the group takes five minutes to describe interests and background. If the individual runs out of things to say before the five minutes are up, the group asks questions for the remaining time. After each person has talked for five minutes, the group feeds back to each participant what they collectively remember about that individual, taking one minute for each. Feedback activity is important to the process and should not be overlooked.

A good way to begin this activity is for the principal to model it by spending the first five minutes talking to all the groups. The groups should also have to provide timed feedback.

Both activities will begin to open up communication lines within the staff and cause new teachers to feel very much a part of the group, as well as help the returning staff to become better acquainted.

Phase two of the orientation should continue with a session conducted by the principal specifically for the new teachers, focusing on basic operating procedures and discussing the schedule, room assignments, discipline, accounting procedures, and records. Ample opportunity should be provided for questions. This session should be conducted in addition to a regular staff update on similar topics, because often a beginning teacher will not feel free to ask certain questions in front of the whole staff. Department heads should also play a major part in this phase of orientation for new teachers.

Phase two should also include an orientation to the instructional program—acquaintance with supplementary texts, library materials, and so on. If the school is organized into teams, the instructional orientation as well as much of the orientation of the basic operating procedures can be automatically handled within the team. Otherwise, a buddy system, with an experienced teacher assigned to a newcomer, should provide counsel and help in orienting the new staff member to the job. The department head may wish to assign a second- or third-year teacher who has performed well and who is often perceptive to the problems of the beginning teacher.

Phase Three

Phase three of orientation takes place during the entire first year of school. The buddy system or team support continue. The principal continues orientation sessions for the new staff, even if there is only one new member. These sessions should be scheduled at anticipated critical times during the school year. As the year proceeds, they will be needed less frequently. The first session should come after the first two weeks of school and have a "how are you doing?" focus. Maintaining a warm, helping relationship with new teachers is important. Another conference should occur near the end of the first marking period to assist new staff members in evaluating students and reporting to parents.

Much of the responsibility for training good teachers falls upon the principal. Colleges cannot provide all the technical detail necessary to operate successfully on the job. The inservice training program, a prime responsibility of the principal, can accomplish much.

SUMMARY

Staff development is a major ongoing responsibility of each school principal. It becomes the way in which school goals and teacher and team job targets are addressed. The most effective programs insist on faculty planning, faculty presentations, and, above all, principal participation.

Orientation of new staff members is also a critical part of staff development. Even though only a few new people may have joined the staff, it is important to provide a series of activities to insure their proper initiation into the organization.

The principal's advisory council should be the major vehicle by which the principal involves the staff in all development activities.

BIBLIOGRAPHY

Burch, Barbara G., and Danley, W. Elzie, Sr. "Self Perception: An Essential in Staff Development." *NASSP Bulletin* 62, no. 417 (April 1978): 15–19, EJ 175 596.

ERIC Clearinghouse on Educational Management. *Staff Development. Research Action Brief Number 10.* Eugene, Ore.: University of Oregon, 1980, ED 189 679.

Halstead, David. "Developing a Professional Growth Program in Small Schools." *NASSP Bulletin* 64, no. 438 (October 1980): 26–32, EJ 232 070.

Joyce, Bruce, and Showers, Beverly. "Improving Inservice Training: The Messages of Research." *Educational Leadership* 37, no. 5 (February 1980): 379–85, EJ 216 055.

Kelley, Edgar A., and Dillion, Elizabeth A. "Staff Development: It Can Work for You." *NASSP Bulletin* 62, no. 417 (April 1978): 1–8, EJ 175 594.

Lawrence, Gordon. *Patterns of Effective Inservice Education: A State of the Art Summary of Research on Materials and Procedures for Changing Teacher Behaviors in Inservice Education* (Tallahassee, Fla.: Division of Elementary and Secondary Education, Florida State Department of Education, 1974), ED 176 424.

McLaughlin, Milbrey Wallin, and Marsh, David D. "Staff Development and School Change." *Teachers College Record* 80, no. 1 (September 1978): 69–94. EJ 195 497.

Olivarez, Ruben Dario, and Berrier, Helen. *School-Based Inservice Teacher Education. A Handbook for Planning and Providing* (Austin, Tex.: College of Education, University of Texas, 1978), ED 186 391.

Trohanis, Pascal, and Jackson, Elouise. "The Technical Assistance Approach to Inservice." *Educational Leadership* 37, no. 5 (February 1980): 386–89, EJ 216 056.

Webster, William E. "Many Resources Available for Staff Development." "Thrust for Staff Development." *Thrust for Educational Leadership* 9, no. 4 (March 1980): 8–10, EJ 221 571.

Wood, Fred H. and Thompson, Steven R. "Guidelines for Better Staff Development." *Educational Leadership* 37, no. 5 (February 1980): 374–78, EJ 216 054.

16

The Principal's Role
in Contract Administration

INTRODUCTION

Written contracts between teacher organizations and school districts cause principals to face the problem of administering personnel arrangements. The school official with the greatest amount of direct contact with the teacher is the building principal who functions in a labor-management sense as the first line supervisor. The principal handles most of the grievances or problems that arise from the formalized teacher-board agreements. As a result of these agreements principals may find that they no longer have the broad discretionary powers they once did. Instead, they must abide by the terms of a formal contract.

Most teacher-board agreements include a procedure to guarantee employees a clear channel of communication to air complaints or grievances within the school system and to seek a just solution to problems. Most contracts state that employees may file a grievance if they believe they have been treated unfairly or if they disagree with their supervisors as to the application of a policy. The word "policy" refers primarily to written agreements negotiated by the teacher organization. However, it may also include written policies, procedures, and standards established by the school administration unilaterally. When differences arise between a negotiated policy and an administrative policy, the negotiated policy controls.

The expression "treated unfairly" relates to matters not covered by policy. It might relate to a substantial deviation from customary practice or might challenge a practice. It might also relate to an action that discriminates against an employee as a person. The concept of unfair treatment does not apply to a disagreement with negotiated policy; an employee who attempts to file a grievance on the basis of such a disagreement would be better advised to present these views to his or her union or association representative.

Occasionally the term "supervisor" will be used interchangeably in contracts with "principal," but more often the term supervisor refers to any administrator with direct responsibility for the actions of a certain group of employees, teachers, and other personnel. The negotiated agreement will probably provide different ways to handle grievances within the district depending on the subject of the grievance, and different administrators will handle different problems.

Some contracts require the person with whom the grievance is being filed to inform the local representative of the teacher organization if the employee is not represented by a union or association, so that the union may take part as provided in the agreement. If the person bringing the grievance to a supervisor is not satisfied with the supervisor's determination, the agreement usually has a carefully defined set of appeal procedures.

While grievance procedures will vary in terminology and the number of appeal levels from contract to contract, they all seem to follow the same basic format. Figure 16-1 presents the grievance-and-complaint section of a recently negotiated contract. This four-level grievance procedure presents an elaborate plan for "communication within the organization."

How to Handle Grievances

What is a principal's role during a grievance procedure? When a grievance is filed, a principal has the opportunity to reestablish the effective relationship with the employee and to improve the relationship. The most can be made of this opportunity by observing the following principles:

Be Approachable. Principals should not place obstacles in the way of employees or their representative that will suggest that the principal is not interested in discussing their problems with them. An appointment should be made for a definite time at a specific place to discuss the grievance in private.

A. A grievance is defined as an alleged violation, misinterpretation, or misapplication of a provision(s) of this contract.

B. Informal Action

If a member of the bargaining unit feels he or she has a grievance, that member shall first discuss the matter in good faith with the immediate supervisor in an effort to resolve the problem informally. This informal action shall take place within twenty (20) teaching days after the grievant knew, or should have known, of the incident which is the basis of the grievance. In this informal action, the grievant shall verbally advise his or her supervisor of the particular section of the Agreement alleged to have been violated. The immediate supervisor will respond verbally to the grievance within six (6) teaching days after the informal meeting.

C. Formal Procedure

Step 1

If the informal action does not resolve the grievance satisfactorily, the grievant shall have the right to lodge a written grievance with his or her immediate supervisor within six (6) teaching days following the verbal response of the supervisor. If such grievance is not lodged within six (6) teaching days following conclusion of the informal action above, the right to proceed with the grievance procedure for this incident is waived. The written grievance shall be on a standard form as contained in the appendices to this contract and shall contain a concise statement of the facts upon which the grievance is based and a reference to the specific section of the negotiated agreement which is allegedly violated. A copy of such grievance shall be filed by the grievant with the superintendent and the association. A response shall be made by the immediate supervisor in writing within six (6) teaching days after the receipt of said grievance by the immediate supervisor. Copies shall be sent by the immediate supervisor to the superintendent and the association.

Step 2

If the grievant is not satisfied with the disposition of the grievance in Step 1, such grievant may appeal, by filing a form, as contained in the appendices to this contract, within six (6) teaching days after receipt of the decision of the immediate supervisor in Step 1, to the assistant to the superintendent for employee relations. At the request of either party to the grievance, within six (6) teaching days, the assistant to the superintendent for employee relations shall meet with the grievant and his or her representative and shall indicate the disposition of the grievance in writing within six (6) teaching days of such a meeting and shall furnish a copy thereof to the grievant, the immediate supervisor, the superintendent, and the association. At this step either party may introduce or present evidence to substantiate his, her, or its position in the matter.

Step 3

If the grievant is not satisfied with the disposition of the grievance at Step 2, he or she may appeal, by filing a form as contained in the appendices of this contract, within six (6) teaching days after receipt of the decision of the assistant to the superintendent for employee relations in Step 2 to the superintendent and request that the grievant be allowed to review the record in Steps 1 and 2 in connection with said grievance. Copies of such notice of the appeal shall be sent to the grievant's immediate supervisor, to the assistant to the superintendent for employee relations, and to the association. The superintendent shall render a decision in writing within ten (10) teaching days after receipt of the appeal. Copies of the decision shall be sent to the grievant, the grievant's immediate supervisor, the assistant to the superintendent for employee relations, and the association.

Step 4

If the association is not satisfied with the decision rendered after the review in Step 3 by the superintendent, the grievance may be submitted for arbitration. The association shall, within fifteen (15) teaching days after receipt of the decision of the superintendent, notify the superintendent of its intent to submit the grievance to arbitration.

FIGURE 16-1. Grievance Procedure.

Listen. Many times the grievance results from an action the principal has taken. The great temptation is for the principal to defend the action without further thought. However, if a principal adopts a defensive attitude the employee may feel even more grieved. When teachers or other employees have a complaint, they should have the opportunity to talk it out. If the employee is excited, or if the basis of the complaint is not clear, the complaint should be clarified. Calm, interested listening is required. Sometimes in the process of putting the complaint into words, the grievance will disappear.

Get the Facts. The principal should repeat the story after the employee has told it to clarify that both parties are discussing the same issue. Those facts agreed upon or accepted as true by both parties should be confirmed. Those aspects not perceived in the same way should be discussed further, and, if an agreement is not reached, more information should be secured before a decision is rendered.

Take Notes. During the discussion the principal should take notes about the facts presented. The notes will be helpful in reviewing the facts with the employee and when the matter is discussed later with the superintendent or personnel director. Notes are also helpful for a written report of a grievance discussion.

Make Decisions with Care. An immediate decision is not usually required, and the principal should carefully weigh all the facts. Employees must be reassured that they will receive a fair hearing based on the facts of an issue.

In all cases it is prudent, even necessary, to discuss the matter with the superintendent or personnel director before making a decision. This is especially important if the issue involves interpretation of a policy or a negotiated agreement. However, undue delay needs to be avoided in acting on the grievance.

Since action taken may result in the employee exercising the right of appeal, the principal's responsibility is to render the initial decision and inform the employee of his or her appeal rights.

It's the Principal's Decision. When the principal makes the decision, it should be clear that it is not that of the board, superintendent, or personnel director. Even though the action that is the subject of the complaint may be based upon some policy of the school district the principal did not help make, it is still the principal who applied that policy and who must accept first-line responsibility.

If grievances at this level are handled properly, most problems covered under the teacher's contract can be solved. If administrators follow reasonable procedures for the rapid but fair handling of grievances, relatively few grievances will need to be appealed to the next level in the established grievance procedure.

Appealed Grievances

When an employee is dissatisfied with the initial responses of the first-level supervisor or principal, a formal hearing may be requested to move the grievance procedure to Level Two. This appeal is usually made by written statements, affidavits, or hearings, or a combination thereof. A hearing is usually held at the request of the employee or the appeal administrator. As grievance procedures become more formal, standard forms may be desirable in processing and recording the grievance decision. Figure 16-2 depicts a suggested format to be used at the building level by the aggrieved employee. The administrator also needs documentation and Figure 16-3 depicts a suggested format.

THE PRINCIPAL'S ROLE IN NEGOTIATION

The school principal has two major responsibilities in the collective negotiation process. The first responsibility is as a member of the administrative team. Every school district should have an administrative team consisting of building-level principals, supervisory staff, and central superintendent staff representing management in negotiation. Occasionally questions arise regarding the principal's role. Formal negotiations recognize that a principal must be part of the management team.

Each principal in small school districts with few principals should be an active member of the administrative team and participate in an advisory capacity during negotiations. In larger communities principals may find it both necessary and effective to have representation on the negotiating team to express their viewpoint. Principals should be represented, because to a great extent negotiation topics represent areas of direct concern to the building principal. In many cases the ensuing negotiations result in the erosion of the power or responsibility of the principal, often reducing administrative effectiveness.[1]

Contract Administration. The principal must be part of the management team because of the basic responsibility of administering the employee contract once it has been negotiated. The grievance procedure outlined above is part of that contract administration.

The principal must be able to interpret the agreement reached with the teachers and to apply it in an acceptable manner. Each year principals should request a briefing about the new contract from the school district negotiator and an interpretation of agreements and information regarding implementa-

---

[1]An increasing number of school districts provide for the direct negotiation of principals or negotiation in cooperation with other administrators or supervisors. Several states already have legislation requiring boards of education to recognize and negotiate with administrator units.

Name _____ Home Phone _____.
        Last   First   Initial

Immediate Supervisor _____ Work Location _____

Contract Section Allegedly Violated _____

Date of Alleged Violation _____

Description:

Redress Sought:

_____ Signature _____ Date _____

STEP I   Date Rec'd _____ Init. ____ Date Reply Rec'd _____ Init. ____

Disposition:

Denied   **Granted**   Reason:

_____ Signature _____ Date _____

STEP II   Date Rec'd _____ Init. ____ Date Reply Rec'd _____ Init. ____

Disposition:

Denied   **Granted**   Reason:

_____ Signature _____ Date _____

STEP III   Date Rec'd _____ Init. ____ Date Reply Rec'd _____ Init. ____

Disposition:

Denied   **Granted**   Reason:

_____ Signature _____ Date _____

STEP IV   Date Rec'd _____ Init. ____ Date Reply Rec'd _____ Init. ____

ASSOCIATION RESPONSE:

( ) We hereby accept the review and decision of the Superintendent in Level III.

( ) We hereby appeal for arbitration of this grievance.

Signature of
Association President _____ Date _____

FIGURE 16-2. Form for Contract Grievances (Members of bargaining unit only).

DECISION OF ADMINISTRATOR

(To be completed by principal, or other appropriate administrator, within 3 days of formal grievance presentation.)

AGGRIEVED PERSON(S) _____

DATE OF FORMAL PRESENTATION _____

SCHOOL _____

PRINCIPAL _____

DECISION OF PRINCIPAL (OR OTHER ADMINISTRATOR) AND REASONS THEREFORE:

DATE OF DECISION _____   _____
                                           (signature of principal)

AGGRIEVED PERSON'S RESPONSE: (To be completed by aggrieved within 3 days of decision.)
   I accept the above decision of principal (or other administrator).
   I hereby refer the above decision to the Association's Professional Rights and Responsibilities Committee for appeal to the superintendent of schools.

DATE OF RESPONSE _____

                                        _____
                                           (signature of aggrieved)

FIGURE 16-3.

---

tion of that contract. Great care must be exercised to stick to the contract. Teachers will readily inform the principal if they are not granted all of the privileges called for in the contract but also will most willingly accept privileges that extend beyond the contract. This is where the danger lies. Principals can inadvertently grant permanent privileges to teachers by on occasion simply giving them certain extra privileges.

Administrators should be aware of a key concept called past practice. It is the acceptance of duties or privileges that teachers have carried out or been granted over an extended period of time. Arbitrators will invoke the term "past practice" in dispute cases when the teacher organization claims that a principal has for an extended period of time allowed a certain privilege or action to take place. Past practices can become a part of the contract and thus a privilege to be exercised by the teachers.

PRINCIPAL INVOLVEMENT IN TEACHER ORGANIZATIONS

A real danger area for the administrator is membership or a leadership role in the teacher organizations of the school district.[2] In many school districts, prior to the institution of negotiations teachers and administrators functioned effectively within the same professional organizations and principals often held leadership responsibilities. Formal negotiations have changed all this; a principal cannot act as an administrator and an employee simultaneously. If the teacher organization decides on militant action and the principal represents the local leadership, that principal is placed in the untenable position of being leader for both parties in a conflict. Numerous cases can be cited where the principal was caught in this dilemma, faced with the demand of the teacher organization to go on strike and the demand of the school district to keep the schools open. In these situations the principal either gains the enmity of the teachers or loses the job, and in some cases both.

SUMMARY

Collective bargaining by teachers has changed the role of the principal. Grievance procedures provide formal guarantees of communication between teachers and administrators; and principals now must abide by a specific set of rules, as spelled out by the contract, in dealing with teachers. Principals must reevaluate their active involvement in professional organizations. If militant teacher action is at hand, principals must consider removing themselves from any active leadership role in the organization and maybe from membership. In many areas the decision no longer rests with the administrator, as the teachers have long since made them unwelcome.

BIBLIOGRAPHY

Castetter, William B. *The Personnel Function in Educational Administration*. New York: Macmillan, 1971.
Lieberman, Myron, and Moskow, Michael. *Collective Negotiations for Teachers: An Approach to School Administration*. Chicago: Rand McNally, 1966.
Stoops, Emory, et al. *Handbook of Educational Administration*. Boston: Allyn and Bacon, 1975, esp. chaps. 25 and 26.

---

[2]This is declining. The AFT does not permit it and the NEA has taken many actions to discourage it.

17

Building Management
and Facility Utilization

INTRODUCTION

Properly housing and equipping the elementary school presents some management priorities for the principal. Creative housing enhances educational programs. This does not mean that innovative programs cannot be housed in traditionally designed buildings. In fact, much evidence exists to the contrary. Whether the building represents the latest in school design or reflects architectural thinking in the 1930s, the principal's responsibility is the same: to insure the maximum efficient use of the school plant for the educational program. An inefficiently used building; a poorly kept building; a building with unpleasant, colorless rooms; a poorly maintained site all inhibit the development of a good educational program and reduce staff and student morale. Similarly, a physical facility that lacks flexibility, is poorly equipped, or has underutilized equipment also inhibits program development. This chapter focuses on management practices that can help get the best out of the school plant.

New Buildings

Open-bay construction and the use of demountable walls are current construction techniques that best meet the need for flexibility. Permanent construction provides large, carpeted, air-conditioned rooms equivalent in size to four or more regular classrooms. Demountable wall panels that press against the ceiling and floor, usually in four- or five-foot widths, can be used to create interior walls and doors where desired. These walls can be installed, moved, or removed by a custodian in a few hours so that changes can be made quickly and frequently. The walls are sound treated and can be purchased with chalkboard or bulletin board surfaces to make them extremely functional. The major advantage of demountable walls is the flexibility to create instructional areas of various sizes and shapes with low-cost, easy transition.

Folding walls are popular in many schools as a way to create flexible spaces. These are less desirable, however, because of high cost, permanency of location, and the tendency of most teachers to leave them either open or closed most of the time.

Open Space

The optimal flexible space is an open space large enough for three or more teachers and their children, with partial dividers such as bookcases and storage carts. Teachers can move these dividers at will and can reorganize space several times each day if necessary. Open space is most functional, however, with team teaching and flexible grouping.

There are many examples of schools designed with open spaces in which a traditional program was implemented. As a result, there was much dissatisfaction with the open areas. Space must follow function, and if traditional teaching is what one has in mind, the more traditional buildings are more appropriate. On the other hand, open areas enhance team teaching, individualized instruction, and flexible grouping. The major advantages of the open area are:

1. The entire curriculum for a group of children can be housed in one area.
2. The open area allows for the easy movement of children from one activity to another.
3. It allows for great variation in group size from one child to the entire group.
4. It allows one teacher to have visual supervision of the entire open area, freeing other teachers for small group work.
5. It allows teachers to coordinate their instructional activities easily with one another because they maintain visual contact.

There are some disadvantages as well, and those most often listed for open spaces include:

1. There are often higher noise levels in the instructional area, because of teaching styles and greater student movement and activity.
2. Some teachers do not like the disturbance caused by other teachers teaching in the same area. Most often the problem is one of inappropriate teacher style for the open area or a lack of team coordination. Good individualized instruction and team coordination will solve this problem.

Space Utilization. Space utilization within the open area is important. An example of good space utilization coordinated with team planning, individualized instruction, flexible grouping, and a varied curriculum is shown in Figure 17-1. Each teacher is responsible for setting up and maintaining one-

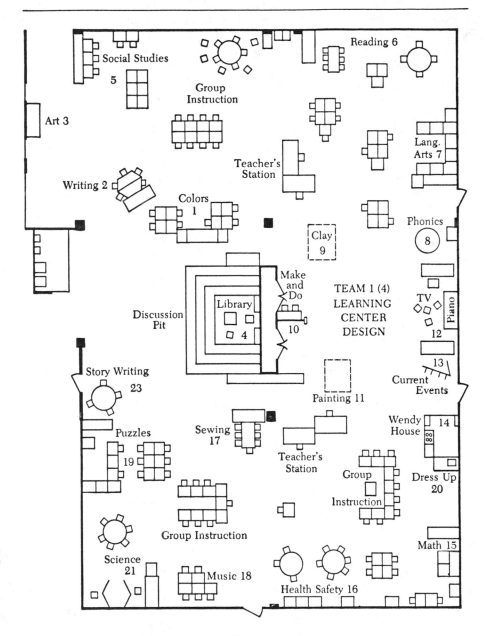

FIGURE 17-1. Space Utilization in an Open-space Classroom.

fourth of the room. Each area includes individual learning centers as well as an area for small groups to meet. Teacher desks are located near the center of the room so teachers can provide supervision of most of the room from their desks. Learning centers are built around the perimeter of the room, adjacent to the wall area for display purposes. Children have access to the entire instructional area, and a broadly based curriculum with a great variety and abundance of learning centers is available. Each learning center has space for student seating and study.

Teachers use the small-group seating area in their portion of the room for skill groups. Supervisory duties for learning centers have teachers moving throughout the entire area; it is possible to schedule large group lessons anywhere in the area appropriate for the instructional program. As a result, teachers have instructional and supervisory responsibilities throughout the room.

Suggestions for Organizing Open Space. Careful arrangement of furniture, equipment, and learning centers will make the maximum use of open-space-designed schools.

1. Place learning centers along the perimeter walls and provide seating at these centers. The student seating area in the learning center permits easier supervision of children and better maintenance of materials and general room appearance.

2. Position room dividers so that they radiate out from the center of the room, allowing teachers stationed in the center to see past the divider to observe students while separating student activities. (See Figure 17-2.)

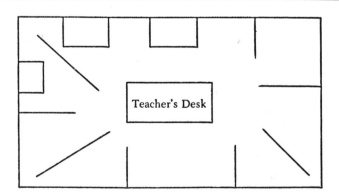

FIGURE 17-2. Room Dividers in an Open-space Classroom.

3. Do not attempt to use permanent large-group seating or assigned seats with many learning centers. This arrangement crowds the room in most cases. If student storage is necessary, a teacher can provide tote trays or large plastic dishpans or boxes for books and personal effects.

4. Set up a number of activities on the floor without furniture. Much of the large-group instruction can be done with children seated on the floor close together, reducing the distance that a teacher needs to project his or her voice. Functioning without furniture also provides greater flexibility for movement of activities.

The Use of Traditional Buildings for Flexible Programs

While open-space buildings are designed with flexibility in mind, with a little planning traditional buildings with separate classroom areas can be used for flexible programs. The most important factor in developing a flexible program in a traditional building is giving teaching teams and students adjacent rooms. Preferably, classrooms should be immediately across the hall. As shown in Figure 17-3, teachers may then set up corridor boundaries for the students and operate the classrooms and the adjacent corridor space as if they were one large open area.

Teachers as well as students should share assigned spaces with each other, moving about as needed. Specific assignment of space will vary from program to program. Greatest flexibility can be maintained if teachers do not

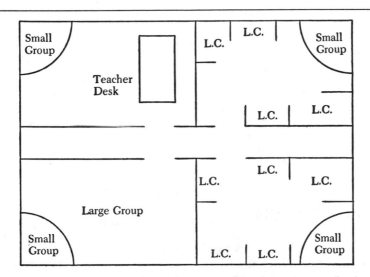

FIGURE 17-3. Open-space Classrooms Arranged by Function.

look upon any particular room as their room. One way to do this is to organize classrooms by function, using one classroom as a quiet independent-study activity area, another for noisy independent-study activity, and a third for small-group activities. A fourth area may also serve for small-group activities and as the location for teachers' desks. (See Figure 17-3.) Learning centers or small-group activities can also be set up in corridors if fire regulations permit.

There are advantages as well as disadvantages to operating a flexible program in a traditional building. One advantage is the reduced visual distraction with more dividers and fewer children in an area. Another advantage is that the separate classrooms provide more perimeter wall space along which to house learning centers.

Major disadvantages include the difficulty of having one teacher supervise more than one-fourth of the full area at a time and the inability to have maximum flexibility in grouping children. For example, extremely large groups cannot be housed in the separate classrooms. This problem can often be overcome, however, by utilizing cafeterias and auditoriums. In no case should a school not start a new instructional program because of limitations imposed by a traditional building. These limitations can almost always be mitigated.

Renovating Existing Facilities

A conventional school building can often be renovated to provide some larger instructional spaces. Removing walls between classrooms or corridors can create a series of two or more classrooms. Occasionally spaces as large as four or more classrooms can be developed. With the addition of carpeting, the improvement of lighting, and the addition of air-conditioners, attractive open areas can be made available for flexible programs. New flexible furniture such as trapizoidal tables and moveable bookcases also add to the attractiveness and function of a renovated building.

Almost any school building, if utilized properly, can be made functional for the instructional program, but the program must be developed first. The building is a tool to enhance the curriculum and facilitate the implementation of the instructional program. Care must be taken not to allow the building to become a stumbling block because of a fixation on previous usage.

EFFECTIVE CARE OF THE SCHOOL PLANT

The principal is not going to spend the day with hammer in hand and a shovel under an arm, but the principal must assume the ultimate responsibility for operating the building at maximum efficiency. There are two important reference groups: classified employees such as custodians, cleaning personnel, cooks, and kitchen personnel who are assigned to the building; and the school-district maintenance department.[1] Working effectively with non-academic personnel to help them do their job requires the same kinds of human relations skills as working with academic staff. Further, as in any decision-making process, the counsel and advice of these persons should be sought and their expertise and insights utilized.

A recent survey of fifty-three "showcase" schools in the Houston Independent School District revealed thirteen common practices which have seemingly resulted in well-kept buildings and grounds:

- Principal (or someone else in supervisory capacity) frequently walks around the building.
- Litter abatement or housekeeping is discussed at teachers' meetings.
- Principal sees that each member of the custodial staff has a specific work schedule.
- Custodial staff sweeps halls regularly during school day.
- Custodial staff inspects and cleans restrooms regularly during school day.
- Custodial staff specifically instructed to pick up litter in and around the school on a daily basis.
- Overall appearance of school is a criterion for evaluating custodial staff members.
- Student organizations assist in responsibility for keeping school clean.
- Parents are involved in effort to maintain or beautify the campus.
- School newspapers print reminders of neatness, cleanliness, trash pick-up, and litter control.
- Students are reprimanded or disciplined for littering.
- Rules restrict the removal of food and beverages from the cafeteria area.
- Teachers stress maintaining the environment as part of their regular curriculum.

Keeping the school site and the building clean and litter-free is everyone's job, but it is up to the principal to set the tone and institute the system so that this occurs. Figure 17-4 depicts a checklist to identify potential trouble spots and provide corrective action.

---

[1]Different school districts are organized differently. In most school districts, custodians and cafeteria personnel are nominally under the jurisdiction of the building executive. However, some districts have a more centralized operation with custodians and maintenance personnel, cafeteria and clerical workers selected and assigned by a central-office division of plant maintenance or a division of business. It is important for the principal to establish the limits of authority and the latitudes of decision making with respect to school-plant operations. In the authors' opinion, those latitudes should be wide indeed and should provide the principal with authority for decision making over all aspects of the operation of the building with the central-office plant division serving as a service unit to provide expert kinds of help when necessary or requested.

Appearance   Yes   No

- Building is well kept in overall appearance.   ___ ___
- No litter is on the grounds.   ___ ___
- Grass is mown.   ___ ___
- Shrubs are trimmed.   ___ ___
- Doormats are in use.   ___ ___
- Walls are void of graffiti.   ___ ___
- Hallways are swept.   ___ ___
- Trash cans are placed in accessible locations.   ___ ___
- Restrooms are clean.   ___ ___
- Restrooms are stocked with appropriate paper products.   ___ ___
- Classrooms are clean and orderly.   ___ ___
- Cafeteria/auditorium is free of food waste and wrappings.   ___ ___
- Service area is without rubbish and debris.   ___ ___

Items sensed, but not observed

- The clean environment is the result of concerted effort,   ___ ___
  not happenstance.
- There is teamwork.   ___ ___
- Custodial staff is efficient   ___ ___
- Principal spends time out of office working with staff and   ___ ___
  making constructive suggestions.
- Good student habits related to building and grounds   ___ ___
  upkeep are reinforced.

Documentation

- School needs are assessed with regard to achieving the   ___ ___
  goal of a clean campus.
- There are specific work schedules for custodial staff.   ___ ___
- Custodial evaluation includes appearance of building.   ___ ___
- Budget shows allocation for cleaning supplies.   ___ ___
- Housekeeping responsibilities are outlined in school   ___ ___
  handbook.
- There is an agenda item for staff meetings re litter abate-   ___ ___
  ment or housekeeping procedures.
- There is a specific program directed at litter abatement, e.g.   ___ ___
  Operation Sparkle.
- Student groups are assigned specific duties for keeping the   ___ ___
  school clean.
- Parent groups have donated plants, equipment, paint, or   ___ ___
  manpower to beautification project.

	Yes	No
• School paper (if applicable) prints reminders of campus appearance.	___	___
• P. A. announcements are made on environmental concerns.	___	___
• There are rules restricting the removal of food and beverages from cafeteria area.	___	___
• Principal maintains listing of appropriate places in curriculum for environmental emphasis.	___	___
• Student schedule permits time to wash hands before lunch.	___	___
• Lesson plans include discussions on cleanliness, sanitation, and neatness.	___	___
• Curriculum content incorporates environmental subject matter.	___	___
• Recognition is given through school paper, programs at events, bulletin boards, and certificates of merit.	___	___

FIGURE 17-4. Clean Building and Grounds Observation Checklist.

SITE UTILIZATION

The high cost of land is often reflected in small school sites and inadequate play areas. This is especially true in urban areas where the children are often most in need of wide open spaces in which to play and experience nature. Nevertheless, there are maintenance and development responsibilities that accrue to the principal regardless of the size of the site. Frequent discussions with the custodial staff can result in maximum effective use of the site.

As a minimum, the site should be kept free of debris and safe, tasks that require daily attention by the custodial staff and regular inspection by an administrator. Playground equipment must be kept in good repair or taken out of service. Preventive maintenance of equipment and the playground surface is the most economical and sensible practice. No principal should tolerate less than this minimum; adequate attention to the site will result in attractiveness, if not beauty.

Attention to the following tasks is important and worthy of administrative supervision:

A. Essential
   1. Daily removal of debris
   2. Weekly preventive maintenance checks and followups (unsafe equipment, unsafe surface—rocks, holes in macadam)

B. Desirable
   1. Creative landscaping
   2. Development of land laboratory

DESIRABLE SITE DEVELOPMENT

The two desirable tasks require some discussion. If the principal is fortunate to be the executive of a building located on a site that is not entirely composed of macadam, some creative opportunities may exist to enhance the attractiveness of the site while providing some excellent educational possibilities.

The professional field of landscape architecture may be of considerable assistance to the principal interested in making a school site both aesthetically pleasing and educationally sound. Help in developing or redeveloping a site may come from such diverse sources as the public library, the United States Department of Agriculture District Office, agricultural extension agents, appropriate university departments, or private landscape architectural firms with some commitment to public service.[2] Such development need not be expensive, and free labor may be available from the PTA/PTO or similar organizations, including a local garden club.

Similarly, in all but the most macadamized of school sites, the development of a land laboratory to enhance the science programs as well as provide other kinds of educational experiences for children is a good possibility, regardless of site size. The size of the site will only determine the nature and kind of flora to be cultivated. Help and inexpensive plantings are readily available, especially from the Department of Agriculture, specifically the Soil Conservation Office. It is possible for schools to become members of a Soil Conservation District through a simple application by the school board. Trees and bushes may be purchased inexpensively with Soil Conservation District help. That office also will assist in the proper placement of plants and give instruction on care and nourishment. Other help in the development of a land laboratory is also available from some of the same agencies mentioned previously in the discussion of appropriate landscaping of the school site. The principal, however, must initiate action in these matters.

MAINTENANCE OF THE BUILDING

The inside of the building requires the same sort of attention to create an attractive and safe learning-living-working environment for pupils and staff. Even old buildings can be attractively maintained. Most large districts have a director of maintenance and operation to employ skilled persons to respond to refurbishment and major maintenance needs of all the buildings in the district. However, the principal, working with the custodial staff, must

---

[2]Creativity and sensitive thinking with respect to the needs of youngsters exist everywhere. One of the authors of this book remembers quite well the rather effective use by one architect of a large quantity of soil that remained on a new school site after excavation for the foundation. In a corner of the school site, the architect had workers form a long sloping hill. When asked why, the architect smiled and said, "Kids need hills to run down." The school was constructed in the midwest in an especially flat area.

identify those major needs ahead of emergency conditions to insure that they are systematically attended to. Even in large districts the day-to-day repairs and light maintenance functions will fall to the building custodial staff.

At the beginning of each school year the principal should meet with the custodian·or the custodial staff to chart the long-range objectives for building maintenance for the year and to work out a systematic plan for addressing those needs. Much of the custodial work, of course, will be routine and daily or weekly in nature. Cooperative development of a work schedule is desirable, and regular inspection by the principal is important.

The principal should anticipate the usual conflicts that occur from time to time between support service personnel, such as custodians, and the instructional staff. Neither, unfortunately, often understands the problems and responsibilities of the other very well, and this often causes disruptive conflicts or, at the least, wary truces. Such conflicts run the gamut from the custodian's refusal to put the chairs in a room back in circles because it is more difficult to clean that way, to out-and-out warfare between a department and the custodial staff over the unwillingness of the instructional staff to have the children reasonably police the area after a unit in art. Many of these problems are simply human relations problems, and a principal must be sensitive to them and take steps to engender equal understanding.

Routinizing Custodial Functions

Effective supervision of building maintenance programs does not require an inordinate amount of time and can be regulated through the use of a simple checklist, as shown in Figure 17-5.

The principal and the custodial staff should give particular attention to common internal building flaws such as inadequate lighting fixtures, roof or wall leaks, dirt in the corners, broken windows, or torn sashes. The entire staff, including instructional staff, should be asked to assist in identifying maintenance needs and reporting them immediately to the office for attention. Many times annoying maintenance defects are allowed to continue simply because a teacher or another staff member has not reported them and they have gone unnoticed by custodial staff. Some defects such as a torn sash or graffiti on a restroom wall, for example, breed others at an almost exponential rate until a major effort and expense is required. Overnight one torn sash becomes sixteen torn sashes, some torn to the point where no repair is possible. Similarly, one clever but obscene statement on a restroom wall provokes others at a geometric rate, to the point where the entire wall has to be repainted.

Scheduling the Work

The custodial staff requires a regular routine consistent with the educational program conducted in the school building. The scheduled projects to be com-

School _____ Date _____

Building _____

Custodians _____

	Condition	Remarks

Roofs
Roofing
Flushing and Coping
Skylights
Gutters
Vents

Exterior Wood Trim
Rakes and Facia
Soffits
Window Frames, Sash
Louvres and Vents
Ceilings
Doors

Exterior Plaster and Concrete
Walls
Ceilings
Arcade Slabs
Platforms
Splash Blocks

Exterior Plumbing and Electrical Fixtures
Hose Bibbs
Fire Hose Cabinet
Fire Extinguishers
Break Glass Alarms
Water S O Valves
Gas S O Valves
Switches and Plates
Exterior Lights
Yard Horns and Bells
Electrical Panels
Drinking Fountains

Exterior Metal
Down Spouts and S Blocks
Columns
Louvres
Grease Traps
Doors
Screens
Sumps, Gratings

	Condition	Remarks

Exterior Concrete, Brickwork, A.C. and D.G.
Curbs and Gutters
Drive-ins
Sidewalks
Incinerators
Water-Meter Boxes
Gas-Meter Boxes
Electrical Vaults
Asphalt-Concrete Areas
Decomposed Granite Areas
Fences and Gates
Bicycle Stands
Flag Pole
Parking Lot
Splash Blocks
Playground Equipment

Exterior Areas
Turf
Lawns
Sprinkler Systems
Trees
Shrubs

Room No. _____

	Condition	Remarks

Floor
Walls
Ceiling
Wood Trim,
Venetian Blinds
Cabinets
Drain Boards
& Splashes
Furniture
Heating &
Controls
Hardware
Electrical
Fixtures
Educational
Equipment

Room No. _____

	Condition	Remarks

Intercom
Amplifier
System
Metal
Partitions
Tile
Plumbing &
Fixtures
Kitchen
Equipment
Stage
Equipment
Towel &
Toilet
Tissue Cab.
Mirrors

Emory Stoops et al., *Handbook of Educational Administration*   (Boston: Allyn and Bacon, 1975), pp. 384–85. Used by permission.

FIGURE 17-5. Checklist for Regular Inspections of Individual Maintenance.

pleted during the school year need to be supplemented by a daily and weekly time schedule that insures routine custodial tasks and maintenance. An example of a work schedule with both a task and time dimension can be seen in Figures 17-6 and 17-7. Figure 17-6 shows a daytime custodial schedule, while Figure 17-7 shows an evening schedule. Times are approximate, of course, and the schedules should be developed in concert with the custodial staff in order that the estimates are reasonable and appropriate to the unique features of each building.

SUPPLIES AND EQUIPMENT MANAGEMENT

A major responsibility of the elementary school principal will be securing, inventorying, and allocating supplies and equipment necessary to facilitate the educational program. It is essential to provide quantities of soft goods (supplies) and the appropriate number of hard goods (equipment) so that they are available ahead of educational needs and secured in the most economical manner possible. It is equally important to provide a management system that won't require the principal to spend an inordinate amount of time on this function. If the school operates under a budget development system such as described in Chapter 18, the selection and purchase of needed supplies and equipment in support of educational goals can become routinized. At most it should require a regular review to see that (1) anticipated needs are met on schedule; (2) that estimated costs remain within budget; (3) that appropriate discounts allowed by suppliers are taken; (4) that inventories are adequate; and (5) that equipment is appropriately tagged, recorded, conveniently stored, and used.

Today's flexible educational programming, which attempts to address the variety of needs of individual learners, requires a great variety of educational materials and equipment, making the task of management somewhat more complex than in the days when uniform sets of texts were the primary means by which the curriculum was implemented. Nevertheless, even though managing supplies and equipment has become more complex, the job can be done effectively when coupled with systematic long- and short-range planning procedures.

Storage and Inventory Control

The day-to-day needs of instructional staff are such that amounts of common educational supplies such as mimeograph paper, art paper, crayons, or chalk, can be relatively easily predicted and kept in sufficient reserve to handle needs over a period of a few months. Schools should avoid taking up valuable storage space with an inordinate oversupply, but a quick comparison of projected needs and past experiences should be sufficient to avoid this. The school secretary or other designated person can have responsibility for insuring that the appropriate amount of day-to-day supplies is available. This task need not and

7:00 AM to 12:00 AM (5-hour worker)	
7:00–8:00 AM	Check heating temperatures.
	Inspect school premises — pick up trash as you enter.
	Put out hose for watering.
	Open administration unit at 7:30 AM
8:00–9:00 AM	Report to office at 8:00 AM — Do this every day!
	Open front gate at 8:15 AM
	Open vehicle gate at 8:15 AM
	Put up flags at 8:30 AM
	Burn trash.
9:00–10:00 AM	Sweep corridors and pick up paper blown and thrown on yard as you water lawns.
	Water lawns. Sweep patio with sweeper.
10:00–12:00 AM	Help set up cafetorium for lunch or special assembly.
	Do any odd jobs requested by principal.

10:00 AM to 6:30 PM (8-hour worker — 30 min. for lunch)	
10:00–10:30 AM	Report to office at 10:00 AM.
	Dust administration unit.
	Inspect women's and men's toilets for paper, soap, towels, etc.
10:30–11:00 AM	Inspect girls' toilets for supplies.
	Set up cafetorium for lunch — morning custodian helping.
11:00–11:30 AM	Spot, wash windows, weed flowers, and do any small cleaning jobs needed.
11:30–12:00 AM	Eat lunch.
12:00–1:00 PM	Spot, wash windows, weed flowers, and do any small cleaning jobs needed.
1:00–3:00 PM	Work in cafetorium. This includes teachers' dining room and setting up for any afternoon or evening cafetorium use.
3:00–4:00 PM	Sweep, dust, clean toilets, clean drinking fountains, empty wastebaskets in rooms 21 and 22. Sweeping takes 20 to 30 minutes per room, depending upon the primary furniture in the rooms and including cleaning toilets and drinking fountains.
4:00–6:00 PM	Sweep, dust, clean toilets, clean drinking fountains, empty wastebaskets in rooms 1, 2, 3, 4, and 5.
6:00–6:30 PM	Clean administration unit.

Emory Stoops et al., *Handbook of Educational Administration* (Boston: Allyn and Bacon, 1975), pp. 392–93. Used by permission.

FIGURE 17-6. Daily Custodial Work Schedule.

should not require much attention by the principal. An inventory control procedure will permit routine replenishment of supplies. Adequate inventories of educational materials and supplies that are unique to special aspects of the program can be maintained by the person responsible for that special aspect of the program. Replenishment of these supplies should also be simply a matter of routine.

2:00 PM to 10:30 PM (8-hour worker — 30 min. for supper)	
2:00–2:30PM	Report to office at 2:00 PM
	Empty garbage cans, clean, scald, let drip — replace.
	Help with cafetorium set-up when needed.
2:30–3:00 PM	Sweep rooms in primary dept. Dust, close windows, turn out lights, etc.
3:00–6:00 PM	Sweep, dust, clean toilets, drinking fountains in primary dept. rooms.
6:00–6:30 PM	Supper.
6:30–9:30 PM	Sweep, dust, clean toilets, drinking fountains in upper grade rooms. Finish by dusting all cleared surfaces in all rooms.
9:30–10:30 PM	Check all doors and windows throughout the plant even though you locked them as you finished in each unit. Check all gates as you lock up.

Emory Stoops et al., *Handbook of Educational Administration* (Boston: Allyn and Bacon, 1975), p. 393. Used by permission.

FIGURE 17-7. Nightly Custodial Work Schedule.

For convenience, most educational equipment should be housed centrally in the building. Supplies used daily or frequently in the classroom or learning spaces should be located throughout the building. For example, equipment such as overheads and tape recorders should be located in almost all of the teaching and learning spaces or classrooms. Similarly, equipment and material supportive of the science program, social studies program, or the arts should be located in that part of the building designated for those programs.

All equipment, irrespective of where it is housed, should be tagged or identified in some manner and inventoried. Further, equipment must be kept in good repair and staff should be aware of their responsibility to report immediately any malfunction of equipment. The principal can give each teacher a supply of mimeographed notices, perhaps printed on red paper, of needed repairs or equipment malfunctions. The notice can identify the particular piece of equipment and describe the nature of the malfunction. These slips should be turned in immediately to the office for action. Figure 17-8 is a sample of such a form.[3]

---

[3]This same form can be used by teachers to identify any needed repair in the building.

Date _____

Instructor _____

HELP!

IT NEEDS FIXING!

_____ What Malfunctioned?

_____ Location and Identifying Number.

_____ Describe what went wrong.

_____

_____

Bring equipment to the office if you can. (Attach this slip to it if you do.)

FIGURE 17-8. Red Flag for Equipment Repair.

Staff Work Areas

Every school needs an instructional staff workroom for the preparation of transparencies, overlays, displays, and so forth. Large school systems may have educational technicians to handle the preparation of elaborate audiovisual aids, but often the school staff itself will want to be able to prepare simple kinds of visuals for immediate use. Supplies and equipment must be provided to make this possible. Often too, the production of less elaborate audiovisual aids can be the responsibility of paraprofessionals or parent volunteers.

Using Equipment

A school will often invest in very expensive equipment only to find that it is not used or is underused by instructional staff. Many times the reason for this is that the staff has not been trained in the use of the equipment or does not understand its instructional possibilities. Thus, instructional and staff support services personnel must receive training in the use and function of the equipment available in the school. Many principals take extensive advantage of the expertise of sales personnel and technicians of the various suppliers and have these individuals available at inservice workshops to work with staff in putting the equipment to best use.

Central Warehousing

Supply management in school systems is frequently handled at the central-office level. Even if the principal has a considerable amount of responsibility with respect to supply management, large systems will have a central warehouse from which most supplies and equipment are secured. There is considerable advantage to this because systems can develop standardized lists of materials, with precise specifications. These can be periodically reviewed to provide maximum use of school system dollar resources.

Further, certain kinds of educational materials can be housed centrally in the school district. Materials such as films, filmstrips, or audio- and videotapes that are used throughout the system but are not required in any individual unit of study except on an infrequent basis are often catalogued, inventoried, and housed centrally in the school district. Where this is the case, teachers must understand the need for more lead time in requisitioning and securing these for classroom use. This is not to say that last-minute requests should not be acted upon to the degree possible—only an unhealthy school system characterized by abundant bureaucratization cannot respond to unplanned "teaching moments"—but in general, staff should anticipate special needs for centrally housed educational materials.

NONACADEMIC SUPPORT PERSONNEL

Before closing this discussion of business management at the building level, some comment is appropriate about the use of nonacademic support personnel in carrying on the business function of the school. Most of the nonacademic personnel will be persons employed to work in the business side of the enterprise. The selection, training, and careful development of responsibilities for these persons is an important managerial function, yet this has received very little attention in professional literature.[4] Improperly trained workers or workers unsure of their responsibility, whether in the cafeteria, in the boiler room, or in the principal's office, are a liability. Similarly, the nonacademic staff member who does not understand or particularly like children, while perhaps not common, is also a liability that a school cannot really afford.

At times entry into nonacademic school positions seems almost casual, and yet such positions are a vital part of a well-functioning school building. For example, a secretary who does not understand that the position requires public relations skills as well as technical skills may produce beautifully type-

---

[4]Such personnel include paraprofessionals, secretarial and clerical staff, cooks and kitchen helpers, custodians, maintenance workers and cleaning personnel, among others. Discussions about building-level operations often overlook the contributions to the educational program made by these noncertificated employees. Yet, nonacademic support staff do have important jobs to perform, and most come into daily contact with pupils.

written reports and books that balance to the penny while doing the school irreparable damage within the community.

It is incumbent on the school system, therefore, to develop personnel policies for the employment, inservice growth, and retention of good nonacademic personnel. Job descriptions, adequate compensation, and other benefits must reflect the school's interest in maintaining a nonacademic work force of the highest quality. The standards of employment should not only evidence an interest in appropriate technical competence but a realization that most of these personnel will be working with children in some way or another. This simply suggests that the appropriate attitudes and understanding about young people may be one of the most important employment and retention criteria. The principal must employ the same kind of leadership skills in working with nonacademic personnel that are used in the academic arena.

SUMMARY

School buildings should be used in the most functional way possible to enhance the implementation of instruction. It doesn't matter if the building is a new open-space structure or an eighty-year-old traditional structure. Nevertheless all designs for curriculum, for student grouping, and for staffing patterns are greatly influenced by the way school buildings are used.

The key word once again is flexibility. As instructional plans change, the utilization of the building must change. In order to have the maximum flexibility in a school, the building requires flexible spaces. These do not necessarily have to be open spaces but preferably will be spaces that can be organized to meet instructional needs with low-cost transitions.

The physical environment of the school contributes mightily to the learning environment. An attractive, well-kept clean school building is essential. It is, in great part, the principal's responsibility to see to it that custodians and other service personnel know what their jobs are and to arrange work conditions so that they can conduct their work with dispatch. Similarly, it is important that the principal provide the appropriate response mechanisms so that teachers can go about their work with the right equipment at the right time.

BIBLIOGRAPHY

Castaldi, Basil. *Educational Facilities: Planning, Remodeling, and Management.* Boston: Allyn and Bacon, 1977.
Day, C. William. "Energy Conservation and School Facilities." *School Business Affairs* 46, no. 3 (March 1980): 28–35.
Feldman, Edward B. "Don't Neglect Your Cleaning Curriculum." *Nation's Schools* 91, no. 5 (May 1973): 66–68.

Graves, Ben E. "How to Turn Old or Obsolete School Space into Really Usable Space." *American School Board Journal* 262, no. 4 (April 1975): 50–52.

Graves, Ben E. "The Recycled School." *Phi Delta Kappan* 56, no. 5 (January 1975): 341–44.

Harroan, Jack T., ed. *Good School Maintenance: A Manual of Programs and Procedures for Buildings, Grounds and Equipment.* Springfield, Ill: Illinois Association of School Boards, 1976.

Hughes, Larry W. and Gordon, William M. "How to Make a School Closing Make Sense." *American School Board Journal* 167, no. 2 (February 1980): 31–33.

Shimanoff, Perry S. "Custodial Management Training for School Principals." *American School and University* 52, no. 5 (January 1980): 9–10.

Stoops, Emory, et al. *Handbook of Educational Administration.* Boston: Allyn and Bacon, 1975.

Williams, Don. "Training School Custodians." *American School and University* 52, no. 8 (April 1980): 10–12.

18

Fiscal Planning
and Recordkeeping

INTRODUCTION

Sounds from the school business office:

"But, why isn't there any more ditto paper; it's only March!"

"Miss Wilson, the state auditors office just called—something about some alleged misappropriated funds. Can you help?"

"And all it will cost for this supplemental reading program is $450 the first year. Sign here."

"The school orchestra needs new uniforms."

"Just remembered—I have to have a metro bus for the annual sixth grade campout."

"Jack, the art department overspent its budget again."

"Well, if you had submitted the purchase order on time, you would have received the lower price. As it is . . ."

"You spent school money for what?"

"Looks like we have a problem here. The federal regulations indicate you can't use project funds the way you did."

"Dr. Davis, the representatives of the Citizens for Economy in Schools are here for their appointment. They look grim."

The principal has a major role to play in the fiscal management of the school. Leading a staff to creative, far-sighted budget development, even causing a staff simply to engage in sensible spending practices after the fact, requires well-honed human relations skills, an intimate knowledge of curricular needs, skill in systematic planning, a good understanding of the fiscal realities of the school district, and a good acquaintance with proper accounting procedures.

A sound budget enhances the ability of the school to deliver on its promises to young people and the ability of the principal to advocate the school's needs persuasively before districtwide budget committees. Knowledge about good accounting procedures insures that the principal will stay out of court and the school out of bankruptcy.

Managing a school budget requires great skill. Poor recordkeeping procedures and other unsound fiscal practices result in mismanaged dollars—indefensible in today's economy of scarce resources.

Schools are big business. In many communities the school system is the single largest employer of personnel and the largest industry in terms of capital flow. School districts receive and disburse huge amounts of money for a variety of services and materials. Similarly, principals in individual school buildings administer sizable financial resources that come from the central district office as a result of local, state, and federal programs, as well as much smaller sums collected from such sources as PTA's, school clubs, and plays.[1]

The fiscal responsibility of the elementary principal is both active and supervisory. It is active in the sense that, within the guidelines set by the central office, the principal establishes the regular procedures governing the fiscal operation of each building. It is supervisory in that the principal regularly monitors the activities of those staff members charged with properly recording and reporting financial transactions involving the school.

The degree of autonomy that an elementary school principal has with respect to the final operation of the school will vary. In some school systems virtually all financial decisions are made in the central office by the superintendent or the superintendent's designate. In other systems the principal has wide latitude in constructing a budget and in the expenditure of funds for personnel, operations, and capital outlay. Principals must know what expectations superordinates have with respect to financial decision making at the building level.

Managing the business side of an elementary school extends from simple recordkeeping of modest amounts of activity-account money to the complexities of program-planning budget procedures, depending upon the size of the school and the school system and the degree of budgetary and financial-decision autonomy accorded individual principals. It is a changing world and the movement toward more decentralization in large school systems has increased fiscal decision-making autonomy and responsibility for many principals.

The Budgeting Process

Good budgeting contains four distinct steps: planning and allocation of all costs, adoption, administration and coordination, and review and appraisal.

---

[1]These latter sources are called internal monies and are frequently unaudited and not accounted for by the central district office.

The budget process itself is cyclical and continuous. The review and appraisal step, for example, immediately precedes the following fiscal year's planning and preparation step. (See Figure 18-1.)

Good budgeting is much more than simply categorically allocating antici- pated revenues and subsequently recording the expenditures made in these categories. Being able to specifically "cost out" the various activities of an educational program is a meagre accomplishment unless such costing out is simply the first step in evaluating the effectiveness of those activities in terms of the attainment of the goals of the institution. Thus, budget development should begin with an examination of the goals and objectives of the various as- pects of the educational program. Total staff participation is desirable in the formative stages.

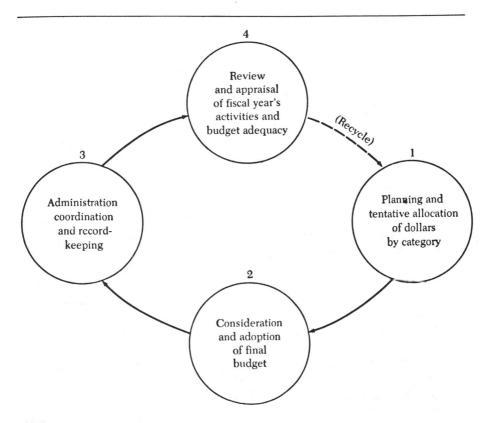

FIGURE 18-1. Budgeting: A Cyclical Process.

Setting Priorities—Where the Dollars Should Go

Foremost in budget building is education planning. The relationship between the educational goals and objectives of the school and the budget that supports these goals must be made obvious. Good budgeting is the result of careful educational planning; it is not a catalog of "outgoes" that lists retrospectively where the money went.

Many school staffs get caught in an incremental budgeting game and, because they do, perform a great disservice to their clients. Incremental budgeting requires simple acceptance of the status quo. Any increases or losses in student population are projected for the next year, and, on the basis of what was required for the current year, dollar needs are established. Such a budget development process is simple, requires very little thought, and can be accomplished in a short period of time with a calculator and a census tract. It is also dysfunctional.

Preferable is a budget development procedure that uses basic elements of Program Planning Budgeting Systems (PPBS).[2]

Program Planning Budgeting System. At its simplest PPBS involves five steps:

1. Establishing the general goals to be achieved
2. Identifying the specific objectives that define this goal
3. Developing the program and processes that it is expected will achieve the objectives and goals
4. Establishing the formative and summative evaluation practices
5. A review and recycle procedure that indicates whether or not, or the degree to which, the program and processes resulted in the achievement of the objectives and goals; this helps determine other procedures, processes, and programs

In other words, PPBS is designed to help a school staff decide specifically what they want to accomplish and how to go about it. PPBS focuses upon goal accomplishment and, if sensitively and sensibly applied, will provide for efficient expenditures of monies.

Education planning is often concerned primarily with the inputs of education. Typically the school budget has been concerned with a numbers game: the number of staff, books, equipment, and buildings that must be secured, purchased, and assembled in order to educate a determined number of children. In this regard PPBS differs substantially from other budget building procedures because it focuses first on desired outputs of the effort (goals and objectives) and afterward considers the number of staff, books, equipment, and buildings needed to obtain the desired end.

---

[2]The following discussion is not intended to supplant a school finance course nor to argue the merits of a full scale PPBS, but the rationale undergirding Program Planning Budget Systems is a sound one.

IMPLEMENTING A SYSTEMATIC BUDGET BUILDING PROCESS

A budget should be the result of planning the educational program. The answer to the question of how one builds an educationally sound budget starts at the base—the educational program—and develops outward. One discovers the program needs by asking the people in the best position to provide the answer—the instructional staff. However, only careful organization provides an effective mechanism to translate the needs of the program efficiently into dollar amounts in the budget. If budget building is to be anything more than a means of classifying outgo, it must consider the future.

Most administrators make at least a modest effort to involve instructional staff in the budget building process, but often this becomes simply a matter of asking the staff for their ideas about needed equipment or supplies. The responses are often uninspired, mundane, and short-sighted suggestions, many of which are of doubtful overall significance to the educational endeavor. The reason for this is that many staffs really haven't had much practice in planning expenditures of significant amounts of money to improve their departments. Frequently the nature of the request from the administrator causes staff members to think solely in terms of additional materials for the department or the school, rather than in terms of the direction the educational program ought to be taking. "What do you need now?" is too often the question, when the question really should be "Where do you see this school, or your department, heading in the next few years, and what is it going to take to get there?" Since staff involvement in decision making is the most effective means for bringing about real change, the effort to involve staff in curricular study and change must extend to budget development.

For the past several years a medium-sized school system with which the authors are familiar has been involved in just such a process, and it evidences values well beyond sound budget making. Not the least of these unanticipated outcomes can be the development of staff concern for the future and a continuous assessment of current curricular and instructional practices. Admittedly, however, when the system began to involve instructional staff more directly in the budget building process, it was because administrators were looking for more exact and educationally sound ways of projecting expenditures for the next fiscal year. What has resulted, however, in addition to a better budget is a far more effective use of materials and equipment (teachers get what they most desire and need), well-planned curriculum change based on attention to long-range goals, continuous evaluation of all aspects of the curriculum by those most instrumental in productive change, and a better teaching and learning climate.[3]

---

[3]An excellent discussion of the intricacies of this process also appears in Walter Garms et al., *School Finance: The Economics and Politics of Public Education* (Englewood Cliffs, N. J.: Prentice-Hall, 1978), chaps. 10 and 11.

Step One: Developing the Five-Year Plan. The planning process begins with the development of a five-year plan well in advance of any specific budget proposals for the next fiscal year. This plan is not quickly developed, and the process provides a good basis for inservice workshops with staff. It lends a substantive focus to faculty meetings and workshops held throughout the school year. The process begins by organizing the preschool workshop to focus on planning for the future and to develop several schoolwide, department, or grade-level brainstorming sessions to consider such topics as "what a child at the end of grade three should know," or "what this school needs is," or "outcomes of the K–6 social studies program should be," or any other topics generative of ideas that focus on curricular or student outcomes. Staff members should be encouraged not to be encumbered by any real-world constraints nor to think solely in terms of the current year, but rather to project their thinking as much as five or ten years in the future. Staff members convert the product of these sessions into a series of goals and objectives by a process of synthesizing, summarizing, and combining.[4]

Once the staff has refined the statements of objectives and goals, they should identify, often through another brainstorming session, the processes, materials, and personnel that will be necessary to implement these goals and objectives. Participants should take care not to get bogged down at this point. The statements are not written on stone and are subject to future modification and change. Less than perfection is acceptable lest the staff and the principal be victimized by the paralysis of analysis. The tentative five-year plan will have four major components:

1. A brief description of the current state of the art or discipline that simply describes where the grade level, or subject matter, or curricular field is at the present time in relation to what the literature and research reveal is the ideal state.

2. A statement of goals, objectives, and reasonable indicators of achievement of objectives for the department or grade level. It is important to establish objective indicators of achievement, but detailed lists do not have to be created at this time. It is important to move the staff as rapidly as possible through the initial five-year-plan development into the actual budget development process so that they may achieve a reward for their hard work reasonably quickly. This establishes credibility and is psychologically most important for a school staff which is engaging in this process for the first time. Again, the authors would stress that less than perfection must be acceptable; staff will become more sophisticated as they engage in the process in sub-

[4]A *goal* may be defined as a direction-setting statement of general worth that is timeless and not specifically measurable. An *objective* explicates the goal statement, is more specific, has a time dimension, and concludes with a series of indicators—subjective and objective evidence—that will be accepted as evidence that the objective has been achieved. These may not be absolutes but simply conditions that, if present, the staff or an individual will accept as being sufficient to show that the objective has been achieved.

sequent years. The five-year plan is subject to modification through the formative evaluation which will occur as it unfolds. Slavishly following the procedures suggested here would be unwise indeed; one must not let the principles of systematic budget development be subverted by unthinking observance of procedures. The sophistication of staff and local conditions must be taken into consideration.

3. A list of processes that will implement the objectives.
4. A list of equipment, materials, personnel, and other resources needed to support the process established in the previous section. (Figure 18-2 provides an outline for a statement of a five-year plan.)

This is the culmination point for the development of the five-year plan. It is subject to refinement and modification and will ultimately be submitted for

Department (or grade level): _____

Prepared by: _____

Submitted to: _____

Date: _____

1. Current state of the art.

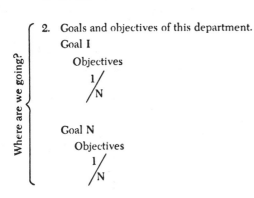

2. Goals and objectives of this department.
   Goal I
      Objectives
      1/N

   Goal N
      Objectives
      1/N

3. Procedures to achieve objectives and goals.

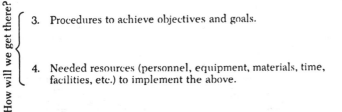

4. Needed resources (personnel, equipment, materials, time, facilities, etc.) to implement the above.

FIGURE 18-2. The Five-Year Plan.

executive review and discussion. It does not yet contain any dollar figures. The process needs adequate time for creative and careful thinking, but definite timelines should be established for the completion of this process. Otherwise, it can become a rather cumbersome, never-ending intellectual exercise.

Step Two: Developing the One-Year Plan. The general direction for the department or grade level will have been plotted in the five-year plan. The one-year plan, in effect, asks the staff to spell out what should happen in the next year if the five-year plan is to be ultimately realized. Figure 18-3 provides the suggested format for the one-year plan.

Department (or Grade Level) _____

Fiscal Year _____

Prepared by _____

Amount Requested _____

Amount Allocated _____

Request (Indicate after each item which long-term objective it supports.)	Estimated Cost	Suggested Source of Supply	Suggested Source of $ (Federal funds; local funds; donation; state experimental funds, etc.)
1. Needed Personnel			
2. Needed equipment and materials			
3. Needed other resources (e.g., travel monies, consultants, etc.)			
N.B. List above in descending order of priority.			
Total Requested _____			

4. Attach a brief statement describing how this proposed budget is consistent with and supportive of the five-year plan.

FIGURE 18-3. The One-Year Plan.

This form translates the one-year plan into needed equipment, supplies, supplementary materials, immediate changes or addition of personnel, remodeling, and other resources such as travel monies and consultants. Justification for each specific item should be available in the one-year-plan document. This need not be elaborate but requires some brief statement about how the budget proposal is consistent with the five-year plan. An additional feature is that the departments or grade levels are asked to list their needs in order of priority. If cutting becomes necessary because of insufficient total dollars, it can begin with the lowest-priority items in each proposal.

Step Three: Setting a Timeline. Ample time must be provided in the initial effort to provide a five-year plan and ultimately translate that into one-year budget proposals. This is an initial timeline only. Obviously, a five-year plan must be addressed totally only every five years, even though adjustments are necessary throughout the period. During the first year of developing a five-year plan, a school should also continue its former budget development procedure because startup and five-year-plan development will require most of the first year and new one-year budget proposals will not be available until the next fiscal year.

Subsequent Steps. These steps involve submitting budget and curriculum proposals to the principal and the administrative staff, their subsequent approval or return for clarification or modification, the preparation of a total school budget in summary form by the principal and staff for submission to the central office, negotiations and approval of the school budget in some form by the ultimate fiscal authority in the school district.

Eventually an approved budget is returned by the principal to each department or grade level that will determine requisitions throughout the year. Each month a recapitulation of purchases to date is returned to the department. Figure 18-4 is an example of a monthly budget sheet for an elementary department.

These procedures may sound quite involved and rather formalized, but in actual operation they need not be. Moreover, the process certainly gives staff much insight into the procedures of school finance as well as a great deal of control over the instructional budget.

Expectations and Product. Involvement of instructional staff in budget building does not make the administrator's job any easier. However, it does supply a principal with much of the data needed to justify increases in the budget to the superintendent or the board of education. Moreover, never will the central office and the board be as well informed about expenditures and the reasons behind them as they will be under this system.

Once the process gets underway, the principal must challenge each department and individual to plan, propose, justify, and defend. Just because the third grade staff thinks it would be nice to have some SRA reading laboratories is not justification. Staff thinking must be made more precise and objec-

DEPARTMENTAL BUDGET, 1984

Mathematics Department   Month _____
Southeast Elementary

Budget Area & Item	Allowable	Exp. this Month	Exp. to Date	Remainder
TEXTS (B–4)				
5th Modern Math	$ 1000.00			
Programmed Texts				
and Temac Binders				
21 @ $10.50	220.50			
Supplementary Texts	450.00			
EQUIPMENT (D–4)				
Volume Demonstration				
Set (1)	60.00			
Graph Board (multi-				
purpose) (1)	35.00			
Tightgrip Chalk-				
holder (6)	1.00			
Rack of Compasses	12.00			
Rack of Protractors	15.00			
SUPPLEMENTARY (B–6)				
Universal Encyclopedia				
of Math (2)	40.00			
Other References	100.00			
AUDIO VISUAL (D–7)				
Overhead Projector	275.00			
DISCRETIONARY				
SUPPLIES	200.00			
SUB TOTAL	$ 2408.50			
PERSONNEL (A–3)				
2 Consultants 2 days				
each for in-service plus				
expenses	1800.00			
SUB TOTAL	$ 1800.00			
TOTAL	$ 4208.50			

FIGURE 18-4. Sample Departmental Budget.

tive. The principal can assist in this with adroit questioning. It takes time to achieve foresighted educational planning. Principals must tolerate less-than-visionary budget proposals during the early years.

The system must remain flexible. If the middle-school social studies department decides it has made a mistake or realizes that certain needs have changed, adjustments in the budget and in the plan must be possible. After three or four years of using this process, the principal and central office administrators can expect some very sophisticated budget proposals. Once a staff becomes accustomed to the idea of planning and is convinced that the challenge is serious, tough decisions and hardnosed proposals and defense sessions will be a reality. At this point the dollar total of the proposals ought to outstrip the amount of money available. If not, staff and the principal are really not doing their job. A staff that has not been involved in such a process will tend to think in terms of nickels and dimes in the beginning when it ought to be thinking in terms of dollars. However, once convinced that the principal's commitment is there, the staff's imagination will pick up.

The budget-building process just described attempts to accomplish three things. It gives the appropriate personnel a large measure of responsibility for initial budget preparation in their areas of instructional expertise. Second, it forces positive, foresighted curriculum planning. Third, it provides substantiation to the board and the community that tax dollars are being spent in an efficient and effective manner. Figure 18-5 depicts the entire process.

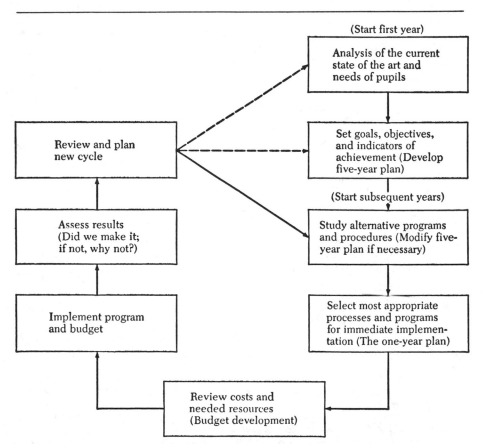

FIGURE 18-5. Systematic Program and Budget Development: Developing and Implementing the Five-Year Plan.

However, as Garms and his associates point out, the process is not quite as rational as it may appear:

> A casual glance at the precise language and impressive detail of a finished budget creates the impression that public school budgeting is a highly rational process. Budgets typically discuss a community's educational needs and social objectives and assert that designated educational programs will accomplish those objectives in an equitable and efficient manner . . .
>
> In fact, public school budgeting is part and parcel of an often heated political process. The final budget for a large district reflects choices constrained by state law, previous budgets, negotiated agreements, and the political influence of key actors. Those choices may have little to do with the rational analysis of alternative means to accomplish the stated objectives. It is important to recognize the political nature of public school budgeting and to design the decision-making process to fairly represent those with an interest in education, including citizens, administrators, teachers, parents, and students.[5]

Once the budget is developed and approved, it becomes the responsibility of the principal to see that it is managed properly. Skillful budget management is the subject of the next section of this chapter.

FINANCIAL RECORDKEEPING

All school systems have accounting procedures with which the principal must be familiar because most school principals at least oversee bookkeeping functions. Because accounting procedures do vary between school systems and states, we will not specifically cover them here.[6]

In general, school principals must keep and properly monitor a journal of receipts and disbursements. (See Figure 18-6.) The principal may also have to maintain appropriate records for specially funded federal projects in the school. The government has established specific procedures that must be followed. In addition, the principal will secure supplies and materials either through a requisition from central warehousing perhaps using a system of transfer vouchers or directly from a supplier. Probably most, if not all, of the principal's accounting responsibilities will occur in the operations—e.g., supplies and equipment—part of the budget. The central office of most school districts will account for personnel and capital income and expenditures.

---

[5]Walter I. Garms, James W. Guthrie, and Lawrence C. Pierce, *School Finance: The Economics and Politics of Public Education* (Englewood Cliffs, N. J.: Prentice-Hall, 1978).

[6]Many states and individual school districts use a standard accounting system employing categories established by the federal government. Such a system results in uniformity and comparability of income and expenditures. See the United States Office of Education, *Financial Accounting: Classification and Standard Terminology for Local and State School Systems,* rev. ed. (Washington, D. C.: Government Printing Office, 1973).

MONTHLY STATEMENT OF RECEIPTS AND DISBURSEMENTS

Report for _____ 19 ____   Prepared by _____

Central
Treasurer

Account	Cash on Hand 1st of Month	Receipts This Month	Total	Disbursements	Balance End of Month

TOTAL $ _____ $ _____ $ _____ $ _____ $ _____

Reconciliation of Bank Statement

Bank balance as of _____ $ _____
Plus deposits not shown on statement $ _____
Plus others _____ $ _____
Minus outstanding checks _____   TOTAL $ _____
                                                              $ _____
Book balance as of _____ $ _____
                                                              $ _____

FIGURE 18-6. A Monthly Report Form.

In most elementary schools a clerk or secretary will be responsible for keeping the books. Under the principal's direction, this person will generally make the journal entries and keep the records in order. This *does not* relieve the principal of any executive responsibility, however. Regular review as well as an independent annual audit is essential. During the first few months on the job the principal should be involved very directly in the accounting procedures to learn intimately the business side of the enterprise. Proper accounting and budget procedures are essential to a well-managed school.

Faculty often misunderstand the need for accounting procedures and view the need for requisitions, invoices, purchase orders, and receipts as unnecessarily cumbersome and designed to get in the way of their securing needed equipment and materials. Nevertheless, any good accounting system requires supportive or original documents such as bank deposit information, requisitions, and purchase orders. The accounting system exists in order for funds to be expended efficiently and in accordance with the plan incorporated in the budget document. In a sense, it also provides a history of spending and may be used to evaluate how the plan developed in the budget document is proceeding.

Financial resources are always in short supply and it is not likely that all the budgetary requests in support of the instructional objectives and school goals can be met in any one year. Thus, the principal interested in educational equity and the most efficient use of available dollars must keep in close touch with outgo, making sure that it is consistent with the budget plan and that sufficient funds remain for the purchase of high-priority items throughout the school year. Often improper accounting procedures result in an inadequate amount of money in April for the purchase of routine supplies necessary to complete the school year. Because of such circumstances, teachers have been known to overpurchase and hoard supplies in their rooms.

Most school districts use an accrual accounting system. This means that as soon as a purchase order is initiated or a requisition is approved, it is entered in the account book. Through such a process the principal knows immediately how much money remains to be expended in any particular account. This system prevents spending beyond the amount of money available.

The faculty and nonacademic personnel will not necessarily understand the intricacies of the accounting system and from time to time individuals on the faculty may view the entire process as a hindrance to the instructional program. Thus, the wise principal will spend some time in faculty and staff meetings—perhaps at a preschool workshop—informing the staff why good recordkeeping and accounting procedures are important to an instructional program. Beyond this, it is the principal's responsibility to make sure that the practices being followed are, in fact, efficient, that they do provide for quick delivery of materials and other services to the classroom, and that decision making with respect to expenditures is consistent with the established instructional budget. Figure 18-7 depicts a flow of purchase requisitions.

The Transgressing Staff Member

From time to time some staff members may transgress and spend monies without approval or make purchases outside the usual channels. How many times should a transgressing employee be bailed out? Once, perhaps, but probably no more. The unfortunate fact is that some people are not aware of the need for regularized accounting of expenditures and incomes, but the principal must be aware of this need as the executive who is ultimately accountable for what goes on in the school, fiscally and otherwise. The principal must develop

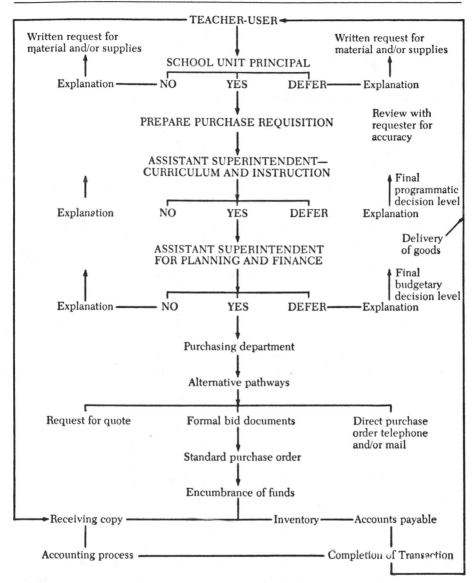

FIGURE 18-7. Flow of a Purchase Requisition.

sensible accounting procedures, instruct staff in their use, and insist that they be followed.

This insistence, of course, should be tempered with sensitivity and understanding. Chastising Mr. Jones because he did not unerringly follow procedures when he purchased an inexpensive instructional gadget from a traveling salesperson is not a good way to engender high morale or creative teaching. So, the principal might bail a teacher out once and use the situation to show that teacher the department budget, the procedures to follow to insure sensible purchasing and good recordkeeping, and the reasons for them.

Yet, a principal must make sure that emergency requests, unplanned expenses, unanticipated instructional opportunities, and similar last minutesorts of things that are important to a good teaching and learning climate do not get lost in a bureaucratic maze. A filmstrip that arrives a month after the completion of a unit is evidence of an unresponsive or inefficient administrative procedure. If this occurs often, it should not be surprising when teachers or staff attempt to circumvent established procedures. In other words, the principal should insure that the procedures actually do facilitate rather than inhibit.

Regular Review

Once systematized, the accounting procedures require only regular monitoring by the principal. Receipt of materials ordered should be noted and materials must be properly inventoried. These are tasks easily performed by the school clerk with a little training. Keeping a separate set of books for district funds will provide the principal with a good check on expenditures against the accounts kept in the central business office. Mistakes are made from time to time and need to be rectified. In many school systems the central business office will supply the principal with periodic financial reports in the form of ledger sheet printouts. These are easily checked against the school's set of books for accuracy. Careful examination of these ledger sheets and a reconciliation with the school's books will provide sufficient financial records, especially if supplemented with additional notations by the principal.

Activity and Other Funds

Many elementary schools receive and distribute monies other than those disbursed by the district office. Such sources and accounts commonly include PTA funds, classroom accounts, insurance monies, candy sales, athletic funds, club treasuries, petty cash, funds from charity drives, and gifts. Individually the accounts are often quite small but collectively often amount to a considerable sum.

A separate set of books should be maintained for these funds, which are generally unaudited by the district. The unwary principal may get into trouble regarding these funds. No less precise bookkeeping procedures are required for these than for the district funds. Many states have passed special legislative acts requiring the establishment of orderly procedures for the administration of school activity funds. Some states as well as local school districts have developed careful policies and procedures to guide individual schools in such financial accounting. Figure 18-8 illustrates internal accounts typical of an elementary school.

MERCHANDISING SERVICE
Bus Ticket
Insurance
Workbooks
PROFIT EARNING
Coke Machine
Pictures
School Store
SPECIAL PURPOSE
Field Trips
Assemblies
Hospitality
Instructional Supplies
ORGANIZATIONS
Faculty Club
Student Council
PTA
Intramural Program
All-School Chorus

FIGURE 18-8. Outline of Typical Internal Ledger Accounts for an Elementary School.

In general, specific procedures must be established to control the collection and disbursement of the activity funds. The following procedures provide a good guide:

1. Official receipts should be issued for all money received.
2. All money expended should be by check, except for small cash purchases made from the petty cash fund.
3. Supporting documents should be kept for all expenditures made.
4. Bank reconciliation statements should be made each month.
5. Monthly and yearly financial statements should be prepared.
6. An audit should be made each year and copies of the audit should be filed with persons having administrative authority for the school.

Figure 18-9 depicts a process for appropriate accounting of activity funds.

Consistent with good financial practice is requiring each group with an account administered by the school to file a simplified budget indicating anticipated income, anticipated expenditures, and persons designated to approve monies to be expended from the account. Further, all school employees who are responsible for the fund should be bonded, with the amount of the bond determined by the estimate of the amount of money the school will handle. Many school districts provide a bond covering all employees in the school sys-

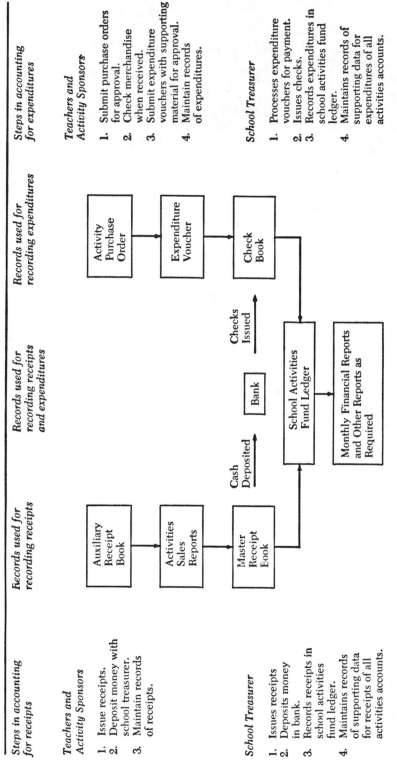

The figure contains the following text, arranged in columns:

Steps in accounting for receipts

Teachers and Activity Sponsors

1. Issue receipts.
2. Deposit money with school treasurer.
3. Maintain records of receipts.

School Treasurer

1. Issues receipts
2. Deposits money in bank.
3. Records receipts in school activities fund ledger.
4. Maintains records of supporting data for receipts of all activities accounts.

Records used for recording receipts

Auxiliary Receipt Book → Activities Sales Reports → Master Receipt Book

Records used for recording receipts and expenditures

Bank

Cash Deposited

Checks Issued

School Activities Fund Ledger

Monthly Financial Reports and Other Reports as Required

Records used for recording expenditures

Activity Purchase Order → Expenditure Voucher → Check Book

Steps in accounting for expenditures

Teachers and Activity Sponsors

1. Submit purchase orders for approval.
2. Check merchandise when received.
3. Submit expenditure vouchers with supporting material for approval.
4. Maintain records of expenditures.

School Treasurer

1. Processes expenditure vouchers for payment.
2. Issues checks.
3. Records expenditures in school activities fund ledger.
4. Maintains records of supporting data for expenditures of all activities accounts.

FIGURE 18-9. Procedures and Records Used in Accounting for School Activity Funds.

tem who are responsible for such funds. The principal should check whether or not this is so in a particular district.

Some school districts require the school principal to make a monthly report about the state of the internal funds in the school. Such a report commonly contains specific and general conditions of the accounts and expenditures. Whether or not this is specifically required by district policy, it is an important procedure for the principal, who should file the report in an appropriate place. It provides substantiation of the expenditure of funds and will assist in the annual audit. Figures 18-10 and 18-11 illustrate a monthly reporting procedure for activity accounts.

FINANCIAL REPORT

School: _____   Report for month of: _____

ASSETS

Cash on hand, petty cash $ _____

Cash in bank, Checking   _____

Cash in bank, Savings   _____

Other, Accounts receivable, etc. (specify)   _____

TOTAL $ _____

FUND BALANCE

Activity	Beginning balance	Receipts		Expenditures		Ending balance
		Month	Year to date	Month	Year to date	
TOTALS						

We certify to the best of our knowledge and belief that this financial report reflects the true condition of the school activity fund.

_____   _____   _____
Principal   School Treasurer   Date

FIGURE 18-10. Monthly Financial Report of the School Activity Fund.

BANK RECONCILIATION

School _____   Report for month of _____

Bank _____

Balance per bank statement _____ $ _____
                              Date

Add   _____

  Deposits in transit   _____

  Other (specify)   _____

Total $ _____

Deduct

  Outstanding checks

Check Number	Date	Payee	Amount

                                                 $ _____

Balance per general ledger _____   _____
                              Date

_____   _____ $ _____
    Principal   School Treasurer   Date

FIGURE 18-11. Monthly Financial Report of the School Activity Fund.

The Audit

Every elementary principal should have the internal account books audited annually by an outside accountant. The product of this audit should be filed with the district office. An audit is not an attack on anyone's integrity. It has two primary purposes: providing good professional suggestions for improving accounting procedures in the individual school and protecting all of those who have been responsible for handling school funds.

Before beginning a position as principal of an elementary school the incoming principal should insist on an audit of all funds as a means of being informed about current practices and improving these as necessary, as well as initially establishing the state of the accounts before assuming responsibility for them. The audit, in effect, red-lines the accounts, and thus the new principal can start with clear fiscal air.

SUMMARY

Financial resources are always in short supply and hard decisions must be made in allocating those monies that are available. Good financial planning—the kind of planning that delivers resources on a systematic basis to the point of greatest need—requires procedures for the involvement of the staff *and* the challenge to look beyond the current year. Incremental budgeting procedures, by definition, stress the status quo and assume that, except for different numbers of students, what was done last year should be done this year.

Once developed, the budget requires careful management. Sound accounting procedures are essential. The principal's role in this is primarily supervisory, but regular monitoring is necessary as is a firm understanding of districtwide fiscal policies.

BIBLIOGRAPHY

Curtis, William H. *Educational Resources Management System.* Chicago: Research Corporation of the Association of School Business Officials, 1971.

Garms, Walter I.; Guthrie, James W.; and Pierce, Lawrence C. *School Finance: The Economics and Politics of Public Education.* Englewood Cliffs, N.J.: Prentice-Hall, Inc., 1978, chaps. 10 and 11.

Greenhalgh, John. *Practitioners Guide to School Business Management.* Boston: Allyn and Bacon, 1978. Chapter 2, "Understanding Accounting and Reporting;" Chapter 3, "Budgeting on a Building Basis;" and Chapter 16, "School Planning Systems" are especially useful to the beginning principal.

Guthrie, James W., ed. *School Finance Policies and Practices: The 1980's—A Decade of Conflict.* Cambridge, Mass.: Ballinger Publishing Co., 1980.

Hentschke, Guilbert C. "Is Zero-Based Budgeting Different From Planning-Programming-Budgeting Systems?" *Planning and Changing* 8 (Summer-Fall 1977): 127–37.

Herman, Jerry T. *Administrator's Practical Guide to School Finance.* West Nyack, N. Y.: Parker Publishing Co., 1977.

Thomas, J. Alan. *The Productive School.* New York: John Wiley and Sons, 1971.

Thompson, Victor A. *Decision Theory, Pure and Applied.* New York: General Learning Press, 1971. This short monograph has an extremely fine critical analysis of Planning Program Budgeting procedures in public organizations.

U.S. Office of Education. *Financial Accounting: Classification and Standard Terminology for Local and State School Systems,* rev. ed. Washington, D. C.: Government Printing Office, 1973.

19

Pupil Transportation and Auxiliary Services and Activities

INTRODUCTION

This chapter focuses on four important auxiliary services and activities within the administrative control of the elementary school principal—transportation, instructional materials centers, food services, and health services. If organized well, each of these services can contribute mightily to an effective instructional program.

The major responsibility for the development of general policies, coordination, and control of transportation services lies at the district level. In larger districts it is handled by a director of transportation. In smaller districts it is often handled by the superintendent, clerk in the district office, or one of the school principals. As noted by Stoops, Rafferty, and Johnson, the principal or the district administrator charged with the overall responsibility for the transportation program needs to determine or provide for:

1. The number of children to be transported
2. Where children live in relation to bus routes
3. Best location for stops and delivery points
4. Loading and unloading methods
5. Effective safety practices
6. Practices for the control of students
7. Degree to which teachers will be involved in supervision
8. Development of records and reports required by law on school district policy.[1]

---

[1]Emory Stoops, et al., *Handbook of Educational Administration* (Boston: Allyn and Bacon, 1975), p. 413. On pages 414–17 is a "Checklist for the Evaluation of Transportation Services."

Most of these responsibilities require much cooperation between administrators. The establishment of coordinated districtwide schoolbus schedules severely restricts the options available to individual school programs. District transportation officials should be encouraged whenever possible to develop independent or autonomous bus schedules for each school. Even if autonomous schedules cannot be developed for regular use, it is desirable to have them available for emergency or special occasions. Thus, if one school wishes to dismiss students early or must dismiss them late, it can without affecting the entire district. Also, when one group of children arrives a half-hour earlier than another group in the morning or leaves a half-hour later in the afternoon as a result of a double-run bus schedule, the school requires a much more complex program of supervision. The wise principal uses staggered bus schedules as an opportunity to develop enrichment programs, avoiding the problems of the "holding tank" and opening creative educational possibilities. If all or most of the children ride a bus to school, the school program is limited to the hours determined by the bus schedule, and most activities sponsored by the school must be established within that time framework. Therefore, a staggered bus schedule can actually be an asset.

The following is only an abbreviated list of possibilities for the use of extra time:

1. Independent study activities for children such as quiet reading time, or continued work on individual student projects

2. Group time for guidance activities: each advisor can take half of the children in the morning and the other half in the afternoon to review the day's or yesterday's activities and to plan for today's or tomorrow's activities

3. Extracurricular activities: the thirty to forty-five minutes often available before and after school with double-load bus schedules is adequate time for many activities such as clubs, craft activities, musical activities, intramural activities; each activity must be run twice, of course, once for the morning and once for the afternoon group.

4. Minicourses in high interest subjects

5. Enrichment activities in such subjects as foreign languages and various art forms

STUDENT CONTROL ON BUSES

The ultimate responsibility for student behavior on buses belongs to the school principal, who must develop reasonable regulations for bus conduct. These should be established with cooperation from students, bus drivers, parents, and teachers. Once the regulations have been agreed upon, they should be well-publicized to all concerned parties.

The responsibility for the safety of the bus and discipline on the bus resides primarily with the driver. It is important that the principal stay in close contact with the bus drivers and remain sensitive to their problems. A procedure should be developed to handle driver and student complaints. In handling discipline cases from the transportation system, due process and formal procedures must be followed just as they are for in-school discipline problems. These procedures should be spelled out in transportation regulations and appropriately disseminated. Figure 19-1 is an example of transportation regulations.

SAMPLE TRANSPORTATION REGULATIONS

To the Parent:
These rules are taken from the administrative policies of the Transportation Department and adopted by the Board of Education. Will you please go over these rules with your children to make them aware of their responsibilities in improving our transportation program.

1. Children should board the bus in a calm and quiet manner and proceed to an empty seat. If the bus is heavily loaded, children should move as close to the rear of the bus as possible and hold on to fixtures provided.
2. Children should remain behind a line of demarcation painted on the floor near the front of the bus. Children must not cross the line except when they are departing from the bus.
3. Children will disembark in an orderly manner. Any child living on the opposite side of the street should cross in front of the bus while traffic is stopped.
4. Children should refrain from holding a seat for another person.
5. Children should refrain from opening and closing a window.
6. Children should refrain from placing any part of body or personal belongings outside the window.
7. Children should keep belongings in their possession at all times.
8. Children should cooperate with the bus driver in providing any information needed to enforce the rules for safety.
9. Children should refrain from talking with the bus driver except when spoken to or when an emergency arises.
10. Children should observe all rules of safety while waiting for the bus.
11. Children should act with courtesy and respect toward private and public property and should expect to be held accountable for committing an act of vandalism.
12. Bus drivers will be instructed not to wait for a child who is not in sight.
13. The name of any child who has to be disciplined by the driver the second time shall be reported to the principal with the reasons for his having been reported. Any child reported to the principal a second time may be suspended from riding the bus.
14. Children should cooperate fully with parents, teachers, and the principal in obeying the rules set up for safety.

FIGURE 19-1.

Good working relationships with the bus drivers will benefit both the principal and the driver. With cooperation and mutual understanding, the principal will find it easier to resolve cases of bus discipline, and drivers will find it easier to work with the school concerning problems the school is having.

Each year should begin with a meeting for the drivers who serve each school. Included in such a meeting for the drivers should be an orientation to the school and its program, an introduction to each of the teachers in the school, a review of the procedures for handling discipline on the buses, a request for the bus drivers to alert the school authority to any pupil personnel needs that they observe in their contact with children, and a reminder that the drivers are an important part of the school team.

FIELD TRIPS

Field trips are almost mandatory for an effective elementary school program today. The principal should encourage teachers to plan field trips. An appropriate rationale stated in the form of learning objectives and anticipated outcomes for each trip are of great importance, however, because of the additional cost and effort that most field trips require. Some districts require the superintendent or the school board to approve all field trips. Teachers should not have to cope with unnecessary red tape, and board policy should be established so that field trips can be carried out, when resources are available, with only the approval of the principal. Central office approval should be limited to special situations such as an overnight trip or a trip covering a particularly great distance.

Special care is necessary when arranging off-campus experiences. Parent consent forms should be required for all trips. Even though parental consent does not remove the legal responsibility of the school personnel for the safety of the children, it is a good accounting procedure to determine which children are going on the trip and whether their parents have approved of their going. A roster should be provided for each off-campus trip so that staff can carefully check attendance to insure that no one has been left behind.

For all field trips, particularly those requiring bus transportation, sufficient supervision of the children must be provided. A good supervision ratio for elementary children is one supervisor for every ten children. It is better to have too many responsible adults than too few. Supervisors other than teachers may be parents or other volunteers. Rules of conduct should be established and communicated to the children before the trip. The faculty can develop a general set of rules for most field trip activities to use as a standard form.

The district office usually coordinates buses. It is best to use buses that must undergo periodic safety examinations by state authority. These may be either school buses or common carrier buses. In general, because of the liability problems involved, it is best to avoid using private automobiles for field trip activities.

INSTRUCTIONAL MATERIALS CENTER

An instructional materials center (IMC) is an integral part of an elementary school. It should house and provide print materials such as books and pamphlets, nonprint materials such as pictures, films, records, and tapes, and the necessary audiovisual equipment for viewing and listening to these materials. The IMC often becomes the repository for all audiovisual equipment in the school.

The IMC should be staffed by at least one full-time professional. This is difficult for many elementary schools because of their small size. If necessary, a school can share a librarian with another school or use the services of a district library supervisor to train paid aides or volunteers to staff the IMC. Staffing an IMC with a traditionally trained librarian and a clerk is not adequate, however, since the person in charge of the IMC, even if only part-time, will require not only training in library science but in the use of the sometimes highly complex audiovisual equipment as well. Graduate programs for media specialists are becoming more common as a result of the development of the library into a multimedia instructional center.

The IMC should be a warm, supportive place where children enjoy working. It should allow frequent convenient access by all children in the school for material selection, research, or just browsing. For those schools without adequate space, the ends of corridors, or even the corridor itself, can become an IMC. Even the foyer at the entrance to the building can be converted to IMC use with a little imagination.

The IMC preferably should be operated to allow free movement of children from the classroom on an unscheduled space available basis. Classes should be scheduled in the IMC only for orientation or specific projects. Regularly scheduled visits are appropriate to encourage book selection and library usage by children as long as they do not prevent free access by others.

General Responsibilities of the IMC Staff. The IMC staff should provide the following services to the school:

1. Gathering resources to be used in the classroom by the teachers and students
2. Participating as resource persons in team planning
3. Making available nonprint as well as print materials, including filmstrips and tapes, directly to the children
4. Conducting special library programs to encourage reading; included should be library clubs, a story time, and special programs illustrating books, such as puppet shows, films, and meet-the-author sessions
5. Managing audiovisual equipment for the school, including:
   a. maintaining an inventory of audiovisual equipment
   b. coordinating the repair and service of audiovisual equipment

    c. coordinating equipment requests from the classroom for permanently assigned equipment as well as convenient access to equipment that must be shared

    d. training and providing student operators for equipment

Major responsibilities of the school librarian include:

1. Being well acquainted with all phases of the school curriculum as an integral part of the instructional team
2. Evaluating, selecting, processing, and distributing instructional materials including tapes, recordings, transparencies, study and art prints, slides, pamphlets, periodicals, realia, filmstrips, and books for use by children and teachers. The librarian should be expected to take the lead in developing selection policies and should chair the library review committee.
3. Motivating teachers and children to use library materials; this will require knowledge about teacher needs and an understanding of how the individual child learns, develops, and behaves
4. Encouraging each child to explore, because the library is wider than the curriculum
5. Working with the classroom and special teachers to develop programs of individualized and group reading and assisting in the guidance of children
6. Instructing children in the skills necessary for the intelligent use of instructional materials
7. Promoting a sequential program of good literature
8. Keeping abreast of the advances in the fields of librarianship and education through study, periodicals, and meetings
9. Assisting the principal in scheduling classes and determining responsibilities in the media center
10. Maintaining current shelf list and inventory of all instructional materials
11. Maintaining an open atmosphere in the library where staff and students feel free to use library resources at unscheduled periods.[2]

A well-functioning Instructional Materials Center is truly the hub of the school program. Its success depends on the cooperation and energy of the IMC staff as well as the teachers whom it serves. An advisory committee made up of members of the various learning communities to assist in the operation of the IMC is an excellent way to provide good communication between the teachers and the librarian. The advisory committee should assist the librarian

---

[2] This list was developed with the assistance of the staff of the Linden Elementary School, Oak Ridge, Tennessee; Dr. Ida Lou Stephens, Principal.

in drawing up rules and regulations for the operation of the IMC as well as in providing specific suggestions how the librarian and staff might better aid the classroom teachers with their tasks.

FOOD SERVICES

A good cafeteria is important in developing positive attitudes and behavior of children and staff in the school. Students and staff respond positively to good food, good menus, and a well-managed cafeteria, while poor management, poor menus, or poor-quality food often lead to increased discipline problems and poor morale in the school.

Often the principal has little or no direct control over the cafeteria staff or the school menus. The staff is often hired and supervised by the district office and menus may be established by a district dietician or other food service employees. However, even under these conditions, the principal can develop a positive working relationship with the food service staff and consequently influence the kind and quality of food served in the building.

Satellite Food Services

Some schools have eliminated the kitchen by bringing in hot food on trucks from a central kitchen, located at one of the nearby schools. A serving line is then set up in a corridor with the food carried on trays by each student to the classroom areas.

Food satellite arrangements are designed to reduce the cost to the district. However, they do increase problems of coordination, sanitation, cleanup, and maintenance at the local school. Instead of limiting food to a part of the building, they distribute it into many areas of the school.

Nutrition and Learning

Whether or not the school lunch and breakfast program is a satellite arrangement or entails preparation on the site, the objectives are the same: to provide nutritional and attractively prepared food at the lowest possible cost. It's not easy to do this, and good management as well as creative cookery is required. In a very real sense, the lunch program is an extension of the health services of the school. Research and literature support the link between nutrition, student learning, and high morale.[3]

---

[3]The research available includes, for example, Rita Bakan, "Malnutrition and Learning," *Phi Delta Kappan* 51, no. 10 (June 1970): 527–29; A. U. Moore et al., "Effect of Food Deprivation on Behavior Patterns," in Scrimshaw and Gordon, eds., *Malnutrition, Learning and Behavior* (Cambridge, Mass.: M.I.T. Press, 1968); Margaret Mead, "The Changing Significance of Food," *American Scientist* 58 (March-April 1970): 176–81.

It's popular to think of school lunch programs as a restaurant operation foisted on the schools by a United States government concerned about agricultural surpluses. Perhaps this was one important reason for initiating the federal support program. Given the important research evidence about learning and nutrition and the social welfare role fulfilled by the public schools, school lunch programs provide an uncommon opportunity as well as the wherewithal to meet a significant need. Recent federal legislation has been aimed at providing nutrition programs in the form of breakfasts, lunches, and snacks for disadvantaged children. Title I of the Elementary and Secondary Education Act, for example, has this as one of its express purposes. The Child Nutrition Act is another program that focuses on providing breakfasts for children who must travel long distances from home with little food, for example when school desegregation requires cross-town busing.

Help is readily available to school cooks and cafeteria workers, even in those districts not large enough for elaborate central office planning and administration. The federal government has prepared pamphlets and books devoted to menu planning using surplus commodities and seasonal foods and cafeteria management. Moreover, frequently state departments of education and intermediate school district offices can provide—and are often mandated to do so—supervisory and management assistance.

HEALTH SERVICES

Health services are often provided within the school district under the direction of the public health officials. Good preventive medicine requires a medical examination for all entering students and the completion of certain vaccinations and inoculations prior to school enrollment. The health form depicted in Chapter 8 is an illustration of such a record to be kept on file in the student's permanent record.

Immediate health problems for some students require exemption from certain school activities. This is most often a request for a reduction or elimination of planned physical education activities, but occasionally will be a request for certain diet exemptions or needed medication intake. A form such as the one shown in Figure 19-2 can be used as a medical excuse report for physical education activities.

School Nurses

There is an important concept that needs reinforcement with respect to the use of school nurses. Stoops, Rafferty, and Johnson point out:

> The administrator should remember that the school nurse does not nurse. Except in cases of minor first aid, she performs no medical services of any kind. She does not diagnose; she does not prescribe if she does not treat. Her function is to advise, evaluate, to organize and to integrate. She works closely with classroom teachers in subject fields of science, homemaking,

MEDICAL EXCUSE REPORT

_____   _____
                Name of School   Date

_____ has presented to me a Medical Excuse Form completed
        (Student's Name)
by Dr._____ .
        This report places this student in activity Group _____ for

_____
        (length of time)
        The Medical Excuse Form is on file in the office of the principal as a part
of this student's permanent record.
                                                    _____
                                                              Instructor's Signature

(Keep one copy and send one to the Physical Education Supervisor)

FIGURE 19-2.

_____

and physical education. Her relations with cafeteria workers are necessarily close; the maintenance and operation personnel will be guided by her recommendations in anything bearing directly upon the health and safety of the children.[4]

The school nurse should be viewed as one more member of the education team, with special expertise well beyond emergency duty.

The Clinic

Children often become ill or receive minor injuries in school. It is desirable to have a nurse on the staff of each elementary school to attend to these children. Often such occurrences of illnesses or injury must receive immediate attention as well as several hours of care until parents can come for the child or the child is feeling better. A school clinic is a necessity to properly deal with these problems.

For schools that do not have a full-time nurse available or on call, clinic supervision is a problem. Some schools have developed effective parent-volunteer programs to staff school clinics. One school known to the authors trained twenty-two volunteers to each work two days a month in teams of two. Each volunteer completed an eighteen-hour first aid course taught by the Red Cross. Two volunteers were assigned to the clinic each day, partly to ensure adequate care in case of emergency and partly to keep each other company.

_____

[4]Emory Stoops et al., *Handbook of Educational Administration* (Boston: Allyn and Bacon, 1975), p. 451.

Each clinic aide was asked to buy a uniform as part of her participation in the program.[5]

Upon the arrival of each child, a health room referral card is completed. (See Figure 19-3.) If the symptoms seem severe or if the temperature of the child is over 100°, the aides notify the parents to come to the school for the child. For less severe problems, the child may remain in the clinic under the aide's care. In case of injury, minor scrapes and bruises are cleaned and dressed. For more serious injuries, first aid is applied as necessary and parents or other medical assistance sought. Aides follow up on injuries by completing an official report filed with the principal and later forwarded to the superintendent's office. (See Figure 19-4.)

The operation of the school clinic by trained volunteers greatly improves the quality and degree of supervision and health care over that of an unstaffed clinic. It also reduces the time required by school clerical staff or the principal to supervise sick and injured children.

DEMONT MIDDLE SCHOOL HEALTH ROOM REFERRALS

CHILD'S NAME _____

TIME OF REFERRAL _____

DATE _____ GRADE _____

TEACHER _____

REASON FOR REFERRAL _____

_____

TIME ARRIVED _____

TIME DEPARTED _____

                                    KMS VOLUNTEER NAME

FIGURE 19-3.

---

[5]In the first year, in addition to their nursing duties, these volunteers assisted in supplying and decorating the clinic area. Decorations included Raggedy Ann bedspreads on the cots as well as on the towels and wall decorations to make the clinic an attractive place for the children.

REPORT OF ACCIDENTS AND INJURIES
Hillman County Schools

Name of Injured _____ School _____

Date of Injury _____ Hour _____

Date of Report _____

Place accident occurred: _____

Description of injury: _____

_____

How did accident occur? _____

_____

Does injured have school insurance? _____

Disposition made of case:

    Insurance report made _____ Date filed _____

    Reported to parents _____ Date reported _____

                              Signature of person filing report

Send to: Office of the Superintendent

Note: Report should be mailed to the Superintendent on *Friday of the week of the accident.*

FIGURE 19-4.

SUMMARY

    Pupil transportation is an important aspect of a school's overall operation, but one that is largely outside of the control of the principal. The individual school's responsibility is largely one of maintaining the safety and control of the students that use the system. Each school should develop with their student body rules for safety around and on the buses. If a principal considers the bus drivers as part of the school staff and develops good communication with them, many of the potential transportation problems relating to student behavior and conduct can be eliminated or dealt with with minimum disruption.

    Auxiliary school services that function outside the regular classroom are a significant part of the school operation. Services such as the instructional materials center and off-campus learning opportunities provided through field trips are an integral part of the learning environment. The food and health services of the school should also be considered an integral part of school life because of the need for quality services in these areas for effective school management.

BIBLIOGRAPHY

Baillie, Susan, and Dewitt, Lawrence B. "The Role of the School as a Site for Social Services." In Steven Goodman, ed. *Handbook on Contemporary Education*. New York: R. R. Bowker Co., 1976.

Cogen, Victor. "Multiaxial Physician-Educator Child Development Team." In Steven Goodman, ed. *Handbook of Contemporary Education*. New York: R. R. Bowker Co., 1976.

Davies, Ruth A. *The School Library: A Force for Educational Excellence*. New York: R. R. Bowker Co., 1969.

Demont, Roger, ed. *Busing, Taxes and Desegregation*, Special Monograph No. 4, Management Series. Danville, Ill.: Interstate Printing and Publishers, 1973.

Eddy, Regina. "Changing Trends in School Health Services." *Thrust for Educational Leadership* 2 (February 1973).

Featherstone, E. Glenn, and Culp, D. P. *Pupil Transportation: State and Local Programs*. New York: Harper and Row Publishers, 1965.

Knezevich, Steven J., and Rye, Glen L., eds. *Instructional Technology and the School Administrator*. Washington, D. C.: American Association of School Administrators, 1970.

National Safety Council (with assistance from Paul T. Stuart and Frank Miskow). "ABC's of Running a Safe Transportation System." *American School Board Journal* 158 (November 1970): 40–44.

Rowell, John, and Heidbreder, M. A. *Educational Media Selection Centers: Identification and Analysis of Current Practices*. Chicago: American Library Association, 1971.

School Bus Task Force. *Pupil Transportation Safety Program Plan*. Washington, D. C.: U. S. Department of Transportation, 1973.

Stoops, Emory, et al. *Handbook of Educational Administration*. Boston: Allyn and Bacon, 1975.

20

Public Relations
Processes and Techniques

INTRODUCTION

The building principalship is the single most potent public relations role in the . . . schools. This position is based upon two factors: (1) the assumption that the most effective and dynamic interpersonal communications channels are those, other things being equal, that make use of direct face-to-face contacts, and (2) the reality that the building principal has regular direct interpersonal communications with a greater number of groups and individuals with legitimate interest in the operation of the schools than any other single school professional.[1]

The school and the community it serves have grown, it seems, increasingly psychologically distant from each other. Efforts to exchange information have often been left largely to report cards, single-spaced ditto bulletins, and slick sheets sent out from a centralized public relations office. The result has been low-level understanding of the nature of the educational enterprise, suspicion, and often an overwhelming lack of support from the public in times of crisis or great need.

Because schools are owned by and operated for the benefit of the community, educators do have a responsibility to keep the community informed about all aspects of the school program. The school, as the largest single public agency serving the community, is most affected by a declining understanding on the part of the various publics. It is crucial that people in a community be made aware of and sensitive to the needs, problems, aims, goals, and directions of the educational enterprise. Keeping the community informed, however, is not an easy task. As the opening quotation makes explicit, the role of the principal in this is fundamental. Consider the complex communications problem implicit in the following case study.

---

[1]David Erlandson, "The Role of the Principal in School-Community Relations," *AASA Professor* 3, no. 4 (Spring 1981): 9.

The Folks Raise a Question

The school system has made a departure from tradition. After considerable study, a decision was made by the system to implement the concept of open education in the junior high and middle schools. Several professional task forces engaged in such necessary activities as material selection, leveling, and developing appropriate inservice activities. Within a little over a year, many of the schools were reorganized in such a way as to provide for flexible scheduling, team teaching, individualized instruction, large group/small group arrangements, independent learning contracts, a new reporting system, and a host of other procedures and processes consistent with open education. Further, some of the buildings were open-space designed. In general, the professional staff in the schools in which the open concept of curriculum was implemented were there because they wanted to be. Teachers who were not favorably disposed to the plan were given the option to join the staff of other more traditional schools. The program has now been in operation two years.

Almost from the start, a number of parents began to complain about the program. The complaints were manifested first in phone calls to the principal, then in some heated discussions at PTO meetings, letters to the editor of local newspapers, a spurious mimeographed neighborhood "newspaper," and ultimately in the formation of a "Return to the Basics" committee. Members of this group called a public meeting in several of the schools to insist that "open education" be discussed, stating the committee's position that it was a fad which was not providing an adequate education for their children.

Specifically, the charges were:

1. The students are not learning the basic skills as well as they were previously.
2. Students are confused by so much independence and freedom.
3. The report card tells only individual progress; it does not tell parents how their child "stacks up" against others in the system or the nation. Thus, parents cannot set realistic goals for their children.
4. Discipline is missing; the students are running amok and "not learning respect."
5. Students need a home base—a teacher who knows them well, not an impersonal team of teachers.
6. The students are not happy with the new program. They say, "Mom, I don't know what's going on and I can't get help from my teachers because there are too many other kids and they get help first."
7. It's a fuzzy-headed idea thought up by left-leaning educators. Children should be told what to do, then made to do it. You can't put kids in charge of their own learning. That's what teachers are paid to do.

Tomorrow evening one of the first citizens' meetings will be held at your school. Indications are that it will be well-attended by parents as well as by some other interested citizens who have followed the controversy as it developed. The meeting was billed as an open-forum discussion of the issue, but you have the nagging feeling that it may turn into a donnybrook.

There are thirty-five hours to prepare for the meeting. What should be done?[2]

An interesting dilemma is presented by this case study: how to overcome the lack of two years of public relations work in a two- or three-hour meeting charged with emotion. This type of situation seems to occur frequently in schools around the nation. While the specifics may vary, one thing is clear—educational decisions will be challenged, sometimes in dramatic confrontations. The public has an inherent right to challenge educational decisions; of that there is little question. However, when such questioning takes place, it should be based on good information. And, to provide that base, an effective, well-organized public relations program must be in place.

This chapter will examine some of the more promising public relations practices so that the public's right to challenge will occur in a setting more likely to result in communication than the one just described.

School-community communication endeavors may take several forms, any of which has limitations. A high quality school-community relations program will use a variety of media, and an alert principal will suit the particular message to be conveyed to the appropriate medium. Too often, however, the communication endeavor has relied almost exclusively on one-way information-dissemination devices. In this chapter, both one-way and two-way information exchanges will be discussed.

ONE-WAY PUBLIC RELATIONS EFFORTS

There are several one-way methods to publicize some aspect or activity in the school. The hope is that the message will reach the intended receivers, be read or listened to, and acted upon in some kind of positive way. The one-way nature of the medium used, however, does not permit much opportunity for the broadcaster to find out whether the message was received.

Newspapers and Other Mass Media

Few communities are not served by at least a weekly newspaper, and no community is outside the reach of radio and television. These mass media are commonly used to impart information about the various public agencies serving the community. The following discussion will focus on newspapers, primarily because of their more localized nature and because the activities of the school

---

[2]This case study also appears in Hughes and Ubben, *The Secondary Principals' Handbook: Guide to Executive Action* (Boston: Allyn and Bacon, 1980).

principal are more likely to involve working with newspapers. Irrespective of which mass medium is utilized, however, the same principles are appropriate.

Newspapers vary all the way from weekly or biweekly advertisers with perhaps a few columns reporting highly localized activities, to urban dailies with several editions. Similarly, depending on the community, a principal's role may vary from writing news releases that will be published mostly word for word to meeting with news reporters who will recast the stories in their own words.

In any case, the development of good relations with the working press is essential. Reporters or editors will ask principals for information about developing stories or news items more often than for stories containing general information about what's going on in the schools.

The news media have their problems too. Newspapers and television stations are businesses, with advertising to sell, bills to pay, and subscribers to satisfy. Further, news editors deal with many pressure groups championing various causes. School administrators are often surprised to learn that only 40 percent of newspaper space is devoted to stories and 60 percent to advertising. This percentage affects the amount of school news that will get printed.

Reporters complain that public agencies tend to engage only in "gold-star" story writing. Many school administrators are only too eager to publicize praiseworthy news items but back away from legitimate adverse criticism. An adverse story is legitimate news and when such a story breaks, the school official and the newspaper both have a job to do. Covering up a weakness or refusing to respond to a legitimate inquiry about a potentially embarrassing situation can only lead to bad press relations and a widening credibility gap.

The Public Information Officer

Increasingly, school systems—even small school systems—are employing public information officers to facilitate and coordinate the one-way flow of information from school to community. The duties vary, and in some school systems the job may be only part-time. (Figure 20-1 depicts a job description for a public information officer in a relatively large suburban system.) Moreover, even where the job is a full-time one and the public relations program well developed, for most of the public and the mass media, it is still the principal who will be sought as the prime source of fast-breaking news or in time of crisis.

Techniques for Dealing with the Mass Media

To insure as nearly as possible that balanced reporting by the media is achieved, there are a number of recommended techniques:

1. *Articles and stories about scheduled events should be prepared well in advance with photographs of speakers or others involved in the program provided to the news media before the event occurs.* Often newspapers do not print information about or report any past event.

The Public Information Officer shall be responsible for keeping the public informed about the goals, programs, and activities in the district, for coordinating all public information activities for the school district, for evaluating current public information activities and practices, and for introducing new programs and activities in order to better inform the public of the programs and progress of the district as well as to receive feedback from the public regarding their attitudes and judgements about the programs within the district.

The Public Information Officer shall report to the superintendent of schools, and shall fulfill the following responsibilities:

1. Prepare and edit special publications such as recruitment brochures, district information pamphlets, district newsletters, special administrative reports, school bond election materials, and other desired publications.

2. Prepare and edit news releases regarding programs and activities within the district for release to the local and area media.

3. Prepare and distribute an internal publication for all district personnel relating matters of interest.

4. Survey the community systematically in cooperation with the Research and Evaluation Committee to solicit significant opinions, suggestions, and recommendations that bear importantly on the policies and operations of the Board of Education and the school district.

5. Provide inservice training in the field of public information for all school personnel.

6. Answer telephone inquiries and correspondence, and meet and guide visitors to the district, to assist the public in gaining an understanding of the programs of the district.

7. Assist staff in the preparation of special public information activities such as open houses, dedications, public school week programs, PTA and PTO programs, and other similar activities.

8. Initiate other public information activities as are necessary and desirable to fulfill the responsibilities of the position.

FIGURE 20-1. Position Description: Public Information Officer.

Source: Courtesy of Alief Independent School District, Houston, Texas.

2. *Followup reports should be prepared for the media as soon as possible after an event.* The school principal should know deadlines, which are crucial for newspapers and television stations. Missing a deadline will mean that the story will not get in at the appropriate time and thus may never get in.

3. A simple and fast way to get radio news coverage is to use a telephone hookup and dictate stories to be taped and played on later newscasts.

4. News releases should be written to conform to the requirements of the different media. Releases for radio and television stations usually must be shorter, more repetitious, and in a more conversational style than those reported by the newspapers.

5. Scheduling programs about local schools may be facilitated by taking advantage of the public service requirements that broadcasting stations must meet. However, Norman and Achilles recommend that "rather than producing programs which are scheduled at off hours, when the listening or viewing audience is small, it is better to concentrate on news stories, audio tapes, slides, and films for regularly scheduled newscasts."

6. Relationships with media representatives will determine if the principal or the public information officer concentrates on writing and distributing releases or on furnishing suggestions and information to journalists who themselves will develop their own stories. In urban settings reporters will probably write more of their own material, but they will ask school administrators to secure material, to identify sources of news, and to arrange interviews. Conversely, in rural or small town settings the school administrator may write much of the material.

7. The public information program should be continually evaluated. It really isn't very valuable to send out large numbers of news releases if few are used, and submitting too much material in an indiscriminate way may result in few stories being published. The lesson is clear: the news media are most impressed by articles that contain only timely and worthwhile information. These will stand the best chance of getting published.[3,4]

The latitude a principal has with the press will depend in great part on the particular school district's press policy. News media personnel, however, are most sensitive to what they perceive to be censorship and normally respond negatively to the suggestion that every story or every interview must be cleared with the central office. A policy that requires all school personnel to refer reporters and editors to the central office rather than answer questions or that sends the news media to the central office for all information, if employed rigidly, will damage press relations. Obviously, fast-breaking news items of a potentially explosive nature will require discretion on the part of the school principal, but to attempt to close off the individual school building to members of the press will do little more than create antagonistic relations.

An especially effective practice is the use of a "School News Item File" depicted in Figure 20-2. Many activities in the school might be newsworthy.

---

[3]Additional insight about good media relations can be found in Douglas C. Norman and Charles M. Achilles, *Public Information Practices in Education: A Study of Techniques* (Knoxville, Tenn.: Bureau of Educational Research and Service, University of Tennessee, 1973). The study contains twenty-eight specific recommended techniques.

[4]An interesting case-study-simulation film dealing with press relations is available from the University Council for Educational Administration, 29 West Woodruff, Columbus, Ohio 43210. Entitled "On The Spot With the Press," the film details a potentially explosive school situation and ends with two questions: "What do we tell the media this afternoon?" and "What should our general policy with respect to relations with the media be?" Discussion materials are included with the film. The film is one component of the Monroe City Simulation set but can be rented or purchased separately.

SCHOOL NEWS ITEM FILE

Type of News Item:

_____ Curriculum Project
_____ Activities of Staff
_____ School Awards
_____ Pupil Activities (field trips, special recognition, etc.)
_____ New or Interesting Instructional Techniques
_____ Continuing Difficult Problems
_____ Other

Title of Project or Item:

Description of Project or Item:

Persons Involved: (how many, and who — names, addresses, titles, etc.)

Dollars Involved and Sources of These Dollars:

Who to Contact for Further Information:

FIGURE 20-2.

Each staff member should have a supply of the news item forms to jot down those projects that should be especially interesting and regularly send these to the principal's office. The principal can then file these reports in a folder labeled according to the kind of project, and a news reporter can simply review the files, selecting any particular items to follow up. This helps both the reporter, whose responsibility is to find news, and the principal whose responsibility is to supply news but not necessarily to write it.

Newsletters, Bulletins, and Report Cards

Frequently the principal and the school staff will attempt to communicate with the home and other agencies through newsletters and bulletins. These can be useful if employed judiciously and if well done. But what kind of a message is conveyed when a newsletter arrives home crumpled in the pocket of a student, printed on a smeared ditto or stencil copy, hard to read, and often containing out-of-date information? If newsletters and bulletins are to be employed, the format should be simple; the information conveyed should be concisely written and to the point, free of educational jargon; and the method of getting them home should be via the mails. Newsletters sent home with children often do little but contribute to the neighborhood litter problem. If the newsletter is not produced with appropriate care and printed in an attractive manner, it is simply not worth the bother.

Certainly, school administrators do not want to talk down to community members, but the education profession does have a language of its own, as do all professions. This language is not well understood outside the profession, and schools should take care to report events and school happenings in such a way that information is shared rather than obfuscated.

Report cards are often overlooked as public relations mechanisms, but they are the single most regular way in which schools communicate with the home. Typically, both teachers and parents like them to be uncomplicated to simplify reporting and understanding. Yet consideration of all of the ways in which a child is growing, developing, and learning defies summing up with a single letter grade. Thus, the development of an appropriate reporting procedure will require careful study by the staff and include the use of a faculty-layperson committee to develop a report form that is easy to understand but also contains important kinds of information relative to the child's progress.

The Message Was Sent—What Happened?

The *co* in communication means a closed loop. That is, communication means that the message was not only sent but that it was received and responded to in a way that indicates it was understood. Following are important questions to ask when examining the quality of one-way informational devices:

1. If the message was received, was it read?
2. If it was read, was it understood?
3. If it was understood, was it understood in the right spirit?
4. If it was understood in the right spirit, will it be acted upon in a positive way?
5. How do you know?

Care should also be taken to recognize the bilingual nature of many neighborhoods.

TWO-WAY COMMUNICATION EFFORTS

Many formal mechanisms provide two-way information sharing. However, nothing about these mechanisms makes them automatically effective. Careful organization is required.

Parent-Teacher Organizations

Everyone is familiar with the PTA or PTO that is a regular part of school-parent relations programs. Their effectiveness has varied markedly throughout the country. In some instances these organizations have served well, with a membership characterized by broad participation in important activities. In other instances, they are moribund groups doing little but spending time listening to speeches and having bake sales in order to buy tape recorders and art paper for the school, with little opportunity for interaction with anybody except themselves. Nothing good automatically happens just because an organization is labeled in such a way as to suggest a formal relationship with the school.

Parent-teacher organizations can provide a useful avenue for interaction between school and community if the meetings are organized to provide an opportunity for both formal and informal interaction and if the organization is given important tasks to perform. The key would seem to be *active involvement in significant tasks*. Parent organizations, just like other community organizations, are competing for the time of their members. Whether or not a parent elects to spend Thursday evening at a PTO meeting will depend upon whether or not that time is viewed as productively occupied. No one wants to give time to an activity that is dull, nonproductive, and not even entertaining.

A working PTO will spend less time meeting formally and more time in subgroups considering important tasks to be performed around the school and the community. Organizing business-industry-education days for the career development program in the school, developing after-school programs for children and adults in the community, training paraprofessionals, and working on curriculum review teams are the kinds of activities developed by an effective parent-school organization.

Another problem is the nature of the membership itself. Many principals have suddenly realized that even though their school may serve a rather heterogeneous population, the active membership of the parent group is very often comprised almost entirely of those who reflect middle-class norms. Thus, the principal should examine the membership rolls of the parent organization carefully. If these organizations are to be used as effective school-community relations devices, a membership that reflects the community at large becomes most important. If those who come to the meetings are the same kinds of people and reflect a consistent ideological unity, then the chances are that important opinions are not being secured nor is there an information exchange with the broader community.

One way to find out the degree to which the parent group reflects the population of the school is to conduct a modified survey about the PTA/PTO membership. Such a survey might be conducted as described in Figure 20-3.

Such a study can determine whether or not the parent-teacher association serving the particular school is truly representative of the student population. If it is not, then it is not an adequate way to communicate with the community. Further, even if it is representative but is not active, or does not

AN INQUIRY TO DETERMINE THE REPRESENTATIVE NATURE OF THE LOCAL PTA/PTO

The initial effort would be to collect representative demographic information about the make-up of the student population of the respective school. Such information as general income levels or the nature and kinds of housing from which children come is what is sought. The kind of classifications that comprise Warner's Social Class Index will prove helpful. Those classifications are "occupation," "source of income," "house type," "dwelling area." These factors can be checked for a random sample of the students in the school if the school size is large.

Once the relevent demographic data about the student population has been collected, a questionnaire may be developed requesting the same general kinds of information and sent to the active membership of the PTA. It is important in this instance to be straightforward and simply explain to the recipients of the questionnaire what you are attempting to find out, that is, the representative nature of the PTA members.

A map of the attendance area served by the school should be developed and by using a color code of some sort, locate active members of the PTA according to where their home is on the map. Are some parts of the attendance area seemingly underrepresented? If it is available, secure a "pupil locator" map and compare the location of students with the location of PTA members. Is there a discrepancy? Using the same parent PTA locator map you can now, by applying the indices of quality of housing, sources of income, occupation, etc., determine whether or not the membership of the PTA is confined to certain social strata.

FIGURE 20-3.

---

have regular meetings, or has a very small membership when compared to the possible membership, it will not serve as an adequate communication medium.

Principal-Organized "Gripe" Sessions

A practice used more frequently in recent years is a regular "tell it to the principal" gripe session. Principals concerned about establishing and maintaining good relationships with students and their parents have initiated two kinds of gripe sessions. One is a student-principal program conducted regularly in the principal's office. Attendance is often limited to about ten students who sign up for the session in advance. An open-forum discussion is the mode, and in these sessions students express interests and discuss grievances they have, making suggestions about the general improvement of the school.

The same thing can be done for parents and other community members. Patrons may be notified by mail or through the newspaper of the meeting dates, and a secretary can take reservations for a dozen or so patrons. The rules for the meeting are that anything goes, except personal complaints about individual teachers. Two or three hours usually provide an adequate amount of time, creating an important opportunity for an informal exchange of ideas in a nonthreatening setting. For the principal it's an excellent sensing mechanism to find out what's on people's minds in the community and to get some notion of impending problem situations. For the patrons it's a good opportunity to find out the inside story of the operation of the school.

One of the problems in engendering community support for the schools is the inadequacy of the information exchange between school and home. Organized informal parent-principal forums address this problem. Complex ideas are difficult to express in the usual one-way bulletins or news stories that serve as major sources of information for parents and other community members. Complex ideas are best tested in a face-to-face setting.

Key Communicators

Many principals capitalize on their knowledge of the influence structure present in the local school community and develop a list of "key communicators" to be used when there is a need to disseminate good information quickly about important developments—positive or negative—in the school. Key communicators are influential people in the immediate community who have a well-known interest in education.[5]

These persons are influential because they interact with large numbers of other people and are trusted and believed. Such persons may be contacted to form a loose organization that meets from time to time with the principal or other professionals in the building to discuss what is going on at the school that would be of general community interest. After an initial meeting, the key communicators are kept informed about such things as school budgets, new curricula, teacher turnover, and new construction. The group, as individuals and in collective feedback sessions, keeps the principal informed about "rumblings and rumors" in the community.[6]

This is not a policy-making nor even an official "advisory" body but simply a loose confederation of important communicators. As always, some care should be taken that the various dimensions of the school community are tapped. The notion of key communicators capitalizes on much research and communications theory which continues to indicate that community members get most of their information and form their attitudes and beliefs in a word-of-mouth fashion, even in this mass media age.

Neighborhood Seminars

Neighborhood seminars have been successful in both large and small school districts. There are two important ingredients: an informed staff and careful

---

[5]See Chapter 4 for a discussion of neighborhood influence patterns.

[6]For a good discussion of this process see Larry Litwin, "Key Communicators—They Lock Out the Rumors," *NASSP Bulletin* 63, no. 420 (January 1979): 17–22.

initial organization. Neighborhood seminars will not be effective if they simply become a way of providing a forum for someone from the school to lecture to a collected group of individuals from the community. A deft discussion leader, careful planning, and an attitude not of propagandizing but rather of providing the opportunity for interchange of ideas and facts are required. Many of the characteristics of a good neighborhood seminar are the same as those of successful principal gripe sessions. The principal doesn't have to do it all; a cadre of well-informed staff who are especially adroit in leading discussions and who have been provided with a sufficient amount of general information about the school can assist the principal.

Properly organized seminars attended by people who represent a cross-section of attitudes and orientation in the community provide a most effective way to begin a new relationship with the community. Once underway, the neighborhood seminar approach creates a basis for sophisticated community involvement programs. Issues and problems discussed often lead to joint task force teams that engage in problem-solving efforts.

Program Analysis by Special Groups

Principals may invite identified groups in the community with an interest in certain parts of the school program to examine, in conjunction with appropriate school personnel, some of the special curricula of the school. A variation may be simply to involve a neighborhood school group in an analysis of the total school program. Many state departments of education have publications that might prove helpful.[7] These or locally developed instruments for analysis can be used to help structure the activities of citizen-school analysis committees.

Citizen Committees

Similar to the special interest committees are general citizens' committees. The basic difference is simply that instead of looking at specific aspects of programs, such committees may be oriented instead toward issues. Asking citizens, students, and staff to study and recommend solutions to specific educational questions does not impinge on the principal's power nor on the school board's power. Various committees can work simultaneously on different educational questions. Citizen involvement in this manner can ease the professional workload, dispel apathy, and lead to valuable recommendations.

Committees may be formed to study and make recommendations about discipline, budget, construction of new schools, or vandalism. When such committees are employed, it is important that good techniques be used in their

---

[7]Further help may be available from such publications as *Profiles of Excellence: Recommended Criteria for Evaluating the Quality of a Local School System* published by the National Education Association, and, of course, the various accrediting bodies such as the North Central Association of Colleges and Secondary Schools, or the Southern Association of Colleges and Schools can provide instruments and suggestions for such an analysis.

formulation; the committees should be representative and have a clear purpose. Forming one more committee simply to occupy people who might become critical of the school is a move transparent to most community members. The purpose of committees is to secure good, creative problem resolution. Better school-community relations will result as a spin-off from such activities, and better school decision making will result because intelligent resources are being tapped.

The committee must know what the anticipated product is, and it must know the limits of its decision-making powers. If the principal is seeking advice and counsel but not final decision making, this should be stated at the outset.

Parent-Teacher Conferences

Planned parent-teacher conferences three times or more a year often are an important element in a school-community relations program. They provide excellent opportunities for direct relationships between the teacher and the home, but they require careful planning. Thought must be given to such factors as working parents, one parent in the home with responsibilities for other children, a parent's occupation that would preclude attendance at parent-teacher conferences scheduled during the normal school day, or transportation difficulties. These and other constraints, however, can be overcome with diligent work on the part of teachers and other school personnel. If the master contract under which the teachers perform precludes night meetings or restricts in other ways the orderly development of parent-teacher conferences, then this might be an item for negotiation at the next contract review.

Organizing for parent-teacher conferences can be a task of a joint community-teacher group although, of course, the group assigned the task of organizing the effort should be generally representative of the neighborhood or the community.

Miniboards and Advisory Councils

The differences between advisory councils and miniboards concern the nature of decision-making authority. Many principals have formed advisory councils to test ideas, but without decision-making authority; that is, the word *advisory* is definitive.

Some schools, where there has been school board mandate to do so, have formed neighborhood miniboards that perform functions much like legally constituted systemwide school boards. In such instances, the miniboard exists as a creature of the system board but may be imbued with broad decision-making powers. In the latter case, the principal of the school may assume a role much like that of the general superintendent.

The community group is involved in a continuous needs assessment process. Addressing the identified needs will require setting goals through a consensus process. This process allows for positive action to meet school needs without blaming anyone. Working together in consensus building activities reduces "we/they" schisms and any accompanying hostility.

Questionnaires and Opinionaires

Surveying community attitudes and opinions can be effective, especially when a school district enters an evaluation phase in an effort to establish or review educational goals, objectives, and priorities. Such a survey can lead to numerous community committees and a revitalization of community involvement in educational policy making and decision making.

There are a number of ways to conduct educational surveys. Mailed questionnaires to a random sample of the population living in a particular school attendance area is the most common, although it is not generally productive of many returns. A good technique to employ if the time and manpower are available is to conduct house-to-house interviews using a structured interview technique, calling on a random sample of the population and making sure that all parts of the community are included in the sample.

Help is available in constructing surveys. The Kettering Foundation publishes a booklet entitled *A Look into Your School District.*[8] Additionally, the National School Public Relations Association is the source of such publications as *Polling and Survey Research*[9] and *Communicating with the Public*[10] that are most useful. Any survey has its limitations, but if conducted on a regular basis, it is a good way to get useful information. If the survey technique is utilized, the information should be acted upon and reported back to the community.

SUMMARY

Schools are a part of the greater social system, and people in the community have a right to be informed about the operation of the school. Similarly, educators have an obligation to see that information flow is facilitated. By failing to interact with the community, the school system or the individual school will stabilize, and become static and unresponsive to changing community needs. The community itself may be undergoing great change, possibly as a result of population mobility or changing attitudes of people. The result is clear: a gap develops between the community and the school it serves.

---

[8] CFK Ltd. Publications, 3333 South Bannock Street, Englewood, Colorado 80110.
[9] John H. Thomas, Stuart C. Smith, and John S. Hall, *Polling and Survey Research* (Arlington, Va.: National School Public Relations Association and ERIC Clearinghouse on Educational Management, 1973).
[10] Ian Templeton, *Communicating with the Public* (Arlington, Va.: National School Public Relations Association and ERIC Clearinghouse on Educational Management, 1972).

Specific objectives for a school-community relations program should include:

1. A communications network that will facilitate two-way communication; traditionally, school-community relations programs have failed to include mechanisms for receiving information back from the intended receiver
2. Procedures for the involvement and participation of community members in the school program development
3. Mechanisms to monitor the community regularly
4. Face-to-face communication between community members and school representatives.

BIBLIOGRAPHY

Erlandson, David A. "The Role of the Principal in School-Community Relations." *AASA Professor* 3, no. 4 (Spring 1981): 9–12.

Glickman, Carl D., and Esposito, James. *Leadership Guide for Elementary School Improvement.* Boston: Allyn and Bacon, 1979, chaps. 20, 21, 22, and 23.

Greenwood, Gordon, et al. "Citizens Advisory Committees." *Theory Into Practice* 16, no. 1 (February 1977): 12–16.

Hines, Susan C., and McCleary, Lloyd. "The Role of the Principal in Community Involvement." *NASSP Bulletin* 64, no. 432 (January 1980): 67–75.

Hughes, Larry W.; Gordon, William M.; and Hillman, Larry W. *Desegregating America's Schools.* New York: Longman, Inc., 1980.

Hughes, Larry W. *Informal and Formal Community Forces: External Influences on Schools and Teachers.* Morristown, N. J.: General Learning Press, 1976.

Hughes, Larry W., and Venditti, Frederick P. *On the Spot with the Press.* Columbus, Ohio: University Council for Educational Administration, URB/SIM Series, 1974. This is a simulation training film.

Hyder, Leslie R. "The Effectiveness of Communications Media used in Tennessee Public School Systems." Unpublished doctoral dissertation, University of Tennessee, 1979.

Kindred, Leslie W.; Bagin, Don; and Gallagher, Donald R. *The School and Community Relations.* Englewood Cliffs, N. J.: Prentice-Hall, 1976.

Lewis, Anne C. *The Schools and the Press.* Washington, D. C.: National School Public Relations Association, n.d. This is a most helpful volume and includes tips on how to organize the news, what to do when there is unfavorable press, how to write copy, and so on.

Litwin, Larry M. "Key Communicators—They Lock Out Rumors." *NASSP Bulletin* 63, no. 420 (January 1979): 17–22.

Norman, Douglas C., and Achilles, Charles M. *Public Information Practices in Education: A Study of Techniques.* Knoxville, Tenn.: Bureau of Educational Research and Service, University of Tennessee, 1973.

Ostrow, Barry J. "Need for Marketing in School Communication Programs." *Educational Digest* 44 (November 1980): 16–19.

Thomas, John H.; Smith, Stuart C.; and Hall, John S. *Polling and Survey Research.* Arlington, Va: National School Public Relations Association and ERIC Clearinghouse on Educational Management, 1973.

Wayson, William W. "Power, Power, Who's Got the Power." *National Elementary Principal* 58 (March 1979): 12–20.

Wiles, David K., and Wiles, Jon. *Practical Politics for School Administrators.* Boston: Allyn and Bacon, 1981.

PART THREE

Management Processes

Being successful as an elementary school principal requires more than understanding the various dimensions of the role and being skilled in the functional aspects of the job. Irrespective of particular issues, there are pervasive needs for decision-making skill, insights about the decision process, and the ability to engage in systematic problem identification and problem resolution. Another pervasive need is the ability to manage one's activities so that the right things get done in a timely manner.

There are three chapters in this final section. Chapter 21 focuses on decision processing and decision making, including when and when not to engage in extensive group involvement. Chapter 22 contains a discussion of project management which embodies the principles of systematic planning, a way of approaching problems in advance that has been revealed to be both efficient and effective. The last chapter examines the problem of too much to do and too little time in which to do it. Principles and operating procedures for managing executive time are presented.

21

Initiating Executive Action
and Decision Processing

> Managerial decision-making is a selection process. Given facts, oppor-
> tunities, threats, problems, risks, strengths, and weaknesses of relative
> positions, the executive makes decisions.[1]

Executive decision making is the essential act of the administrator. Ultimately, of course, all that goes on in and around the school building is the responsibility of the principal. If the school is moving effectively to discharge its
responsibilities to achieve appropriate goals, the principal will take the bows;
conversely, if things are not all that they should be, then, justly, the principal
will be held accountable. This does not mean, however, that the principal
must personally do all of the important decision making that needs to be
accomplished in order for the school to be a good one. And, the principal who
attempts to manage by personal direction rather than by exception will do little but spend time reacting to a variety of brush fires with little time left over
for either planning activities or working with staff in goal-setting or goal-im-
plementing endeavors.

This chapter will look at decision making and problem resolution not as
single acts, but as a process that considers the people in the organization and
views them as a rich resource in the process.

THREE DECISION PROCESSES

It is possible to distinguish among three kinds of problem-resolution processes: unilateral, majority opinion, and consensus. The labels just
used suggest something about the nature of the involvement of others in the
process.

---

[1] George Odiorne, *Management and the Activity Trap* (New York: Harper and Row, Publishers, 1974), p. 114.

Unilateral Decision Making

By definition the principal is in an authoritative role. To be sure, the degree to which the person occupying this role can make unilateral decisions is circumscribed by public laws, the rules and policies of the school system, the actions of the superordinate decision structure, as well as by informal constraints such as community customs. Nevertheless, in most districts the individual school executive does enjoy considerable latitude in decision making.

Further, there is both an organizational (superordinate structure) expectation and an expectation of those people within the school building (subordinate structure) that the principal will engage in judgmental actions to insure the maintenance of order and the delivery of services to the appropriate point at the appropriate time. In short, the principal is supposed to keep the school functioning with a minimum of disruption of teaching and learning. Such decision making, or problem-anticipation and problem-responding acts, comprises an important part of the principal's role. But not all problems, nor indeed very many complex problems, can be adequately resolved through purely unilateral acts.

Nothing magic occurs when a state department of education confers an administrative certificate licensing a person to be a principal. That person does not, by virtue of certificate, or even, alas, by virtue of training, become all-knowing. One hopes the person will have acquired some skills and technical competence and insight into educational problems, but no administrator can function effectively from the cloister of the office, ruling by an assumed divine right accorded by a shiny state department certificate.

Is it necessary to state this? The authors would argue that it is, because of their observation of the behavior of too many administrators and teachers that suggests that while everyone may know better, many act as if all intelligence *vis-à-vis* the school operation resides in the principal's office. This misunderstanding of role, often coupled with the inability to distinguish between routine maintenance decisions and futuristic decisions requiring more complex processes, impedes the school. The lack of skills and mechanisms to tap the collective intelligence of the work group has resulted in uncreative, poorly implemented solutions to the many difficult problems confronting the school.

Majority Opinion

Simple vote taking is an appropriate way to resolve a simple problem. It's fast and relatively easy. The issue is described to the group, some discussion of pros and cons ensues, and the group decides, with one vote over half sufficient to determine the decision. This process is especially effective when no one in the group really cares what the decision is.

Making a decision should not be confused with implementing a decision. If the decision will require people to behave much differently than they have been behaving, as in the case of an important curricular change or a reorganization of the school, majority opinion is not sufficient to the task. Consider, for example, the instance of the faculty which voted 18 to 17 to move to a team-teaching arrangement. It would not have required an Indian mystic to predict the outcome of that venture.

Yet unfortunately, such a process has gone on untold times in the name of democratic decision making, and with predictable results. The process is useful for the ultimate resolution of legislature or procedural matters in large groups, but a well-working task group—and a school faculty *is* a task group—seldom can rely on vote taking as a means for creative problem resolution.

If a decision requiring important behavior changes is to be acted upon appropriately, it requires commitment and understanding by the participants. Simple changes in schedules, hours of work, and the like, that require only modest behavior changes might rather easily be effected by majority opinion. Issues of curricular change, crisis management, goal setting and goal implementation, and similar questions of overriding importance require a more thoughtful process, such as consensus decision making.

Consensus Decision Making

Consensus decision making is a process that provides: (1) maximum participation of group members in the examination of the issue at hand, (2) sharing of pertinent information bearing on the problem(s), and (3) emergent situational leadership based on expertise concerning the issue being confronted irrespective of formal position in the organization.

The problem and subproblems to be addressed must be clearly defined. That is, the group must understand what it is attempting to resolve. If one is looking for a quick decision, a consensus process is probably inappropriate; if one is looking for a decision that relies on group intelligence and that will receive maximum individual commitment in its implementation, then the consensus process offers great possibilities. The consensus process, then, is best employed for policy decision making, for difficult changes requiring substantial organizational readjustment, and for the development of new response mechanisms to anticipate problems of some complexity.

Engaging in a consensus decision-making process does put stress on a task group. In consensus decision making, differences of opinion (conflict) must be expected if the group is ultimately to resolve the problem in a productive manner. Groups lacking cohesion or newly formed groups are less likely to be able to manage this conflict. Therefore, the principal who sees value in forming faculty task force teams, or administrative teams, to engage in collective decision making should confront such groups initially with problems of low intensity. It has been found, for example, that established groups (people who have worked on tasks together a number of times before) in the face of conflict will tend to come up with unique solutions that are creative in nature. In contrast, newly formed groups in conflict situations will tend to rely more on compromise techniques, vote taking, and the like, which often are unsatisfactory to most of the members but do avoid conflict.

The consensus process begins with the creation of a task force team, probably no more than seven or eight people, likely to be affected by a developing problem situation. The composition of the group may at times be cross-sectional in nature as when, for example, the problem to be confronted is buildingwide or when several kinds of expertise and insight are needed. At other times members may represent a complete unit in a department or grade level or the administrative team. Time is spent initially defining the nature of the developing problem, setting the limits of decision-making authority (for example, is the group's role solely advisory or is it to be charged with final decision making?), and identifying any existing rules, policies, and laws that would affect the nature of the decision to be rendered.

Adequate time must be set aside for the task. There is no sense attempting to resolve a complex issue through a consensus process if inadequate time exists to examine the underlying issues thoroughly. Time strictures always exist, of course, but when these are too severe, group members quickly recognize it, resign themselves to an inadequate resolution, and refuse to engage in what is perceived to be an exercise in futility. Group members may be polite about this, of course, but when the time allocated is insufficient to provide maximum achievement, it is unrealistic to expect individual group members to address the task very seriously.

The principal's role in a true consensus process is that of a peer among peers; the ascribed authority implicit in the title "principal" must be discarded. If the authority were sufficient to the task, there would be little reason to use the consensus process—unless the principal wishes simply to engage in a game-playing kind of involvement. This latter practice, however, is quickly perceived by any intelligent group and, again, while group members may remain polite and play the game, few productive results from such charades can be expected.

Several techniques to facilitate consensus building are available. Brainstorming, discussed elsewhere in this chapter, is one such technique. Figure 21-1 describes yet another technique. In the process described in Figure 21-1 group members are asked to generate alternative solutions rather than quickly committing themselves to a single course of action. This has the effect of keeping the discussion open. Also important in the process is that attention be given to the anticipated consequences of actions that might be taken in any of the alternatives. In the process, the group attempts to anticipate what the result of the action taken will be with respect to any of the receivers of the action.

Training a Group in Consensus Decision Making. As previously noted, newly formed groups often have difficulty with the consensus process, largely because it generates conflict as differing views and proposals are advanced and discussed. It is possible, however, to train even newly formed groups in the consensus process rather quickly. One way, mentioned earlier, is initially to confront such groups with less complex problems. Another way is to explain

A MINIVERSION OF PROBLEM SOLVING AND ACTION PLANNING*

The following process is intended to provide general guidelines for a group wishing to methodically, yet quickly, engage in problem solving and action planning activities.

An organizational problem is herein defined as any issue the whole group wishes to consider, and which can be planned or decided in a short period of time.

Stage 1: Define the problem

Given the issue for which you have convened, discuss some of its broad parameters as a problem. Why is it a problem? What are some of the facets? What are the underlying issues that present problems?

Stage 2: Suggest alternative solutions

Each member of the group should try to think of two viable solutions to the problem. Take some time to think about these solutions and to list them. Then share them with the group.

Stage 3: Choose some solutions (not more than five)

From all of the alternatives before you, you must as a group choose about five of the most promising solutions. This must be a group decision based on consensus.

In arriving at a consensus group decision, (1) everyone should feel free to state his reasons why one or more solutions should be listed among the five; (2) the communication skills learned earlier should be used; (3) a survey should be taken when actually making the choices; (4) every member of the group should "own" or be willing to support the five alternatives finally chosen.

Stage 4: Make some action plans

Outline, based upon the solutions you chose, some plans for implementing those solutions and for resolving the problem. The plans should be as specific as possible, including when, where, who, and how. All of the members of the group should agree to help implement the plans. The plans should be recorded and every member of the group should receive a copy of them.

*Courtesy of Professor C. Brooklyn Derr, University of Utah.

FIGURE 21-1.

---

the rules of the game and clearly indicate at the outset that conflict and difference of opinion are to be expected. Once a task group realizes that it is not seeking total unanimity, rarely achieved on a complex problem, but rather a *maximum feasible decision* to which all can commit themselves, progress in consensus decision making can be made.

A Case in Point

To illustrate and synthesize the concepts presented in this section about different modes of decision making, consider the following case:

You are principal of a six-grade elementary school and lately have become aware that all might not be well with the reading program in your school. The children in grades four through six do not seem to be reading as well as might be expected. There are a number of troubling indicators. As you review test scores on the standardized reading series used, you see that your students are, in the main, well below the norms for the system as a whole and for the nation. Various teachers have expressed concern about the reading skills of their students. The librarian has mentioned the low circulation rate among even the usually more popular children's books. Your junior high school and senior high school principal colleagues have remarked frequently that students from your school seem to have less well-developed reading skills when they arrive in their schools. As you systematically examine the situation you reach the conclusion that there is something functionally wrong with the reading program, and the anticipated outcome, adequately skilled readers, is not being realized. A quick review tells you that there is a heterogeneous student body with perhaps a bit more children at the lower end of the economic continuum than usual for the system as a whole. But, as an educator, you aren't satisfied with the aphorism that "it's the home that makes the difference." This seems to beg the question.

A decision point has been reached. Given your information base you have alternative routes to take in decision making and decision implementation. You could, for example, take one kind of specific unilateral action to correct what is perceived to be the problem. You do a little professional reading, talk with the reading supervisor, maybe consult a teacher or two and decide to (a) inform your staff of the low level of reading achievement of their students in general, (b) purchase a set of SRA reading labs and place them in classrooms, and (c) have an intensive inservice workshop on the teaching of reading. This program now becomes, in the eyes of staff, the "principal's new reading program." *Your* program? That's right, yours. Yours to implement, yours to check, yours to evaluate, yours when it fails—you don't even teach, but it's yours. Take a bow.

But, whether or not you yourself are a reading expert, the people who will be charged with implementing any new program are the staff, people who, if the program requires substantially different procedures and material, will be required to behave (teach) differently and organize their classes differently than they have been doing. Giving up old, comfortable practices and procedures requires a commitment to change; such a commitment is difficult to achieve by total reliance on unilateral decision making.

Other kinds of executive action are available in the resolution of this problem. Restructuring the reading program, or even studying the need for restructuring the reading program, is a complex event. Implementing new processes that appear to have, on the basis of information and insight, a reasonable chance of solving the problem are even more complex.[2] It is

---

[2]"New" processes probably are best thought of as "hypotheses to be tested." That is, the effect of the new process should be continually evaluated. The "what are we doing," "why are we doing it," "can it be done a better way" approach is important.

axiomatic that for a change to be implemented successfully those charged with the implementation should be aware of the need to change (i.e., see that a problem exists), be reasonably committed to doing something about it, and be provided with the wherewithal (material resources, decision latitude, and removal of organizational constraints) to facilitate the change.

Unilateral action by the principal may proceed through the same first three steps as before (professional reading, consultation with reading specialists, discussion with key staff) but following this the action of the principal diverges considerably from the previous example. It is at this point that the principal begins to tap the group's wisdom and its collective energy, a synergistic approach more likely to result in program success.

Consider the following steps: Following the initial exploration of the perceived problem by the principal and the beginning data collection process, interested faculty members are contacted to form a task force team. Their charge might be two-fold: (1) investigate more fully the nature of the problem and (2) propose alternative solutions to the problems. It is important that the task force team be given some realistic decision-making perimeters.

Setting Realistic Task Force Decision-Making Parameters. Few task forces can operate completely unfettered. Real-world constraints must always be contended with. Any group charged with completing a task needs to know the "rules of the game" if they are expected to render a decision that can be implemented. The following are important considerations and should be the basis for initial discussions between the task force group and the principal:

1. Decide if the task force team is to be advisory in nature. That is, are its decisions to be suggestions only, not very satisfying to a group that has worked hard, but sometimes appropriate and necessary, or is the group to be charged with coming up with a series of decisions that, with your help, will result in a new program?
2. Cooperatively set some realistic target dates concerning further investigation and data collection, the preparation of final reports, the generation of new program alternatives, the anticipated implementation date, and so on.
3. Establish a tentative budget for the project phases. Possible line items include released time costs, materials costs, transportation.
4. Review any districtwide policies or state laws that might impinge on the nature of any new program proposed. For example, is there a systemwide or statewide adopted basal reading series that must be "lived with" no matter what; does the state provide for experimental programs?
5. Set up regular reporting dates to you and to the rest of the staff (interaction sessions) about progress and findings to date.

This procedure is not a magic wand, to be sure, but the prognosis for successful problem resolution is much more optimistic than in the first example given, and the solution will become "our new program" instead of the "principal's new program."

PARTICIPATORY DECISION MAKING

Much is heard these days about participatory decision making as the way to achieve effective problem resolution. The question that arises in many minds is whether this means the creation of committees for everything, with principals serving as a kind of coordinator and implementor of other people's decisions. How would anything get done with this arrangement?

Set aside, for the moment, all that you have read and heard about the term "democratic administration." This term has become virtually nondefinitive. Instead, think of situations requiring decisions, of problems requiring resolution. Further, think about the kinds of people who comprise the professional as well as the noncertificated staff in the school; think about the clients of the school; think about the goals and objectives of the school; and finally, think about the processes that must be used to put all these things together to achieve those goals. Creating an organizational climate within which active leadership and good decision making will emerge from the staff is necessary. Hughes has written:

> Basic to the creation of such a climate . . . would seem to be the principal's assumptions about those with whom he works. If a principal sees his fellow workers—whether they be teachers, supervisors, custodians, or students—as drone-like, lazy, requiring close supervision, and unresponsive [then his] patterns of interpersonal behavior will likely manifest these assumptions.[3]

If these are the assumptions of the principal, creative decision making from the staff cannot be expected. In order genuinely to make use of the group intelligence, one must believe it exists.

Assumptions About the Staff

In 1960 Douglas McGregor identified two sets of assumptions that administrators might have about subordinates.[4] He labeled these assumptions *Theory X* and *Theory Y*. Essentially, Theory X holds that people are by nature indolent, will avoid work wherever possible, and are not goal oriented except perhaps in

---

[3]From *Performance Objectives for School Principals: Concepts and Instruments* by Jack A. Culbertson, Curtis Henson and Ruel Morrison, materials from Chapter Five, "Achieving Effective Human Relations and Morale" by Larry W. Hughes, © 1974 permission by McCutchan Publishing Corporation.

[4]Douglas McGregor, *The Human Side of the Enterprise* (New York: McGraw-Hill, 1960).

selfish kinds of ways. The task of the administrator, given these assumptions, is to direct the efforts of subordinates actively, to attempt overtly or covertly to control their actions, and to narrowly describe the subordinate's job so that close supervision is possible. Unless this is done, Theory X assumes, subordinates will be passive, perhaps even resistant to organizational goals. In short, subordinates need to be closely controlled, persuaded, rewarded, and punished; their activities must be directed, otherwise nothing good will get done.

It can be readily seen that there would occur little participatory decision making or that there would be little latitude for creative task accomplishment in a management system built on these assumptions. Sadly, many schools are organized in such a way, and inevitably the benefits of the group intelligence for complex problem identification and problem resolution are totally lost. The principal who behaves on the basis of such assumptions is victimized and spends time responding to brush fires, controlling by close supervision the activities of the subordinates, and interpreting and applying minute aspects of the policy manual. Staff, in responding to such a management system, will indeed be passive and at times resistant, but the management system itself causes these reactions, not an inherent human characteristic.

Theory Y is based on a much different set of assumptions. It assumes that most people are basically capable of self-direction and given the opportunity will contribute to organizational goal achievement without intense supervision and close control. It also assumes that creativity and decision-making ability are widely distributed in the population.

Assuming that the motivation, potential for development, capacity to accept responsibility, and a willingness to work toward organizational goals are present in all people, the administrator's task becomes somewhat different. The task of the principal under a Theory Y set of assumptions becomes that of arranging organizational conditions so that the staff can satisfy their own personal needs best by directing their efforts toward the objectives of the organization.

Summarizing the application of the X and Y dichotomy to the tasks of the principal it has been written:

> *Theory X* basically assumes the need for a vast array of external control mechanisms, while *Theory Y* assumes much employee self-control and self-direction and implies a participatory management system. In neither instance are the goals of the organization forgotten, but the means of achieving them vary widely. A principal who accepts the assumptions of *Theory Y* might provide more opportunities for leadership on a particular project or task to emerge from the staff rather than considering himself to be the sole source of initiation. Such a principal would encourage activities designed to enlarge the decision-making authority of individual teachers or groups of teachers, thereby giving them more control over their daily professional life. Clearly, too, performance appraisal of teachers and other employees would result from cooperative target setting, rather than

the predetermined expectations of a single administrator. Such procedures require greater faith in one's co-workers.[5]

Cooperative Goal Setting Facilitates Decision Making

It is axiomatic that any well-functioning organization and hence any units of that organization, for example, the individual school building, must have a clear sense of direction, a sense of what the unit or the system is all about, where it is desirably headed (goals), and what it will take to get there (processes). These goals[6] and processes should be the result of the joint thinking of all those to be affected by the school—the staff, the student, parents of the student, and the community as a whole. Once developed and written down, goals need to be explicated by specific statements of objectives and subjected at regular intervals to a review in the light of (a) whether or not, or the degree that they are being achieved; (b) whether, in view of changing social dynamics and social needs, they continue to be appropriate.

Thus, a focus is provided for school system and school building endeavors, and a means exists to evaluate the efficacy of these endeavors. New program proposals, responses to problem situations, alternative decisions, all may be evaluated in the light of such goals and objectives. Of course, within the goals there must be objectives and processes with latitude for individual contribution and creative behavior. Practically speaking, specific goal setting and subsequent progress toward these goals becomes a mechanism whereby an individual or department or school staff can show its worth—always important, but increasingly so in these days of accountability. As important, however, are the positive psychological effects that such cooperative goal setting engenders in a staff. Characteristic of the healthy organization is a considerable degree of congruence between individual goals and objectives and organizational goals and objectives. Where no stated goals or objectives exist or where there is uncertainty about what they are, one can expect to find at best accidental excellence and incidental staff and client growth, even though individual staff members may be expending great personal energies in the accomplishment of their own professional or personal goals. With clearly defined and accepted goals there may be energy in an organization but not synergy.

The key then would appear to be to utilize human resources in an organization in such a way that people behave congruently with the organizational goals, and by carrying out their responsibilities in this way they are also maximally engaged in meeting their own personal objectives and goals. How can this be achieved? The best way is to provide mechanisms and opportunities for

---

[5]From *Performance Objectives for School Principals: Concepts and Instruments,* by Jack A. Culbertson, Curtis Henson and Ruel Morrison, materials from Chapter Five, "Achieving Effective Human Relations and Morale" by Larry W. Hughes, © 1974 permission by McCutchan Publishing Corporation.

[6]For the purposes of this discussion a goal is defined as a timeless, direction-setting statement of general worth. Goals need to be explicated into a series of more specific and measurable objectives if they are to be put into operation.

participation in goal-setting endeavors and decision making by those who are to be most affected by the goals that are developed and the decisions that are ultimately to be made. Such a mode requires administrative confidence in staff abilities and motivations.

Defining the Tasks

There are two ways of assigning specific tasks in the organization. Figures 21-2 and 21-3 depict polar concepts in task assignments. At one end of the continuum are jobs in which behavior is very carefully and tightly defined. Thus, assigning tasks becomes a matter of defining the job and making the person fit that job. At the other end of the continuum are jobs with freedom for the individual to define the job and to enjoy much autonomy with respect to the processes employed in carrying out that job.

Few, if any, formal organizations have jobs that are totally at one pole or another. To be sure, in highly mechanized industries the person on the production line often has virtually no autonomy, no decision making on the job. Often this person becomes a virtual automaton. Conversely, of course, in very

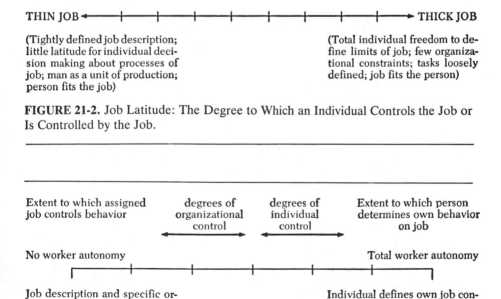

THIN JOB ◄——+——+——+——+——+——+——+——► THICK JOB

(Tightly defined job description; little latitude for individual decision making about processes of job; man as a unit of production; person fits the job)

(Total individual freedom to define limits of job; few organizational constraints; tasks loosely defined; job fits the person)

FIGURE 21-2. Job Latitude: The Degree to Which an Individual Controls the Job or Is Controlled by the Job.

Extent to which assigned job controls behavior | degrees of organizational control | degrees of individual control | Extent to which person determines own behavior on job

No worker autonomy ◄——————► Total worker autonomy

Job description and specific organizational expectations tightly define individual's activity.

Individual defines own job consistent with goals of organization and carries it out.

◄——— THIN JOBS   THICK JOBS ———►

FIGURE 21-3. Organizational Job Latitude Model.

loosely developed organizations of people, such as an artist colony, one may find almost total individual job autonomy.

In the school organization, however, neither mode is present in its pure form. There are tendencies toward one end of the continuum or the other, however. In the school organization teachers, for example, often do have wide latitude for certain kinds of decision making with respect to how the day will be organized and which teaching methodologies will be executed. However, much of the teacher decision making in traditional schools is confined to the limits of the classroom itself. Figure 21-4 illustrates where various organizational "jobs" might commonly be placed on the continuum. The authors and most organizational theorists believe that the degree to which the school organization can operate in a mode tending toward the autonomous end of the continuum will determine the degree to which the rich resources of human intelligence in the organization are appropriately utilized to provide for effective decision making and organizational goal accomplishment. The "work force" in the schools is uncommonly well trained. The means for capitalizing on this resource for better problem resolution are available to the principal.

All of the positions on the "thin-thick" scale could probably be given more autonomy to good effect. The primary reason for doing so is not to achieve high morale, it is to get better results. High morale frequently occurs because of greater job autonomy and this is good, but unless the administrative focus is also to achieve greater movement toward organizational goals, the principal will simply be presiding over a country club. Much energy may be expended, but unless this results in better learning by students, what is the point? There are techniques that the principal can employ to achieve both increased job satisfaction and organizational goal achievement. Job target setting and job thickening are two such techniques.

FIGURE 21-4. Organizational Job Latitude Model: Examples of Kinds of Jobs by Degree of Organizational Control and Worker Autonomy.

Job Target Setting

Essentially, individual job target setting requires that the principal and staff members mutually establish for each staff member some year-end goals ("targets"). These targets are to be congruent with the general direction in which the school is desirably headed. It is anticipated that the achievement of these staff goals will result in more effective staff performance and movement to organizational goals.

The principal's responsibility is to help the staff member develop instructional, curricular, and professional growth targets that are realistically addressable and consistent with the curricular goals of the school. It is also the principal's responsibility to provide the resources (e.g., time, budget allocations, technical assistance) to assist staff members in achieving the established targets.

It is the responsibility of each staff member to engage in a self- and organizational analysis, after which appropriate year-end targets are generated for subsequent discussion with the principal. In addition to the target statements, the staff member establishes what will be accepted as indicators of whether or not, or the degree to which, the targets have been reached. Figure 21-5 is an example of a series of targets generated by a teacher in collaboration

---

Professional Targets
School Year_____
Gordon Elementary School

Name_____ Dept._____

I. Instructional Target(s)
   Individualize instruction in Basic arithmetic course.
   Indicators of Achievement:
   1. Develop self-instructional modules for Units 1–4
   2. Revise preinstruction assessment instruments for basic arithmetic
   3. Devise at least four enrichment activities or games for low-interest students

II. Curriculum Target(s)
   Institute one section of accelerated sixth grade mathematics
   Indicators of Achievement:
   1. Initiate interdepartmental study group
   2. Develop objectives for course
   3. Identify potential students
   4. Develop syllabus

III. Professional Growth Target(s)
   Improve diagnostic and prescriptive skills
   Indicators of Achievement:
   1. Review Buros, *Mental Measurements*
   2. Successfully complete EPSY 6380 at University of Houston

FIGURE 21-5. An Example of a Teacher's Job Targets.

with the principal; Figure 21-6 shows principal job targets. Care must be exercised to avoid the extremes of either unrealistically high targets or statements of low-level accomplishments.

Initially, a process such as that just described may require some intensive inservice training for staff. If the technical expertise is not available in the district, help may be secured from such varied sources as local university departments of administration and supervision, professional associations, and private educational consultants.

Job Thickening

Providing a work environment wherein staff may exercise a greater degree of professional or technical autonomy can result in a highly productive and often creative release of energy. The illogic of the person who thinks the principal must make all of the important decisions and closely supervise individual staff member activities has been stressed several times in this book. Stressed too, though, has been that certain kinds of decision making and administrative control logically and expectedly accrue to the principal. Therefore, what are some specific decision areas that might best be matters of individual staff member or at least departmental discretion? The following decision areas would seem appropriate for delegation to departments and individuals.

Teaching methodology
Selection of instructional materials

Activity: Administration of the School Unit

General Objective: Provide for instructional leadership

Specific Targets:

1. The principal will organize his or her time in such a way that he or she visits each classroom in the building for a minimum of one hour per month.
2. The principal will require each teacher in the building to submit behavioral objectives each year for Instructional Council review and will meet individually with each teacher to discuss these.
3. The principal will organize an instructional council which will not meet less than once monthly to advise on school policy curriculum development and instructional practices.
4. The principal will introduce at least one instructional or curricular innovation adjudged by research evidence to be a significant new approach to the teaching/learning process each school year and will develop a PERT network to implement the change.

FIGURE 21-6. An Example of a Principal's Job Targets.

Course content

Inservice training in subject matter

Relationships and roles of teachers and students

Student scheduling

Scope and sequence of curricular area

Assignment of advisors

Evaluation practices and procedures

Scheduling of class periods

Sequencing of instructional modules

Job descriptions and assignments of paraprofessionals

Objectives of the courses, modules, and department

Public relations programs

Schoolwide issues such as truancy, vandalism, and enrichment programs

Why Participatory Decision Making?

The school executive is looking for the best decision, the maximal feasible solution. Such solutions will not occur in an organization of interacting humans unless processes are employed that make great use of the collective intelligence of these humans.

Four assumptions guide the executive who engages in participatory decision making:

1. People at the working level tend to know the problems best.
2. The face-to-face work group is the best unit for diagnosis and change.
3. People will work hard to achieve objectives they have helped develop.
4. Initiative and creativity are widely distributed in the population.

We hear a lot about trust these days; about how we must "trust" each other if the outcome is to be an effective faculty team and a hospitable organizational environment. Trust is not developed by talking about it or by exhortation. Productive and trusting relationships develop as a result of people engaging in important activities together—through which the strengths and weaknesses of fellow members are revealed—to learn who can be counted on for what kinds of expertise. Knowing where certain kinds of expertise exist permits the principal to constitute effective task force teams to focus on troubling schoolwide issues, existent or anticipated.

When to Involve Others in Decision Making

It is not possible to know unerringly when to involve others in a decision-making process, who those others should be, or what the nature of their involvement should be. Decision making and decision implementation require varying degrees of expertise and varying degrees of faculty commitment. It depends in great part on the complexity of the problem to be solved and the degree to which those affected by the decision will be required to behave differently in order for the decision to be properly implemented. Using the two factors of technical expertise (quality of decision required) and need for group acceptance (hearty compliance and/or behavior change required) as prime determinants, a quadrant model can be developed to help determine the answer to the involvement question. Figure 21-7 displays such a model.

Quadrant I in the model contains those decisions that require much technical expertise and knowledge in order for a high-quality solution to be

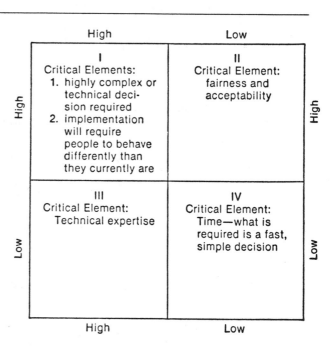

Need for group acceptance and great concern for feelings of persons who must execute the decision. Implementation of decision will occur through behavioral change and group commitment.

	High	Low
High	**I** Critical Elements: 1. highly complex or technical decision required 2. implementation will require people to behave differently than they currently are	**II** Critical Element: fairness and acceptability
Low	**III** Critical Element: Technical expertise	**IV** Critical Element: Time—what is required is a fast, simple decision

High   Low

Need for a high-quality decision. Decision must be based on expertise, facts, and research evidence.

FIGURE 21-7. When to Involve Others in Decision Making.

Source: Adapted from J. L. Franklin, A. Wissler, and G. J. Spencer, *Survey-Guided Development III: A Manual for Concepts Training* (San Diego, CA: University Associates, 1977). Used with permission.

achieved. Quadrant I also describes a situation wherein no matter how technically superior the solution may be, in order for this solution to be put into effect much work-group acceptance will be necessary. Hearty acceptance may be questionable for several reasons: because an apparent solution is contrary to present practice or present attitudes; because it requires work-group members to perform in ways that are initially more difficult, or for which they have not been trained; because of a simple lack of agreement about the efficacy of the decision; or for any number of other reasons including threat, fear, distrust of administrators, or anger. Also, some, if not all, of these reasons may have substance other than emotion.

What kinds of issues might fall within this quadrant? Any curricular change certainly would, as would budget development. Changes in school policies affecting large numbers of students, and school constitutional questions would also seem to fit here. A problem such as that described in the case study earlier in this chapter illustrates this kind of decision situation. Operating in this quadrant will require good human relations skills and technical competence in the subject under review.

Quadrant II depicts those situations where group feelings may be intense, but great technical expertise is not required because the subject is not a complex one. Any number of resolution schemes are available; the appropriate one must be that which is fair and sensitive to the needs and desires of the work group. Assignment of unpaid extracurricular duties, balanced work schedules for routine duties, school calendar development, among a myriad of decision situations, might fall in this category. Among appropriate ways to handle problems in this quadrant would be the formation of advisory committees, complete delegation of decision making to standing or ad hoc bodies, or informal consultation with leaders of the group affected.

Quadrant III contains those kinds of decisions that affect the quality of the operation in a technical sense, but do not impact much on the human side of the enterprise. Equipment selection once needs have been identified, development of conflict-free schedules and the design of a management information system, among other examples, might be found in this quadrant.

In the fourth quadrant neither great technical competence nor sensitive human relations is a critical consideration. (No decision can ever be entirely devoid of these, however.) What is needed is a concrete act to resolve a simple problem. Time is the only critical element. The decision has to be made in a timely manner so that people in the organization can go about their work in an orderly, efficient, and knowledgeable manner.

The model is helpful as an analytical tool. It emphasizes that the good school principal will have a repertoire of decision-making processes from which to select and that the process selected will be a result of the nature of the problem. Neither the use of committees for everything nor total exercise of the raw power of expertise will uniformly serve. Also, involvement is a rich term extending from situations where persons will be asked their opinions to situations where broad decision limits will be set and task forces asked to engage in final decision making for the entire high school, with a number of points in between.[7]

ROUTINE AND NONROUTINE DECISION MAKING

Decisions come in a variety of forms, differing in content, in the process by which the problem is addressed, and in the kind of impact they make on the organization and the people in the organization. Too, there is always the problem of matching the appropriate problem-resolution process with the type of decisional situation. When should one make a straightforward, from-the-hips, unilateral decision; when should one involve groups in the agonizing process of consensus?

The answer is not hard to see in the extreme. If the situation is a fire in the basement, one issues the order to clear the building; one does not call a committee together to achieve consensus on which fire exits to use. However, it would be appropriate to involve affected groups or individuals in advance in the development of policies and procedures for coping with such anticipated emergencies.

There are many ways to classify decisions, but beyond a certain point it really doesn't do much good except for retrospective analysis. That is, knowing a taxonomy of decisions would hardly put a person in the position of unerringly knowing when to do what. Unfortunately that kind of written wisdom doesn't exist. Helpful to this discussion, however, may be some examination of general decision categories occurring in any organization. Decision situations, for example, can be either routine or nonroutine.

Routine Decision Making

Any organization, of course, must accommodate itself to many unanticipated situations but generally the basis for an orderly goal-oriented school is a "repertory of proven, reliable, productive activities that are activated, monitored, and terminated by an appropriate set of habituated routine decisions."[8]

Many ongoing activities in the school organization are recurring in nature. Although it is important that procedural or routine decision-making practices be reviewed from time to time to make sure they are still adequate to the task, that is, to make sure that the social or organizational conditions to

---

[7]Many readers will be familiar with the Tannenbaum and Schmidt model which depicts points on a decision continuum from "Boss Tells" to "Boss Accepts any Group Decision," the nature of decision involvement depending on latitudes of leader and subordinate autonomy. Robert Tannenbaum and Warren H. Schmidt, "How to Choose a Leadership Pattern," *Harvard Business Review* 51 (May-June, 1973): 178.

[8]William J. Gore, "Decision-Making Research: Some Prospects and Limitations," in Stanley Mailick and Edward Van Ness, eds., *Concepts and Issues in Administrative Behavior* (Englewood Cliffs, N. J.: Prentice-Hall, 1962), p. 53.

which they respond have not changed, the decisions and decision processes that respond to these recurring activities should be routinized. The principal can expect certain kinds of problems to recur with frequency, given a particular environment or set of circumstances. Routine response mechanisms to these are expected by the staff so that they can go about their work with a minimum of disruption.

Arranging conditions in the school so that routine, recurring problems are resolved with a minimum of disruption and false starts can be achieved readily. A school building policy and rules and regulations manual carefully developed with staff, and students, can provide much assistance. Such a manual should contain statements of basic responsibilities accruing to teachers, counselors, administrators, and classified personnel, perhaps in each of the major decision categories of pupil personnel services, staffing and staff relations, building financial operations, public relations, curriculum and instructional development. In such a manual the roles and responsibilities of various personnel with respect to matters pertaining to the decision category would be carefully delineated, lines of communication spelled out, and common procedural questions answered.

Delegation of specific management tasks to designated people will also insure a degree of stability, not only because it clarifies the "who is to do what" question but also because it permits the principal to manage by exception rather than by direct participation in all decisions.

It is important, however, to provide a review process whereby policies, procedures, rules and regulations, and delegation practices are systematically examined to insure that they continue to serve efficiently and effectively. The reason for the development of policies and procedures is to facilitate the delivery of services to classrooms. When it becomes evident that a particular procedure is no longer appropriate or is actually inhibiting problem resolution, it must be revised. Effective use can be made of a staff-student advisory council for regular reviews of the routine procedures. The question sequence for such reviews is simply: "What are we doing?" "Why are we doing it?" "Can it be done a better way?"

A final word is necessary before closing this discussion of routine decision making. Do not assume that because a decision is termed routine or programmed that that decision is unimportant; it means only that the situations recur, that the school organization has developed procedures for dealing with these problems, and that certain requisite role behaviors have been established.

A properly managed school can carry on routine day-to-day activities without the constant involvement of the principal. The primary responsibility of the principal is not the building's routine operation but to create organizational conditions whereby the school may modify its operations to meet changing demand and opportunities.

Thus, routine, regularized, or programmed decision making, while encompassing problem situations running from the highly important to the mundane, is most often formalized to the extent that relatively little stress on individuals or organization occurs as decisions are promulgated and implemented. Such is often not the case with nonroutine decision making.

Nonroutine Decision Making

Unanticipated problems, unique situations, and fast-changing conditions are also characteristics of organizational life. Decisions concerning these situations often require "leaps into the unknown" that by their very nature produce both individual and organizational stress.

Establishing conditions for creative problem resolution is an important task of the principal, perhaps the most important task. Routinizing responses to recurring problems requires good management skills, to be sure; creative problem resolution requires as well the ability to tolerate ambiguity over a period of time and effective human relations skills.

As noted earlier, the most important resource for creative problem resolution is the combined intelligence and insight of the work group itself, the faculty, classified personnel, and students in the school. Lipham describes this process at its best:

> In heuristic or creative decision-making there is a lack of emphasis upon hierarchical structure. Role behavior is characterized by each individual being free to explore all ideas bearing on the problem, and the processes utilized are characterized by full and free discussion. The emotional or social tone is relatively relaxed and characterized by openness and originality. Working with students or teachers in solving a curricular issue is an example of heuristic decision-making, particularly if there is no agreed-upon method for dealing with the issue.[9]

Brainstorming

Many techniques exist for tapping the collective intelligence of a staff for creative or nonroutine decision making. One effective technique is brainstorming.

Brainstorming has as its only purpose the generation of ideas, no matter how wild or impractical the ideas may seem at first consideration. Whereas the usual kinds of meetings or conferences tend to be rather noncreative, a brainstorming group devotes itself *solely to creative thinking*. To function properly, the group must remain, during the period of the brainstorm, completely divorced from the mundane world. The rules described in Figure 21-8 must be followed precisely if the maximum result is to be gained from the brainstorming activity.

---

[9]James M. Lipham, "Improving the Decision-Making Skills of the Principal," in Culbertson et al., *Performance Objectives for School Principals,* chapter 4.

Rules of the Game:
1. *The problem that the group is going to work on must be stated clearly.* That is, everyone must know the problem that is to be solved.
2. *Criticism in the brainstorming session is not permitted.* The group facilitator must not permit any adverse judgment of ideas during the period of the brainstorming. Any idea is a good idea no matter how apparently ridiculous it may seem at the moment to some other member of the group.
3. *"Free wheeling" is welcome and encouraged.* The wilder the idea, the better. The reason for engaging in a brainstorming session is to try to find new ways of approaching a problem and any group, or any individuals in the group, that becomes infected with the "that won't work because" syndrome will be most ineffective.
4. *Quantity is what the group is after.* The greater the number of ideas the more likelihood one or more of those ideas will be a winner.
5. *Combination and improvement are sought.* In addition to contributing ideas of their own, participants should suggest how ideas of others can be combined or changed in some way to produce yet another idea. Idea "stealing" and modification is encouraged; the common rules governing social convention do not apply in brainstorming sessions.
6. *Maximum participation of group members is required.* It is for this reason that brainstorming groups should be kept relatively small, probably no more than ten. It is hard to drop out when one is in a small group—it is so noticeable, and, thus, smaller groups tend to promote maximum participation. Everybody has something to contribute to a brainstorming group and the ideas of everyone are sought.
7. *The only role of the group leader is that of facilitator and participant.* He does not serve as a chairman in a usual sense and *Robert's Rules of Order* are out. A brainstorming group is a very impolite group.

FIGURE 21-8. Rules of Brainstorming.

The role of the group leader is one of facilitator rather than gatekeeper. The best method to record ideas is a flip chart, on which ideas may be quickly and easily displayed. Using flip charts keeps the ideas visible and thus stimulates other ideas. Moreover, when the session ends, the paper can be given to a secretary for duplication on ditto paper for subsequent circulation.

Judgment and Refinement of Ideas. Later, the group reconvenes for the purpose of judging and modifying the ideas. This session is one of analysis. Its purpose is to select those ideas that singly or in combination with other ideas seem to provide a creative solution to the problem.

From the analysis session the group decides on the four or five solutions that offer a basis for the systematic resolution of the problem. At this point a group may engage in any number of systematic planning approaches and work the solutions into an implementation phase. (See Chapter 22 for approaches to systematic planning.)

GUIDELINES FOR EXECUTIVE DECISION MAKING

The overriding question in decision making is what goal or outcome are the pupils or staff attempting to reach and by what process can it be best achieved. Decision making may be seen as a six-step process:

1. Identifying the true problem and subproblems
2. Collecting the relevant facts
3. Identifying alternative actions from which to choose the best course; as a part of this step it is important to anticipate for each of the alternatives what the possible consequences of the action will be with respect to any of several reference groups who may be affected by the decisions
4. Commitment to a single choice or single course of action
5. Implementing the preferred choice
6 Providing for evaluation and feedback about the decision

What Is the Problem?

Until the problem is adequately defined, no effective decision can be reached. Also, the real problem is often not presented verbally or readily apparent, and investigation beneath the surface is always justified. Some redefinition of the problem may become apparent in the data collection procedure. Thus, the first task is to identify the real problem and the impinging subproblems. When any problem is first presented, an individual or a group is an immediate captive of insufficient data. A staff complaint or parent complaint may simply be an iceberg with the real problem far below the surface. Treating symptoms instead of causes is an administrative trap.

Alternative Actions

There are usually several approaches to any problem and several alternative actions that can be taken to resolve the immediate issue. One good way to decide which alternative is the best, once all the facts are in, is to list the alternatives and ask the following questions of each:

1. Does this action treat the real problem or merely the symptom?
2. What kinds of other problems does this alternative decision create?
3. Who and what will be affected by the decision?
4. What probable reaction can be expected from those affected by the alternative?
5. Is the alternative consistent with general school policy, rules, and regulations and with the law?
6. Can the decision be reasonably well understood and implemented?

It is sound to withhold judgment initially. Rarely does an immediate seat-of-the-pants decision have to be made. Good decision making requires taking the necessary time to gather relevant facts that have a bearing on the problem at hand. Further, there are usually many sides to an issue or problem and the avoidance of commitment in the first flush of reaction will stand decision makers in good stead.

Organizational and Personal Barriers

Good ideas and good decisions often fail because the attempt to put them into action may not take into consideration the traditions, norms, and informal dimensions of the organization, nor the abilities and understanding of those who will be charged with implementing the desired action. Ignoring any of the five following barriers will defeat even the best decision:

1. *Vested interests, territoriality, and organizational boundaries.* Every change affects or threatens someone's privileges, someone's status, someone's ordered life. Recognizing this is the first step to mitigating any negative effect.

2. *Lack of clarity of the issue or problem to be addressed.* Until a group is able to state the problem clearly there is no sense in moving on. The first step is to distinguish between problems and symptoms. Placing a bandaid on an aching head does little good. Fuzzy objectives result in ill-conceived solutions to which few staff members can become committed.

3. *Lack of attention to the consequences of the proposed action.* Before a change process or a solution is implemented, attention must be directed to possible negative outcomes in addition to the desired outcome. If the proposed solution will create other problems, perhaps an alternative would be better. Failure to consider the effects of a proposed action can have serious consequences.

4. *Lack of technical skill of those to be charged with implementing the change or solution.* Any change must take into consideration the abilities of those who will be actively involved in it. Before any particular solution can be achieved there may be a need for retraining staff, employing additional personnel with special skills, or reassigning or replacing existing personnel.

5. *Two-valued thinking.* Issues and problems are rarely two-sided; things are rarely either/or. Seldom is there but one solution. Putting things into such a context effectively shuts off thinking about alternatives. Creative eclecticism might better serve. One way to avoid two-valued thinking is to define the problem carefully and then engage in a series of brainstorming sessions with the staff before becoming committed to a single course of action.

Inattention to these barriers will result in staff uncertainty, anxiety, disorientation, and often out-and-out sabotage. It will also result in organizational dysfunction and decisions that will not get translated into action.

Good Communication Is Essential

Implementing decisions is in large part dependent upon good communication. The way in which the decision is communicated will say much about the importance of the decision. Using the ditto machine to communicate a major policy change says loudly and clearly that the decision is not a very important one. If the problem is a complex one and important behavior change is required in order to have a decision properly implemented, more is required than a simple written statement from the principal's office or the task group. Further, there is a need to know whether or not those affected by the decision know what it is they are supposed to do. Feedback and evaluation are necessary in any decision process. In its simplest form the question is, "Is the decision working; was the goal achieved; if not, why not?"

SUMMARY

This chapter has focused on decision making. Three kinds of decision processing are available to the principal: unilateral, majority opinion, and consensus. Each has its place, but for those decisions that require important changes in the behavior of staff members, students, or patrons or that require significant organizational readjustment, neither rule by administrative fiat nor rule by a vote of one-over-half-the-membership is sufficient to the task.

A school organization is composed of several interacting parts and a hierarchical structure. Individuals have impact on their work environment and that environment has an impact on them. In such an environment, bringing about important changes is difficult and requires sensitivity and the adroit use of appropriate decision processes.

Techniques such as task force teams, consensus decision making, and systematic problem solving are necessary. Each of these taps the "group wisdom" and provides a strong basis for the effective implementation of solutions.

BIBLIOGRAPHY

Bridges, Edwin M. "A Model for School Decision Making in the School Principalship." *Educational Administration Quarterly* (January 1967): 49–61. This work is an analysis of the dimensions and implications of three kinds of arrangements in which school faculties may arrive at decisions.

Culbertson, Jack A. et al., eds. *Performance Objectives for School Principals.* Berkeley, Calif.: McCutchan Publishing Corp., 1974.

Drucker, Peter. *Management: Tasks, Responsibilities, Practices.* New York: Harper and Row, Publishers, 1974.

Glickman, Carl D., and Esposito, James P. *Leadership for Elementary School Improvement.* Boston: Allyn and Bacon, 1979, esp. chaps. 18 and 19.

Hughes, Larry W. "Effective Human Relations and Morale." In Culbertson et al., *Performance Objectives for School Principals,* chap. 5.

Hughes, Larry W. *Effective Decision-Making: A Principal's Primer.* New London, Conn.: Croft Educational Services, 1970.

Hughes, Larry W., and Robertson, Thomas. "Principals and the Management of Conflict." *Planning and Changing* 11, no. 1 (Spring 1980): 3–15.

Likert, Rensis, and Likert, Jane Gibson. *New Ways of Managing Conflict.* New York: McGraw-Hill, 1976.

Lipham, James M. "Improving the Decision-Making Skills of the Principal." In Culbertson et al., *Performance Objectives for School Principals,* chap. 4.

McGregor, Douglas. *The Human Side of the Enterprise.* New York: McGraw-Hill, 1960.

Odiorne, George S. *Management and the Activity Trap.* New York: Harper and Row, Publishers, 1974.

Sergiovanni, Thomas J., and Carver, Fred D. *The New School Executive.* New York: Harper and Row, Publishers, 1980.

22

Systematic Planning and Project Management

INTRODUCTION

"Something's got to be done!" said Ogg. "There are too many alligators, that's the problem." "No," replied Ogg's spouse, "the problem is the swamp. It needs to be drained. Then the alligators would go away. But better than that, this place would then be habitable in all ways."

So, what to do? Should the focus be on the immediate crisis of too many alligators (a symptom) or should something be done about the problem—providing a habitable area? Problems of great proportion frequently confront the school administrator, and moving from crisis to crisis in alligator fighting fashion provides little hope of ever achieving a long-lasting resolution.

Much has been written about project management and systematic planning as processes for effecting change or solving problems. Great scientific achievements have occurred largely as a result of systematically disaggregating a desired goal into a series of interrelated, interdependent tasks or activities. These tasks or activities are then organized into manageable components. Completing the tasks of the components result in the attainment of the goal. Task-force teams based on technical expertise are formed under the direction of a project manager, who coordinates the efforts of the team in the completion of a component.

Putting a man on the moon (a goal) was an infinitely complex project. The number of people and agencies involved in the effort was myriad. Yet, in a relatively short span of time—less than a decade after President Kennedy made the initial decision—the mission was accomplished. How could a task with such magnitude be completed so quickly? Using concepts and procedures that were developed during the building of the Polaris submarine, often summed up under the acronym PERT (Program Evaluation Review Technique), thousands of people from a variety of agencies were involved in a step-by-step progression to the moon. Groups, often working independently of each other, systematically focused on components of the master plan.

The following were characteristic:

1. Problem definition
2. Task-specific expertise of personnel
3. Clarity of function and clear designation of responsibility
4. A specified time line
5. Allocation of dollars and other resources
6. Intergroup communications systems
7. A general master plan specifying each of the interrelated components and the nature of the interrelationship

Educating young people is also a complex act. Moreover, a school, even the smallest elementary school, is itself a complex organism faced continually with problems and pressures from within and without. There is a need to adapt to new social conditions, to revise curricula, to address issues ranging from vandalism to the creative use of external grants of money, to plan in-service education programs, to develop more effective ways to communicate with the public, to respond to apparent learning deficiencies of clients, and the list could go on and on. The point is that often too many of these issues never do get resolved; they don't go away, either. They linger, forming and reforming, manifesting themselves in different ways, and result not only in an ineffective operation but also reduced morale of staff, students, and members of the community, who may feel as though they are on some sort of treadmill. Often a school year is completed with survival being the only identifiable accomplishment.

A better way exists. While systematic planning and project management is no panacea, it will result in an orderly progression to problem resolution and something far more sound and satisfying than simple survival as the major year-end accomplishment.

It is possible to become battle-weary and overwhelmed with the terms and acronyms that permeate written works about systematic planning. PERT, CPM, PPBS, Gantt charts, and complicated formulae for predicting completion dates might all appear to the novitiate planner to confound rather than solve a problem. It need not be so. One does not have to be a graduate systems analysis engineer or a college major in educational futures to lead a staff in systematic-planning endeavors. Systematic planning will facilitate goal achievement, not get in its way, and it does not make much difference what words or labels are used as long as certain identifiable and logical procedures are employed. Ultimately the stress is on goal achievement, what it is that one is attempting to accomplish, and how it can be done most efficiently. What follows is an explication of this process.

PROBLEM IDENTIFICATION OR GOAL STATEMENT

A problem exists. Students don't seem to be reading as well as expected, or all is not well with the school-community relations program, or the social studies curriculum needs revision, or the incidence of vandalism is on the rise. Something is wrong.[1]

Participants must take care in the problem identification phase to define the real issue, to avoid stating problems as solutions, and to avoid focusing on symptoms rather than problems. Suppose for example that school personnel realize that the children in the intermediate grades do not seem to be reading as well as expected. To state the problem as "the need to implement a new reading program" presupposes a solution. Similarly, to state the problem as "how to get pupils to read more books" focuses on a symptom. The problem, stated after careful collection and examination of facts, might be "to improve the functional reading skills of intermediate students at Hudson Elementary School."

To be sure, one solution might indeed be a revamping of the reading program and one desired outcome might be that intermediate youngsters read more books, but neither of these is the basic problem. If this seems tautological, it isn't. Moving too hastily to solutions on the basis of uncertain facts will result in faulty planning, displaced energy, and unresolved problems. Changing the reading program when what was needed were better-trained teachers, a new partnership with the home, and wider varieties of experiences for learners will end with predictably poor results.

Once the problem has been clarified and the specific desired outcomes identified, project management, using a systematic problem resolution process, is possible.

PURPOSE OF THE PROJECT

The initial step in project management is to state specifically the purpose of the project. The purpose may be as simple as organizing a two-day workshop on techniques of teaching reading for intermediate grade teachers or more complex such as developing a coordinated public relations program for Hudson Elementary School or very complex and long range, such as instituting a K–6 program of individualized instruction.

For the purpose of illustration, assume that one problem confronting a school is increasing social distance between the school and the community.

---

[1]Uncovering issues to be addressed in the upcoming school year provides an excellent activity at preschool or year-end inservice workshops. Groups of teachers, and perhaps community members, may be set to work generating items, large and small, that seem to be getting in the way of maximum effectiveness. This list can then be turned over to a representative steering committee for refinement and the ultimate identification of major issues for review by the staff.

Several symptoms lead the principal and the staff to this conclusion. Attendance at school-sponsored programs and PTO meetings is poor or not representative of the community at large, criticism of the school curriculum often becomes emotional, pupil tardiness and attendance rates are not what is desired, communication with the home seems limited to report cards, student morale is low, student attitudes toward the school seem to reflect parental disinterest, perhaps even distrust. These, among other symptoms, lead the principal and staff to conclude that the relationship between the home and school needs to be improved. The project goal is stated "to improve home-school communications."

FORCE FIELDING THE PROBLEM

Kurt Lewin concluded that in an organization things stay as they are because a field of opposing forces is in balance.[2] His force field theory provides a useful way to engage in problem analysis as well as a basis for engaging in problem solution. One way to conceptualize a situation is to regard it as a product of forces pushing and pulling in opposite directions.

There are restraining forces and facilitating forces. The restraining forces are current conditions or actions which are such that change is inhibited. One might think of these forces as negative or "minus" forces. The facilitating forces are current conditions or actions which are such that change is encouraged. These may be thought of as positive or "plus" forces.

The force field concept issues from the physical law that a body at rest (in equilibrium) will remain at rest when the sum of all the forces operating on it is zero. The body will move only when the sum is not zero, and it will move only in the direction of the unbalancing force.

This can be observed in an organization, whether one is examining the productivity of staff, the state of the intramural program, or the status of home-school communication, among any of a number of examples. A thing is where it is because the counterbalancing plus and minus forces together equal zero. That is, conditions are such that the forces militating against improvement are equal to the existing forces pushing for positive change.

A school staff or project team dissatisfied with the current state of home-school communication should ask the question, "Why are things as they are?" This question leads to a force field analysis. A beginning analysis is shown in Figure 22-1.

Movement or change will take place when an imbalance is created. An imbalance is created either by eliminating forces or by affecting the intensity

---

[2]See Kurt Lewin, "Quasi-Stationary Social Equilibria and the Problem of Social Change," in Bennis, Benne, and Chin, eds., *The Planning of Change* (New York: Holt, Rinehart and Winston, 1961), pp. 235–38. See also, in the same volume, David H. Jenkins, "Force Field Analysis Applied to a School Situation," pp. 238–44.

Facilitating forces for change (+)	Forces militating against change (−)
1. Faculty interest	1. Perceived community apathy
2. External monies available	2. High student turnover
3. Media interest	3. Moribund PTO
4. Consultant help available	4. Little released time for teachers
5. State mandate	5. Lack of budget to support new approaches
6. . . .	6. . . .

FIGURE 22-1. Force Field Analysis: Why Aren't Home-School Communications Better?

or power of the forces. The imbalance "unfreezes" the current situation, and the level will change to a new position where balance will be once again achieved (new state of equilibrium). An imbalance may be created by:

1. The addition of a new force (in the example given, the allocation of some external monies for budget support)
2. The deletion of a force (e. g., revitalization of the PTO)
3. A change in the magnitude or strength of force(s)

Any plan that is developed after the force field analysis will probably use all three processes to some degree. Also, as can be seen from the above example, some forces may appear almost reciprocal, so that an increase in one necessarily reduces the other in direct proportion. Other forces are such that there may be little direct action that can be taken. For example, it is not likely that a school faculty could do much to reduce transience of the school population.

In general, increasing only facilitating forces will likely increase tension in the system, and the restraining forces may correspondingly increase. It is often more effective to attempt first to reduce the intensity of the restraining forces.

Engaging in a force field analysis will help a task force focus its thinking on those specific environmental conditions in need of change, if the project goal is to be reached.

THE PROJECT PLAN

Figure 22-2 illustrates a comprehensive problem-resolution document that reveals the project goal, delineates the components comprising the solution to the problem, establishes target dates for completion, and identifies the specific persons who have accepted responsibility for seeing to it that the various activities are carried out. There is also a project director who assumes overall responsibility, and each component has a designated coordinator.

In a sense, the specific components are hypotheses. That is, the staff or the task force team involved in the problem-definition phase has decided that if all of these activities are carried out, better home-school relations will result.[3]

Component Coordinators and Other Key Personnel

Different people will be affected by the project. Some will be involved directly by coordinating components or carrying out other agreed-upon responsibilities. Others will be involved in ancillary ways, ranging from giving approval for certain acts to simply being kept informed. Figure 22-3 illustrates a way for the project manager, component coordinator, and the staff to keep track of who is to do what, who is affected by the action, and what needs to be done about it.

Two things must be considered when responsibilities are assigned: the person accepting the responsibility must be capable of carrying it out and that person must agree to and understand the nature of the assignment. The assignment of responsibility must not occur in the cloister of an office by an individual unaccompanied by anything more than a sharp pencil. More jobs have been bungled because of unclear, unaccepted assignments than because of any other single factor. Further, the unique talents and interests of staff members should be capitalized on and their inabilities mitigated.

Beyond the task force team charged with the implementation of the project will be others who are affected by the project, some in positions of authority, others who have a special competence to be used, and still others who simply have a need or a right to know. The key personnel checklist depicted in Figure 22-3 takes these into account.

Key personnel or groups should be identified along with the several components comprising the project. The nature of the relationship of each person or group to each component should be indicated.

Putting the Specific Components into Operation

The project has now been disaggregated into a series of components that provide greater specificity. Depending on the nature of its complexity, each component may require further subdivision into a series of specific tasks, the carrying out of which will result in the accomplishment of the component. For this component, coordinators may need to develop a document similar to the

---

[3]The need for an evaluation component is apparent. It is important to provide checkpoints throughout the project to see if desired outcomes are being achieved and, if they are not, to make midpoint corrections. Additionally, of course, a final evaluation and recycling stage must be provided.

Project: To Improve Home-School Communication; Hudson Elementary School

Project manager: Charles Achilles

Completion date: July 1, 19--

Start date: September 1, 19--

Resolution components	Date for completion	Relationship to force field (if any). State which "plus" or "minus" the component relates to.	Component coordinator	Special notes
1. Monthly newsletters to clients	11/15	See Facilitating 2 and 3 See Inhibitors 4 and 5	Fred Hay	
2. Congratulatory letters system	11/1	See Inhibitor 1	Dennis Spuck	Trusty should facilitate
3. Parent rap sessions schedule	11/15	See Facilitating 4	Dorothy Kilburn	
4. Student rap sessions schedule	11/15	See Inhibitor 1	Brian Rocksborough	
5. Visitation days organized	1/1	See Inhibitors 1 and 3	Peter Husen	Get PTO involved
6. Report cards revised	3/1		John Croft	
7. Parent advisory council organized	7/1	Inhibitor 3	Jody Stevens	Board must be kept informed
Budget to support approved 8/15 (Date)		Amount $1700 (initial)	FY 19-- (current)	

FIGURE 22-2. Comprehensive Problem-resolution Document.

comprehensive problem resolution document that disaggregates complex components into manageable units. Figure 22-4 depicts such a disaggregation. Again, target dates are established for each of the major units comprising components, and responsibilities are assigned. For those units that are themselves complex or composed of several related identifiable events, a further disaggregation may be required. It is important for component coordinators to note also what resources will be needed in the way of personnel, money, and facilities and then to advise the project director about these.

Establishing Realistic Completion Dates

Establishing precise starting and completion times for the project as a whole as well as for the components of the project is very important. In not all cases will the completion of one component depend upon another, but often this will be so.[4] Even when this is not so, it is vital that all components be completed on time.

The best method of establishing realistic completion dates requires that those involved in the project understand: a) the nuances of the problem, b) certain organizational realities, and c) the capabilities of the staff. Then, the project team can ask itself, "If unanticipated problems arose, what is the most pessimistic date by which this activity could be completed?" And then, "If all went well, what is the most optimistic date by which this activity could be completed?" The realistic date is a point midway between the pessimistic and the optimistic dates.

The project manager's responsibility is to help the task force stay on schedule. This does not mean daily supervision; it means regular conversations with the component coordinators about how the activity is going so that help can be provided at the point of need.

The Project Calendar: Gantt Charting

After the comments have been delineated, responsibilities assigned and accepted, and specific tasks comprising the more complex components established, an important responsibility of the project manager[5] is to develop the master schedule. The master schedule is a chronology of the project, and it is developed in the form of a Gantt Chart (Figure 22-5). Each major component

---

[4]When the project is very complex and has several interdependent parts, it may be necessary to develop a PERT chart that depicts the order in which each of the activities has to occur and the relationship of one activity to another. An especially good treatment of this process can be found in Thomas Seragiovanni, *Handbook for Effective Department Leadership* (Boston: Allyn and Bacon, 1977), chaps. 7 and 8.

[5]The project manager is not necessarily the principal. He or she might be, of course, but any staff member with the requisite administrative abilities or other special expertise may serve in this position.

PROJECT: To Improve Home-School Communication at Hudson Elementary School

Project component	Who needs to know?	What part do they play?			
		Must approve	Keep informed	Special skill	Other
1. Monthly newsletter	Secretary, PTO			X	
	Faculty Council		X		
	Achilles or Spuck	X			
	News Media		X		
2. Congratulatory letters	Class Advisors, PTO			X	
	Achilles			X	
3. Parent rap session	Achilles	X			
	Trusty			X	
	News Media		X		
	PTO		X		
	Board of Education		X		
	Superintendent		X		
4. Student rap session	Achilles, Spuck, Trusty, Stevens, Waters	X		X	
				X	
	Faculty Council		X		
	Board of Education				
	Superintendent				Monthly reports
5. School visitation days	Achilles, Spuck, Husen			X	
	News Media		X		
	PTO		X		
6. Report card revision	Faculty Council	X			
	Superintendent, PTO	X			
	News Media		X		
7. Parent advisory council	Achilles	X			
	Faculty Council		X		
	Superintendent		X		
	Board of Education		X		
	Trusty, Hay			X	

FIGURE 22-3. Key Personnel Checklist for Component Coordinators.

Project: Improve Home-School Communication at Hudson Elementary School

Component: Development of Newsletter

Coordinator: Fred Hay

Completion date: 11/15 and continuing

Units	Completion date	Person responsible	Special notes
1. Develop format	10/1	Hay (with committee)	Limited to 4 pages
2. New sources identified	10/1	Hay (with committee)	Use Student Council if possible
3. Reproduction mechanics developed	10/15	Barbara Greer	Postage meter required
4. Copy assignments out and collected	11/1	Hay	
5. Material edited	11/8	Leah Dunaway	Released time required
6. Reproduce and mail out	11/15	Barbara Greer	Released time required

Budget to support: $500 start up; $200 per quarter thereafter — TOTAL This FY $1300
Equipment and Space: Reproductive (available), postage meter, designated workroom.

FIGURE 22-4. Problem-resolution Component Sheet.

is listed along with the units comprising the component and a calendar of beginning and intended completion dates. The chart serves three purposes: (1) it provides the project manager with a ready reference for checking progress; (2) posted prominently, it serves as a motivator for individual-activity supervisors and participants; and (3) posted prominently, it communicates to a wider audience the nature and intent of the project.

The Master Project Document

An important responsibility of the project manager is to prepare a master project document. This may simply be a looseleaf binder in which is placed the comprehensive problem-resolution document, key personnel checklists, complex component documents, and the master schedule. This will make the project easier to monitor. Component coordinators should prepare a similar document for their specific part of the project.

EVALUATION

One last step remains: evaluation. Did the project result in the desired goal? At the outset of this discussion, it was indicated that the several activities developed were actually hypotheses: the project team or the entire school staff thought that if these activities were carried out, better home-school relations would result. These hypotheses must be checked, for it is pointless to engage in a series of activities designed to achieve an outcome if one does not provide a means to determine if the results were sufficient to justify the expenditure of resources.

At the beginning of a project, it is essential to state the indicators of achievement that the project staff is willing to accept as evidence of desired outcomes. These indicators may best come from restatements of the symptoms of the problem originally identified. In the previous illustration dealing with deteriorating home-school relations, those symptoms were:

1. Attendance at PTO meetings was poor.
2. The PTO membership was not representative.
3. Attendance at school-sponsored events was small.
4. Criticism of the school program was emotional.
5. Attendance and tardiness rates of pupils was unsatisfactory.
6. Student morale was low.
7. Communication with the home was limited to report cards.
8. Student attitudes about learning were negative.

Changes in such conditions provide a means for evaluating the effectiveness of a project. Parent- and student-attitude inventories, attendance

Project: To improve home-school communication at Hudson Elementary School

Target date: July 1, 19--

Activity Description	Month: Sept. week 1	2	3	4	Month: Oct. week 1	2	3	4	Month: Nov. week 1	2	3	4	Month: Dec. week 1	2	3	4	Month: etc. week 1	2	3	4
A 1 Newsletter	X	---	---	---	---	---	---	---	X											
t 1 Format		X	---	X																
t News 2 Sources			X	---	X															
t 3 Reproduction			X	---	---	X														
t 4 Copy out						X	---	X												
t 5 Mat'l edited								X	---	X										
t 6 Reproduction									X	---	X									
A Congratulatory 2 Letters				X	---	---	---	---	X											

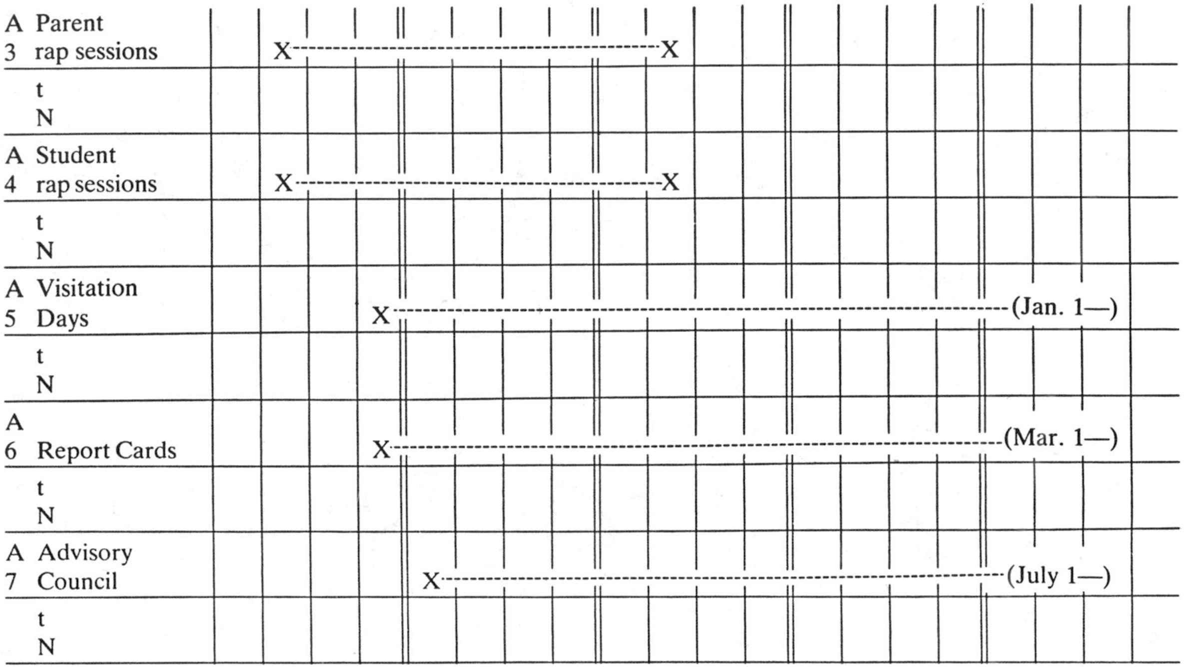

A Parent
3 rap sessions
t
N

A Student
4 rap sessions
t
N

A Visitation
5 Days
t
N

A
6 Report Cards
t
N

A Advisory
7 Council
t
N

(Jan. 1—)

(Mar. 1—)

(July 1—)

FIGURE 22-5. Project Calendar of Events.

records, and informal and formal feedback from school and community persons and groups all serve as data sources to determine project effectiveness. Further, it may be that certain activities were efficacious and others were not. This, too, will need to be investigated.

SUMMARY

The process of systematic planning is applicable to any problem situation. It is designed to do two things: (1) engender commitment to problem resolution by involving those who have expertise, insight, and interest in the specific problem in question and (2) marshal those resources through a systematic process to get from problem identification to problem resolution. The result of such an endeavor will be productive change.

BIBLIOGRAPHY

Bennis, Warren; Benne, Kenneth D.; and Chin, Robert, eds. *The Planning of Change.* New York: Holt, Rinehart and Winston, 1961.

McGrath, J. H. *Planning Systems for School Executives.* San Francisco: Intext Educational Publishers, 1972.

Sergiovanni, Thomas J. *Handbook for Effective Department Leadership,* Boston: Allyn and Bacon, 1977, esp. chaps. 8 and 9. Also Carver, Fred D. *The New School Executive.* New York: Harper and Row, Publishers, 1980, esp. chap. 15.

Tanner, C. Kenneth. *Designs for Educational Planning.* Lexington, Mass.: D. C. Heath and Co., 1971.

Woodcock, Mike, and Francis, Dave. *Unblocking Your Organization.* La Jolla, Calif.: University Associates, Inc., 1979. This is a most useful volume for the practicing school administrator. It provides analytical techniques and exercises designed for immediate use with work groups and project task forces.

23

Managing Executive Time

INTRODUCTION

There are twenty-four hours in a day, 168 hours in a week—no more, no less. For a principal to make the best use of the available hours requires planning and conscious action. Unless this occurs there will be missed deadlines, unaccomplished goals, and a briefcase filled with after-dinner tasks to be done. And it starts all over again the next morning. The result is a less-than-satisfying professional and personal life. The focus of this chapter is on the principles of good time management. There is no magic wand that can be waved, but there are practices to insure that the right things get done, in a timely fashion.

Distinguishing between the Principal and the Principalship

The "principal" is a person; the "principalship" is a collection of responsibilities and specific tasks. The principal's job is to see that these responsibilities are met and the tasks performed well. We distinguish between principal and principalship to point out that while the principal is ultimately responsible for what goes on in and around the school, this does not imply that the principal must personally perform all of the management and leadership acts. Only a foolish person would attempt to do so, for not only would it violate the precepts of good administration, it would also be impossible. The principal should perform some tasks directly—because of their complexity or because the tasks are those for which the principal has great skill.

Distinguishing between the terms "principal" and "principalship" suggests, therefore, that two of the most important skills a principal must possess are the appropriate organization and development of personnel and the delegation of authority. An example of the effective implementation of these skills can be found in the typical physician's office.

Physicians try to draw a tight circle around their professional activities and spend time and talent doing only those things that they alone can do.

Other persons, with varying degrees of professional training and medical expertise, are assigned the tasks that fall outside the circle but are also of importance to the health of the patient. Thus, by doing only a limited number of tasks, the physician is able to minister effectively to a great number of patients every day and still frequently make it home for dinner on time. Similarly, the principal can effectively carry out all of the functions of the principalship with the same attention to good administrative practice. It is, of course, somewhat more difficult to draw a circle around the principal's job, but unless this is done, principals will find themselves spending entire days on tasks that someone else could and should be performing.

Establishing a Responsibility Circle. Good management is mostly the science and art of achieving *stated objectives* through the efforts of other people. Those things that require only the principal's attention must be identified. These things include tasks which, because of special training, insight, or superordinate delegation, can be performed only by the principal or those tasks of an important kind for which the principal has the greatest skill. Once these tasks have been identified, the principal establishes the nature of his or her involvement. Does the task require that the principal actually do it or only that it gets done under the principal's general supervision or initiation? All activities that do not require physical performance by the principal should be done by someone else!

The latter approach will require that the principal spend time initially working with appropriate staff so they will (1) know what is required and by when and (2) be trained in the proper dispatch of these responsibilities. The principal can effectively manage all of the functions of the principalship with attention to good delegative practices.

How to Get It All Done: Time Management

The first chapter of this book suggested that it was unrealistic to expect principals to be either administrative paragons or obsequious bookkeepers. The position does require a person with well-developed human, conceptual, and technical skills. It also requires an individual who can make maximum use of the time available for task accomplishment.

THE ACTIVITY TRAP

The frenetic activity characteristics of administrative offices at all levels of elementary and secondary education often suggests accomplishment that is more apparent than real. Principals frequently find themselves parceled out in so many different directions, responding directly to so many requests of others, that the important tasks do not get done or get done in an inadequate way. But, even if the product of the effort is minuscule, the energy expended was great, and the principal is tired. Odiorne calls this the "activity trap."

> Most people get caught in the Activity Trap! They become so enmeshed in activity they lose sight of why they are doing it, and the activity becomes a false goal, an end in itself. Successful people never lose sight of their goals; the hoped-for outputs.[1]

Successful school executives know how to manage their time and avoid the activity trap. It's not easy but it can be done. It's not easy, because the busy executive often has the least control over time. Principals spend a great deal of their time reacting to the problems of others. The issue in time management is how to get more time free to *act* rather than *react*, how to spend more time on policy development and other leadership activities and less time focusing on other people's crises or engaging in pointless activity.

The key to spending time productively is in goal setting and the consequent establishment of job priorities in support of the goals. This will result in effectiveness rather than just efficiency. Efficiency is doing things right; effectiveness is doing the *right things right*. The first question to answer when confronted with a task always is, "should this thing be done?" This is a goal-and-priority question. The issue the principal must confront is not how to get more time, but rather how to spend more time on those things that are most important. The latter is achievable.

Four Questions to Ask before Agreeing
to Take On "One More Task"

1. How important is this?
2. Can someone else handle it with equal or better facility *OR* is there a more appropriate person who should handle it?
3. Does it need *immediate* attention from me or someone else?
4. What kinds of information will be required for the job to get done, and where or from whom is this information available?

Chapter 1 of this book identified five functions as comprising the principalship: community-school relations, staff personnel development, pupil-personnel development, educational program development, and business and building management. The skills necessary for the implementation of these functions are the subject of this concluding chapter.

---

[1]George Odiorne, *Management and the Activity Trap* (New York: Harper and Row, Publishers, 1974), p. 6.

IDEAL/PERCEIVED/REAL USE OF TIME

How would elementary principals prefer to spend their time? How do elementary principals think they spend their time? How do elementary principals *actually* spend their time? These are three very different questions, and the answers seem always to be at some variance with each other. Perhaps it is not surprising that how principals prefer to spend time is different from how they think they spend time, because few people can always spend their professional or personal hours exactly as they want. Others in the school organization will by right impinge upon the principal's work time. Similarly, the needs of family members and friends or other personal responsibilities will interfere with plans for nonwork time.

The most surprising thing is that the way principals perceive they are spending professional time and the way they are actually spending time *invariably reveals a disparity!* That is, principals, and other executives as well, are not only unable to spend time the way they most desire, they are not even aware of how they really are using their time.

Job Analysis

The first step in getting control of time is to engage in a job analysis. An instrument such as that depicted in Figure 23-1 is useful for this purpose. Based on the five identified functions of the principalship, it requires a frank assessment of the way in which time would be allocated "if it were the best of all possible worlds," compared to the way one perceives time is currently being spent and the way time is actually being spent. (The "actual" column requires data collected over a few weeks' period, about which more later.) The instrument also helps identify organizational roadblocks.[2]

Question 6 of the questionnaire asks respondents to tell what percentage of time they would ideally allocate among the five functions of the principalship. (There are two additional categories: unoccupied and other. The latter category is listed in case the respondent doesn't feel the first five categories are adequate.) Question 7 requests respondents to identify what percentage of their time they think they are currently spending in these same categories. The remainder of the questionnaire is used for further time analysis and other data collection.

Ideal Time Usage. A typical group of principal responses to Question 6 is recorded in Figure 23-2. Ideally, most of the principals would spend only 10 percent of their professional time on building and business management activities. They would devote about one-quarter time each to pupil personnel,

---

[2]The authors have made frequent use of this instrument in time management seminars they have conducted, and the data presented in subsequent figures are from one such seminar. Typically the instruments are completed by the participants a few weeks ahead of a scheduled seminar.

NAME

SCHOOL

QUESTIONS

1. ____ What is your present position?
2. ____ If you are a principal, do you have an assistant?
3. ____ What is the student enrollment of your school?
4. ____ Level of school (h.s.; jr. high; elem.)?
5. ____ Best description of school population served; e.g., inner city; urban but not inner city; suburban.
6. If it were the best of all possible worlds, I would allocate my time as follows:
   ____ % Community-school relations activities (meeting with parents and civic groups; doing news releases; etc.)
   ____ % Developing personnel (helping teachers; in-service activities)
   ____ % Working with students
   ____ % Educational programming (developing innovative curricula; future planning; etc.)
   ____ % Managing the building (report writing; keeping the toilets flushing; keeping kids in and intruders out; etc.)
   ____ % Unoccupied (woolgathering; Monday morning quarterbacking; coffee drinking; etc.)
   ____ % Other (please specify)
7. Alas, it's not the best of all worlds and here's how I think I actually spend my time:
   ____ % Community-school relations activities (meeting with parents and civic groups; doing news releases; etc.)
   ____ % Developing personnel (helping teachers; in-service activities; etc.)
   ____ % Working with students
   ____ % Educational programming (developing innovative curricula; future planning; etc.)
   ____ % Managing the building (report writing; keeping the toilets flushing; keeping kids in and intruders out; etc.)
   ____ % Unoccupied (woolgathering; Monday morning quarterbacking; coffee drinking; etc.)
   ____ % Other (please specify)
8. The things (people, objects, organizational constraints, whatever or whoever) that most often keep me from allocating my time the way I would like to are: (list 2 or 3)

   _____

   _____

9. Respond to the following statement in a short, sweet and "from the hips" fashion. "I've got a good school (or this is a good system), but it could be better if _____

   _____

   _____."

FIGURE 23-1. Initial Job Analysis Questionnaire.

"IDEAL" TIME USAGE

A Typical Group of Elementary School Principals' Responses to the Statement:[1]
"If it were the best of all possible worlds, I would allocate my time as follows."

	Mode	Avg.	High	Low
Community-School Relations	15%	16%	20%	10%
Staff Personnel	20	26	45	20
Pupil Personnel	25	22	35	4
Educational Programming	25	21	25	15
Building Management	10	10	15	5
Unoccupied	5	3	5	0
Other*	0	2	7	0

[1] N = 12 (All were from the same district.)
* Statements: Attendance at workshops; graduate work; visiting classrooms.

FIGURE 23-2.

staff personnel, and educational programming. School-community relations activities would occupy about 15 percent of their time.[3]

Perceived Time Usage. How do these principals think they really have to spend their time? Quite differently, as can be viewed in Figure 23-3. The modal response on school-community relations was 10 percent, although the average was 14 percent. Principals perceived themselves as spending about 20 percent of their time in each of the categories of staff personnel and pupil personnel. Half of the principals thought they devoted 10 percent of their time to curriculum development; the other half, 20 percent. They thought building management activities occupied 25 percent or more of their time.

Thus, in most instances these principals do not believe they are able to spend their time as they really would prefer. A discrepancy exists between ideal and perceived. But one more step must be taken before the principal can effectively address the time management issue. That step is collecting information about how the principal actually spends time—because, and our studies strongly support this, how principals perceive they spend time does not correlate very closely with how they really do spend time.

[3]No judgment is made here about how an individual principal ought to spend time. The principalship contains five functions, and these functions must be performed adequately by somebody, either the principal or by someone who has been delegated that authority by the principal. In either case, of course, it is the principal who is ultimately responsible.

PERCEIVED TIME USAGE

A Typical Group of Elementary School Principals' Responses to the Statement:[1]
"Alas, it's not the best of all worlds and here's how I think I actually spend my time."

	Mode	Avg.	High	Low
Community-School Relations	10%	14%	25%	20%
Staff Personnel	20	19	25	15
Pupil Personnel	20	17	50	4
Educational Programming	10 and 20	15	20	10
Building Management	25	27	45	15
Unoccupied	5	3	10	0
Other*	5	5	10	0

[1] N = 12 (All were from the same district.)
* Self renewal; attendance at workshops out of district.

FIGURE 23-3.

Real Time Usage. The only way to gain insight into how time is actually allocated is to record activities in a systematic way. The same principals whose responses are recorded in Figures 23-2 and 23-3 kept a log of their activities for several days over an extended period of time. These logs were then analyzed by persons outside the system using the seven categories listed. This analysis provided insight into their real use of time.

Principals actually spent an average of less than 10 percent of their time on community-school relations, 15 percent or less on staff personnel and educational programming, and a whopping 35 percent of their time on building-management activities.

REAL USE OF TIME BY ELEMENTARY PRINCIPALS [1]

Function	Average % of Time
Community-School Relations	8%
Staff Personnel	15
Pupil Personnel	25
Educational Programming	10
Building Management	35
Unoccupied	5
Other	2

[1] N = 12 (All were from the same district.)

FIGURE 23-4.

Reducing the Discrepancies

Something is wrong when the principals spend 35 percent or more of their time at a task they ideally think should require only 10 percent of their time. The problem becomes how to control the administrative day to spend time on those tasks that are high priority. Deciding how time should be spent is the first step. This also involves carefully analyzing one's own skills and interests. Taking stock of actual time allocation is the second step in gaining control. The third and final step is organizing time to place the maximum effort on high-priority tasks and providing an administrative structure that appropriately delegates other tasks.

The Administrative Log

Keeping a time log is the best way to find out how the principal is actually spending time. This is necessary to determine if time is to be managed wisely, because, as was pointed out earlier, depending on perception alone often results in faulty judgments. Keeping a log of activities recorded at fifteen-minute intervals on random days over a several-week period will provide the kind of insight needed. The use of an activity-and-time-recording sheet such as that depicted in Figure 23-5 will help.

A fellow administrator or some other person knowledgeable about the principalship should probably be asked to do the initial analysis. This involves judging which of the seven categories the activities recorded fall into. To be sure, it is at times a very subjective judgment, but if the log has been kept for several days, a definite pattern will emerge, and a few erroneous subjective judgments will not skew the information. Computing the percentage of time spent in each of the categories is a simple arithmetic exercise. Since categorical designations are made in fifteen-minute intervals, an eight-hour day would result in thirty-two intervals.

How to Keep an Administrative Time Log

1. The log should cover different days of the week over an extended period of time (at least four weeks).
2. Avoid the first and last months of the regular school year.
3. The log must be as complete as possible with items listed every few minutes. Something needs to be written down at intervals no greater than fifteen minutes. There is no way that one can recall or reconstruct conversations, conferences, phone calls, personal dealings after several hours.
4. When you are in your office, ask the secretary to be a shadow and keep the log. Otherwise carry the log on a clipboard.
5. If the press of a particular situation makes it impossible to write it out in detail, make a brief note at the moment regarding that activity so it may be recalled and written in more detail at the end of the day.

ADMINISTRATOR'S LOG

(Record major activities in appropriate fifteen-minute blocks and indicate leading action taken.)

Day_____	ACTIVITIES (What are you doing; who are you talking with; what is it about?)	LEADING ACTION TAKEN (Or, minutes wasted and why)
7:00 a.m.		
7:15 a.m.		
7:30 a.m.		
7:45 a.m.		
8:00 a.m.		
8:15 a.m.		
8:30 a.m.		
8:45 a.m.		
9:00 a.m.		
9:15 a.m.		
9:30 a.m.		
9:45 a.m.		
10:00 a.m.		
10:15 a.m.		
10:30 a.m.		
Etc.		

FIGURE 23-5.

Once the categorical percentages have been computed, the principal has information upon which to act. If there are discrepancies between the "what is" and the "what is desired," then it's time to examine some principles and procedures of good time management. Moreover, if an examination of the individual activities performed suggests that these activities run to the trivial, then this too must be a subject for reflection.

Task Analysis

Categorical analysis is an initial step; task analysis provides greater specificity and will uncover the real timewasters. Frequently, much of the day is taken up with tasks that someone else could and should be doing. Not only is this time inefficient, but it also does not give other people in the organization the opportunity to develop job skills.

To identify these timewasters requires only a reexamination of the administrator's time log and the recasting of the activities listed therein into a series of entries on the task analysis form depicted in Figure 23-6. The "litany"

TASK ANALYSIS			
What did I do?	Why did I do it?	Must it be me? Yes	No

FIGURE 23-6. Task Analysis.

is: what did I do; why did I do it; must it be me? Every check in the "no" column is a task that can be eliminated either by delegating it to a more appropriate person or by not doing it at all. Answering the telephone on calls coming into the building, opening one's own mail, unnecessarily attending meetings, making bookkeeping entries, or otherwise doing someone else's work are all too typical entries. In other words, every check in the "no" column means minutes that can be converted to important work.

Analysis usually reveals that others are consistently wasting an executive's time in a variety of ways and that the executive is consistently wasting other people's time. It will also reveal that the school executive is spending too much time on relatively unplanned and relatively unimportant work, that he or she is not focusing energies and rather is jumping from task to task in random fashion. Planning and priority setting are the keys to good use of time.

PRIORITY SETTING

What's important anyhow? In a sense, this question can be answered by the responses to the "best of all worlds" part of the question depicted in Figure 23-1, because it asks principals to indicate how they would ideally spend their time. The degree to which responses to the question of "ideal" use of time are true, of course, depends on the candor and insight of the particular respondent. The first step in getting better control of time, therefore, is to make an honest appraisal of what ought to be done. This appraisal should consist of a careful self-examination of organizational expectations, personal skills, and personal interests. These three forces in balance will provide a basis for job satisfaction and maximum productivity.

The most effective executives concentrate their energies on a few major tasks where superior performance will produce outstanding results. Contrast this approach with those executives who get caught up in the activity trap discussed earlier. The effective use of time requires the highest form of self-discipline.

Steps in Priority Setting. Once a decision has been made about how the individual principal can best utilize time, the task becomes one of establishing goals and setting priorities. The principal then spends time mainly in those predetermined task areas.[4] The individual, in a very real sense, draws a circle around those tasks and activities that he or she is most competent to do, and activities and tasks that fall outside of the circle become tasks for other persons.

The first step in this process is to establish specific year-long goals or targets for the school, things that the principal would like to see accomplished. Goals might be stated for each of the five functional aspects of the principalship. The next question becomes which of these goals require primary energy, and these become the high-priority items in terms of personal time usage.

Each goal is defined by a series of activities, the completion of which will result in the achievement of the goal over an established period of time, in this instance a school year. Figure 23-7 depicts part of such a list. The principal who developed the list in Figure 23-7 intends to devote 30 percent of the time during the current school year to curriculum development activities. This principal, after analysis of personal interest and skills, believes that his/her time can be most effectively spent in an instructional leadership role. In order to

---

[4]"Mainly" is the word used because no executive can totally control time; there are always emergencies, unplanned interruptions, and other unanticipated inside and outside organizational demands.

Functional area	% Time to be allotted	Goal	Activities
Curriculum development	30	To provide instructional and curricular leadership.	1. Visit each classroom four times per year. 2. Require teachers to develop behavioral objectives. 3. Organize an instructional council. 4. Introduce instructional or curricular innovation and provide for implementation.
School-community relations	25	Better relationships with the community.	1. Develop regular newsletter home. 2. Organize Parent Advisory Council. 3. Organize neighborhood resources file.
Pupil personnel	15		
Staff development	15		
Business	10		
Self-renewal	5		

FIGURE 23-7. An Example of an Elementary Principal's Priority List for a School.

reach this goal, several priority activities have been developed. The principal in question will also devote considerable energy to the development of better school-community relations and again has specified a series of priority activities. Such a list can be developed very easily into an evaluation device as well. Figure 23-8 depicts an administrative performance objective derived from such a priority list.

The establishment of priority administrative goals and specific activities permits the principal to develop daily and weekly "to do" lists. (See Figure 23-9.) The title "to do" is self-explanatory, except that the principal also attaches a priority to each item. Generally speaking, these priorities should reflect the statements of goals and activities developed for the year. If they do not, too much time is being spent on low-priority or emergency items. This can be corrected if detected early.

Goal: Provide more instructional leadership.
Performance Objective —

1. The principal will visit each classroom in the building for a minimum of one hour per nine-week period.
2. The principal will organize an instructional council that will meet once monthly to advise on school policy, curriculum development, and instructional practices.
3. The principal will require each teacher in the building to submit behavioral objectives each year for Instructional Council review and will meet individually with each teacher to discuss these.
4. The principal will introduce at least one instructional or curricular innovation adjudged by research evidence to be an important new approach to the teaching/learning process and will develop a PERT network to describe the implementation procedure.

FIGURE 23-8. An Example of a Principal's Performance Objective.

Date   Monday   , November 6

To do	Priority
Set up conference with parents re: Advisory Council	1
Set up grade-level meetings	2
Review monthly ADM	3
Visit Mr. Shelton	1
Ms. Bratton	2
Ms. Svec	2
Review school health insurance package	3
Meet with custodian re: faulty swings	1
Counsel Billy Nichols	2
Call Bob Roney re: Principal Association Program	2
Delta Kappa Meeting 3:15	2

FIGURE 23-9. A "To Do" List.

Managing Is Not Doing. One question often arises as priority lists are developed: how can a principal get away with spending so much time on curriculum development and school-community relations when there are books to be balanced, kids to be seen, inservice programs to be run, faculty meetings to be directed, and so on? To be sure, there are other functions of the principalship and they must be adequately performed or the school will not operate well, but managing does not mean personally doing everything. The "principalship" is not the "principal." Careful assignment of tasks to others and delegation of authority will provide a structure for others to make decisions and help administer the school. Then, the principal can spend time on those tasks performed best.

Planning Time. Obviously not all events and emergencies can be foreseen. Just as obvious is that the principal can control only a portion of the time. A principal is required to spend much time reacting to the problems presented by others. Nevertheless, much of the workday can be planned and that plan can be followed.

Planning does require a willingness not to be dominated by urgent events. MacKenzie has written:

> Urgency engulfs the manager; yet the most urgent task is not always the most important. The tyranny of the urgent lies in its distortion of priorities—its subtle cloaking of minor projects with major status, often under the guise of "crisis." One of the measures of the manager is his ability to distinguish the important from the urgent, to refuse to be tyrannized by the urgent, to refuse to be managed by crisis.[5]

Being managed by crisis is the result of a failure to plan. In order to insure that time is spent on the most important tasks rather than just the urgent, it is essential to prepare a daily planning document.

The document should be developed at the end of each day or at the beginning of the next. (See Figure 23-10 for an example.) The document is divided into three priority areas: those of highest priority (priority 1), those of some importance (priority 2), and those of less importance (priority 3). It requires estimates of time needed to complete activities, judgments about when during the day the time is available, and a determination whether or not someone else can do it. Further, the document requires a determination about whether or not priority activities are related to the yearly goals.

Next, a firm resolve is necessary: the principal will not work on any priority 2 activity until completing all priority 1 activities, no matter what! If time has to be stolen, it must be taken from priority 2 and 3 activities. If the principal completes all priority 1 activities, priority 2 activities may be engaged in, and the principal will not work on any priority 3 activities until completing all priority 2 activities. At the beginning of each day, the principal should spend fifteen minutes to half an hour going over the daily planning document to develop the day's routine. One half-hour spent this way will save four hours later.

A weekly analysis of the planning document will help insure that progress is being made toward the year-long goals and that high-priority activities are taking precedence.

---

[5]R. Alec MacKenzie, *The Time Trap* (New York: AMACOM, 1972), pp. 42–43.

DAILY PLANNING DOCUMENT

PRIORITY 1 Activities	Relates to what goal?	Estimated time needed for completion	When is this time available?	Who else could do it?
PRIORITY 2 Activities				
PRIORITY 3 Activities				

FIGURE 23-10. Daily Planning Document.

WHAT GETS IN THE WAY?

Robert Burns said it: "The best laid schemes o' mice and men gang aft a-gley." Emergencies do occur and a carefully planned day or week can explode in a flurry of unanticipated crises. These can be expected and need not have long-range effects on the orderly achievement of the priorities of the week or the goals of the year.[6] Studies conducted over the years in a variety of management settings have consistently revealed fifteen common sources of management time control problems:[7]

1. Telephone
2. Drop-in visitors
3. Meetings (scheduled and unscheduled)
4. Crises
5. Lack of objectives

[6]If the principal does appear to be moving continuously from crisis to crisis, something is wrong. A reassessment of the principal's role, of organizational structure, of delegation practices, and of time management practices is immediately required.

[7]Charles A. Lutzow, "Effective Time Management for the Public School Principal," *Chicago Principal's Reporter* (Spring 1978): 10.

6. Cluttered desk and personal disorganization
7. Ineffective delegation and involvement in routine
8. Attempting too much at once; unrealistic time estimates
9. Confused responsibility and authority
10. Inadequate, inaccurate, and delayed information
11. Procrastination
12. Lack of or unclear instruction
13. Inability to say no
14. Lack of controls
15. Fatigue

A review of this list indicates many items over which the principal has control. Telephone interruptions, for example, can be controlled by a secretary who takes names for the principal to call back and who is able to refer the caller to another person. Using a "call back" system will save much time. Telephones should not be tyrants.

Drop-in visitors can be controlled. For one thing, the principal can close the door when there is a project to be worked on. Or, if a closed door is contrary to the ethos of the place, the principal can find a "hideaway" that few know about. The point is, it is essential that the principal have periods of uninterrupted time so that major projects can be accomplished and so that something more than cursory attention can be given to important educational issues.

Meetings can be made more efficient and need not interfere with the effective use of the principal's time. Some meetings need not be held at all; the same kind of analysis of meetings can be made that was made of the administrator's log. Moreover, time spent at those meetings can often be shortened either by sending a subordinate or reserving the right to speak and leave.

Good managers always work from tightly developed agenda with stated anticipated outcomes which other participants have had an opportunity to see in advance. Selective participation will save everyone's time. Individuals who have a need to meet frequently can organize those meetings to make maximum use of time. The key is to meet less frequently and cover more items. Figure 23-11 displays a conference planner that, if used to set up conferences with those who frequently have a need to see each other, will save hours per week.

Delegation

One of the important tasks of the administrator is that of helping others develop. An underutilized staff is a serious indictment of the management practices of the administrator. Additionally, making inadequate use of the talents of subordinates simply means that the administrator will personally have to perform more tasks than it is possible to perform well, leaving no time for those conceptual activities for which the executive has been given "a title on the door and a carpet on the floor." There is some wisdom in the only partly facetious statement: "Whatever is worth doing is worth getting someone else to do."

Instructions:

    In the spaces below enter the names of those with whom you have frequent conferences. As you are reminded of items you need to discuss with each, jot them down. When the timing is right for a conference, number the items in order of their priority. Eliminate unnecessary items or those that can best be dealt with in another way and strike them out. Work toward avoiding one-or-two-item conferences. Be sure to include your secretary. Bosses interrupt their secretaries far more often than necessary!

NAME	*NAME*	*NAME*
NAME	*NAME*	*NAME*

FIGURE 23-11.

    Done properly, good delegation will result in greater productivity, a better staff, and more hours to be devoted to the priority tasks. It must be realized, however, that in the beginning delegation will require an expenditure of executive time. Those staff members to whom tasks are to be given must be prepared. Time must be spent adequately explaining the nature of what is being assigned, the limits of authority, the timeline, and the expected outcome. Before some staff members will be able to take on additional duties, more training may be required. Without adequate preparation, disastrous results can ensue, and even if not, the executive may be left with a job to be done over.

    Neither can delegation be seen as a way of avoiding responsibility; it is a way of getting more done in an expeditious manner. It is a way of developing staff. Accountability rests permanently and unavoidedly with the top executive in the building, regardless of who performs the work. Nevertheless the inveterate "do it all" or perfectionist, who does what others with a little instruction could be doing, is wasting valuable time and is overpaid.

    It may be helpful to think of delegation as moving through several developmental stages (developmental for both the principal and the staff member). As a staff member moves through these stages, more time will be saved by the executive and greater job enrichment will occur for the staff member.

    Figure 23-12 depicts six degrees of delegation. The nature of the project or problem to be solved, the general situation, and the ability of the staff member will determine the degree of delegation. One can see, however, that each succeeding degree of delegation requires less administrator involvement and

DEGREES OF DELEGATION

1. "Look into this and give me the particulars. I will decide."
2. "Give me your analysis and recommendation for my review."
3. "Decide and let me know your decision. But wait for my go-ahead."
4. "Decide and let me know your decision. Then take action unless I say not to" (within some specified time).
5. "Decide and take action, but let me know what you did."
6. "Decide and take action. You need not check back with me."

FIGURE 23-12.

more staff member autonomy. The principal may not get to the final degree very often or with very many staff members, but the frequency with which the principal can have staff members perform at the various levels will determine his or her own effectiveness.

The Myth of the Open Door

The principal must be accessible. What has developed from this belief in reasonable accessibility is something called the open-door policy. Unfortunately, "open door" has come to mean the door is supposed to be open all the time. How foolish. This is a certain way to insure that the principal will spend virtually all of the working day responding to other people's problems or engaging in Monday-morning quarterbacking with anybody with extra time. The always-available principal will find it impossible to work.

All executives need planned unavailability. If this is impossible to get in the office, then a principal should find a hideaway to develop projects that require longer periods of time.

Some executives seem to have an illusion of indispensability and conclude that the organization could not survive without their immediate and continuous attention. Vacations and weekends are given up as the executive stays on the firing line, making decisions and putting out fires. This refusal to delegate authority leaves the principal with an underdeveloped staff, an overworked secretary, and no recourse but to wade daily through mountains of paperwork and a morass of other people's problems.

Let no one misunderstand, however. This discussion is not to suggest that the successful principal should become some kind of rigid clock-watching phantom. Good time-management practices and a door that is closed against unwarranted interruption releases the principal from time domination so that there is more productive availability. Good time-management practices will provide more opportunities to chat with students and teachers, visit with custodians and cooks, take the secretary to lunch, feel the pulse of the school, and to see and be seen. Time consciousness and priority setting are not a licenses to disappear behind the door and never be seen again.

SUMMARY

How to get the job done, done well, and on time has been the subject of this concluding chapter. The five functions of the principalship are not manageable if the principal believes in personally performing each task. Rather, the effective school executive organizes time so all the important things get done by those best suited by disposition, training, interest, and availability. Skills in delegation and time management are basic to this goal.

BIBLIOGRAPHY

Cross, Ray. "How to Beat the Clock: Tips on Time Management." *National Elementary Principal* (March 1980): 27–30.

Hughes, Larry W. "Organizing and Managing Time," chap. 3 in *Skills for Effective Supervision*, edited by James Cooper. New York: Longman, Inc., 1984.

Lakein, Alan. *How to Get Control of Your Time and Life.* New York: Peter H. Wyden, 1973.

Loen, Raymond O. *Manage More By Doing Less.* New York: McGraw-Hill, 1971.

Martin, William J., and Willower, Donald J. "The Managerial Behavior of High School Principals." *Educational Administration Quarterly* 17, no. 1 (Winter 1980): 69–90. Although the focus of this article was five high school principals, the discussion of the press of time has much relevance to elementary principals as well.

McConkey, Dale D. *No-Nonsense Delegation.* New York: AMACOM, 1974.

Odiorne, George S. *Management and the Activity Trap.* New York: Harper and Row, Publishers, 1974.

Stellar, Arthur. Quit Wasting Time: Get Organized." *Executive Educator* (April 1981): 21–22.

Index

Accountability
and blind faith good will, 11
financial, 289–290
role of principal, 10–11
Achilles, Charles M., and Ralph
Norman, 328
Action planning
forms for, 373, 376, 377, 378–379
mini-version, 345
Activity funds, 304, 307
Activity trap, 382–383
Administration
aides, 200
grievances, 262–265
negotiation, 265–267
Administrator time log, 388–389
Advisor-advisee, 167–168
advisement schedule, 173
establishing, 171
selection of advisor, 170
Agger, Robert, 69
Appropriate objectives, 88
Audits, 308

Bernard, Jesse, 72
Brainstorming
refinement of ideas, 361
rules for, 361
Buckley amendment, 55–56
Budgeting
cyclical process, 291
implementing a budget, 293–300
P.P.B.S., 292
process, 290–292
recordkeeping, 300–302
Bulletins, briefings, and benedictions, 16

Communication
basic understandings, 23
bulletins and briefings, 16
closed loop, 330
and decision-making, 364
levels of, 21
mass media, 325
one-way, 325–330
public information officers, 326–327
questionnaires, 336
two-way, 330–336
Computers
student records, 137
Community
blut und bod, 72
conflict, 73
idealogical disunity, 63
influence systems, 70
pluralistic, 70
power structures, 66–70
sacred, 63–64
secular, 63–64
Conference planner, 395
Corporal punishment, 51–52
Croft, Don, 6
Counseling, 166–167
advisor-advisee, 167–168
developmental, 169
referral services, 175
role of guidance counselor, 173–175
selection of advisors, 170–171
Curriculum
basic skills, 115–116
common learning, 115–117
continuity, 113
emphasis, 113

Curriculum (*continued*)
exploratory, 115–118, 120
Fisher, Charles, Richard Marliave, and
Nikola Filby, 117
flexibility, 112
gifted, 118
handicapped students, 118
interrelationships, 116
a model, 112–114
organization, 111–112
specialization, 115–117
vertical selection, 117–118
Custodians
routinizing functions of, 279
work schedules, 279, 280, 282–283

Dahl, Robert, 67
Decision making
barriers to, 363
community, 66–70
consensus, 343–348
delegation of, 386–398
and goal setting, 350
majority rule, 342
maximum feasible, 345
participatory, 348–350
routine and non-routine, 358–360
unilateral, 342
when to involve others in, 356
Desegregation
distinguished from integration, 35
legal frameworks, 36
school environment, 35, 37–38
Discipline
bus control, 312–313
corporal punishment, 51–52
field trips, 314
Gallup Poll, 162
Glasser on, 164, 169
Human Development Training Institute, 169
in-school suspension, 164
Memphis city schools, 163
preventive program, 163
student conduct, 50
student control, 162
suspension/expulsion, 53
ten steps to good behavior, 164–166
Due process
guidelines, 43

procedural, 44–45
substantive, 42

Education credibility gap, 11
Educational engineer, 5–7
Erlandson, David, 323

Family Educational Rights to Privacy
Act, 55–56
Fiedler, Fred, 9–10
Field trips
off-campus trip request, 48
planning for, 314
Food services, 317–318
Force field analysis, 370
Forehand, Garlie A., and Marjorie
Ragosta, 37, 38–39
Fourteenth Amendment, 29–30

Gantt chart, 348, 378–379
Garms, Walter I., 300
Gifted students, 118
Goal setting
and decision making, 86–87
determination, 87
elementary school, 88–89
guidelines, 87
instruction, 127
National Study of School Evaluation,
87
objectives, 88–89
use in evaluation, 232
Grades
letter vs. other symbols, 154–155
Grouping, 91–109
ability, 91–92, 100–103
achievement, 91–92, 105–106
bases, 103–104
Board of Regents, 106
Class Size: A Summary of Research, 99
composition, 100
Cook, Walter W., 103
Cook, Walter W., and Theodore
Clymer, 92
Dewey, John, 95
differences in learning styles, 92–93
Esposito, Dominick, 101
flexibility, 106
Glass, Gene V., and Mary Lee Smith,
99

growth and maturity, 95
guidelines, 108
heterogeneous, 104
homogeneous, 104
IGE Unit Operations and Roles, 106
interest, 105
learning interests, 95
multi-age, 105, 191
Olson, Martin N., 98
regrouping, 106–107
retention, 103
Rosenthal, Robert, and Lenore
Jacobson, 101
Shanisky, Aida, 94
size, 98–100
skill, 105
Taylor, Calvin, 95
Goldhammer, Keith, 5

Halpin, Andrew, 6
Handicapped students, 118. *See also*
Mainstreaming
Hughes, Larry W., 5, 6–7, 35–36, 64, 156,
222, 348, 349–350
Hunter, Floyd, 66, 67

In loco parentis, 28
Individual differences
instruction, 125
learning styles, 92, 126
needs, 96
Instruction
definition, 123
French, Russell L., 126
goals, 87
implications for organization, 126
independent study, 130–131
individual differences, 125–126
learning centers, 129–130
learning packages, 129
organizing, 123–125
overtones, 126
questions, 123
studies on teacher evaluation, 125
systems, 126–128
tools for individualization, 128–129
Instructional materials center, 315–316

Job analysis, 384–388, 390
Job latitude model, 351–352

Job target setting, 353–355

Legal framework
federal constitution, 28–29
local authority, 27
Learning styles, 92–94
interests, 95
Lewin, Kurt, 370
Likert, Rensis, 7
Lipham, James, 5, 360

Mainstreaming
individualized educational program, **34**
P.L. 93-112, 33
P.L. 94-142, 33
P.L. 94-143, 33
rights to, 33
zero reject policy, 34
MacKenzie, R. Alec, 394
McGregor, Douglas, 348
Motivating work environment, **7**
Music Man, The, 61

Norman, Ralph, and Charles M.
Achilles, 328

Open spaces
flexibility of, 270
organizing for, 272
utilization of, 271
Organizational Climate Descriptive
Questionnaire, 6
Organizations
behavior in, 15
climate, 6
informal groups in, 19
loosely coupled, 20
multi-dimensional, 17

Parents
home visits, 158
organizing, 156
parent participation, 157
parent-teacher, 155
praise calls, 157
scheduling parents, 157
Program organization, 83–90
balance, 85
capability, 84
components, 84

Program organization (*continued*)
  flexibility, 85
  interdependence, 84
  National School Public Relations Association, 83
Pressure groups
  defined, 73
  evaluating legitimacy of, 75–76
  negotiating with, 74
  policies to deal with, 76–78
Principal
  distinguished from principalship, 4, 381
  educational engineer, 5–7
  performance statement sample, 8
  school-community relations specialist, 11
  special demands on, 4
Principalship
  dimensions of, 4
  five functions of, 4
Privacy
  F.E.R.P.A., 58–56
  student records, 55–57
Public information officers, 326–327
Public relations
  changing community and, 61, 65
  key communicators, 333
  National School Public Relations Association, 83
  objectives of a p.r. program, 337
  one-way communication, 325–330
  policies, 76–77
  techniques with mass media, 326–327
  two-way communication, 330–337
Pupil conduct. *See* Discipline
Pupil injuries
  health services, 318
  liability for, 45–48
  reporting, 321

Ragosta, Marjorie, and Garlie Forehand, 37, 38–39
Retention, 103
Rules and regulations
  guidelines for, 41
  what is reasonable, 39
Rutter, Michael, 6

Sacred society, 63–64

Scheduling
  block, 205
  decision level, 204
  flexibility, 203
  middle school, 210–214
  middle school team, 212–213
  parallel, 210
  rotating, 205
  sample schedule, 207–209
  simplicity and complexity, 204
  skill groups, 206
  students' daily, 209
  team daily, 208
  team planning time, 209–210
  techniques, 204–207
  timeless, 204
Secular society, 63–64
Sergiovanni, Thomas, and Fred D. Carver, 62–63
Sex discrimination, 31–32
Shannon, Patrick, 30
Site
  development, 278
  utilization, 277
Sovereign immunity, 25
Special programs. *See also* Mainstreaming
  gifted, 118
  handicapped, 118–120
Staff
  administration, 200
  aides, 198
  analysis, 179
  atmosphere, 200
  contract administration, 260–261
  court cases related to due process-teacher dismissal, 224
  design, 180
  dismissal procedure, 223–226
  due process, 223
  federal regulations, 219–220
  grievance appeals, 265
  grievance form, 266
  grievance procedure, 262–265
  Hughes, Larry W., and William M. Gordon, 222
  interview, 220–221
  job description, 216–218
  liability, 200

National School Volunteer Program, 197
orientation and training, 199, 256
paraprofessionals, 197
participatory management, 196
person description, 216
position description, 216–218
probation, 221–222
recruitment, 198, 215–219
reduction in force, 225
selection process, 220, 198
tenure, 222
termination (involuntary), 222–227
termination (voluntary), 227
Ubben, Gerald C., 220
Staff development
Berman, Paul, and Melbrey W. McLaghlin, 249
Brimm, Jack L., and Daniel Tollett, 249
characteristics of good plan, 251
evaluation, 255–256
ideas, 251
implementation, 255
Lawrence, Gordon, 250
planning, 251
planning model, 252
problems, 249
purposes, 250
specification, 254
steps, 252–255
Staff evaluation
activities, 233
attributes of a model, 230–231
calendar, 236
characteristics, 229–230
cycle, 231–233
evaluation instruments, 238–241
evaluation form, 234
Institute for the Development of Educational Activities, 232
job targets, 233–234, 237
observation tools, 237
orientation, 256–258
purposes, 229
relationship to staff development, 244–245
Staffing patterns, 179–193
complex, 180

design, 180
differentiated, 180, 182, 183
generalization vs. specialization, 181–183
matrix management, 196
participatory management, 196
schoolwide, 196
team integration, 195
utilization of staff specialists, 193
Student records
computerized, 137
cumulation, 139–144
developing new record forms, 136
federal law, 135
guidelines, 135
Hughes, Larry W., 156
maintenance, 136
parent letter, 148
personal data, 138
physical education letter form, 148–149
release form, 146
report card, 152–153, 155
Russell Sage Foundation, 136
sample records, 139–154
student medical, 145
student transfer, 150–151
Supervision
clinical, 236
collection of data, 237
cyclical process, 242–246
Educational Research Service, 237–242
planning, 237
postobservation conference, 237

Team organization
aides, 191, 197–200
compatibility, 185
design, 186
disciplinary, 184
evaluation, 189
grouping, 188
integration, 195
interdisciplinary, 184–185, 195
matrix management, 196
meetings, 186–189
models, 189, 194, 195
paraprofessionals, 197–200
planning, 186
schedule, 189

Team organization (*continued*)
  situational, 188
  specialists, 193–194
  teaching, 190
Theory X and Theory Y, 348–350
Title IX of Education Act, 32
Tort liability, 45–46
Transportation
  field trips, 314

principal's responsibility, 311
regulations, 313
student control, 312–313

Ubben, Gerald C., 220

Weick, Karl, 20

Ziegler, Harmon, 19